ARISTOPH

ARISTOPHANES FROGS

EDITED WITH INTRODUCTION, REVISED TEXT,
COMMENTARY AND INDEX
BY W.B. STANFORD
EMERITUS FELLOW OF TRINITY COLLEGE, DUBLIN
AND REGIUS PROFESSOR OF GREEK IN THE UNIVERSITY OF DUBLIN
1940-1980

PUBLISHED BY BRISTOL CLASSICAL PRESS
GENERAL EDITOR: JOHN H. BETTS
(BY ARRANGEMENT WITH MACMILLAN EDUCATION LTD)

Cover illustration: Dionysus, from the interior of an Attic red-figure *kylix* by the painter Makron, ca. 490 BC; Villa Guilia, Rome. [Drawing by Marion Perry.]

First published in 1958 by Macmillan Education Ltd

This edition published in 1983 by
Bristol Classical Press
an imprint of
Gerald Duckworth & Co. Ltd
61 Frith Street
London W1D 3JL
e-mail: inquiries@duckworth-publishers.co.uk
Website: www.ducknet.co.uk

Reprinted 1991, 1993, 2001

A catalogue record for this book is available
from the British Library

ISBN 0-86292-115-5

Printed in Great Britain by
Antony Rowe Ltd, Eastbourne

PREFACE

ARISTOPHANES's *Frogs*, though a favourite play, has not been edited in English for over fifty years. Tucker's edition, the most recent and in many ways the best for general use, is now out of print. Merry's judicious and economical edition was last revised in 1905. Rogers's, renowned for its superb translation, appeared in 1902. Meanwhile Aristophanic studies have continued to advance, and new editions of *Frogs* have been produced in Austria, France, and Italy. So it seemed worth while to prepare a new introduction, text, and commentary, designed primarily for English-speaking students in schools and universities. Accomplished scholars will find much of it elementary and familiar; but I hope that it may at least be useful for their classes and lectures.

The play is so rich and varied in its contents and technique that an editor's gravest difficulty is to decide how long his commentary should be. Fritzsche in 1845 took some four hundred and fifty pages to expound the fifty pages of his text. On the other hand, Merry thought that seventy-four pages would be enough. Some readers of the present volume, then, may find it too long; others, too short. In fact, what I have published amounts to about a half of my first draft. For those who seek more information I have given fairly full references to other publications. Like Heracles in the play I have tried to present a 'short, well-beaten path'; but I hope readers will not, like Dionysos, think it 'cold and wintry'.

Among the many recent studies to which this edition is indebted I must especially mention those of Cantarella, Coulon, Denniston, Dover, Ehrenberg, Erbse, Koster, Kraus, Pickard-Cambridge, Radermacher, Schmid, Süss, and Webster, as cited in my book list. Professor Coulon kindly allowed me to use his text as the basis of mine. I was particularly fortunate in being enabled by Mr. T. F. Higham to include excerpts from his lectures and from those of the late Mr. J. D. Denniston (by kind permission of Mrs. Denniston). Others have generously helped me with advice and amendment: Professor J. A. Davison, Mr. J. V. Luce, Professor H. W. Parke, Professor W. H. Porter, Professor L. J. D. Richardson, Mr. R. G. Ussher, and Professor D. E. W. Wormell. Miss A. M. Dale and Professor Paul Maas kindly guided me in some of the more fearsome metrical problems ; but they must not be held responsible for my final temerarious steps in these quicksands. I am also indebted to the staffs of Messrs. Macmillan & Co. and Messrs. R. & R. Clark for their co-operation, and to my wife for her assiduous help in every stage of the work.

Finally, as a member of Trinity College, Dublin, I would like to take this opportunity of paying tribute to those former Fellows of the College who have greatly en-riched Aristophanic studies during the last eighty years : to Beare, Bury, Palmer, Starkie, Tyrrell, and, with special personal regard, to W. A. Goligher, whose terse, lively, and sensible lecture notes on the *Frogs* have guided me in many perplexities. To these γόνιμοι διδάσκαλοι I dedicate this βιβλιδάριον.

SECOND EDITION

Errors have been corrected and some new material added so far as was possible within the existing pagina-tion. I am grateful to reviewers (especially G. J. de Vries in *Mnemosyne* 1960 and H.-J. Newiger in *Gnomon* 1960) and to friends (especially J. A. Richmond) for many of these improvements.

December, 1962

W. B. S.

CONTENTS

INTRODUCTION

§ 1. THE FIRST PRODUCTION

ONE winter's morning in 405 B.C. the Athenians came crowding into their open-air theatre to see the new comedies written for the Lenaean Festival. They could expect good entertainment. The programme was:

> *The Muses*, a literary comedy, by Phrynichus:
> *Cleophon*, a political comedy, by Plato;
> *Frogs*, a mixed comedy, by Aristophanes.

Both Phrynichus and Plato (not the philosopher) had previously won the prize for the best play. Aristophanes was now at the height of his dramatic powers.[1]

The competition resulted in a triumph for Aristophanes. *Frogs* won the prize (*The Muses* being second). Its parabasis (see § 13) was so greatly admired that the play was given the unusual honour of a second

---

[1] He was born about 450 B.C., probably a full Athenian citizen. His first play was *Banqueters* in 427: next *Babylonians* in 426. *Acharnians* (425) is the earliest of his plays that has survived. He wrote, with great popular success (see n. 91 below), 40 plays (or 44: 4 are dubious) in all: only 11 survive (see § 14). He presumably died shortly after the production of his *Plutus* in 388, since his son produced two new plays of his after his death. For details of his life and work see Murray, Rose, Lever, and (most fully) Schmid, as cited in the Book List at the end of this edition. Cantarella, vols. i and ii, gives the most recent survey of the evidence: see also Kraus.

production.[2] *Frogs* remained one of the most popular
of Aristophanes's plays. Many modern critics have con-
sidered it his masterpiece.

The prizes at the Lenaia were probably awarded (as in
the City Dionysia[3]) on the vote of judges selected from
the ten tribes. In so democratic a state as Athens their
voting was likely to be influenced by the applause of the
audiences in the theatre. Consequently a playwright who
wanted to win first prize would have to compose his play
to please the mind and mood of a mixed assembly. So
if we wish to understand Aristophanes's dramatic motives
and methods, we may do well to glance for a moment at
those Athenians crowded on the southern slopes of the
Acropolis [4] on that winter's morning in 405. What kind
of people are they ? What mood are they in ? Why have
they left their homes and work and come here on this
special day ?

§ 2. THE LENAEAN FESTIVAL

Every wise community has cheerful winter festivals
to brighten the gloom of the darker and colder days.

---

[2] It is uncertain when : presumably soon after the first pro-
duction while popular approval was fresh and the political situa-
tion unchanged. The likeliest time seems to be at the following
City Dionysia. See Schmid 212 and refs. in n. 25 below.
    [3] See Pickard-Cambridge, *Dramatic Festivals* 96 ff.
    [4] The site of the later fifth-century Lenaean performances is
still .disputed. Anti, Bieber (*Entrances and Exits*), and others
believe it was in the Lenaean precincts as located by Dorpfeld,
west of the Acropolis, between the Propylaea and the Pnyx.
Pickard-Cambridge (*Dramatic Festivals* 38) and others place it (in
Aristophanes's time, at least) in the Theatre of Dionysos, S.E. of
the Acropolis. I believe the second view is correct, for reasons
given in *Hermathena* lxxxix (1957).

The Athenians had three winter festivals of Dionysos (the god of wine, energy, and growth). These were the Rustic Dionysia in December, the Lenaea at the end of January or beginning of February,[5] and the Anthesteria later in February.[6]

During these festivals the Athenians were accustomed to leave their work and enjoy themselves under the relaxing influence of Dionysos and his wine. The Lenaean Festival included competitions for writers of comedy. Normally five comedies, but during the stringencies of the Peloponnesian War only three, were performed. All free-born Athenians (except, presumably, young children) attended the theatre,[7] primarily as a religious duty but also in pleasant expectation of free-and-easy fun. Public business was suspended in the parliament and law courts ; prisoners were released from jail ; trade and work were forbidden. All came in holiday mood, as to a carnival or fiesta in Latin countries today ; and many were—to put it mildly—exhilarated by wine.[8]

The performances began in the morning and took place in the open air—in contrast with our modern

[5] For uncertainties in the Attic calendar see *Oxford Classical Dictionary* 155-6.

[6] See note on 216 ff., and in general Pickard-Cambridge, *Dramatic Festivals* 1-22. The name *Lenaea* probably derives from Λῆναι, female followers of Dionysos, not from ληνός, a wine-press.

[7] Here I follow Pickard-Cambridge (*Dramatic Festivals* 268 f.) against Schmid 66, and Ehrenberg 27 (who thinks that only male citizens were admitted). The testimonia are uncertain : but we should keep in mind the strong feminine element in the Dionysiac cults and also the fact that women attended other Attic and Ionic festivals. Difficulties of accommodation arise : but I take it that many spectators watched from the surrounding slopes.

[8] See Philochoros as cited in Athenaeus 464 f, Pherecrates, fr. 95, and Plato, *Laws* 637 B.

indoor evening performances.[9] Fresh-minded and relaxed,
the Athenians watched the comedies in a setting of
superb natural beauty. From where they sat or stood
on the steep southerly slope of the Acropolis they could
look across the plain of Attica to the southernmost
slopes of Hymettos and the Saronic Gulf. But beyond
this, if the air was clear, they could also see the territory
of their Peloponnesian enemies.

§ 3. THE AUDIENCE

What kind of people were those Athenians in the
Theatre of Dionysos? Let us, in imagination, look
round the audience at the first production of *Frogs*.
There in the front row are the principal magistrates and
priests of the city—the Priest of Dionysos in the
seat of honour.[10] Near them, perhaps, are the party
politicians—the demagogues and their supporters.
They may well be wondering which of them Aristophanes
will choose to mock in his new play. (In fact he does
mock *Archedemos*, *Cleophon*, *Theramenes*,[11] and others.)
Over there, looking, perhaps, rather scornful and fas-
tidious, sit the followers of the Sophists. Aristophanes
will not spare them either. Other intellectuals are here,
too : philosophers (Socrates and young Plato probably

[9] For the effects of the open-air setting on Greek drama see
Virginia Woolf's sympathetic essay 'On not knowing Greek' in
The Common Reader (London, 1925).

[10] See on **297** ; and note how Aristophanes sometimes brings re-
ferences to the audience into his plays : *cf.* on **274-6**. For the
Athenian social groups mentioned in this section see especially
Ehrenberg. For Aristophanes's special sympathy with the
countryfolk see Schmid 178.

[11] See index for italicized names (except literary titles) and
topics,

among them), playwrights (but Sophocles and Euripides died last year), historians, orators, poets, literary critics, and wits. The last two with their 'sniffy nostrils' (*Frogs* 893) will be hard to please. They will demand subtlety, originality, and a polished style before they approve of any play.

In contrast with these sophisticated cityfolk, those less self-assured people further back, with badly cut clothes and awkward gestures, are from the country parts of Attica. In normal times they would be easy enough to amuse. But they have a special reason now for being glum. The Peloponnesian invaders have occupied most of the Attic countryside since 413, and these countryfolk have been cooped up in the city for several years. If Aristophanes wants to make them laugh, he will have to crack plenty of broad, earthy jokes and bring in amiable references to their beloved countryside with a chorus of, say, country frogs or birds or wasps to make them feel at home. They will like it, too, if he makes fun of the city people—and so he does.

Other groups will expect notice and sympathy, too : the city workers suffering from high wartime prices ; traders anxious about shortages of supplies ; aristocrats deploring the loss of their ancestral privileges and properties ; out-of-office politicians eager for revolution and reform ; and—a pathetic group this—those citizens who have lost their political rights as the result of *ἄτιμοι* recent plots and counter-plots (see on **686** ff.).

These will all want to feel, as they watch the play, that they are 'in the picture', that the playwright is at least sometimes on *their* side, and that he can laugh *with* them as well as *at* them. And, as will be seen in *Frogs.* Aristophanes does in fact show great skill in catering for all these multifarious interests among the audience. In contrast his two rivals in the dramatic competition had appealed, if we may judge from the titles of their plays, to special sections of the audience—Phrynichus in *The Muses* to those interested in literature, Plato in *Cleophon* to the political factions. But Aristophanes, universal in his appeal then and now, had something for everyone, and won the first prize.

§ 4. THE HISTORICAL BACKGROUND

But this was in 405 B.C.—no easy time for making Athenians laugh and forget their cares. The Peloponnesian War had been dragging on (apart from a short interval of uneasy peace) for over twenty-five years.[12] The naval victory at Arginusae in the previous year, despite its unhappy political sequel (see § 5), had encouraged the war party to demand further military efforts. But many Athenians must have known that ultimate victory was unlikely. In fact Arginusae was their last success. Six months after the first production of *Frogs* came the final Athenian defeat at Aegospotami.

Economically the city had been suffering greatly. The Peloponnesian occupation of Attica had deprived the Athenians of their normal agricultural supplies from the neighbourhood. The population had to depend for

---

[12] Noteworthy dates: 431, outbreak of War; 430, the plague of Athens; 429, death of Pericles; 427–421, ascendancy of *Cleon*; 421, Peace of Nicias; 420–417, ascendancy of *Hyperbolos*; 415–413, Sicilian expedition and its disastrous failure; 413, Spartan occupation of Deceleia; 412–411, revolts of Athenian allies; 411, oligarchical revolution of the Four Hundred; 410, restoration of democracy at Athens, Athenian victory at Cyzicus; 407, victory of Spartans (under Lysander) at Notion; 406, Athenian victory at *Arginusae*, trial of the Generals; 405, Aegospotami; 404, surrender of Athens.

their food mainly on hard-pressed convoys of ships from overseas. Depreciation of the currency and wartime inflation (see on **718 ff.**) had probably harmed all but the most adroit financiers and traders. The health and hygiene of the city cannot have been good : besides the over-crowding, ill effects probably still remained from the plague which had swept through the city at the begininng of the war.

Intellectually, too, the Athenians were coming near to what historians have called 'the failure of nerve'. The influence of the *Sophists* had undermined traditional beliefs and loyalties. Ethical standards were being disputed : religion was being challenged and doubted. Drastic changes of fashion in poetry and *Music* were having an unsettling effect on education and art. In the world of literature the deaths of Euripides and Sophocles in the previous year may have seemed to mark the end of a great epoch. In fact only one great masterpiece of the high classical period remained to be written—the *Frogs* of Aristophanes.

§ 5. THE POLITICAL BACKGROUND

The Athenian citizen was, in Aristotle's phrase, intensely 'a political animal'. He played a direct and active part in the government of the country—in the Assembly, the Council, and the Presiding Committee—, and he had a good chance of becoming a magistrate or an official. On the other hand the man who avoided his political responsibilities was generally despised (see on **459**). In so keenly political an atmosphere a comic poet who neglected political affairs in composing his plays would clearly lose many good targets for mockery and caricature. Further, if he himself had a serious interest in politics, a comedian could use his plays to give effective political advice to the audience.

Most of Aristophanes's comedies are political in the sense that he constantly makes fun of political personalities and sometimes offers serious political advice from his own point of view. But we must not go on to assume that his main purpose in writing his plays was political.[13] Primarily and essentially he wanted to make his audience laugh, and to win the prize. For this purpose he constantly ridicules the absurdities of politics and politicians. But on the other hand when, as an Athenian citizen, he wants to talk seriously on politics, he usually confines it to the *Parabasis.* In other words, Aristophanes is a dramatist with a typically Athenian interest in politics, not a party politician using drama primarily as a means of propaganda.

In 405 the political scene was confused and perplexing. Since the abortive oligarchical revolution in 411 the feud between the democratic and oligarchical parties had been bitter and dangerous. (In 404 the oligarchs would regain control for a short while again.) As a result of this revolution, many citizens had been deprived of political privileges. For them Aristophanes specially pleads in 686 ff. A second source of political unrest lay in the controversy between those who wished to continue the War and those who wished to end it. This controversy seems to have become exacerbated after Arginusae when the Spartans had offered peace again, but, thanks mainly to *Cleophon*, the Athenians had refused it. A third

---

[13] See Schmid 31ff. and 397-8, Dover 102-3, Hugill. Against Couat and Murray, who over-emphasize Aristophanes's political motives (especially his oligarchical or pacifist inclinations), see Croiset and Gomme.

trouble was the economic competition, heightened by wartime conditions, between the rich and the poor, the 'haves' and the 'have-nots'.

In these anxious times three politicians (all mentioned in *Frogs*) stood out. *Cleophon* led the majority of the common people and supported a war policy. *Theramenes* was apparently trying to form a coalition between democrats and oligarchs under his personal leadership. The aristocratic *Alcibiades*, in many ways the most brilliant as well as the most unstable of all Athenians in his time, was in voluntary exile from Athens (since the defeat at Notion); but in the minds of many Athenians he seemed the only person likely to lead Athens to victory.[14] Hence Aristophanes makes the conclusive question in the contest between Aeschylus and Euripides, 'What do you think about Alcibiades?' (1422-3).

Political grievances and anxieties had been increased by the deplorable aftermath of the victory at *Arginusae*. After that battle the Strategoi (generally translated 'Generals', but usually in fact naval commanders) had neglected to save the crews of the wrecked ships. Politicians at Athens indicted them for negligence. Eight were condemned to death. Six, including *Erasinides* and a son of Pericles, were executed: the other two had wisely kept away from Athens. *Theramenes* and *Archedemos* played a leading part in the indictment. Socrates in vain tried to preserve the proper forms of law. The condemnation was illegal and malicious. Its general effect in Athens was to spoil the optimism caused by a major victory and to increase political mistrust.

[14] For Athenian optimism based on Alcibiades after Cyzicus see Diodorus Siculus, 13, 68, 4-6.

§ 6. THE RELIGIOUS BACKGROUND

From among the complex religious forces of late fifth-century Athens three elements deserve special attention here—the Olympian gods, the Mystery Cults, and the rationalists.[15] The Olympian gods and goddesses are, of course, prominent in Greek literature from the time of Homer (and most of them are mentioned in the Linear-B Mycenaean tablets). Their shrines filled Athens, and their festivals occupied many days in the Athenian year. In *Frogs* Aristophanes mentions nine out of the twelve chief Olympians: *Zeus, Poseidon, Demeter, Apollo, Artemis, Hermes, Aphrodite, Ares*, and, of course, *Dionysos*. He also mentions some minor Olympians: *Pan, Persephone, Pluto*, and *Heracles*.

What is most surprising to modern hearers in some of these references is the apparent lack of reverence shown to the gods. *Dionysos* (see § 8) appears at times as a contemptible weakling, *Heracles* as a glutton. Similarly, religious formulae are parodied in what seems very like blasphemy to modern ears (see, *e.g.*, on **479**). But it would be wrong to assume anti-religious sentiments here.[16] The comic performances were themselves religious ceremonies, performed on consecrated ground during a festival presided over by the chief priest of Dionysos. Dionysos was, so to speak, the host at these entertainments, and, like a genial host at a Christmas party today, he could dress up and play the clown without dishonour. Whatever was said or done in good humour under his patronage was deemed to be a good-humoured joke and nothing more. No comedian was ever tried for impiety

[15] See Guthrie, and C. Seltman, *The Twelve Olympians* (London, 1952).

[16] See Schmid 401-2; Dover 100-1; Lever 108-9.

in fifth-century Athens.   Even if the host-god Dionysos himself was caricatured—well, his priests were confident enough in his prestige and popularity to laugh indulgently. What the religious leaders feared was not the fun of the comedians, but the arguments of the rationalists.

Besides the public and domestic worship of the Olympians, the Mystery Cults had a strong influence in the Athens of Aristophanes's time.   These,[17] unlike the Olympian ceremonies, were not open to all.   The chief rites of the Mysteries were held in secret and witnessed only by those who had gone through certain initiation ceremonies.   The initiates were promised a degree of bliss after death which was inaccessible to all outside the cult (see especially on 454 ff.).   There were two chief varieties of these Mysteries at Athens in the late fifth century— first the Mysteries of Demeter and Persephone which had their central shrine in the precinct of Demeter at Eleusis, and, second, the Orphic-Dionysiac Mysteries.

Here another vexed question has arisen for the inter-pretation of *Frogs*.   The Chorus in 324 ff. consists of Initiates (see on 336) and their first lyrics abound in allusions to mystic doctrines.   Did Aristophanes intend his audience to identify these allusions as specifically Eleusinian or Orphic-Dionysiac or what?   Opinions have varied, but on the whole the Dionysiac kind, perhaps a type directly connected with the Lenaean Festival (§ 2), seems the most likely,[18] though possibly Aristophanes was presenting an eclectic [19] impression derived from more than one cult—to please as many members of the audience as possible.

[17] See Tierney and Lapalus for their significance in *Frogs* and in general, Guthrie.

[18] See especially Tierney on this.

[19] Pickard-Cambridge in *Dramatic Festivals* 43 thinks that the Lenaean ceremonies had Eleusinian connexions.

Whatever its precise reference may be, the presence of the Initiates has three noteworthy aspects for our appreciation of *Frogs*. First: even such sacred and awe-inspiring rites as theirs could be brought into a comedy and parodied (or at least adapted to comic purposes) without risking a charge of irreverence. Second: as the main Eleusinian ceremonies had been prevented since 413 by the enemy occupation of Attica (except in 408 when Alcibiades escorted the Initiates with an armed guard), a presentation of this kind in the theatre would have special poignancy for Eleusinian initiates in the audience. Third: as the ritual and doctrine of the mysteries centred on the life after death, a Chorus of Mystic Initiates had a special aptness in a play describing a journey to Hades.

Another element in Athenian religious thought at this time was the doctrine of the rationalists. These—philosophers, scientists, and sophists among them—had derived their views from the Ionian scientists who had explained phenomena, once thought to be divine, in terms of natural processes. Their beliefs varied from dogmatic atheism (like that of *Diagoras*) through various grades of agnosticism to an attitude that combined religious faith with a desire to purge conventional beliefs from superstition and error. Religious leaders feared this tendency. Thus the execution of *Socrates* in 399 B.C. seems to have been partly due to his attacks on popular beliefs about the gods (though in essence he was a most religious man himself). Other Athenians before him—notably Euripides and Anaxagoras—were suspected of, or accused of, similar 'impiety'.

Aristophanes ridiculed all such 'impiety' and attacked alleged rationalists and materialists like Euripides and Socrates. These attacks are less prominent in *Frogs* than in, say, *Clouds*, but some passing gibes will be found in **99** ff., **1082, 1477-8**, and **1491-9**. As with so many of his personal caricatures, we cannot assume that they are even mostly true.

§ 7. THE ACTION OF THE PLAY AND THE LITERARY CONTEST

In the anxious days of winter 406/5 Aristophanes prudently decided that the Athenians would best enjoy a play which transported them in imagination right away from Athens for a while. Already during the Sicilian Expedition in 414 his *Birds* had brought the audience to a Cloudcuckooland in the sky. Now in *Frogs* he takes them below the earth, to Hades the realm of Persephone and Pluto [20]—a sadder place to visit, this, but he does his best to make it enjoyable.

At the beginning of the play the god Dionysos, dressed as Heracles (who had already gone to Hades and returned safely) and accompanied by his slave Xanthias, visits the house of Heracles to ask advice for a journey. He wants to go to Hades to bring back Euripides, as there are no living poets worthy of the Athenian theatre. After Heracles has described the way they must go, they set out. Meeting a Corpse who is also going their way, D. tries to hire him to carry the baggage for X.; but he finally refuses to pay the price the Corpse demands. Then D. and X. come to a lake on the borders of Hades. D. crosses it in Charon's boat: X., being a slave, has to go round it on foot. During the crossing D. hears the song of the marsh-frogs, has a shouting-contest with them—and wins it. On the other side of the lake

[20] For the motif of a descent into Hades see on **137** ff.

D. and X. encounter an imaginary ghost. A Chorus
of Initiates enters. They sing a mixture of songs on
religious, political, and personal themes. At the entrance
to Pluto's house the gate-keeper Aeacus (but see on
464 ff.) terrifies D. by his threats. When Aeacus has
gone for the police, D. asks X. to exchange costume with
him, hoping that Aeacus will be deceived. X. puts on
D.'s Heracles-costume. Instead of Aeacus, a servant
returns with an invitation for the pseudo-Heracles to a
banquet with Queen Persephone. When he goes out,
D., eager for the feast, makes X. give him back his
clothes. Two inn-keepers enter. They denounce the
pseudo-Heracles for having robbed them on his previous
visit, and go out, with threats of vengeance, to seek help.
D. manages to persuade X. to put on the Heracles-
costume once more. Aeacus returns with a squad of
ferocious policemen. They attack X., believing him to
be Heracles. X. denies that he has ever been to Hades
before. He offers to hand over his apparent slave, D.,
for torture to prove the truth of this assertion. D.
proclaims that he is not a slave but a god, and that X.
is the slave. X. denies this. They agree to a test by
whipping: whichever of them cries out and shows he is
hurt when he receives the lash will obviously not be a
god, since the gods feel no pain. After some ludicrous
efforts Aeacus fails to determine which is which. He
decides to leave the question to Pluto and Persephone.
D., sore from his whipping, wishes Aeacus had thought
of this sooner. All the actors go inside.

Here there is a pause in the action while the Chorus
deliver the *Parabasis* expressing the author's own
political opinions. Then X. comes out with a servant
of Pluto (but see on **738 ff.**). They exchange slavish
confidences. Soon they hear the sound of quarrelling

from inside Pluto's house. It is Aeschylus and Euripides disputing which of them should have the Chair of Tragedy. After the Chorus has sung an introductory ode, they enter. Dionysos accompanies them. It has been agreed that he should judge between them.

After a mock-ceremonial prelude—with incense, hymn, and prayer—D. opens the contest. First Euripides denounces Aeschylus as a cheat and an impostor in his plays. He accuses him of using absurdly long words, grotesque images, and a ridiculously inflated style. He claims that he, Euripides, restored tragedy to health by purging it of its superfluous bulk and by making the characters speak and act like intelligent human beings. Aeschylus begins by defending his plays on ethical rather than on stylistic grounds. His plays, he claims, taught the Athenians to be brave, honourable, and disciplined : Euripides's plays taught them to be cowardly, immoral, and argumentative.[21]

This bout being inconclusive, Euripides· launches an attack on Aeschylus's prologues : they are obscure and repetitive in their phrasing. Aeschylus counter-attacks with the accusation that Euripides's own prologues are, first, untrue to the facts, and, second, all capable of being 'destroyed by one single little oil-jar' (see on 1208 ff.). He proves this by a remarkable demonstration. Euripides, undaunted by this attack, sings—doubtless with grotesque exaggeration—some of Aeschylus's lyrics to show their monotony. Aeschylus replies with two devastating parodies of Euripides's

[21] For details of this far-reaching literary discussion see Schmid 345 ff. and Radermacher, and notes on 907 ff. For wider aspects see Snell, chap. 6 (he notes how much Plato was influenced by Aristophanes's views here) ; J. W. H. Atkins, *Literary Criticism in Antiquity*, i (Cambridge, 1934), 25-32 ; E. E. Sikes, *The Greek View of Poetry* (London, 1931), 37 ff.

lyrical style.   Dionysos, still undecided, passes on to a
'scientific' test: he will weigh the verses of each poet.
A comic weighing-scales is brought forward, and each
poet speaks some verses into the opposite scale-pans.
Aeschylus has the better of this ; but D. is still reluctant
to give judgement.   At Pluto's request he proposes a
final test.   It is a political one: what does each poet
think should be done about *Alcibiades* ?   He finds both
poets' opinions good in their way, and still hesitates to
decide on the winner.   Pluto insists.   D., without giving
any serious reason, decides for Aeschylus, much to
Euripides's disgust.   After an off-stage banquet, Aes-
chylus and Dionysos set off for Athens escorted by the
Chorus with triumphal songs and torches.

Some critics have complained [22] of incoherence and
inconsistency in this plot.   For example, they point out
that Dionysos's original intention of bringing back
Euripides is entirely ignored in the contest for the Chair
of Tragedy and in the final choice of Aeschylus.   Further,
why does nothing come of the elaborate description of
Hades (**136** ff.), or of the promised appeal to Cleon
(**569**) ?   And why does the Weighing Scene end so
abruptly (**1413**) ?

These objections are based on a misunderstanding of
Aristophanes's dramatic technique.[23]   His plots have
little in common with the clear and logical construction
of a Sophoclean tragedy.   Sophocles (and to some
extent the other Greek tragedians and also the writers of
Menandrian comedies) based his plays on a clear-cut
central problem or conflict ;   he avoided irrelevant side-

[22] See especially Radermacher 355-7 and the works cited there :
also Erbse 273, Schmid 358.

[23] For this view see Schmid 358, Süss, *Scheinbare* etc., Krause,
and Dover (98 and n. 6).

issues and inconsistencies of character. Aristophanes
cares little if his endings are inconsistent with his begin-
nings, and loves to chase an amusing side-issue for as
long as there is a laugh in it. Instead of a carefully
constructed plot, Aristophanes often uses one general
idea as the foundation of his play. In planning *Frogs*,
for example, he seems to have thought something like
this : 'Let's send Dionysos off to Hades in search of a
poet, give him plenty of adventures and surprises, have
a contest between Euripides and Aeschylus, decide it
quite whimsically, and end up with the usual victory-
scene'. The more variety and absurdity he can insert
into this loose framework, the better. He knows that
laughter is soon wearied by sameness and mental con-
centration. His one and only principle is that he must
not break the continuity or confuse the spectators about
what is happening at *any particular moment*.

In other words the sequence of action in an Aristo-
phanic play is more like that of a dream or reverie than
that of a normal play or story.[24]

In a dream we have a general idea of what is going
on at the moment : we are climbing a mountain, say,
or talking with the animals in the zoo. But in that
given situation almost anything may *emerge* without any
shock to our sense of logic or consistency. Similarly in
an Aristophanic play there is often only the most slender
link of time, space, or mood, between each episode. In
terms of such wide-awake logic as some critics would
impose on Aristophanic comedy, this produces 'glaring
inconsistencies' : but it is a critical error to impose
normal rules of consistency on Aristophanes. It must

[24] For a development of this view, suggesting similarities with
Lewis Carroll's technique in the Alice books, see *Icarus* 17 (Nov.
1955), 3-8.

be remembered that the spectators were relaxed, exhilarated, and probably partly intoxicated by ritual potations (§ 2). In this state people are capable of close attention only to what is going on at any particular moment: their minds become blurred about both the past and the future. 'Live in the moment and enjoy it' was a central doctrine of the Dionysiac cult. Critics who (like Pentheus in the *Bacchae*) try to imprison Dionysiac drama in the stricter rules of dramatic plot-making are trying to measure wine with an inch-tape.[25]

§ 8. THE CHARACTERS AND CHORUS

Aristophanes has five main kinds of characters in his plays. The first kind consists of gods, heroes, and mythological figures: such are Dionysos, Heracles, Charon, Aeacus, and Pluto, in *Frogs*. The second: eminent contemporary Athenians, like Aeschylus and Euripides here. The third: type-figures, like Xanthias (the clever slave), Plathane (the angry inn-keeper), and to some extent Aeacus (as angry door-keeper: but see on **464 ff.**). Fourth: animals (like the Frogs here, and, most effectively, the Birds in *Birds*), natural phenomena (like the Clouds in *Clouds*), and abstractions (like the

[25] But the incoherence of 1431-53 (see notes) can hardly be excused on grounds of comic licence. Here scholars have suggested that some of the alleged anomalies in the plot may be due to one or both of two causes: (*o*) the death of Sophocles after (it is suggested) Aristophanes had planned his play, (*b*) alterations made for the second performance of the play (see n. 2). Against the first view see Ruppel, and against the second, Süss (*Scheinbare* etc.) and van Leeuwen. See also Radermacher 355-7 (and works discussed there) and Schmid 333, 336, 358. The whole question is speculative: there is in fact no clear evidence whatever about any changes of text after the first performance.

Just Argument in *Clouds*). The fifth kind, consisting of figures possessed by some ruling passion and called by a descriptive name (such as Cleon-lover and Cleon-loather in *Wasps*), is not represented in *Frogs*.[26] Besides these, Aristophanes often introduces fanciful minor characters to serve a brief episode : such are the Corpse in *Frogs* and the Pseudo-Persian in *Acharnians*.

Most of the characters in *Frogs* are conventional figures. Simplest are : *Pluto*, King of Hades (no doubt regally impressive in costume and behaviour), whose only function is to wind up the plot; *Charon*, presented as a gruff, sardonic ferryman ; Persephone's *Servant* ; the *Innkeepers* ; *Acacus* (first an irascible door-keeper ; then a callous slave-whipper) ; and the *Corpse*. *Heracles* is the traditional comic hero [27] — gluttonous, boisterous, inclined to throw his massive weight around, and crude in intellectual matters. *Xanthias* is a clever, unprincipled rascal, but he shows an endearing touch of loyalty to his master in 178-9. *Aeschylus* and *Euripides* [28] are more elaborately portrayed : Aeschylus, exponent of the grand style in literature, was probably presented here

[26] Some critics have preferred to view Aristophanes's characters in terms of stock characters, *e.g.* as Scurrilous Jesters (βωμολόχοι : *cf.* on 358), Boastful Imposters (ἀλαζόνες : *cf.* on 909), Parasites, Pedants, etc. : see especially Süss, *De personarum antiq. com. usu*, Cornford, chap. 8, Grene. But this approach, though illuminating to the modern reader, seems to me to impose categories on Aristophanes's characterization which are too rigid and too abstract. On A.'s characters in general see Schmid 415 ff. and Dover 103.

[27] In *Wasps* 60 (see Starkie's note) Aristophanes had already dismissed Heracles the Glutton as a worn-out figure. It is typical of his genius (and impudence) to present him again successfully here. For the Heracles-figure in general see Schmid 539 ff.

[28] Aristophanes likes to introduce grotesquely contrasting pairs : so, too, Dionysos and Xanthias (*cf.* Don Quixote and Sancho Panza, Pickwick and Samuel Weller) : see Schmid 419.

as an exaggerated specimen of The Great Man with deep, resonant voice, grandiose gestures, and imposing costume ; in contrast Euripides, representing the fastidious, subtle kind of writer and critic, probably spoke in a high-pitched precise voice, using deft, delicate gestures.

But since Euripides and Aeschylus were also actual people, a problem arises: how true to life are their portraits here, and do these portraits represent Aristophanes's personal opinion about these two poets ? On the first point one can probably say with safety that Aristophanes's figures of the two poets were outrageous caricatures—but, like all caricatures, were contrived by exaggerating actual features of the victims. Physically and temperamentally Euripides and Aeschylus *may* have contrasted like this—but much less blatantly. The second point comes to this: did Aristophanes personally agree with the criticisms of Euripides and Aeschylus as expressed in his *Frogs* ; and, further, does the final rejection of Euripides in favour of Aeschylus indicate Aristophanes's own personal verdict ? This has been much disputed.[29] Without going into details, one can point to the likelihood that the defeat of Euripides and the triumph of Aeschylus (who, having died fifty years before Euripides, was probably the more popular with the average Athenian: for popular taste moves slowly) was contrived mainly for theatrical and political effects (surprise, and praise of the Old Style in literature and life) ; and, secondly, that in fact Aristophanes may have had a profound respect for Euripides's poetic

---

[29] See C. Prato, *Euripide nella critica di Aristophane* (Lecce, 1955), Schmid-Stählin 1, 3, 1, 819-22, Steiger, Murray 107 ff., and Wycherley. Some other recent studies are listed by Murphy. In what follows I follow mainly Schmid-Stählin, Murray, Stevens, and Wycherley.

ability.[30] In *Frogs* Euripides is *not* rejected for any clear
inferiority in poetic skill or political sagacity. The
Chorus, it is true, does tend to be on Aeschylus's side
in showing him more respect than his rival (*e.g.* **997,
1004-5, 1253** ff.). But Dionysos's judicial remarks are
ambiguous (**1413, 1434**), and his final decision is based
on flagrantly frivolous grounds. Indeed, though the
more old-fashioned members of the audience were
probably pleased at good old Aeschylus's victory,
Aristophanes may have intended his more sympathetic
hearers to be sorry for Euripides's largely undeserved
defeat.

Dionysos is in action in every episode except one. In
fact—since the scene and the chorus change, and
Xanthias disappears in the last half of the play—
he is the single continuing element, the slender thread
of continuity, in the play. But he is no hero of firm
character and purpose like Oedipus or Pentheus, against
whose resolve the waves of destiny beat remorselessly.
On the contrary, so supple, fickle, wayward, panicky,
opportunistic, and unscrupulous is he that he rather
resembles the oil which helps to blend a salad or lubricate
a machine, than any solid substance. He abandons his
purpose in undertaking the journey to Hades—to bring
back Euripides—without any serious explanation in the
end. In fact he is a kind of personified *Oxymoron*, self-
contradictory but with a kind of irrational reason for
his actions which prevents him from becoming a mere
bundle of contradictions. He changes like a chameleon

---

[30] Cratinos (fr. 307) seems to have accused Aristophanes of
'Euripidizing', and a scholium on Plato, *Apology* 19 c, says A.
was ridiculed for imitating Euripides while mocking him. Good
parody is impossible without intimate knowledge, and does not
imply dislike.

—in turn haughty master, yearning poet-lover, adventurous traveller, clownish oarsman, disgusting coward, timorous visitor, feckless opportunist, squealing whipping-boy, impressionable judge, vulgar buffoon, unscrupulous umpire, and so on.   Yet for all his follies, faults, and weaknesses, he is not an unlikable fellow.   At least he is never utterly defeated (how stubbornly he resists the Frog Chorus !) and never entirely loses his good spirits.

All this is clear enough.   But when we begin to ask whether Aristophanes intended any symbolism in his portrait of Dionysos, uncertainty returns.   Is Dionysos intended to represent (or burlesque) a fickle, wayward Athenian of the time, the 'average Athenian ass' as Verrall put it ?   Or is he a caricature of the Euripides-loving intellectuals ?   Or is this a covert attack on orthodox religion ?   The last (see § 6) is least likely, I think.[31] The other views are possible.   But it seems safest to take it that Dionysos's chief functions in the play are to maintain the continuity of the plot, to exhibit in himself many ludicrous features of human nature, to act as a kind of neutral buffer-state in the conflict between Aeschylus and Euripides, and alternately to disgust and delight the spectators with his delinquencies and ingenuities. The fact that Dionysos was also a god hardly matters at all in the play, except to increase the humour of his antics, as if an Archbishop were to dress up as Santa Claus at a Christmas party.[32]

The Chorus (twenty-four in number) has to play a

[31] See especially Lapalus against Pascal's view that Aristophanes is hostile to Dionysos as a god : also Schmid 334.

[32] Perhaps the primary reason why Aristophanes chose Dionysos and not some ordinary Athenian poetry-lover for the part was because Dionysos had special associations with the Mysteries and the underworld and, besides, was able to meet Heracles and Pluto as fellow-gods and fellow-initiates (see further in Lapalus).

double part. First unseen (see on **209** ff.) the Choreutai sing the delicious frog-song—this partly, no doubt, to please rustic members of the audience with agreeable memories of the countryside (§ 3). But it is as Initiates of the Mysteries (§ 6) that they first appear. After their impressive *Parodos* with its many allusions to mystic ceremonies, they rather lose their identity and adopt the passive role of introducing and commenting on the characters and the action. Occasionally the leader (*Coryphaios*) speaks by himself, like a separate actor.[33]

For the minor parts see *Characters in the Play*. They are sometimes given some special idiosyncrasies of speech (see, *e.g.*, on **193, 562-3**). Some silent 'walk-on' figures also appear: attendants carrying the Corpse's bier, inn-keepers' servants (**569**), policemen to help Aeacus in **605** ff., a comic Muse in **1305** ff. Stage-hands also probably came into the *Orchestra* to roll in Charon's boat (see on **180**) and to set up the weighing-scales for **1364** ff.

§ 9. THEATRE, MASKS, COSTUMES [34]

Aristophanes's comedies were produced in an open-air theatre, probably in the great theatre of Dionysos on the S.E. slope of the Acropolis (see n. 4). The spectators sat in ascending tiers above the circular dancing-floor (*Orchestra*) on which the actors and chorus performed.[35]

[33] See J. W. White in *Harvard Studies in Classical Philology* xvii (1906), 103-29. See further in § 12.

[34] See Pickard-Cambridge, *Theatre of D.* and *Dramatic Festivals*, Dover 114-15, and especially Webster who lists the important and now plentiful evidence from vase-paintings.

[35] Webster believes that a platform may have been used for some of the performances. But the evidence is hardly conclusive yet. For criticism of Anti's theories of a trapezoidal Lenaean

Behind the Orchestra there was a building in which the actors could dress and wait. The front of this *Scene-building* (σκηνή: originally 'tent, booth': at first probably a mere shelter) was designed to represent the street-front of a house with one or more doors in it.[36] Just how much additional scenery was used is quite uncertain. The *Frogs* needs none; the words supply all we need to imagine about the scenes on earth and in Hades. But some accessories are needed: a club for Dionysos, a donkey and a porter's pole for Xanthias, a bier for the Corpse, a boat for Charon, a whip for Aeacus, measuring instruments and a weighing-scales for the judgement scenes, and torches for the final procession.

The actors and chorus wore masks, which might caricature some personal feature, such as baldness or a snub nose, or else might indicate identity or character. Their costume, too, seems to have been grotesquely exaggerated.[37] Sometimes padding was used: so Dionysos, who is called 'fatty' by Charon in 200, may have been wearing a stomach-pad under his tunic. There is no clear reference in *Frogs* to the other traditional features of comic costume.

theatre see Pickard-Cambridge in *Classical Review* lxii (1948), 125-9, and C. F. Russo in *Atti d. Accademia dei Lincei* xi (Rome, 1956), 14-27.

[36] It seems to me to be still a matter of pure conjecture whether or not in *Frogs* there were separate doors in the Scene-building for the House of Heracles and the House of Pluto. But Webster 8 ff. makes a reasonable case for a wide central door with a narrower door on each side. *Cf.* Radermacher, Krause, C. Fensterbusch, *Die Bühne des A.* (Leipzig, 1912), and Bieber.

[37] W. Beare in *Classical Quarterly*, n.s. iv (1954), 64-75, has argued that at least some characters wore the costume of ordinary life, but Webster in *C.Q.*, n.s. v (1955), 94-5, rejects this view. The evidence is very fragmentary. Webster holds that tights were always worn under the costumes.

§ 10. THE COMIC TECHNIQUE OF ARISTOPHANES

Aristophanes used both the eye and the ear for making his audience laugh. Visually he amused them by inventing grotesque and incongruous costumes; [38] by making his characters use funny gestures and antics,[39] besides those strictly demanded by the action; and by involving them in ludicrous predicaments (as when Dionysos finds himself being whipped as a slave). This kind of comedy could be conveyed in mime alone (as in the silent films).

But Aristophanes is supremely a master of words; and for us especially (since little knowledge of the visual production of *Frogs* has survived) his verbal humour matters most. In this he shows supreme mastery of almost every known means of making people laugh. In *Frogs* he goes through the whole comic scale from the lowest levels—personal abuse, references to physical abnormalities (*e.g.*, fatness, thinness, excessive height: see **1089 ff., 1437-8, 55**), and references to bodily parts or processes usually unmentioned in polite society [40]—to

[38] Thus Dionysos's costume absurdly combines Heracles's club and lion-skin with his own yellow tunic and boots (as if a character came on to a modern stage wearing battle-dress with an umbrella and spats); and probably, too, the masks and costumes of Aeschylus, Aeacus, Euripides, and others were grotesquely designed. For such grotesquerie as an important element in the humour of Aristophanes see especially Steiger and Jernigan.

[39] '*Business*' is the modern theatrical term: for examples see Pickard-Cambridge, *Dram. Fest.* 169 ff. and index. Comic dances were a special form of this: see § 12.

[40] For example 237, 308, 422 ff., and see on 3-4. As there is some confusion of thought about these 'scatological' jokes, it may be noted that whatever may be said about their politeness there is and was nothing strictly immoral about them. Aristophanes's

exquisite touches of wit and fantasy. In other words, he provides congenial humour for as many as he can of the various intellectual and social elements in his audience (§ 3).

Sometimes his humour lies in the sound or form of the words rather than in their meaning: as in comic exclamations (*e.g.* **63, 649, 1073**), *Assonance, Onomatopoeia, Polysyllables*,[41] grotesque *Coined Words, Comic Distortions, Comic Terminations, Comic Names.*[42] Mere repetitions of words and phrases can also have a comic effect (*e.g.* **3/30, 5/20, 58/60, 305/6**) ;[43] so too a flood of verbiage spoken at high speed (*e.g.* **465 ff.**).[44]

More often the joke depends on the witty manipulation of word-meanings. Thus the *Pun* exploits *Ambiguities* (as when a clerical debater once remarked : 'I gave Canon Brush no handle for such sweeping statements '). So too an absurd *Comparison* wins a smile by

alleged immorality lies elsewhere : but on this I agree with Rose 231 : 'Of all surviving Greek authors he is one of the most moral and sympathetic, while remaining, in many places, superficially one of the most indecent ': *cf.* Ehrenberg 194 ff. C. S. Lewis has discussed some problems of vocabulary in modern renderings of these physiological jokes ('Prudery and Philosophy', *Spectator* for January 21, 1955).

[41] See G. Meyer, 'Die stilistische Verwendung der Nominal-komposition im Griechischen', *Philologus*, supplement-volume, xvi (1923), 3, 146 ff. and Américo da Costa Ramalho, 'Dipla onomata no estilo de A.', *Humanitas*, suppl. iv (1952). The longest polysyllable in Greek is the gargantuan 169-letter word for a banquet in *Eccl.* 1169. For polysyllabic humour in general see H. W. Fowler's *Modern English Usage* (Oxford, 1937).

[42] See especially Peppler. One thinks here of Dickens's intrinsically funny names, like Chuzzlewit, or of actual place-names like Timbuctoo, Sallynoggin. *Cf.* on **475**.

[43] See Miller.

[44] The technical term is λαλιά. For analyses of rhetorical terms for comedy see Rutherford, *Scholia Aristophanica* 3, 435 ff. and Starkie, *Ach.* xxxviii ff., and Lane Cooper as cited in n. 51.

its incongruity (as when Sidney Smith told a child who was stroking the back of a giant tortoise in the Zoo, 'You might as well stroke the dome of St. Paul's to please the Dean and Chapter'). An unexpected comical change in direction of thought (called the παρὰ προσδο-κίαν or 'contrary-to-expectation' joke : see index) is one of Aristophanes's favourite tricks : it is exemplified in Oscar Wilde's description of a person as having a 'face once seen never . . . remembered'. A special form of this is the *Bathos* joke, in which the level of discourse suddenly slumps : thus Dionysos tries to explain literary taste in terms of . . . soup. The effect here is rather like what happens if one is climbing stairs in the dark, raises one's foot for the last step, and finds that it isn't there.

Aristophanes's humour becomes more elaborate and complex as the element of fantasy increases. We can see this in the phantasmagorical imagery in the introduction to the contest between Aeschylus and Euripides in 814-29, where wild boars and lions and chariots and whirlwinds merge in a Jabberwockian vortex, and in Aeacus's rhapsodic imprecations in 470-7.

These last two examples also depend for their total effect on another humorous technique. This is *Parody*, perhaps the most complex of Aristophanes's ways of amusing his audience.[45] His methods vary widely. Either he quotes a lofty line in an absurd context (*e.g.* 844, 992) ; or he quotes with some absurd alteration (*e.g.* 304, 282) ; or else he ludicrously paraphrases (*e.g.*

---

[45] See, *e.g.*, Schlesinger, Householder, Hope, Schmid 422-5 (with refs. to previous studies), and F. J. Lelièvre in *Greece and Rome* i (2nd series), 1954, 68-81. Fowler's (see n. 41) distinction between parody and cognate terms is helpful: *burlesque* applies to actors and acting, *caricature* to physical form and features, *parody* to verbal expression, *travesty* in general for any misrepresentation whether intended to be humorous or not. Steiger takes a different view.

101-2); or he jumbles together a mass of exalted terms
(*e.g.* 311, 470 ff.), or makes an absurd patchwork of
striking phrases (*e.g.* 1264 ff., 1285 ff.); or sometimes he
writes quite new verses as, say, Euripides or Aeschylus
might have written them (838-9 and 1331 ff.).[46] And
sometimes he parodies the linguistic methods of un-
poetic people like the Sophists (*e.g.* 25 ff.) or even the
language of a ferryman (185 ff.). Many other examples
will be mentioned in the notes (see on *Parody*). It is
one of the hardest of Aristophanes's jests for modern
readers to appreciate. But the Athenians apparently
delighted in it.[47]

Characterization, too, obviously contributes to comic
effect (see § 8). It depends mainly on words, appearances,
and actions. But it also depends on less tangible quali-
ties—ways of thinking, principles, decisions. Naturally
Dionysos, Xanthias, Aeschylus, and Euripides (and to
some extent the minor characters) exhibit comic manner-
isms, do comic things, think comic thoughts, and make
comic decisions—like any humorous figure in Dickens,
Rabelais, or Cervantes. One example out of dozens
must serve : when Dionysos, with utter faithlessness and
superb impudence, rejects his favourite Euripides with
two (misused) lines from Euripides's own plays (1471 ff.)
what an absurd, disgraceful, and laughable decision it is
—and yet how paradoxically apt for all we have seen
of Dionysos up to that point !

But drama is essentially a matter of action (δρᾶμα,

[46] But since much of the literature that A. parodies is lost, we
can rarely be quite sure that he is composing a new passage and
not just quoting or distorting some lost work : see, *e.g.*, on 1320-2
and 1330 ff.

[47] How the average Athenian came to have the literary know-
ledge and taste to appreciate such varied forms of parody is
discussed by Sedgwick.

δράω) : humour of action and situation is an essential
of the comedian's art. Once again one cannot com-
pletely separate it [48] from appearances, words, and char-
acterization. But many scenes in *Frogs* must have won
the loudest and most prolonged laughter by sheer plot-
contrivance, as, for example, when Dionysos by an ill-
judged manœuvre lets himself in for being whipped as
a slave (605 ff.) : the memory of this gloriously incon-
gruous situation and its results would be likely to tickle
the spectators' minds long after some of the verbal jokes
and parodies were forgotten.

It must be emphasized here that very often Aris-
tophanes uses several of these comic devices at once.[49]
Like Rabelais and Shakespeare in his broader comedy,
Aristophanes assaults the solemnity and sobriety of his
audience simultaneously with every comic weapon he
can lay hands on—the more, the merrier—and he pre-
fers a general hurly-burly of fun to the rapier-attacks of
wit and fantasy which more fastidious writers prefer.
In other words, he is a poet of fulness and exuberance,
not of precision and restraint. In this he truly repre-
sents the spirit of the Old Comedy in contrast with that
of the New. For originally the Old Comedy was derived
from a mixture of festive revelry, primitive fertility-
cults, and licensed invective.[50] It would lead too far

---

[48] On this see the valuable discussion in H. House, *Aristotle's
Poetics* (London, 1956), 68-81.

[49] For his comic use of metre, music, and dancing see § 12.
For comic terminations see on 587-8.

[50] For the recent discussion of origins of comedy, and its
constituent κῶμος, φαλλός, and ψόγος mentioned here, see Hans
Herter, *Vom dionysischen Tanz zum komischen Spiel* (Iserlohn,
1947), M. Pohlenz, ' Die Entstehung der attischen Komödie ', *Nach.
Akad. Göttingen* (1949), 31-44 : see also Pickard-Cambridge, *Di-
thyramb* 225 ff., Schmid-Stählin 1, 2, 1, 523 ff., Schmid 4 ff.,
Dover 113.

afield here to try to analyse the underlying principles of Aristophanes's comic technique.[51] Incongruity, surprise, topsyturvydom, exaggeration, anti-climax, disorderliness, absurdity, mimicry, stupidity, indecency, derision, exuberance, deformity, illogicality, nonsense, garrulity, *Mystification*,[52] the overthrow of proud or powerful personages, novelty, bewilderment, deception, freakishness, flouting of conventions, childishness—these and many other qualities contribute to the laughter-working technique of every accomplished comedian, and are all to be found in the comedies of Aristophanes.[53]

§ 11. THE LANGUAGE OF ARISTOPHANES [54]

Aristophanes's Greek is extraordinarily varied. Other Greek authors tend to confine themselves to one consistent level of style. Aristophanes uses terms from

[51] For Aristotelian and pseudo-Aristotelian definitions of humour see Lane Cooper, *An Aristotelian Theory of Comedy* (Oxford, 1924) and refs. in n. 44 above. For general discussion of the sources of laughter see W. McDougall, *An Outline of Psychology*, 3rd edn. (London, 1926), 165-70, J. C. Gregory, *The Nature of Laughter* (London, 1924), J. Y. T. Greig, *The Psychology of Laughter* (London, 1923).

[52] This occurs when elaborate preparations are made for some purpose unknown as yet to the audience (who will laugh at the relief from curiosity and tension when the purpose is finally revealed).

[53] I have not attempted here to discuss A.'s way of mixing the serious and the comic at times—τὸ σπουδογέλοιον, as it has been called: *cf.* Horace's principle of *ridentem dicere verum*. See Schmid 410 and on **389**.

[54] As Schmid (425) notes, there is no comprehensive study of Aristophanes's language. He (56, 425) lists the chief contributions to the subject down to 1945: see further in Murphy. Schmid's own discussion (425-34) is the most comprehensive as yet. In English see especially Tucker xxxiv-lvi, Richards 116-59, Lever 135 ff.

current speech, formal prose, and poetry : he expresses his actors' thoughts and feelings in the lowest or loftiest phrases imaginable : and he extends the range of contemporary Greek by inventing many new words.

Within each play marked variations [55] are to be found between (a) dialogue and speeches (in iambic trimeters, or in iambic, anapaestic, or trochaic tetrameters) ; (b) choral songs in pure lyric metre ; and (c) choral commentaries on the action, delivered in shorter iambic, trochaic, or anapaestic, lines.

We shall consider these variations under three heads : dialect, vocabulary, syntax. In the dialogue and speeches the language approximates (so far as we can judge) to the speech of everyday Athens in 405 B.C. The dialect is generally New Attic.[56] Similarly the vocabulary of the dialogues and speeches is mainly that of everyday Athenian life, with some admixture of such technical terms as medical doctors, or Sophists, or literary critics, or craftsmen used.[57]

In the syntax of his dialogues he tends to avoid certain non-colloquial and poetic uses such as ὡς for ὡσπερ in similes, πρός or ἐκ for ὑπό in the sense of 'by', and the omission of ἄν with the subjunctive after πρίν,

[55] On this see especially Richards. In what follows I have substituted three broader divisions for his five (iambic trimeters ; trochaic tetrameters ; other iambic and trochaic metres ; anapaests ; lyric metres).

[56] This, in contrast with the Old Attic of Thucydides and the tragedians, uses σύν for ξύν in the preposition and its compounds (e.g. σύνεσις for ξύνεσις : but see n. 75), -ττ- for -σσ- (τάττω for τάσσω), -ρρ- for -ρσ- (θαρρεῖν for θαρσεῖν) : see further in C. D. Buck, The Greek Dialects, 2nd edn. (Chicago, 1955), Tucker xxxvii and Schmid 426. For Doric words in dialogue see index.

[57] See Miller, Denniston (Technical Terms etc.), Murphy (A. and Art of Rhetoric), and index at Medical Terms, Sophists. For craft terms see, e.g., **799** ff.

εἰ, ἕως, ὅς, and other relatives. He allows himself more freedom than stricter Greek writers in the use of *Elision* (*e.g.* of -αι in the infinitive and in verbal forms in -μαι, -νται (as, *e.g.*, εἶν' ἐν in 692)), *Aphaeresis* (*e.g.* ἀξιῶ 'γώ), *Crasis* (κἄστι 183), *Synizesis* ('Απόλλω‿ού, Πηλέᾳ), as well. as *Hiatus* and *Deictic Iota*. His flexible use of *Particles* in the dialogue and speeches shows the genius of Greek for expressing subtle nuances of thought and feeling : only Plato rivals him in this. The colloquial idiom is also clear in his use of current phrases and proverbs (191, 438).

A peculiarly charming feature—this, too, derived from popular speech—is his use of *Diminutives*.[58] These may express affection (*e.g.* Ξανθίδιον in 582), depreciation (172), contempt (89), and other mental attitudes, simple or mixed (*e.g.* affection and pity or contempt in ὠδελφίδιον in 60). They are formed by adding simple endings like -ιον (παιδίον in 37), -αριον (usually contemptuous, *e.g.* πλοιάριον in 139), -ισκος, -η, -ον (σανδαλίσκον in 405) ; or double endings like -ιδ-ιον, (Ξανθίδιον in 582), -ιδ-αριον (κῳδάριον in 1203), -ισκιον (χλανίσκιον), -ύλλ-ιον (ἐπύλλιον in 942) ; or even a triple form -ισκ-ίδ-ιον (χλανισκίδιον). These—like the diminutives of the colloquial Latin writers (*e.g.* Catullus's *misellus, molliculus, pusillus*) and the remarkable variety of diminutives in contemporary Italian—combine intimacy and expressiveness with extraordinary subtlety. No other Greek writer approaches Aristophanes in this, or in the vigorous use of abusive terms (*e.g.* 465 ff.), curses, oaths, and appeals to the gods.[59]

In contrast with the free-and-easy, often coarse,

[58] See Peppler, Pauly-Wissowa xvi, 1640, Tucker liii, and P'. Chantraine, *La formation des noms* etc. (Paris, 1933).
[59] See further in Tucker liv-lvi and Werres. For some other

always vigorous, language of his dialogues and speeches, Aristophanes's choral odes are at times beautiful examples of pure lyric style (*e.g.* the Frogs' songs in 209 ff. and 229 ff.—but with deliberately low-comedy insertions—and the Initiates' Parodos in 323 ff.). Here the vocabulary and syntax are mainly those of the traditional Greek lyric, and the dialect is mainly literary Doric (with its most noticeable feature of -ā for -η).[60]

The contrast between the lyrical purity of these passages, in style and thought, and the general tone of the other parts of the play is sometimes poignant, sometimes (deliberately) shocking. At one moment we may be involved in some sordid street wrangle : the next, breathing an air of beauty and imagination as pure as in Pindar or Keats.

Between these contrasting extremes lies the inter-mediate style of some of the shorter iambic, trochaic, and anapaestic rhythms. These are generally nearer in language and tone to the colloquial style of the dialogue, but a greater degree of poeticism is sometimes observable (especially in the anapaests).[61]

In trying to separate the different levels of Aristo-phanes's language we must reckon with a disruptive element. This is *Parody* (§ 10). When Aristophanes intends parody, the level of the dialogue-language may suddenly shoot up to absurd heights, its dialect and metre being altered to suit ; or, contrarily, the level of

figures of speech see Index at *Ambiguities, Asyndeton, Oxymoron, Tmesis*. For A.'s use of interjections, exclamations, rhetorical questions, wish-formulas, and ellipses see W. Dittmar, *Sprach-liche Untersuchungen zu A. und Menander* (Weida, 1937). See also Poultney, G. K. Gardikas in *Athena* xxxiii (1921), 25-60, and G. P. Anagnostopoulos in *Athena* xxxvi (1924), 1-60.

[60] See especially Björck.
[61] Richards gives examples : but further study is needed.

his tetrameters and lyrics may suddenly slump into equally absurd depths. So the tetrameters in 1004 ff. begin in lofty style but soon descend into 'twaddle and spouting': so, too, the Frogs' song is interspersed with deliberate vulgarities and absurdities (see on 210 ff. and 249). Sometimes the mixture of styles becomes fantastically complex (see on 814 ff.). One can only repeat here that an essential quality of Aristophanes's genius is fluidity and variability.

Much of Aristophanes's copious language and varied style is derived from predecessors and contemporaries. But—though the scantiness of surviving early Greek literature prevents complete proof of this—much seems to have been his own original contribution to the Greek literary tradition. We can probably see this originality in many of his fantastic *Coined Words*, *Diminutives*, *Comic Terminations*, and *Comic Names*; and—the surest mark of imaginative genius, this—in his brilliant *Metaphors* and comparisons.[61a]

As a result of this prodigal profusion, the total effect of Aristophanes's language is quite unlike that of the homogeneous and disciplined styles which are usually taken to represent the classical tradition—the style of Homer, or Sophocles, or Plato, for example, or in English that of Dryden, Pope, or Gibbon. Its nearer equivalents in modern languages are the works of Rabelais, Shakespeare, or James Joyce. This contrast corresponds to the difference between two profound influences on Greek life and thought: the influence of the cult of Apollo with its emphasis on discipline, orderliness, restraint, self-control, and regularity, and the influence of the cult of Dionysos with its emphasis on freedom and exuberance.

[61a] See H. J. Newiger, *Metaphor u. Allegorie* (in A.), Munich, 1957.

§ 12. METRE, MUSIC, DELIVERY, DANCING

No Greek author displays a wider range of *Metres* than Aristophanes. The *Iambic trimeters* of his dialogue are much freer than those of the tragedians ; the variety of his *Tetrameters* and *Dimeters* (iambic, trochaic, anapaestic) is unparalleled ; his *Lyric metres* (choriambic, ionic a minore, etc.) are as subtle as any outside Pindar ; and he even uses the heroic dactylic *Hexameter* at times. Details of these rhythms will be discussed in the notes, as they occur in the text (see index). Here only a few general observations will be made.

As has been noticed in the previous section, Aristophanes's language varies with his metres, from the colloquial Attic of the trimeters to the artificial and elaborate diction of the lyrics. Further, Aristophanes's humour depends at times on a skilful manipulation of rhythms, as when, for example, Dionysos fights with iambics against the trochees of the Frog-chorus (see on **209** ff.). Metre, too, can help to point to parody. Thus when he wants to mock the tragic style in his dialogue he generally restricts his trimeter to the rules of tragic iambics. In **814** ff. he uses dactylic hexameters for describing Aeschylus and the *Lecythion* metre for Euripides. The Lecythion-scene (**1200** ff.), too, depends partly on metre for its effect, though its main point is probably not metrical. Similarly in one of Euripides's attacks on Aeschylus (**1261** ff.) the main point is metrical ; and Aeschylus counter-attacks partly in metrical terms. Other examples of humour and characterization by *Metre* will be mentioned in the notes.[62]

[62] On A.'s metres in general see J. W. White, Wilamowitz, *Gr. Vers.*, Schmid 57-61, Dale, Platnauer, and Koster, who examine problems of colometry, periodic structure, and responsion, not discussed here. For the iambic trimeters see Descroix.

The music of the voices and of their instrumental accompaniment is entirely lost.[63] As in modern operas or films, it could provide an effective means of expressing the underlying moods and emotions of the singers (*e.g.* sentimentality in **1346** ff., religious exaltation in **340** ff., warlike vigour in **1356** ff., triumphal joy in **1528** ff.). At times, too, it formed a part of the humour and satire (see on **1264** ff.). Whatever were the tone-values of its tunes, we can be reasonably sure of two features : first, the words generally dominated the music ; second, the music was melodic, without any of the elaborate harmonies and instrumental complexities of modern choral music. Plainsong is perhaps its nearest tonal equivalent in modern times.

The lyrical parts, then, were sung to appropriate melodies. The dialogues were spoken more or less as in ordinary speech—except that the pronunciation, no doubt, became more mannered and orotund when tragic diction was being parodied. There is evidence (*cf.* on **303**) that the Athenian actors usually spoke with superb clarity, as was necessary in open-air performances. Besides the spoken delivery of the dialogue and the singing of the pure lyric passages there was an intermediate kind of declamation in a sing-song reciting-style halfway between speaking and singing [64] which was used in reciting the tetrameters. To these broad divisions we must, of course, add the natural variations resulting from changes of mood and character : for example, Xanthias the slave would not speak like King Pluto, nor would the Frogs sing quite like the Initiates.[65]

[63] See on *Music* and Schmid 61. Normally lyrics were accompanied by a flute ; but a lyre is used in *Frogs* 1284 ff. and *Thesm.* 124.

[64] For this (and the dubious παρακαταλογή) see White 20, 368-71, Pickard-Cambridge, *Dram. Fest.* 153-65, and Schmid 433.

[65] On actors' voices and gestures see Pickard-Cambridge, *Dram. Fest.* 165-74.

Dancing normally accompanied the lyrics, tetra-
meters, and dimeters.[66] There were two kinds of dance :
group-dances by the Chorus, and solo-dances. In the
first the Chorus of twenty-four (consisting of male
citizens trained for the purpose) moved in symmetrical
arrangements with co-ordinated gestures and postures,
led by the *Coryphaios* and, when necessary for divided
groupings, by sub-leaders. There were also the solo-
dances (see, *e.g.*, on **1305-6**). The characteristic dance
of Old Comedy was the *kordax*, associated with drunken-
ness.

§ 13. THE FORMAL STRUCTURE OF AN ARISTOPHANIC COMEDY

It is a characteristic of Greek art that many of its
apparently spontaneous and free-flowing productions are
constructed on rigorous structural principles. The life-
like statues of Polycleitos conform to a strict canon of
measurement. The flexible and fluent odes of Pindar
obey minute laws of symmetry. Aristophanes's comedies,
for all their apparent spontaneity and looseness, exem-
plify the same Greek love of formal discipline.

As we have seen, Aristophanes's plays were all subject
to the discipline of metre. But they also in part con-
formed to certain precise rules of structure.[67] This can

---

[66] See Pickard-Cambridge, *Dram. Fest.* 251-62, E. Roos, *Die
tragische Orchestik im Zerrbild der altattischen Komödie*, Lund,
1951 (with copious bibliography), L. Lawler in *Transactions
American Phil. Assocn.* lxxix, lxxx, lxxxi, lxxxii (1948–51), and
American Journal of Phil. lxxii (1951), 300-7.

[67] The pioneer in the study of formal structure in Aristophanes's
plays was Zielinski : see also Mazon, Starkie (*Wasps* ix-xxxi),
Schmid 43 ff., Wüst, Pickard-Cambridge (*Dithyramb* 292 ff.), and
Radermacher. I agree with Cornford, Norwood, Starkie, and
Pickard-Cambridge, that schematization has sometimes been
pressed too far.

be most clearly seen in the Parabasis and the Epir-
rhematic Syzygy as described below.

The formal structure of an Aristophanic comedy
goes like this :

1. The play opens with a **Prologue** in iambic trimeters :
   dialogue or monologue.
2. The Chorus enters in the **Parodos**.[68]
3. Various **Episodes** follow.
4. There is a **Parabasis**. This seems to have been an
   essential part—some think, the original nucleus
   —of Old Comedy, going back, apparently, to its
   early sources.[69] In it the Chorus apparently took
   off their costumes, abandoned all pretence of
   dramatic action, and spoke directly like orators to
   the spectators. Aristophanes generally used this
   part of the play for expressing his own personal
   opinions on literature or politics.

The seven parts of a full Parabasis were :

A. The κομμάτιον : a choral prelude.
B. The παράβασις proper : generally in anapaestic
   tetrameters.
C. The πνῖγος (literally 'choker') or μακρόν : a passage
   delivered at high speed (like a modern 'patter'
   song).
D. The στροφή or ᾠδή : lyric song and dance in free
   rhythms.

[68] See Kranz on *Parodos* in Pauly-Wissowa xviii, 4.

[69] See Schmid 43 ff., Pickard-Cambridge, *Dithyramb* 235, Kranz
on *Parabasis* in Pauly-Wissowa xviii, 3. The name Parabasis
(from παραβαίνειν 'to come forward' towards the audience) occurs
first in the *Scholia*. Ar. does not use the term, but refers to part
B as his 'anapaests'. The term Parabasis is unfortunately used
ambiguously to describe either the whole complex of A to G as
described here (or its truncated form D-G as used in *Frogs*) or
else B (*i.e.* the 'anapaests') alone.

E. The ἐπίρρημα : another address to the audience : usually in trochaic tetrameters.

F. The ἀντιστροφή or ἀντῳδή, corresponding with D in metre and similar in tone.

G. The ἀντεπίρρημα, corresponding with E and similar in tone.

The last four comprise what is called the Epirrhematic Syzygy. (This structure is sometimes also used elsewhere in the plays : see n. 72.) The numbers of lines in E and G are invariably multiples of four (see on 737), presumably to allow symmetrical dance-groupings.[70]

5. Further **Episodes** interspersed with comments or songs by the Chorus.

6. The **Exodos** ('going out'), in which the actors and chorus withdraw, often with songs of victory.

The remarkable feature here is the strictly symmetrical Parabasis-complex. Nothing quite like it recurs in any other form of classical drama. On the other hand, it is obvious that every play which has a chorus and is presented in a theatre without any curtain must have some kind of Parodos and Exodos ; and no play can begin without some kind of prologue or continue without episodes.

These formal divisions are identifiable in *Frogs*.[71] But the construction of its Prologue and Parodos is complicated by the introduction (off-scene) of the Frog Chorus so that we have a kind of false Parodos before the Chorus actually appears.

[70] This is a mere sketch of a very complicated matter : for details see citations in n. 67 above. Starkie, *Wasps* xix-xxi, shows how Aristophanes gradually discarded the Parabasis, until in *Eccl.* and *Plutus* there is 'no genuine Parabasis'.

[71] See especially Mazon, Pickard-Cambridge as cited in n. 67, and Wüst.

1. Prologue: **1-208** (or to **322**: see 3 below).   See also end of note on **738** ff.
2. False Parodos: song of the Frogs (**209-68**).
3. Prologue (continued) or Episode: **269-322**.
4. True Parodos: Chorus of Initiates.   (**323-459**: note a kind of abortive Parabasis in anapaests in **354-71**).
5. Episodes (iambic) and Choral Interventions (**460-673**).
6. Parabasis (**674-737**).   Here the first three parts of the full Parabasis are omitted, and only D-E-F-G (the epirrhematic syzygy) are left.   The address to the audience is transferred to E and G.   Thus:

   D. Ode (**674-85**).
   E. Epirrhema (**686-705**).
   F. Antode (**706-16**).
   G. Antepirrhema (**718-37**).

7. Episodes (tetrameters as well as iambic trimeters) and Choral Interventions (**738-1499**).[72]
8. Exodos with victory songs and procession (**1500** to end of play).

Some other broader divisions of Aristophanic comedy deserve notice.   In these the emphasis is on content not on formal construction.   Every play of Aristophanes

---

[72] These include a formal *Agon* (see next paragraph) constructed on a pattern that approximates to the formal Parabasis-complex thus: Ode (**895-904**), Epirrhema (**905-70**), Pnigos (**971-91**), Antode (**992-1003**), Antepirrhema (**1004-76**), Antipnigos (**1078-98**).   Note also the corresponding Keleusmos (**905-6**) and Antikeleusmos (**1004-5**).   For amplification of this very curt treatment of a highly complicated matter see Pickard-Cambridge, *Dithyramb* 326-7, Cantarella, *Rane* 29-31, and refs. in n. 67.   Outside the Parabasis the epirrhematic structure is not, I think, always so clearly identifiable as disciples of Zielinski allege.

contains a major contest or argument (called the ἀγών)
as well as various minor conflicts. It (or part of it) is
generally constructed epirrhematically (see, *e.g.*, n. 72).
In *Frogs* the main Agon is that between Euripides and
Aeschylus in **905** ff. (Elsewhere it usually comes before
the Parabasis.) His plays also generally end with a
Wedding or a Feast, and a triumphal procession or revel-
rout (κῶμος). In *Frogs* 1500 ff. we have a triumphal
procession after a feast. Some scholars have also held
that occasional passages of sustained abuse (ψόγος) (see
on **368** and **374**) deserve recognition as a formal element
in the Old Comedy. Possibly all of these, together with
what seem to be survivals from fertility cults, may go
back to ritual sources.[73] But, on the other hand, conflicts,
quarrels, arguments, abuse, feasts, weddings, and revel-
ries, must have been normal features of Athenian life
during the wine-festivals.

§ 14. THE TRANSMISSION OF THE TEXT: COPYISTS AND COMMENTATORS [74]

How has the *Frogs* been preserved from 405 B.C. to
the present day? How closely does the text of the
present edition resemble what Aristophanes or his scribe
wrote out in Athens for the first production? [75]

[73] See references in n. 50.

[74] See especially Schmid's survey (387-92) of the literature
on this, and more recently Dover (see p. 207 n. 1), W. J. W.
Koster's articles in *Revue des Etudes Grecques* lxvi (1953), 1-33,
Dioniso xv (1952), 143-52, and *Mnemosyne*, 4th ser., vii (1954),
136-56 and ix (1956), 225-31. See also the introductions to the
edns. of Radermacher and Coulon, van Leeuwen's *Prolegomena*,
Coulon's *Essai*, Boudreaux, and G. Pasquali, *Storia della tradi-
zione*, etc. (Florence, 1952), 194 ff.

[75] Some clear differences are : A. used capital letters through-
out, used no accents, did not normally mark divisions between

In answering these questions we shall find that two kinds of people are chiefly involved : the copyist (first scribe, then printer) who makes each new version of the text, and the scholar who directs their work and adds his interpretations. (At times the two merge in a scholar-scribe or scholar-printer.)

Nothing is known of the text's history for over a century.[76] But after the death of Alexander the Great the foundation of the Library at Alexandria and the encouragement of scholars by the Ptolemies of Egypt led to energetic study of Aristophanes's plays in the third and second centuries B.C., notably by Lycophron, Eratosthenes, Euphronios, Aristophanes of Byzantium (who seems to have produced a critical edition, paying special attention to orthography), Timachidas, and the great *Aristarchus*. A rival school at Pergamon under the Attalid monarchs in the third and second centuries B.C.

words, probably did not divide up the lyrics into lines (on this see K. Holzinger, Χαριστήρια *A. Rzach*, Prague, 1930, 70 ff.). Aristophanes probably wrote the opening line of *Frogs* thus : ΕΙΠΩΤΙΤΩΝΕΙΩΘΟΤΩΝΩΔΕΣΠΟΤΑ (if he used the Ionic alphabet : if not, he wrote O for Ω, E for H, etc. : on this dubiety see especially Boudreaux 7). In questions of orthography (see especially Coulon i, xxviii and Boudreaux) editors have generally assumed that A.'s *Spelling* was always consistent. But from what we know of many later poets (*e.g.* Shakespeare, Yeats) this is dubious ; so when the MSS. of *Frogs* vary between Old Attic ξυν (see n. 56) and New Attic συν, I have followed the stronger MS. tradition (except, of course, when the metre is decisive : see Starkie on *Wasps* 359) regardless of consistency (see on 699 ff.) : *cf.* the frequent variation in English between -*ise* and -*ize*. *Cf.* on 328-36 (end of n.). In the numbering of the lines (which ultimately depends on the colometry of the lyrics : see n. 62) I have adapted the traditional system (derived from Brunck's edn. of 1810) to meet recent metrical views.

[76] On the question whether A. rewrote parts of the play for the second performance see n. 25.

produced works on Aristophanes by Crates and others.[77]
Later Aristophanic scholars included Didymus (died
c. A.D. 10) and Symmachus (c. A.D. 100). It was Sym-
machus, apparently, who first produced an edition of
selected plays of Aristophanes. He chose the eleven
which now survive : the rest were subsequently lost. A
later edition reduced the number to three: *Plutus*,
Clouds, *Frogs* : cf. n. 84.

No writings of these scholars have survived in en-
tirety. We owe our knowledge of them mainly to the
citations from them written in the margins of the MSS.
—the *Scholia* as they are called.[78] The Scholia on
Aristophanes are among the fullest that have survived
from antiquity and provide a rich store of miscellaneous
information. Modern editors owe much to them.

One other ancient source of knowledge about the text
of Aristophanes may be briefly mentioned—ancient
lexicographers, metricians, anecdotists, and grammarians,
such as *Athenaeus*, *Hesychius*, *Photius*, and *Suidas*, who
quote or comment on passages from Aristophanes.[79]

To turn to the text as it now survives. The earliest
existing fragment of *Frogs* is that on a Rhodian inscrip-
tion of the first century B.C.[80] Next come the *Papyrus*
fragments, dating from about A.D. 100–600.[81] The
earliest complete text is preserved in the Ravenna MS. (R).

[77] For the methods of the Alexandrian and Pergamene scholars
see J. E. Sandys, *History of Classical Scholarship* i (3rd edn.,
Cambridge, 1921), chaps. 8-9.

[78] A new edition of these to supersede F. Duebner's (Paris,
1855) has been promised by Koster (see n. 74). Rutherford un-
fortunately ignored the scholia of V.

[79] For these miscellaneous 'testimonia' see Kraus. Suidas is
a particularly rich source : see especially G. Bünger, *De A.
Ranarum apud Suidam reliquiis* (Freiburg, 1881).

[80] See on 454-9.

[81] See Coulon i, xxii-xxv, Pack 13-14, and n. 92.

It was written about A.D. 1000, contains all eleven plays of the Symmachus collection—the only MS. to do so.[82] Next in age and value comes the Marcianus or Venetian codex (V). It contains fuller Scholia than R and probably dates from the twelfth century.[83] Others of importance are the Vaticanus Urbinas (U), the Ambrosianus (M), and the Parisinus (A), all dating from the fourteenth century. There are many others.[84] On these MSS. (together with the slight help of the papyri, quotations in other works, and the Rhodian inscription) all our modern editions depend.[85] Editors have made alterations by conjectural emendation. But over 95 per cent of a modern text corresponds with R and/or V.[86]

A new epoch in the textual history of the classics begins with the invention of printing, through which

[82] For an analysis of the various distributions of plays in the chief MSS. see Radermacher 66-7. R was discovered by Invernizi and first used in modern times in his edition of 1794.

[83] Photographic facsimiles of R and V have been edited by J. van Leeuwen (Leyden, 1904) and T. W. Allen (London, 1902). I am grateful to the library officials in Ravenna and Venice who allowed me to consult the MSS. there.

[84] 237 MSS. of A. in all according to Schmid 387. Of these 148 contain *Plutus*, 127 *Clouds*, 76 *Frogs*, these being the 3 most popular plays in late classical and in post-Renaissance times. It is possible that RVUMA derive from a single archetype of the 9th century (see G. Zuntz in *Byzantion* xiv, 1939, 545 ff.). How many copies lie between that source and A.'s own MS., no one can tell.

[85] The fact that the papyri and the inscription generally agree with our best MSS. suggests that the post-classical corruption has been slight. For the chief kinds of error and disagreement between the MSS. see Coulon i, xiii ff. and his *Essai*, also Starkie, *Wasps* lii-lviii. Von Velsen gives the fullest account of the variants.

[86] In one respect, however, the MSS. are often inadequate or unreliable—in the distribution of dialogue between the various speakers: see Coulon i, xxx f. and, *e.g.*, on **738** ff., **568** ff., **645**.

hundreds or thousands of copies of a work could be produced by a single process—and much more clearly, on the whole, than by hand. The first printed edition of Aristophanes was the beautifully executed Aldine (Venice, 1498), edited by a Cretan scholar, Marcus Musurus. But it lacked two plays, *Lysistrata* and *Thesmophoriazusae*. The second Juntine edition (Florence, 1525 : 1st edn. 1510) was the first to print all eleven plays. Since then there have been about forty complete editions and twenty notable separate editions of *Frogs*.[87]

Since the seventeenth century many eminent scholars have worked on the text and interpretation of Aristophanes : Casaubon, *Bentley*, *Porson* (who, it is said, wept with joy to find that some of his emendations in Aristophanes had been anticipated by Bentley),[88] *Wilamowitz*, and many others. Gifted translators [89]—in English notably J. H. Frere, B. B. Rogers and Gilbert Murray—have also done much to popularize Aristophanes's humour. But he remains—alone, perhaps, with Pindar in this—one of the hardest of authors to appreciate in any other language but his own subtle and elegant Greek.

[87] Listed in Blaydes xxiv-xxvi and Schmid 391-2, 332. More recently part of Cantarella's complete edition has been published.

[88] See H. R. Luard, 'Porson', *Cambridge Essays*, 1857, 153. Porson's notes on Aristophanes were published by his friend Dobree in 1820. The Greek type of the text of the present edition is called 'Small Pica Porson' and is derived from Porson's own Greek script.

[89] The earliest known full translation (into Latin) was that of Andreas Divus at Venice, 1538 (but see next section) : the earliest of any play into a modern language (Italian) was in 1545 : earliest translation of *Frogs* into English, Dunster (1780 ?). For other English translations see *Cambridge Bibliography of English Literature* (index at *Aristophanes*).

§ 15. ARISTOPHANES'S INFLUENCE AND REPUTATION [90]

Though Aristophanes's plays enjoyed great popularity during his lifetime,[91] soon afterwards dramatic taste and fashion turned away from his kind of comedy. Menander, the master of the New Comedy, became the pattern for later classical comedy ; [92] and he, through his Latin imitators, Terence and Plautus (though Plautus had some Aristophanic traits), dominated the main evolution of Western comedy to the present day. On the other hand the non-dramatic satirical writers of Greece (notably Lucian) and of Rome (notably Lucilius and Horace) imitated Aristophanes. But no classical author inherited the fullness of his comic genius.

His plays were apparently unknown in the Middle Ages outside Greek lands. But they were not neglected in the western revival of Greek learning in the fifteenth

[90] See, in general, L. E. Lord, *A., his Plays and Influence* (London, 1925) ; W. Süss, *A. und die Nachwelt* (Leipzig, 1911) ; G. Highet, *The Classical Tradition* (Oxford, 1949) ; and Schmid 359 ff. and 450 ff. (Some modifications of Schmid's account of the German tradition can be deduced from Stuart Atkins, 'A. and the Classical Walpurgisnacht', *Comparative Literature* vi, 1945, 64-78, who argues that Goethe retained a strong interest in A. ; and from R. Wellek, *A History of Modern Criticism*, i-ii, London, 1955 : see indexes at *Aristophanes*.) For the English tradition see especially L. Rechner, *A. in England* (Frankfurt-on-Main, 1914). For A.'s influence on W. S. Gilbert see P. Fiddian in *Proceedings of the Classical Association* lii (1955), 20-1.

[91] Out of 9 known results he was first with 4 (*Babylonians, Acharnians, Knights, Frogs*), second with 4 (*Banqueters, Wasps, Birds, Peace*), and last only with *Clouds*.

[92] It is perhaps a sign of disfavour that only 2 or 3 out of some 50 Egyptian fragments referring to Aristophanes (as cited by Pack) date from before A.D. 100.

century. Italian scholars owned copies as early as 1408
and 1423 ; [93] and the first printed edition, the Aldine of
1498 (see § 14), was one of the earlier volumes in that
famous series. But the first vernacular translation (into
Italian) came, rather late, in 1545.[94] On the whole the
difficulty of his language and the apparent formlessness
of his plots, together with the grossness and extreme
topicality of his humour, prevented him from having
much influence on early Renaissance writers.

In France, however, one genuinely Aristophanic spirit
emerged early in the sixteenth century—Rabelais (b.
1483).[95] He is one of the few writers who equals Aristo-
phanes in style, humour, satire, and fantasy : but he
lacks Aristophanes's purer lyrical moods, lightness of
touch, and structural discipline. In France, too, Aristo-
phanes had the advantage of being partly translated by
Ronsard ; and Racine and Molière copied him in their
early work. In Germany during the sixteenth century
several authors, most notably Hans Sachs, imitated him,
and contemporary critics praised him.

In England *Plutus* and *Peace* were produced at
Cambridge in 1536 and 1546 ; and soon such influential
writers as More and Ascham were referring to him. But
Shakespeare, in many ways a kindred spirit,[96] seems to
have ignored him, preferring to model his comedies on
Plautus. Ben Jonson (b. 1573) followed Aristophanes

[93] R. R. Bolgar, *The Classical Heritage and its Beneficiaries*
(Cambridge, 1954), 495-6 and 509.

[94] Efforts to translate some of the *Plutus*, the easiest and least
Aristophanic of the plays, into Latin date from before 1444.
See D. P. Lockwood in *Transactions Amer. Phil. Assocn.* xl (1909).

[95] See especially Steiger 430 ff. Rabelais owned a copy of A.'s
plays, but probably acquired much of his Aristophanic quality
through Lucian.

[96] For parallels see Starkie, *Ach.* xxxix ff. and in *Hermathena*
xlii (1920), 26 ff.

closely in his *Poetaster* and *Epicoene*; and other con-
temporary English dramatists were clearly interested in
his works.[97]   Later in the seventeenth century, puritan-
ism in England, and, in France, a stricter theory of classi-
cism, brought him into a period of disfavour that lasted
until the end of the eighteenth century.   Early in the
nineteenth century the Romantic Movement, with its
emphasis on exuberance and freedom, welcomed Aristo-
phanes as a powerful ally in the Classical camp.   Writers
like Shelley (though his *Swellfoot the Tyrant*, an Aristo-
phanic onslaught on George IV, was not a success),
Browning, and Swinburne admired and imitated him;
and translations became more numerous and more
popular (see n. 89 above).   W. S. Gilbert had Aristo-
phanes very much in mind when he wrote his comic
operas in collaboration with Sir Arthur Sullivan.   No
English writer has so successfully reproduced the quality
of Aristophanes's lyrics as he.   More recently T. S. Eliot
began, but did not complete a remarkable 'Aristophanic
Melodrama', *Sweeney Agonistes*.   Within the last few
years adaptations of Aristophanes's plays have been
frequently presented in the theatre and by broadcasting.
But the main tradition of European comedy has remained
Plautine-Menandrian on the whole—depending for its
humour on character, irony, and plot, rather than on
broad comedy, caricature, and fantasy.   In the con-
temporary theatre the Aristophanic style is best exempli-
fied (though without direct imitation) in pantomime,
music-hall, and revue.

Among writers specially interested in education [98] the

[97] *Cambridge Hist. of English Lit.* vi, 362-3; also viii, 164;
x, 25, and index to *Bibliography*.

[98] See Bolgar (*op. cit.* in n. 93) as indicated in his index. A.'s
own interest in education is expressed in *Frogs* 1008 ff. (especially
1054-5).

work of Aristophanes has on the whole been more often recommended than rejected. Quintilian (10, 1, 65) praised the Old Comedy (especially as composed by Aristophanes, Eupolis, and Cratinus) for its purity, charm, and grace of style and for its vigour in attacking faults ; and he recommended it as next best to Homer's poetry as a model for orators. In the time of Hadrian grammarians and stylists particularly admired the Attic purity of his Greek. Byzantine scholars continued to study his plays, especially in the fourth, fifth, and ninth centuries. In the sixteenth century Erasmus and the Reformers praised him highly, and the Jesuits recommended *Plutus* as a text-book for their schools in Italy—a happy example of the unifying effects of the classical tradition in times of controversy. Disfavour, as we have seen, came in the seventeenth and eighteenth centuries. But within the last century several plays besides *Plutus* have become popular as school-books, especially *Clouds*, *Birds*, *Wasps*. The nineteenth-century editors of school editions, following the precepts and practice of Dr. Bowdler, tended to omit passages deemed to be unsuitable for younger readers.

As might be expected in the case of so many-sided a genius, Aristophanes's reputation has varied greatly. Plato, who knew him personally, seems to have liked and admired him, to judge from the genial portrait in *Symposium* and the epigram to be quoted later. He apparently bore no ill will against him for his remarks on Socrates (see on **1491**). But the whole tendency of Plato's ethics and of his hostile attitude to the freedom of literature (as expressed in his *Republic*) weighed against the Aristophanic drama.[99] So, too, in the fourth century a greater

[99] Though in fact the germ of much of Plato's moralistic attitude to literature is, paradoxically, to be found in *Frogs* 1008 ff.

aesthetic fastidiousness [100] rejected the coarseness of the
Old Comedy in favour of the suaver (but in many ways
more immoral) New Comedy of Menander. This ethical
and moral revulsion from Aristophanes finds its strongest
expression in extant classical literature in Plutarch's
Judgement between Aristophanes and Menander. Here
Plutarch condemns Aristophanes's kind of comedy for
its vulgarity, untidiness, licence, scurrility, baseness, and
nauseating garrulity. But other influential critics thought
differently. Quintilian's praise of his style has already
been mentioned. The Emperor Marcus Aurelius (*Medita-
tions* 11, 6), no lover of base or frivolous things, admired
the Old Comedy for its outspokenness and its denuncia-
tions of pretentiousness. Cicero (*Laws* 2, 37) acknow-
ledged Aristophanes's wit and moral influence. One of
the greatest Fathers of the Church, St. John Chrysostom
(345–407), must have admired and loved Aristophanes's
works, if we can believe Aldus Manutius's statement in
the Aldine edition that the Saint even used twenty-
eight of them as his pillow at night.[101]
    The same difference of opinion has already been

[100] See, *e.g.*, Aristotle's strictures on αἰσχρολογία in *Nicoma-
cheian Ethics*, 1128 a 3 ff. and *Politics*, 1336 b 3 ff. But Aristotle
ranks Aristophanes himself with Sophocles (*Poetics*, 1448 a 27).
See further in Schmid 451 ff. and 445 ff.

[101] *Hunc item Ioanes Chrysostomus tanti fecisse dicitur, ut
duodetriginta comoedias Aristophanis, semper haberet in manibus,
adeo ut pro puluillo dormiens uteretur: hinc itaque et eloquentiam
et seueritatem, quibus est mirabilis, didicisse dicitur.* Q. Cataudella
in *Athenaeum* xviii (1940), 236–43 dismisses the story as a fabri-
cation by some detractor of Chrysostom ; but there is no evi-
dence for this (and is it not a frequent characteristic of saints
to do surprising things ?). It is idle to speculate which 28 plays
the saintly head rested on (if the number is not exaggerated).
Aristophanic influences have not been detected in Chrysostom's
writings.

noticed in post-Renaissance times. Sixteenth-century
critics generally admired him; but some very scathing
criticisms could be quoted from the seventeenth and
eighteenth centuries. Even then a few critics—Madame
Dacier among them—continued to praise him. The
majority, however, affected to despise him as a scurrilous
buffoon. Dean Swift, a far from unaristophanic writer
himself, complained (in an atrocious rhyme) that 'Aristo-
phánes/ . . . too bawdy and too prophane is'.

In the nineteenth century he returned to favour
among literary critics as well as among creative writers.
Two examples will illustrate prevailing views. Matthew
Arnold in his essay *On the Modern Element in Literature*
(1869) praised the underlying seriousness of Aristophanes's
thought, and found in his work 'the instinct of self-
preservation in humanity' and 'the seed of life' in
contrast with 'the seed of death' in Menander's plays.
George Meredith in his *Essay on Comedy* (1897) wrote:
'We may build up a conception of his powers if we mount
Rabelais upon Hudibras, lift him with the songfulness
of Shelley, give him a vein of Heinrich Heine, and cover
him with the mantle of the Anti-Jacobin, adding (that
there may be some Irish in him) a dash of Grattan . . .'.

But the finest tribute ever written to Aristophanes's
genius and charm is the epigram by his friend Plato the
philosopher:

> The Graces, seeking for a sanctuary
>   that Time would spare,
> came to the soul of Aristophanes
>   and rested there.

Αἱ Χάριτες, τέμενός τι λαβεῖν ὅπερ οὐχὶ πεσεῖται
ζητοῦσαι, ψυχὴν ηὗρον Ἀριστοφάνους.

CHARACTERS IN THE PLAY

(in order of their speaking) [1]

XANTHIAS, a slave
DIONYSOS, the god
HERACLES, the hero
CORPSE
CHARON, ferryman of the Dead
CHORUS OF FROGS (unseen)
CHORUS OF INITIATES
AEACUS, a door-keeper (see on **464** ff.)
SERVANT (see on **503** and **738**)
FIRST INNKEEPER
SECOND INNKEEPER (PLATHANE: see on **552** and **570**)
SERVANT OF PLUTO
EURIPIDES, the tragedian
AESCHYLUS, the tragedian
PLUTO, King of Hades

Also (silent parts): Bier-bearers, Servants of Aeacus, Policemen, Comic Muse.

[1] For the many variants and uncertainties in the MSS. lists of characters see Radermacher.

ΒΑΤΡΑΧΟΙ

ΞΑΝΘΙΑΣ

Εἴπω τι τῶν εἰωθότων, ὦ δέσποτα,
ἐφ᾽ οἷς ἀεὶ γελῶσιν οἱ θεώμενοι;

ΔΙΟΝΥΣΟΣ

νὴ τὸν Δί᾽ ὅ τι βούλει γε, πλὴν ʹ πιέζομαι.ʹ
τοῦτο δὲ φύλαξαι· πάνυ γάρ ἐστ᾽ ἤδη χολή.

ΞΑ. μηδ᾽ ἕτερον ἀστεῖόν τι;
ΔΙ.   πλήν γ᾽ ὡς θλίβομαι.   5
ΞΑ. τί δαί; τὸ πάνυ γέλοιον εἴπω;
ΔΙ.   νὴ Δία
θαρρῶν γε· μόνον ἐκεῖν᾽ ὅπως μὴ ʼρεῖς —
ΞΑ.   τὸ τί;
ΔΙ. μεταβαλλόμενος τἀνάφορον ὅτι χεζητιᾷς.
ΞΑ. μηδ᾽ ὅτι τοσοῦτον ἄχθος ἐπ᾽ ἐμαυτῷ φέρων,
εἰ μὴ καθαιρήσει τις, ἀποπαρδήσομαι;   10
ΔΙ. μὴ δῆθ᾽, ἱκετεύω, πλήν γ᾽ ὅταν μέλλω ʼξεμεῖν.
ΞΑ. τί δῆτ᾽ ἔδει με ταῦτα τὰ σκεύη φέρειν,
εἴπερ ποήσω μηδὲν ὧνπερ Φρύνιχος
εἴωθε ποιεῖν καὶ Λύκις κἀμειψίας
σκεύη ʼφέρουσ᾽ ἑκάστοτ᾽ ἐν κωμῳδίᾳ;   15
ΔΙ. μή νυν ποήσῃς· ὡς ἐγὼ θεώμενος,
ὅταν τι τούτων τῶν σοφισμάτων ἴδω,
πλεῖν ἢ ʼνιαυτῷ πρεσβύτερος ἀπέρχομαι.

1

ΞΑ. ὦ τρισκακοδαίμων ἄρ' ὁ τράχηλος οὑτοσί,
ὅτι θλίβεται μέν, τὸ δὲ γέλοιον οὐκ ἐρεῖ.   20

ΔΙ. εἶτ' οὐχ ὕβρις ταῦτ' ἐστὶ καὶ πολλὴ τρυφή,
ὅτ' ἐγὼ μὲν ὢν Διόνυσος, υἱὸς Σταμνίου,
αὐτὸς βαδίζω καὶ πονῶ, τοῦτον δ' ὀχῶ,
ἵνα μὴ ταλαιπωροῖτο μηδ' ἄχθος φέροι;

ΞΑ. οὐ γὰρ φέρω 'γώ;

ΔΙ.   πῶς φέρεις γὰρ ὅς γ' ὀχεῖ;   25

ΞΑ. φέρων γε ταυτί.

ΔΙ.   τίνα τρόπον;

ΞΑ.   βαρέως πάνυ.

ΔΙ. οὔκουν τὸ βάρος τοῦθ' ὃ σὺ φέρεις ὄνος φέρει;

ΞΑ. οὐ δῆθ' ὅ γ' ἔχω 'γὼ καὶ φέρω, μὰ τὸν Δί' οὔ.

ΔΙ. πῶς γὰρ φέρεις, ὅς γ' αὐτὸς ὑφ' ἑτέρου φέρει;

ΞΑ. οὐκ οἶδ'· ὁ δ' ὦμος οὑτοσὶ πιέζεται.   30

ΔΙ. σὺ δ' οὖν ἐπειδὴ τὸν ὄνον οὐ φῄς σ' ὠφελεῖν,
ἐν τῷ μέρει σὺ τὸν ὄνον ἀράμενος φέρε.

ΞΑ. οἴμοι κακοδαίμων· τί γὰρ ἐγὼ οὐκ ἐναυμάχουν;
ἦ τἄν σε κωκύειν ἂν ἐκέλευον μακρά.

ΔΙ. κατάβα, πανοῦργε. καὶ γὰρ ἐγγὺς τῆς θύρας   35
ἤδη βαδίζων εἰμὶ τῆσδ', οἷ πρῶτά με
ἔδει τραπέσθαι. παιδίον, παῖ, ἠμί, παῖ.

ΗΡΑΚΛΗΣ

τίς τὴν θύραν ἐπάταξεν; ὡς κενταυρικῶς
ἐνήλαθ' ὅστις. . . . εἰπέ μοι, τουτὶ τί ἦν;

ΔΙ. ὁ παῖς.

ΞΑ.   τί ἐστιν;

ΔΙ.   οὐκ ἐνεθυμήθης;

ΞΑ.   τὸ τί;   40

ΔΙ. ὡς σφόδρα μ᾽ ἔδεισε.

ΞΑ.   νὴ Δία, μή μαίνοιό γε.

ΗΡ. οὔ τοι μὰ τὴν Δήμητρα δύναμαι μὴ γελᾶν.
καίτοι δάκνω γ᾽ ἐμαυτόν· ἀλλ᾽ ὅμως γελῶ.

ΔΙ. ὦ δαιμόνιε, πρόσελθε· δέομαι γάρ τί σου.

ΗΡ. ἀλλ᾽ οὐχ οἷός τ᾽ εἴμ᾽ ἀποσοβῆσαι τὸν γέλων   45
ὁρῶν λεοντῆν ἐπὶ κροκωτῷ κειμένην.
τίς ὁ νοῦς; τί κόθορνος καὶ ῥόπαλον ξυνηλθέτην;
ποῖ γῆς ἀπεδήμεις;

ΔΙ.   ἐπεβάτευον Κλεισθένει.

ΗΡ. κἀναυμάχησας;

ΔΙ.   καὶ κατεδύσαμέν γε ναῦς
τῶν πολεμίων ἢ δώδεκ᾽ ἢ τρισκαίδεκα.   50

ΗΡ. σφώ;

ΔΙ.   νὴ τὸν Ἀπόλλω.

ΞΑ.   κᾆτ᾽ ἔγωγ᾽ ἐξηγρόμην.

ΔΙ. καὶ δῆτ᾽ ἐπὶ τῆς νεὼς ἀναγιγνώσκοντί μοι
τὴν Ἀνδρομέδαν πρὸς ἐμαυτὸν ἐξαίφνης πόθος
τὴν καρδίαν ἐπάταξε πῶς οἴει σφόδρα.

ΗΡ. πόθος; πόσος τις;

ΔΙ.   σμικρός, ἡλίκος Μόλων.   55

ΗΡ. γυναικός;

ΔΙ.   οὐ δῆτ᾽.

ΗΡ.   ἀλλὰ παιδός;

ΔΙ.   οὐδαμῶς.

ΗΡ. ἀλλ᾽ ἀνδρός;

ΔΙ.   ἀπαπαῖ.

ΗΡ..   ξυνεγένου τῷ Κλεισθένει;

ΔΙ. μὴ σκῶπτέ μ᾽, ὠδέλφ᾽· οὐ γὰρ ἀλλ᾽ ἔχω κακῶς·
τοιοῦτος ἵμερός με διαλυμαίνεται.

ΗΡ. ποῖός τις, ὦδελφίδιον;
ΔΙ.   οὐκ ἔχω φράσαι.   60
ὅμως γε μέντοι σοι δι᾽ αἰνιγμῶν ἐρῶ.
ἤδη ποτ᾽ ἐπεθύμησας ἐξαίφνης ἔτνους;
ΗΡ. ἔτνους; βαβαιάξ, μυριάκις γ᾽ ἐν τῷ βίῳ.
ΔΙ. ἆρ᾽ ἐκδιδάσκω τὸ σαφὲς ἢ ᾽τέρᾳ φράσω;
ΗΡ. μὴ δῆτα περὶ ἔτνους γε· πάνυ γὰρ μανθάνω.   65
ΔΙ. τοιουτοσὶ τοίνυν με δαρδάπτει πόθος
Εὐριπίδου.
ΗΡ.   καὶ ταῦτα τοῦ τεθνηκότος;
ΔΙ. κοὐδείς γέ μ᾽ ἂν πείσειεν ἀνθρώπων τὸ μὴ οὐκ
ἐλθεῖν ἐπ᾽ ἐκεῖνον.
ΗΡ.   πότερον εἰς Ἅιδου κάτω;
ΔΙ. καὶ νὴ Δί᾽ εἴ τί γ᾽ ἔστιν ἔτι κατωτέρω.   70
ΗΡ. τί βουλόμενος;
ΔΙ.   δέομαι ποιητοῦ δεξιοῦ.
οἱ μὲν γὰρ οὐκέτ᾽ εἰσίν, οἱ δ᾽ ὄντες κακοί.
ΗΡ. τί δ᾽; οὐκ Ἰοφῶν ζῇ;
ΔΙ.   τοῦτο γάρ τοι καὶ μόνον
ἔτ᾽ ἐστὶ λοιπὸν ἀγαθόν, εἰ καὶ τοῦτ᾽ ἄρα·
οὐ γὰρ σάφ᾽ οἶδ᾽ οὐδ᾽ αὐτὸ τοῦθ᾽ ὅπως ἔχει.   75
ΗΡ. εἶτ᾽ οὐχὶ Σοφοκλέα πρότερον ὄντ᾽ Εὐριπίδου
μέλλεις ἀναγαγεῖν, εἴπερ ἐκεῖθεν δεῖ σ᾽ ἄγειν;
ΔΙ. οὔ, πρίν γ᾽ ἂν Ἰοφῶντ᾽, ἀπολαβὼν αὐτὸν μόνον,
ἄνευ Σοφοκλέους ὅ τι ποεῖ κωδωνίσω.
κἄλλως ὁ μέν γ᾽ Εὐριπίδης πανοῦργος ὢν   80
κἂν ξυναποδρᾶναι δεῦρ᾽ ἐπιχειρήσειέ μοι·
ὁ δ᾽ εὔκολος μὲν ἐνθάδ᾽, εὔκολος δ᾽ ἐκεῖ.
ΗΡ. Ἀγάθων δὲ ποῦ ᾽στιν;
ΔΙ.   ἀπολιπών μ᾽ ἀποίχεται,

ἀγαθὸς ποιητὴς καὶ ποθεινὸς τοῖς φίλοις.
ΗΡ. ποῖ γῆς ὁ τλήμων;
ΔΙ.   ἐς μακάρων εὐωχίαν.   85
ΗΡ. ὁ δὲ Ξενοκλέης;
ΔΙ.   ἐξόλοιτο νὴ Δία.
ΗΡ. Πυθάγγελος δέ;
ΞΑ.   περὶ ἐμοῦ δ' οὐδεὶς λόγος
ἐπιτριβομένου τὸν ὦμον οὑτωσὶ σφόδρα.
ΗΡ. οὔκουν ἕτερ' ἔστ' ἐνταῦθα μειρακύλλια
τραγῳδίας ποιοῦντα πλεῖν ἢ μυρία,   90
Εὐριπίδου πλεῖν ἢ σταδίῳ λαλίστερα;
ΔΙ. ἐπιφυλλίδες ταῦτ' ἐστὶ καὶ στωμύλματα,
χελιδόνων μουσεῖα, λωβηταὶ τέχνης,
ἃ φροῦδα θᾶττον, ἢν μόνον χορὸν λάβῃ,
ἅπαξ προσουρήσαντα τῇ τραγῳδίᾳ.   95
γόνιμον δὲ ποιητὴν ἂν οὐχ εὕροις ἔτι
ζητῶν ἄν, ὅστις ῥῆμα γενναῖον λάκοι.
ΗΡ. πῶς γόνιμον;
ΔΙ.   ὡδὶ γόνιμον, ὅστις φθέγξεται
τοιουτονί τι παρακεκινδυνευμένον,
' αἰθέρα Διὸς δωμάτιον,' ἢ ' Χρόνου πόδα,'   100
ἢ ' φρένα μὲν οὐκ ἐθέλουσαν ὀμόσαι καθ' ἱερῶν,
γλῶτταν δ' ἐπιορκήσασαν ἰδίᾳ τῆς φρενός.'
ΗΡ. σὲ δὲ ταῦτ' ἀρέσκει;
ΔΙ.   μᾶλλὰ πλεῖν ἢ μαίνομαι.
ΗΡ. ἦ μὴν κόβαλά γ' ἐστίν — ὡς καὶ σοὶ δοκεῖ.
ΔΙ. μὴ τὸν ἐμὸν οἴκει νοῦν· ἔχεις γὰρ οἰκίαν.   105
ΗΡ. καὶ μὴν ἀτεχνῶς γε παμπόνηρα φαίνεται.
ΔΙ. δειπνεῖν με δίδασκε.
ΞΑ.   περὶ ἐμοῦ δ' οὐδεὶς λόγος.

ΔΙ. ἀλλ' ὧνπερ ἕνεκα τήνδε τὴν σκευὴν ἔχων
ἦλθον, κατὰ σὴν μίμησιν — ἵνα μοι τοὺς ξένους
τοὺς σοὺς φράσειας, εἰ δεοίμην, οἷσι σὺ   110
ἐχρῶ τόθ', ἡνίκ' ἦλθες ἐπὶ τὸν Κέρβερον.
τούτους φράσον μοι, λιμένας, ἀρτοπώλια,
πορνεῖ', ἀναπαύλας, ἐκτροπάς, κρήνας, ὁδούς,
πόλεις, διαίτας, πανδοκευτρίας, ὅπου
κόρεις ὀλίγιστοι.
ΞΑ.   περὶ ἐμοῦ δ' οὐδεὶς λόγος.   115
ΗΡ. ὦ σχέτλιε, τολμήσεις γὰρ ἰέναι καὶ σύ γε;
ΔΙ. μηδὲν ἔτι πρὸς ταῦτ', ἀλλὰ φράζε τῶν ὁδῶν
ὅπῃ τάχιστ' ἀφιξόμεθ' εἰς Ἅιδου κάτω·
καὶ μήτε θερμὴν μήτ' ἄγαν ψυχρὰν φράσῃς.
ΗΡ. φέρε δή, τίν' αὐτῶν σοι φράσω πρώτην; τίνα;   120
μία μὲν γὰρ ἔστιν ἀπὸ κάλω καὶ θρανίου —
κρεμάσαντι σαυτόν.
ΔΙ.   παῦε, πνιγηρὰν λέγεις.
ΗΡ. ἀλλ' ἔστιν ἀτραπὸς σύντομος τετριμμένη,
ἡ διὰ θυείας.
ΔΙ.   ἆρα κώνειον λέγεις;
ΗΡ. μάλιστά γε.
ΔΙ.   ψυχράν γε καὶ δυσχείμερον·   125
εὐθὺς γὰρ ἀποπήγνυσι τἀντικνήμια.
ΗΡ. βούλει ταχεῖαν καὶ κατάντη σοι φράσω;
ΔΙ. νὴ τὸν Δί', ὡς ὄντος γε μὴ βαδιστικοῦ.
ΗΡ. καθέρπυσον νῦν εἰς Κεραμεικόν.
ΔΙ.   κᾆτα τί;
ΗΡ. ἀναβὰς ἐπὶ τὸν πύργον τὸν ὑψηλόν —
ΔΙ.   τί δρῶ;   130
ΗΡ. ἀφιεμένην τὴν λαμπάδ' ἐντεῦθεν θεῶ,

κἄπειτ' ἐπειδὰν φῶσιν οἱ θεώμενοι
εἶναι, τόθ' εἶναι καὶ σὺ σαυτόν.
ΔΙ.   ποῖ;
ΗΡ.   κάτω.
ΔΙ. ἀλλ' ἀπολέσαιμ' ἂν ἐγκεφάλου θρίω δύο.
οὐκ ἂν βαδίσαιμι τὴν ὁδὸν ταύτην.
ΗΡ.   τί δαί;   135
ΔΙ. ἥνπερ σὺ τότε κατῆλθες.
ΗΡ.   ἀλλ' ὁ πλοῦς πολύς.
εὐθὺς γὰρ ἐπὶ λίμνην μεγάλην ἥξεις πάνυ
ἄβυσσον.
ΔΙ.   εἶτα πῶς γε περαιωθήσομαι;
ΗΡ. ἐν πλοιαρίῳ τυννουτῳί σ' ἀνὴρ γέρων
ναύτης διάξει δύ' ὀβολὼ μισθὸν λαβών.   140
ΔΙ. φεῦ.
ὡς μέγα δύνασθον πανταχοῦ τὼ δύ' ὀβολώ.
πῶς ἠλθέτην κἀκεῖσε;
ΗΡ.   Θησεὺς ἤγαγεν.
μετὰ ταῦτ' ὄφεις καὶ θηρί' ὄψει μυρία
δεινότατα.
ΔΙ.   μή μ' ἔκπληττε μηδὲ δειμάτου·
οὐ γάρ μ' ἀποτρέψεις.
ΗΡ.   εἶτα βόρβορον πολὺν   145
καὶ σκῶρ ἀείνων· ἐν δὲ τούτῳ κειμένους,
εἴ που ξένον τις ἠδίκησε πώποτε,
ἢ παῖδα κινῶν τἀργύριον ὑφείλετο,
ἢ μητέρ' ἠλόησεν, ἢ πατρὸς γνάθον
ἐπάταξεν, ἢ 'πίορκον ὅρκον ὤμοσεν,   150
ἢ Μορσίμου τις ῥῆσιν ἐξεγράψατο.
ΔΙ. νὴ τοὺς θεοὺς ἐχρῆν γε πρὸς τούτοισι κεἰ

τὴν πυρρίχην τις ἔμαθε τὴν Κινησίου.
HP. ἐντεῦθεν αὐλῶν τίς σε περίεισιν πνοή.
ὄψει τε φῶς κάλλιστον ὥσπερ ἐνθάδε,　　　155
καὶ μυρρινῶνας καὶ θιάσους εὐδαίμονας
ἀνδρῶν γυναικῶν καὶ κρότον χειρῶν πολύν.
ΔΙ. οὗτοι δὲ δὴ τίνες εἰσίν;
HP.　　　　　　　　　οἱ μεμυημένοι —
ΞΑ. νὴ τὸν Δί’ ἐγὼ γοῦν ὄνος ἄγω μυστήρια.
ἀτὰρ οὐ καθέξω ταῦτα τὸν πλείω χρόνον.　　　160
HP. οἵ σοι φράσουσ’ ἀπαξάπανθ’ ὧν ἂν δέῃ.
οὗτοι γὰρ ἐγγύτατα παρ’ αὐτὴν τὴν ὁδὸν
ἐπὶ ταῖσι τοῦ Πλούτωνος οἰκοῦσιν θύραις.
καὶ χαῖρε πόλλ’, ὦδελφέ.
ΔΙ.　　　　　　　　νὴ Δία καὶ σύ γε
ὑγίαινε. σὺ δὲ τὰ στρώματ’ αὖθις λάμβανε.　　　165
ΞΑ. πρὶν καὶ καταθέσθαι;
ΔΙ.　　　　　　　καὶ ταχέως μέντοι πάνυ.
ΞΑ. μὴ δῆθ’, ἱκετεύω σ’, ἀλλὰ μίσθωσαί τινα
τῶν ἐκφερομένων, ὅστις ἐπὶ τοῦτ’ ἔρχεται.
ΔΙ. ἐὰν δὲ μηὕρω;
ΞΑ.　　　　　　τότ’ ἔμ’ ἄγειν.
ΔΙ.　　　　　　　　καλῶς λέγεις.
καὶ γάρ τιν’ ἐκφέρουσι τουτονὶ νεκρόν.　　　170
οὗτος, σὲ λέγω μέντοι, σὲ τὸν τεθνηκότα.
ἄνθρωπε, βούλει σκευάρι’ εἰς Ἅιδου φέρειν;

ΝΕΚΡΟΣ

πόσ’ ἄττα;
ΔΙ.　　　ταυτί.
ΝΕ.　　　　　δύο δραχμὰς μισθὸν τελεῖς;

ΔΙ. μὰ Δί', ἀλλ' ἔλαττον.

ΝΕ.   ὑπάγεθ' ὑμεῖς τῆς ὁδοῦ.

ΔΙ. ἀνάμεινον, ὦ δαιμόνι', ἐὰν ξυμβῶ τί σοι.   175

ΝΕ. εἰ μὴ καταθήσεις δύο δραχμάς, μὴ διαλέγου.

ΔΙ. λάβ' ἐννέ' ὀβολούς.

ΝΕ.   ἀναβιοίην νῦν πάλιν.

ΔΙ. ὡς σεμνὸς ὁ κατάρατος.

ΞΑ.   οὐκ οἰμώξεται;
ἐγὼ βαδιοῦμαι.

ΔΙ.   χρηστὸς εἶ καὶ γεννάδας.
χωρῶμεν ἐπὶ τὸ πλοῖον.

ΧΑΡΩΝ

           ὠόπ, παραβαλοῦ.   180

ΞΑ. τουτὶ τί ἐστι;

ΔΙ.   τοῦτο; λίμνη νὴ Δία
αὕτη 'στὶν ἣν ἔφραζε, καὶ πλοῖόν γ' ὁρῶ.

ΞΑ. νὴ τὸν Ποσειδῶ κἄστι γ' ὁ Χάρων οὑτοσί.

ΔΙ. χαῖρ', ὦ Χάρων, χαῖρ', ὦ Χάρων, χαῖρ', ὦ Χάρων.

ΧΑ. τίς εἰς ἀναπαύλας ἐκ κακῶν καὶ πραγμάτων;   185
τίς εἰς τὸ Λήθης πεδίον, ἢ 's Ὀνουπόκας,
ἢ 's Κερβερίους, ἢ 's Κόρακας, ἢ 'πὶ Ταίναρον;

ΔΙ. ἐγώ.

ΧΑ.   ταχέως ἔμβαινε.

ΔΙ.   ποῦ σχήσειν δοκεῖς —
ἐς κόρακας ὄντως;

ΧΑ.   ναὶ μὰ Δία — σοῦ γ' εἵνεκα.
εἴσβαινε δή.

ΔΙ.   παῖ, δεῦρο.

ΧΑ.   δοῦλον οὐκ ἄγω,   190

εἰ μὴ νεναυμάχηκε τὴν περὶ τῶν κρεῶν.

ΞΑ. μὰ τὸν Δί' οὐ γάρ, ἀλλ' ἔτυχον ὀφθαλμιῶν.

ΧΑ. οὔκουν περιθρέξει δῆτα τὴν λίμνην κύκλῳ;

ΞΑ. ποῦ δῆτ' ἀναμενῶ;

ΧΑ.   παρὰ τὸν Αὑαίνου λίθον,
ἐπὶ ταῖς ἀναπαύλαις.

ΔΙ.   μανθάνεις;

ΞΑ.   πάνυ μανθάνω.   195
οἴμοι κακοδαίμων, τῷ ξυνέτυχον ἐξιών;

ΧΑ. κάθιζ' ἐπὶ κώπην. εἴ τις ἔτι πλεῖ, σπευδέτω.
οὗτος, τί ποιεῖς;

ΔΙ.   ὅ τι ποιῶ; τί δ' ἄλλο γ' ἢ
ἵζω 'πὶ κώπην, οὗπερ ἐκέλευές με σύ;

ΧΑ. οὔκουν καθεδεῖ δῆτ' ἐνθαδί, γάστρων;

ΔΙ.   ἰδού.   200

ΧΑ. οὔκουν προβαλεῖ τὼ χεῖρε κἀκτενεῖς;

ΔΙ.   ἰδού.

ΧΑ. οὐ μὴ φλυαρήσεις ἔχων, ἀλλ' ἀντιβὰς
ἐλᾷς προθύμως.

ΔΙ.   κᾆτα πῶς δυνήσομαι
ἄπειρος, ἀθαλάττωτος, ἀσαλαμίνιος
ὢν εἶτ' ἐλαύνειν;

ΧΑ.   ῥᾷστ'· ἀκούσει γὰρ μέλη   205
κάλλιστ', ἐπειδὰν ἐμβάλῃς ἅπαξ.

ΔΙ.   τίνων;

ΧΑ. βατράχων κύκνων θαυμαστά.

ΔΙ.   κατακέλευε δή.

ΧΑ. ὦ ὄποπ, ὦ ὄποπ.

BATPAXOI

βρεκεκεκὲξ κοὰξ κοάξ,
βρεκεκεκὲξ κοὰξ κοάξ.   210
λιμναῖα κρηνῶν τέκνα,
ξύναυλον ὕμνων βοὰν
φθεγξώμεθ᾽, εὔγηρυν ἐμὰν
ἀοιδάν, κοὰξ κοάξ,
ἣν ἀμφὶ Νυσήιον   215
Διὸς Διώνυσον ἐν
Λίμναισιν ἰαχήσαμεν,
ἡνίχ᾽ ὁ κραιπαλόκωμος
τοῖς ἱεροῖσι Χύτροισι
χωρεῖ κατ᾽ ἐμὸν τέμενος λαῶν ὄχλος.   219a
βρεκεκεκὲξ κοὰξ κοάξ.   220
ΔΙ.   ἐγὼ δέ γ᾽ ἀλγεῖν ἄρχομαι
        τὸν ὄρρον, ὦ κοὰξ κοάξ.
ΒΑ.   βρεκεκεκὲξ κοὰξ κοάξ.
ΔΙ.   ὑμῖν δ᾽ ἴσως οὐδὲν μέλει.
ΒΑ.   βρεκεκεκὲξ κοὰξ κοάξ.   225
ΔΙ.   ἀλλ᾽ ἐξόλοισθ᾽ αὐτῷ κοάξ·
        οὐδὲν γάρ ἐστ᾽ ἀλλ᾽ ἢ κοάξ.
ΒΑ.   εἰκότως γ᾽, ὦ πολλὰ πράττων.
        ἐμὲ γὰρ ἔστερξαν εὔλυροί τε Μοῦσαι
        καὶ κεροβάτας Πάν, ὁ καλαμόφθογγα παίζων· 230
        προσεπιτέρπεται δ᾽ ὁ φορμικτὰς Ἀπόλλων.
          ἕνεκα δόνακος, ὃν ὑπολύριον
          ἔνυδρον ἐν λίμναις τρέφω.   233/4
          βρεκεκεκὲξ κοὰξ κοάξ.   235
ΔΙ.   ἐγὼ δὲ φλυκταίνας γ᾽ ἔχω,
        χὠ πρωκτὸς ἰδίει πάλαι,

κᾆτ' αὐτίκ' ἐγκύψας ἐρεῖ —

ΒΑ. βρεκεκεκὲξ κοὰξ κοάξ.

ΔΙ. ἀλλ', ὦ φιλῳδὸν γένος,   240
παύσασθε.

ΒΑ.   μᾶλλον μὲν οὖν
φθεγξόμεσθ', εἰ δή ποτ' εὐ-
ηλίοις ἐν ἀμέραισιν
ἡλάμεσθα διὰ κυπείρου
καὶ φλέω, χαίροντες ᾠδῆς   244a
πολυκολύμβοισι μέλεσιν·   245
ἢ Διὸς φεύγοντες ὄμβρον
ἔνυδρον ἐν βυθῷ χορείαν
αἰόλαν ἐφθεγξάμεσθα
πομφολυγοπαφλάσμασιν.

ΔΙ. βρεκεκεκὲξ κοὰξ κοάξ.
τουτὶ παρ' ὑμῶν λαμβάνω.

ΒΑ. δεινὰ τἄρα πεισόμεσθα.   252

ΔΙ. δεινότερα δ' ἔγωγ', ἐλαύνων   253/4
εἰ διαρραγήσομαι.   255

ΒΑ. βρεκεκεκὲξ κοὰξ κοάξ.

ΔΙ. οἰμώζετ'· οὐ γάρ μοι μέλει.

ΒΑ. ἀλλὰ μὴν κεκραξόμεσθά γ'
ὁπόσον ἡ φάρυξ ἂν ἡμῶν
χανδάνῃ δι' ἡμέρας —   260

ΔΙ. βρεκεκεκὲξ κοὰξ κοάξ.
τούτῳ γὰρ οὐ νικήσετε.

ΒΑ. οὐδὲ μὴν ἡμᾶς σὺ πάντως.

ΔΙ. οὐδὲ μὴν ὑμεῖς γ' ἐμέ.
οὐδέποτε· κεκράξομαι γὰρ   264a
κἄν με δῇ δι' ἡμέρας,   265

ἕως ἂν ὑμῶν ἐπικρατήσω τῷ κοάξ,
βρεκεκεκὲξ κοὰξ κοάξ.
ἔμελλον ἄρα παύσειν ποθ' ὑμᾶς τοῦ κοάξ.

ΧΑ. ὦ παῦε, παῦε, παραβαλοῦ τῷ κωπίῳ.
ἔκβαιν', ἀπόδος τὸν ναῦλον.

ΔΙ.   ἔχε δὴ τὠβολώ.   270
ὁ Ξανθίας.   ποῦ Ξανθίας; ἤ, Ξανθία.

ΞΑ. ἰαῦ.

ΔΙ. βάδιζε δεῦρο.

ΞΑ.   χαῖρ', ὦ δέσποτα.

ΔΙ. τί ἐστι τἀνταυθοῖ;

ΞΑ.   σκότος καὶ βόρβορος.

ΔΙ. κατεῖδες οὖν που τοὺς πατραλοίας αὐτόθι
καὶ τοὺς ἐπιόρκους, οὓς ἔλεγεν ἡμῖν;

ΞΑ.   σὺ δ' οὔ;   275

ΔΙ. νὴ τὸν Ποσειδῶ 'γωγε, καὶ νυνί γ' ὁρῶ.
ἄγε δή, τί δρῶμεν;

ΞΑ.   προϊέναι βέλτιστα νῷν,
ὡς οὗτος ὁ τόπος ἐστὶν οὗ τὰ θηρία
τὰ δείν' ἔφασκ' ἐκεῖνος —

ΔΙ.   ὡς οἰμώξεται.
ἠλαζονεύεθ' ἵνα φοβηθείην ἐγώ,   280
εἰδώς με μάχιμον ὄντα, φιλοτιμούμενος.
οὐδὲν γὰρ οὕτω γαῦρόν ἐσθ' ὡς Ἡρακλῆς.
ἐγὼ δέ γ' εὐξαίμην ἂν ἐντυχεῖν τινι
λαβεῖν τ' ἀγώνισμ' ἄξιόν τι τῆς ὁδοῦ.

ΞΑ. νὴ τὸν Δία· καὶ μὴν αἰσθάνομαι ψόφου τινός.   285

ΔΙ. ποῦ ποῦ 'στιν;

ΞΑ.   ἐξόπισθεν.

ΔΙ.   ἐξόπισθ' ἴθι.

ΞΑ. ἀλλ' ἔστιν ἐν τῷ πρόσθε.

ΔΙ.   πρόσθε νυν ἴθι.

ΞΑ. καὶ μὴν ὁρῶ νὴ τὸν Δία θηρίον μέγα.

ΔΙ. ποῖόν τι;

ΞΑ.   δεινόν. παντοδαπὸν γοῦν γίγνεται·
τοτὲ μέν γε βοῦς, νυνὶ δ' ὀρεύς, τοτὲ δ' αὖ γυνὴ
ὡραιοτάτη τις.

ΔΙ.   ποῦ 'στι; φέρ' ἐπ' αὐτὴν ἴω.   291

ΞΑ. ἀλλ' οὐκέτ' αὖ γυνή 'στιν, ἀλλ' ἤδη κύων.

ΔΙ. Ἔμπουσα τοίνυν ἐστί.

ΞΑ.   πυρὶ γοῦν λάμπεται
ἅπαν τὸ πρόσωπον.

ΔΙ.   καὶ σκέλος χαλκοῦν ἔχει;

ΞΑ. νὴ τὸν Ποσειδῶ, καὶ βολίτινον θἄτερον,   295
σάφ' ἴσθι.

ΔΙ.   ποῖ δῆτ' ἂν τραποίμην;

ΞΑ.   ποῖ δ' ἐγώ;

ΔΙ. ἱερεῦ, διαφύλαξόν μ', ἵν' ὦ σοι ξυμπότης.

ΞΑ. ἀπολούμεθ', ὦναξ Ἡράκλεις.

ΔΙ.   οὐ μὴ καλεῖς μ',
ὦνθρωφ', ἱκετεύω, μηδὲ κατερεῖς τοὔνομα.

ΞΑ. Διόνυσε τοίνυν.

ΔΙ.   τοῦτ' ἔθ' ἧττον θἀτέρου.   300

ΞΑ. ἴθ' ᾗπερ ἔρχει. δεῦρο δεῦρ', ὦ δέσποτα.

ΔΙ. τί δ' ἐστί;

ΞΑ.   θάρρει· πάντ' ἀγαθὰ πεπράγαμεν,
ἔξεστί θ' ὥσπερ Ἡγέλοχος ἡμῖν λέγειν·
' ἐκ κυμάτων γὰρ αὖθις αὖ γαλῆν ὁρῶ.'
Ἔμπουσα φρούδη.

ΔΙ.   κατόμοσον.

ΞΑ.   νὴ τὸν Δία. 305
ΔΙ. καῦθις κατόμοσον.
ΞΑ.   νὴ Δί'.
ΔΙ.   ὅμοσον.
ΞΑ.   νὴ Δία.
ΔΙ. οἴμοι τάλας, ὡς ὠχρίασ' αὐτὴν ἰδών.
ΞΑ. ὁδὶ δὲ δείσας ὑπερεπυρρίασέ σου.
ΔΙ. οἴμοι, πόθεν μοι τὰ κακὰ ταυτὶ προσέπεσεν;
    τίν' αἰτιάσομαι θεῶν μ' ἀπολλύναι; 310
ΞΑ. αἰθέρα Διὸς δωμάτιον ἢ Χρόνου πόδα;
                 [αὐλεῖ τις ἔνδοθεν]
ΞΑ. οὗτος.
ΔΙ.   τί ἐστιν;
ΞΑ.   οὐ κατήκουσας;
ΔΙ.   τίνος;
ΞΑ. αὐλῶν πνοῆς.
ΔΙ.   ἔγωγε, καὶ δᾴδων γέ με
    αὔρα τις εἰσέπνευσε μυστικωτάτη.
    ἀλλ' ἠρεμεὶ πτήξαντες ἀκροασώμεθα. 315

ΧΟΡΟΣ

    Ἴακχ', ὦ Ἴακχε.
    Ἴακχ', ὦ Ἴακχε.
ΞΑ. τοῦτ' ἔστ' ἐκεῖν', ὦ δέσποθ'· οἱ μεμυημένοι
    ἐνταῦθά που παίζουσιν, οὓς ἔφραζε νῷν.
    ᾄδουσι γοῦν τὸν Ἴακχον ὅνπερ Διαγόρας. 320
ΔΙ. κἀμοὶ δοκοῦσιν. ἡσυχίαν τοίνυν ἄγειν
    βέλτιστόν ἐστιν, ὡς ἂν εἰδῶμεν σαφῶς.

ΧΟ. Ἴακχ', ὦ πολυτίμητ' ἐν ἕδραις ἐνθάδε ναίων,

Ἴακχ᾽, ὦ Ἴακχε,   325
ἐλθὲ τόνδ᾽ ἀνὰ λειμῶνα χορεύσων
ὁσίους εἰς θιασώτας,
πολύκαρπον μὲν τινάσσων
περὶ κρατὶ σῷ βρύοντα
στέφανον μύρτων, θρασεῖ δ᾽ ἐγκατακρούων 330/1
ποδὶ τὰν ἀκόλαστον
φιλοπαίγμονα τιμήν,   333/4
Χαρίτων πλεῖστον ἔχουσαν μέρος, ἀγνήν, ἱερὰν 335
ὁσίοις μύσταις χορείαν.

ΞΑ. ὦ πότνια πολυτίμητε Δήμητρος κόρη,
   ὡς ἡδύ μοι προσέπνευσε χοιρείων κρεῶν.
ΔΙ. οὔκουν ἀτρέμ᾽ ἕξεις, ἤν τι καὶ χορδῆς λάβῃς;

ΧΟ. ἔγειρε φλογέας λαμπάδας ἐν χερσί· παρήκεις,
     Ἴακχ᾽, ὦ Ἴακχε,   341
   νυκτέρου τελετῆς φωσφόρος ἀστήρ. 342
     φλογὶ φέγγεται δὲ λειμών· 343/4
     γόνυ πάλλεται γερόντων· 345
     ἀποσείονται δὲ λύπας 346
   χρονίους τ᾽ ἐτῶν παλαιῶν ἐνιαυτοὺς 347
   ἱερᾶς ὑπὸ τιμῆς. 348/9
     σὺ δὲ λαμπάδι φέγγων 350
   προβάδην ἔξαγ᾽ ἐπ᾽ ἀνθηρὸν ἕλειον δάπεδον
   χοροποιόν, μάκαρ, ἥβαν.

εὐφημεῖν χρὴ κἀξίστασθαι τοῖς ἡμετέροισι χοροῖ-
   σιν,
ὅστις ἄπειρος τοιῶνδε λόγων ἢ γνώμην μὴ καθα-
   ρεύει,   355

ἢ γενναίων ὄργια Μουσῶν μήτ᾽ εἶδεν μήτ᾽ ἐχό-
ρευσεν,
μηδὲ Κρατίνου τοῦ ταυροφάγου γλώττης Βακχεῖ᾽
ἐτελέσθη,
ἢ βωμολόχοις ἔπεσιν χαίρει μὴ ᾽ν καιρῷ τοῦτο
ποιοῦσιν,
ἢ στάσιν ἐχθρὰν μὴ καταλύει μηδ᾽ εὔκολός ἐστι
πολίταις,
ἀλλ᾽ ἀνεγείρει καὶ ῥιπίζει κερδῶν ἰδίων ἐπιθυ-
μῶν, 360
ἢ τῆς πόλεως χειμαζομένης ἄρχων καταδωρο-
δοκεῖται,
ἢ προδίδωσιν φρούριον ἢ ναῦς, ἢ τἀπόρρητ᾽ ἀπο-
πέμπει
ἐξ Αἰγίνης Θωρυκίων ὢν εἰκοστολόγος κακοδαί-
μων,
ἀσκώματα καὶ λίνα καὶ πίτταν διαπέμπων εἰς
Ἐπίδαυρον,
ἢ χρήματα ταῖς τῶν ἀντιπάλων ναυσὶν παρέχειν
τινὰ πείθει, 365
ἢ κατατιλᾷ τῶν Ἑκατείων κυκλίοισι χοροῖσιν
ὑπᾴδων,
ἢ τοὺς μισθοὺς τῶν ποιητῶν ῥήτωρ ὢν εἶτ᾽ ἀπο-
τρώγει,
κωμῳδηθεὶς ἐν ταῖς πατρίοις τελεταῖς ταῖς τοῦ
Διονύσου.
τοῖς μὲν ἀπαυδῶ καὖθις ἀπαυδῶ καὖθις τὸ τρίτον
μάλ᾽ ἀπαυδῶ
ἐξίστασθαι μύσταισι χοροῖς· ὑμεῖς δ᾽ ἀνεγείρετε
μολπὴν 370

καὶ παννυχίδας τὰς ἡμετέρας αἳ τῇδε πρέπουσιν
ἑορτῇ.

χώρει νυν πᾶς ἀνδρείως
εἰς τοὺς εὐανθεῖς κόλπους
λειμώνων ἐγκρούων
κἀπισκώπτων
καὶ παίζων καὶ χλευάζων.   375
ἠρίστηται δ᾽ ἐξαρκούντως. —

ἀλλ᾽ ἔμβα χὤπως ἀρεῖς
τὴν Σώτειραν γενναίως
τῇ φωνῇ μολπάζων,
ἢ τὴν χώραν   380
σῴζειν φήσ᾽ εἰς τὰς ὥρας,
κἂν Θωρυκίων μὴ βούληται.

ἄγε νυν ἑτέραν ὕμνων ἰδέαν τὴν καρποφόρον βα-
σίλειαν,
Δήμητρα θεάν, ἐπικοσμοῦντες ζαθέαις μολπαῖς
κελαδεῖτε.

Δήμητερ, ἁγνῶν ὀργίων   384a
ἄνασσα, συμπαραστάτει,   385
καὶ σῷζε τὸν σαυτῆς χορόν·
καί μ᾽ ἀσφαλῶς πανήμερον
παῖσαί τε καὶ χορεῦσαι. —

καὶ πολλὰ μὲν γέλοιά μ᾽ εἰ-
πεῖν, πολλὰ δὲ σπουδαῖα, καὶ   390
τῆς σῆς ἑορτῆς ἀξίως
παίσαντα καὶ σκώψαντα νι-
κήσαντα ταινιοῦσθαι.

ἄγ᾽ εἶα
νῦν καὶ τὸν ὡραῖον θεὸν παρακαλεῖτε δεῦρο   395
ᾠδαῖσι, τὸν ξυνέμπορον τῆσδε τῆς χορείας.

Ἴακχε πολυτίμητε, μέλος ἑορτῆς
ἥδιστον εὑρών, δεῦρο συνακολούθει   398/9
πρὸς τὴν θεὸν   400
καὶ δεῖξον ὡς ἄνευ πόνου
πολλὴν ὁδὸν περαίνεις.
Ἴακχε φιλοχορευτά, συμπρόπεμπέ με. —

σὺ γὰρ κατεσχίσω μὲν ἐπὶ γέλωτι
κἀπ᾽ εὐτελείᾳ τόδε τὸ σανδαλίσκον   405
καὶ τὸ ῥάκος,
κἀξηῦρες ὥστ᾽ ἀζημίους
παίζειν τε καὶ χορεύειν.
Ἴακχε φιλοχορευτά, συμπρόπεμπέ με. —

καὶ γὰρ παραβλέψας τι μειρακίσκης
νῦν δὴ κατεῖδον καὶ μάλ᾽ εὐπροσώπου,   410
συμπαιστρίας,
χιτωνίου παραρραγέν-   411
τος τιτθίον προκύψαν.
Ἴακχε φιλοχορευτά, συμπρόπεμπέ με.   413

ΞΑ.   ἐγὼ δ᾽ ἀεί πως φιλακόλου-   414
θός εἰμι καὶ μετ᾽ αὐτῆς
παίζων χορεύειν βούλομαι.
ΔΙ.   κἄγωγε πρός.   415
ΧΟ.   βούλεσθε δῆτα κοινῇ
σκώψωμεν Ἀρχέδημον,

ὃς ἑπτέτης ὢν οὐκ ἔφυσε φράτερας; —
νυνὶ δὲ δημαγωγεῖ
ἐν τοῖς ἄνω νεκροῖσι,   420
κἄστιν τὰ πρῶτα τῆς ἐκεῖ μοχθηρίας. —
τὸν Κλεισθένους δ᾽ ἀκούω
ἐν ταῖς ταφαῖσι πρωκτὸν
τίλλειν ἑαυτοῦ καὶ σπαράττειν τὰς γνάθους. —
κἀκόπτετ᾽ ἐγκεκυφώς,   425
κἄκλαε κἀκεκράγει
Σεβῖνον ὅστις ἐστὶν ἀναφλύστιος.—
καὶ Καλλίαν γέ φασι
τοῦτον τὸν Ἱπποβίνου
κύσθου λεοντῆν ναυμαχεῖν ἐνημμένον.   430
ΔΙ.   ἔχοιτ᾽ ἂν οὖν φράσαι νῷν
       Πλούτων᾽ ὅπου ᾽νθάδ᾽ οἰκεῖ;
       ξένω γάρ ἐσμεν ἀρτίως ἀφιγμένω.
ΧΟ.   μηδὲν μακρὰν ἀπέλθῃς,
       μηδ᾽ αὖθις ἐπανέρῃ με,   435
ἀλλ᾽ ἴσθ᾽ ἐπ᾽ αὐτὴν τὴν θύραν ἀφιγμένος.
ΔΙ.   αἴροι᾽ ἂν αὖθις, ὦ παῖ.
ΞΑ.   τουτὶ τί ἦν τὸ πρᾶγμα
       ἀλλ᾽ ἢ Διὸς Κόρινθος ἐν τοῖς στρώμασιν;

ΧΟ. χωρεῖτε   440
νῦν ἱερὸν ἀνὰ κύκλον θεᾶς, ἀνθοφόρον ἀν᾽ ἄλ-
σος   441/2
παίζοντες οἷς μετουσία θεοφιλοῦς ἑορτῆς.   443/4
ἐγὼ δὲ σὺν ταῖσιν κόραις εἶμι καὶ γυναιξίν,   445
οὗ παννυχίζουσιν θεᾷ, φέγγος ἱερὸν οἴσων.
χωρῶμεν εἰς πολυρρόδους

λειμῶνας ἀνθεμώδεις,
τὸν ἡμέτερον τρόπον,   450
τὸν καλλιχορώτατον,
παίζοντες, ὃν ὄλβιαι
Μοῖραι ξυνάγουσιν. —

μόνοις γὰρ ἡμῖν ἥλιος
  καὶ φέγγος ἱερόν ἐστιν,   455
ὅσοι μεμνήμεθ' εὐ-
σεβῆ τε διήγομεν
τρόπον περὶ τοὺς ξένους
καὶ τοὺς ἰδιώτας.

ΔΙ. ἄγε δὴ τίνα τρόπον τὴν θύραν κόψω; τίνα;   460
  πῶς ἐνθάδ' ἄρα κόπτουσιν οὑπιχώριοι;
ΞΑ. οὐ μὴ διατρίψεις, ἀλλὰ γεῦσαι τῆς θύρας,
  καθ' Ἡρακλέα τὸ σχῆμα καὶ τὸ λῆμ' ἔχων.
ΔΙ. παῖ παῖ.
ΑΙΑΚΟΣ
  τίς οὗτος;
ΔΙ.   Ἡρακλῆς ὁ καρτερός.
ΑΙ. ὦ βδελυρὲ κἀναίσχυντε καὶ τολμηρὲ σὺ   465
  καὶ μιαρὲ καὶ παμμίαρε καὶ μιαρώτατε,
  ὃς τὸν κύν' ἡμῶν ἐξελάσας τὸν Κέρβερον
  ἀπῇξας ἄγχων κἀποδρὰς ᾤχου λαβών,
  ὃν ἐγὼ 'φύλαττον. ἀλλὰ νῦν ἔχει μέσος·
  τοία Στυγός σε μελανοκάρδιος πέτρα   470
  Ἀχερόντιός τε σκόπελος αἱματοσταγὴς
  φρουροῦσι, Κωκυτοῦ τε περίδρομοι κύνες,
  ἔχιδνά θ' ἑκατογκέφαλος, ἣ τὰ σπλάγχνα σου
  διασπαράξει· πλευμόνων τ' ἀνθάψεται

Ταρτησσία μύραινα, τὼ νεφρὼ δέ σου   475
αὐτοῖσιν ἐντέροισιν ἡματωμένω
διασπάσονται Γοργόνες Τειθράσιαι,
ἐφ' ἃς ἐγὼ δρομαῖον ὁρμήσω πόδα.
ΞΑ. οὗτος, τί δέδρακας;
ΔΙ.   ἐγκέχοδα· κάλει θεόν.
ΞΑ. ὦ καταγέλαστ', οὔκουν ἀναστήσει ταχὺ   480
πρίν τινά σ' ἰδεῖν ἀλλότριον;
ΔΙ.   ἀλλ' ὡρακιῶ.
ἀλλ' οἶσε πρὸς τὴν καρδίαν μου σπογγιάν.
ΞΑ. ἰδοὺ λαβέ· προσθοῦ. — ποῦ 'στιν; ὦ χρυσοῖ θεοί,
ἐνταῦθ' ἔχεις τὴν καρδίαν;
ΔΙ.   δείσασα γὰρ
εἰς τὴν κάτω μου κοιλίαν καθείρπυσεν.   485
ΞΑ. ὦ δειλότατε θεῶν σὺ κἀνθρώπων·
ΔΙ.   ἐγώ;
πῶς δειλὸς ὅστις σπογγιὰν ᾔτησά σε;
οὐ τἂν ἕτερός γ' αὔτ' εἰργάσατ' ἀνήρ.
ΞΑ.   ἀλλὰ τί;
ΔΙ. κατέκειτ' ἂν ὀσφραινόμενος, εἴπερ δειλὸς ἦν·
ἐγὼ δ' ἀνέστην καὶ προσέτ' ἀπεψησάμην.   490
ΞΑ. ἀνδρεῖά γ', ὦ Πόσειδον.
ΔΙ.   οἶμαι νὴ Δία.
σὺ δ' οὐκ ἔδεισας τὸν ψόφον τῶν ῥημάτων
καὶ τὰς ἀπειλάς;
ΞΑ.   οὐ μὰ Δί' οὐδ' ἐφρόντισα.
ΔΙ. ἴθι νυν, ἐπειδὴ λημᾶτιᾷ κἀνδρεῖος εἶ,
σὺ μὲν γενοῦ 'γὼ τὸ ῥόπαλον τουτὶ λαβὼν   495
καὶ τὴν λεοντῆν, εἴπερ ἀφοβόσπλαγχνος εἶ·
ἐγὼ δ' ἔσομαί σοι σκευοφόρος ἐν τῷ μέρει.

ΞΑ. φέρε δὴ ταχέως αὖτ'· οὐ γὰρ ἀλλὰ πειστέον.
 καὶ βλέψον εἰς τὸν Ἡρακλειοξανθίαν,
 εἰ δειλὸς ἔσομαι καὶ κατὰ σὲ τὸ λῆμ' ἔχων.   500
ΔΙ. μὰ Δί' ἀλλ' ἀληθῶς οὐκ Μελίτης μαστιγίας.
 φέρε νῦν, ἐγὼ τὰ στρώματ' αἴρωμαι ταδί.

ΘΕΡΑΠΩΝ

ὦ φίλταθ' ἥκεις Ἡράκλεις; δεῦρ' εἴσιθι.
ἡ γὰρ θεός σ' ὡς ἐπύθεθ' ἥκοντ', εὐθέως
ἔπεττεν ἄρτους, ἧψε κατερικτῶν χύτρας   505
ἔτνους δύ' ἢ τρεῖς, βοῦν ἀπηνθράκιζ' ὅλον,
πλακοῦντας ὤπτα, κολλάβους — ἀλλ' εἴσιθι.
ΞΑ. κάλλιστ', ἐπαινῶ.
ΘΕ.   μὰ τὸν Ἀπόλλω οὐ μή σ' ἐγὼ
περιόψομἀπελθόντ', ἐπεί τοι καὶ κρέα
ἀνέβραττεν ὀρνίθεια, καὶ τραγήματα   510
ἔφρυγε, κῶνον ἀνεκεράννυ γλυκύτατον.
ἀλλ' εἴσιθ' ἅμ' ἐμοί.
ΞΑ.   πάνυ καλῶς.
ΘΕ.   ληρεῖς ἔχων·
οὐ γάρ σ' ἀφήσω. καὶ γὰρ αὐλητρίς τέ σοι
ἤδη 'νδον ἔσθ' ὡραιοτάτη κὠρχηστρίδες
ἔτεραι δύ' ἢ τρεῖς —
ΞΑ.   πῶς λέγεις; ὀρχηστρίδες;   515
ΘΕ. ἡβυλλιῶσαι κἄρτι παρατετιλμέναι.
ἀλλ' εἴσιθ', ὡς ὁ μάγειρος ἤδη τὰ τεμάχη
ἔμελλ' ἀφαιρεῖν χἠ τράπεζ' εἰσήρετο.
ΞΑ. ἴθι νυν, φράσον πρώτιστα ταῖς ὀρχηστρίσιν
ταῖς ἔνδον οὔσαις αὐτὸς ὅτι εἰσέρχομαι.   520
ὁ παῖς, ἀκολούθει δεῦρο τὰ σκεύη φέρων.

ΔΙ. ἐπίσχες, οὗτος. οὔ τί που σπουδὴν ποεῖ,
ὁτιή σε παίζων Ἡρακλέα 'νεσκεύασα;
οὐ μὴ φλυαρήσεις ἔχων, ὦ Ξανθία,
ἀλλ' ἀράμενος οἴσεις πάλιν τὰ στρώματα.   525
ΞΑ. τί δ' ἐστίν; οὔ τί πού μ' ἀφελέσθαι διανοεῖ
ἅδωκας αὐτός;
ΔΙ.   οὐ τάχ', ἀλλ' ἤδη ποιῶ.
κατάθου τὸ δέρμα.
ΞΑ.   ταῦτ' ἐγὼ μαρτύρομαι
καὶ τοῖς θεοῖσιν ἐπιτρέπω.
ΔΙ.   ποίοις θεοῖς;
τὸ δὲ προσδοκῆσαί σ' — οὐκ ἀνόητον καὶ κε-
νόν; —   530
ὡς δοῦλος ὢν καὶ θνητὸς Ἀλκμήνης ἔσει.
ΞΑ. ἀμέλει, καλῶς· ἔχ' αὔτ'. ἴσως γάρ τοί ποτε
ἐμοῦ δεηθείης ἄν, εἰ θεὸς θέλοι.

ΧΟ.   ταῦτα μὲν πρὸς ἀνδρός ἐστι
νοῦν ἔχοντος καὶ φρένας καὶ   534a
πολλὰ περιπεπλευκότος,   535
μετακυλίνδειν αὐτὸν ἀεὶ
πρὸς τὸν εὖ πράττοντα τοῖχον
μᾶλλον ἢ γεγραμμένην
εἰκόν' ἑστάναι, λαβόνθ' ἓν
σχῆμα· τὸ δὲ μεταστρέφεσθαι   539a
πρὸς τὸ μαλθακώτερον   539b
δεξιοῦ πρὸς ἀνδρός ἐστι   540
καὶ φύσει Θηραμένους.
ΔΙ.   οὐ γὰρ ἂν γέλοιον ἦν, εἰ
Ξανθίας μὲν δοῦλος ὢν ἐν

στρώμασιν Μιλησίοις
ἀνατετραμμένος κυνῶν ὀρ-
χηστρίδ᾽ εἶτ᾽ ᾔτησεν ἀμίδ᾽, ἐ-   544a
γὼ δὲ πρὸς τοῦτον βλέπων   544b
τοὐρεβίνθου ᾽δραττόμην, οὗ-   545
τος δ᾽ ἆτ᾽ ὢν αὐτὸς πανοῦργος
εἶδε, κᾆτ᾽ ἐκ τῆς γνάθου
πὺξ πατάξας μοὐξέκοψε   548a
τοὺς χοροὺς τοὺς προσθίους;   548b

ΠΑΝΔΟΚΕΥΤΡΙΑ Α´

Πλαθάνη, Πλαθάνη, δεῦρ᾽ ἔλθ᾽. ὁ πανοῦργος οὑ-
τοσί,
ὃς εἰς τὸ πανδοκεῖον εἰσελθών ποτε   550
ἑκκαίδεκ᾽ ἄρτους κατέφαγ᾽ ἡμῶν —

ΠΑΝΔΟΚΕΥΤΡΙΑ Β´

                                        νὴ Δία,
ἐκεῖνος αὐτὸς δῆτα.
ΞΑ.   κακὸν ἥκει τινί.
ΠΑ. Α´ καὶ κρέα γε πρὸς τούτοισιν ἀνάβραστ᾽ εἴκοσιν
ἂν᾽ ἡμιωβολιαῖα —
ΞΑ.   δώσει τις δίκην.
ΠΑ. Α´ καὶ τὰ σκόροδα τὰ πολλά.
ΔΙ.   ληρεῖς, ὦ γύναι,   555
κοὐκ οἶσθ᾽ ὅ τι λέγεις.
ΠΑ. Α´   οὐ μὲν οὖν με προσεδόκας,
ὁτιὴ κοθόρνους εἶχες, ἂν γνῶναί σ᾽ ἔτι.
τί δαί; τὸ πολὺ τάριχος οὐκ εἴρηκά πω.
ΠΑ. Β´ μὰ Δί᾽ οὐδὲ τὸν τυρόν γε τὸν χλωρόν, τάλαν,

ὃν οὗτος αὐτοῖς τοῖς ταλάροις κατήσθιεν. 560

ΠΑ. Α΄ κἄπειτ᾽ ἐπειδὴ τἀργύριον ἐπραττόμην,
ἔβλεψεν εἴς με δριμὺ κἀμυκᾶτό γε —

ΞΑ. τούτου πάνυ τοὔργον· οὗτος ὁ τρόπος παντα-
χοῦ.

ΠΑ. Α΄ καὶ τὸ ξίφος γ᾽ ἐσπᾶτο μαίνεσθαι δοκῶν.

ΠΑ. Β΄ νὴ Δία, τάλαινα.

ΠΑ. Α΄ νὼ δὲ δεισάσα γέ που 565
ἐπὶ τὴν κατήλιφ᾽ εὐθὺς ἀνεπηδήσαμεν·
ὁ δ᾽ ᾤχετ᾽ ἐξᾴξας γε τὰς ψιάθους λαβών.

ΞΑ. καὶ τοῦτο τούτου τοὔργον.

ΠΑ. Α΄ ἀλλ᾽ ἐχρῆν τι δρᾶν.
ἴθι δὴ κάλεσον τὸν προστάτην Κλέωνά μοι —

ΠΑ. Β΄ σὺ δ᾽ ἔμοιγ᾽ ἐάνπερ ἐπιτύχῃς Ὑπέρβολον 570
ἵν᾽ αὐτὸν ἐπιτρίψωμεν.

ΠΑ. Α΄ ὦ μιαρὰ φάρυξ,
ὡς ἡδέως ἄν σου λίθῳ τοὺς γομφίους
κόπτοιμ᾽ ἄν, οἷς μου κατέφαγες τὰ φορτία.

ΔΙ. ἐγὼ δέ γ᾽ εἰς τὸ βάραθρον ἐμβάλοιμί σε.

ΠΑ. Β΄ ἐγὼ δὲ τὸν λάρυγγ᾽ ἂν ἐκτέμοιμί σου 575
δρέπανον λαβοῦσ᾽, ᾧ τὰς χόλικας κατέσπασας.
ἀλλ᾽ εἶμ᾽ ἐπὶ τὸν Κλέων᾽, ὃς αὐτοῦ τήμερον
ἐκπηνιεῖται ταῦτα προσκαλούμενος.

ΔΙ. κάκιστ᾽ ἀπολοίμην, Ξανθίαν εἰ μὴ φιλῶ.

ΞΑ. οἶδ᾽ οἶδα τὸν νοῦν· παῦε παῦε τοῦ λόγου. 580
οὐκ ἂν γενοίμην Ἡρακλῆς ἄν.

ΔΙ. μηδαμῶς,
ὦ Ξανθίδιον.

ΞΑ. καὶ πῶς ἂν Ἀλκμήνης ἐγὼ

υἱὸς γενοίμην δοῦλος ἅμα καὶ θνητὸς ὤν;
ΔΙ. οἶδ' οἶδ' ὅτι θυμοῖ, καὶ δικαίως αὐτὸ δρᾷς·
κἂν εἴ με τύπτοις, οὐκ ἂν ἀντείποιμί σοι.   585
ἀλλ' ἤν σε τοῦ λοιποῦ ποτ' ἀφέλωμαι χρόνου,
πρόρριζος αὐτός, ἡ γυνή, τὰ παιδία,
κάκιστ' ἀπολοίμην, κἀρχέδημος ὁ γλάμων.
ΞΑ. δέχομαι τὸν ὅρκον κἀπὶ τούτοις λαμβάνω.

ΧΟ.   νῦν σὸν ἔργον ἔστ', ἐπειδὴ   589a
τὴν στολὴν εἴληφας ἥνπερ   590
εἶχες, ἐξ ἀρχῆς πάλιν
ἀνανεάζειν . . .
καὶ βλέπειν αὖθις τὸ δεινόν,
τοῦ θεοῦ μεμνημένον
ὧπερ εἰκάζεις σεαυτόν.   594a
ἢν δὲ παραληρῶν ἁλῷς ἢ   594b
κἀκβάλῃς τι μαλθακόν,   595
αὖθις αἴρεσθαί σ' ἀνάγκη
'σται πάλιν τὰ στρώματα.
ΞΑ.   οὐ κακῶς, ὦνδρες, παραινεῖτ',
ἀλλὰ καὐτὸς τυγχάνω ταῦτ'
ἄρτι συννοούμενος.   599a
ὅτι μὲν οὖν, ἢν χρηστὸν ᾖ τι,   599b
ταῦτ' ἀφαιρεῖσθαι πάλιν πει-   600
ράσεταί μ' εὖ οἶδ' ὅτι.
ἀλλ' ὅμως ἐγὼ παρέξω
'μαυτὸν ἀνδρεῖον τὸ λῆμα
καὶ βλέποντ' ὀρίγανον.
δεῖν δ' ἔοικεν, ὡς ἀκούω   604a
τῆς θύρας καὶ δὴ ψόφον.   604b

ΑΙ. ξυνδεῖτε ταχέως τουτονὶ τὸν κυνοκλόπον,   605
   ἵνα δῷ δίκην· ἀνύετον.

ΔΙ.   ἥκει τῳ κακόν.

ΞΑ. οὐκ ἐς κόρακας; μὴ πρόσιτον.

ΑΙ.   εἶέν, καὶ μάχει;
   ὁ Διτύλας χὠ Σκεβλύας χὠ Παρδόκας,
   χωρεῖτε δευρὶ καὶ μάχεσθε τουτῳί.

ΔΙ. εἶτ' οὐχὶ δεινὰ ταῦτα, τύπτειν τουτονὶ   610
   κλέπτοντα πρὸς τἀλλότρια;

ΑΙ.   μᾶλλ' ὑπερφυᾶ.

ΔΙ. σχέτλια μὲν οὖν καὶ δεινά.

ΞΑ.   καὶ μὴν νὴ Δία,
   εἰ πώποτ' ἦλθον δεῦρ', ἐθέλω τεθνηκέναι,
   ἢ 'κλεψα τῶν σῶν ἄξιόν τι καὶ τριχός.
   καί σοι ποήσω πρᾶγμα γενναῖον πάνυ·   615
   βασάνιζε γὰρ τὸν παῖδα τουτονὶ λαβών,
   κἄν ποτέ μ' ἕλῃς ἀδικοῦντ', ἀπόκτεινόν μ' ἄγων.

ΛΙ. καὶ πῶς βασανίζω;

ΞΑ.   πάντα τρόπον· ἐν κλίμακι
   δήσας, κρεμάσας, ὑστριχίδι μαστιγῶν, δέρων,
   στρεβλῶν, ἔτι δ' εἰς τὰς ῥῖνας ὄξος ἐγχέων,   620
   πλίνθους ἐπιτιθείς, πάντα τἄλλα, πλὴν πράσῳ
   μὴ τύπτε τοῦτον μηδὲ γητείῳ νέῳ.

ΛΙ. δίκαιος ὁ λόγος· κἄν τι πηρώσω γέ σοι
   τὸν παῖδα τύπτων, τἀργύριόν σοι κείσεται.

ΞΑ. μὴ δῆτ' ἔμοιγ'. οὕτω δὲ βασάνιζ' ἀπαγαγών.   625

ΑΙ. αὐτοῦ μὲν οὖν, ἵνα σοι κατ' ὀφθαλμοὺς λέγῃ.
   κατάθου σὺ τὰ σκεύη ταχέως, χὤπως ἐρεῖς
   ἐνταῦθα μηδὲν ψεῦδος.

ΔΙ   ἀγορεύω τινὶ

ἐμὲ μὴ βασανίζειν ἀθάνατον ὄντ'· εἰ δὲ μή,
αὐτὸς σεαυτὸν αἰτιῶ.

ΑΙ.   λέγεις δὲ τί;   630

ΔΙ. ἀθάνατος εἶναί φημι, Διόνυσος Διός,
τοῦτον δὲ δοῦλον.

ΑΙ.   ταῦτ' ἀκούεις;

ΞΑ.   φήμ' ἐγώ.
καὶ πολύ γε μᾶλλόν ἐστι μαστιγωτέος·
εἴπερ θεὸς γάρ ἐστιν, οὐκ αἰσθήσεται.

ΔΙ. τί δῆτ', ἐπειδή καὶ σὺ φῂς εἶναι θεός,   635
οὐ καὶ σὺ τύπτει τὰς ἴσας πληγὰς ἐμοί;

ΞΑ. δίκαιος ὁ λόγος· χὠπότερόν γ' ἂν νῷν ἴδῃς
κλαύσαντα πρότερον ἢ προτιμήσαντά τι
τυπτόμενον, εἶναι τοῦτον ἡγοῦ μὴ θεόν.

ΑΙ. οὐκ ἔσθ' ὅπως οὐκ εἶ σὺ γεννάδας ἀνήρ·   640
χωρεῖς γὰρ εἰς τὸ δίκαιον.   ἀποδύεσθε δή.

ΞΑ. πῶς οὖν βασανιεῖς νὼ δικαίως;

ΑΙ.   ῥᾳδίως·
πληγὴν παρὰ πληγὴν ἑκάτερον.

ΞΑ.   καλῶς λέγεις.

ΑΙ. ἰδού.

ΞΑ.   σκόπει νυν ἤν μ' ὑποκινήσαντ' ἴδῃς.

ΑΙ. ἤδη 'πάταξά σ'.

ΞΑ.   οὐ μὰ Δί' οὐδέπω δοκεῖς.   645

ΑΙ. ἀλλ' εἶμ' ἐπὶ τονδὶ καὶ πατάξω.

ΔΙ.   πηνίκα;

ΑΙ. καὶ δὴ 'πάταξα.

ΔΙ.   κᾆτα πῶς οὐκ ἔπταρον;

ΑΙ. οὐκ οἶδα· τουδὶ δ' αὖθις ἀποπειράσομαι.

ΞΑ. οὔκουν ἀνύσεις; ἰατταταῖ.

ΑΙ.   τί τάτταταῖ;
μῶν ὠδυνήθης;

ΞΑ.   οὐ μὰ Δί' ἀλλ' ἐφρόντισα   650
ὁπόθ' Ἡράκλεια τὰν Διομείοις γίγνεται.

ΑΙ. ἄνθρωπος ἱερός. δεῦρο πάλιν βαδιστέον.

ΔΙ. ἰοὺ ἰού.

ΑΙ.   τί ἐστιν;

ΔΙ.   ἱππέας ὁρῶ.

ΑΙ. τί δῆτα κλάεις;

ΔΙ.   κρομμύων ὀσφραίνομαι.

ΑΙ. ἐπεὶ προτιμᾷς γ' οὐδέν;

ΔΙ.   οὐδέν μοι μέλει.   655

ΑΙ. βαδιστέον τἄρ' ἐστὶν ἐπὶ τονδὶ πάλιν.

ΞΑ. οἴμοι.

ΑΙ.   τί ἐστι;

ΞΑ.   τὴν ἄκανθαν ἔξελε.

ΑΙ. τί τὸ πρᾶγμα τουτί; δεῦρο πάλιν βαδιστέον.

ΔΙ. Ἄπολλον, — ὅς που Δῆλον ἢ Πυθῶν' ἔχεις.

ΞΑ. ἤλγησεν· οὐκ ἤκουσας;

ΔΙ.   οὐκ ἔγωγ', ἐπεὶ   660
ἴαμβον Ἱππώνακτος ἀνεμιμνησκόμην.

ΞΑ. οὐδὲν ποεῖς γάρ· ἀλλὰ τὰς λαγόνας σπόδει.

ΑΙ. μὰ τὸν Δί', ἀλλ' ἤδη πάρεχε τὴν γαστέρα.

ΔΙ. Πόσειδον, —

ΞΑ.   ἤλγησέν τις.

ΔΙ.   ἁλὸς ἐν βένθεσιν
ὃς Αἰγαίου πρωνὸς ἢ γλαυκᾶς μέδεις —   665

ΑΙ. οὔ τοι μὰ τὴν Δήμητρα δύναμαί πω μαθεῖν   668
ὁπότερος ὑμῶν ἐστι θεός. ἀλλ' εἴσιτον·
ὁ δεσπότης γὰρ αὐτὸς ὑμᾶς γνώσεται   670

χἠ Φερρέφατθ', ἅτ' ὄντε κἀκείνω θεώ.

ΔΙ. ὀρθῶς λέγεις· ἐβουλόμην δ' ἂν τοῦτό σε
προτέρον νοῆσαι, πρὶν ἐμὲ τὰς πληγὰς λαβεῖν.

ΧΟ. Μοῦσα, χορῶν ἱερῶν ἐπίβηθι καὶ ἔλθ' ἐπὶ τέρψιν
   ἀοιδᾶς ἐμᾶς,   675
 τὸν πολὺν ὀψομένη λαῶν ὄχλον, οὗ σοφίαι
   μυρίαι κάθηνται
 φιλοτιμότεραι Κλεοφῶντος, ἐφ' οὗ δὴ
 χείλεσιν ἀμφιλάλοις δεινὸν ἐπιβρέμεται   680
   Θρηκία χελιδὼν
 ἐπὶ βάρβαρον ἑζομένη πέταλον·
 κελαδεῖ δ' ἐπίκλαυτον ἀηδόνιον νόμον, ὡς ἀπο-
   λεῖται,
  κἂν ἴσαι γένωνται.   685

τὸν ἱερὸν χορὸν δίκαιόν ἐστι χρηστὰ τῇ πόλει
ξυμπαραινεῖν καὶ διδάσκειν. πρῶτον οὖν ἡμῖν
  δοκεῖ
ἐξισῶσαι τοὺς πολίτας κἀφελεῖν τὰ δείματα.
κεἴ τις ἥμαρτε σφαλείς τι Φρυνίχου παλαίσμασιν,
ἐγγενέσθαι φημὶ χρῆναι τοῖς ὀλισθοῦσιν τότε   690
αἰτίαν ἐκθεῖσι λῦσαι τὰς πρότερον ἁμαρτίας.
εἶτ' ἄτιμόν φημι χρῆναι μηδέν' εἶν' ἐν τῇ πόλει.
καὶ γὰρ αἰσχρόν ἐστι τοὺς μὲν ναυμαχήσαντας
  μίαν
καὶ Πλαταιᾶς εὐθὺς εἶναι κἀντὶ δούλων δεσπότας.
κοὐδὲ ταῦτ' ἔγωγ' ἔχοιμ' ἂν μὴ οὐ καλῶς φάσκειν
  ἔχειν,   695
ἀλλ' ἐπαινῶ· μόνα γὰρ αὐτὰ νοῦν ἔχοντ' ἐδράσατε.
πρὸς δὲ τούτοις εἰκὸς ὑμᾶς, οἳ μεθ' ὑμῶν πολλὰ δὴ

χοὶ πατέρες ἐναυμάχησαν καὶ προσήκουσιν γένει
τὴν μίαν ταύτην παρεῖναι συμφορὰν αἰτουμένοις.
ἀλλὰ τῆς ὀργῆς ἀνέντες, ὦ σοφώτατοι φύσει,   700
πάντας ἀνθρώπους ἑκόντες συγγενεῖς κτησώμεθα
κἀπιτίμους καὶ πολίτας, ὅστις ἂν ξυνναυμαχῇ.
εἰ δὲ ταῦτ' ὀγκωσόμεσθα κἀποσεμνυνούμεθα,
τὴν πόλιν καὶ ταῦτ' ἔχοντες κυμάτων ἐν ἀγκάλαις,
ὑστέρῳ χρόνῳ ποτ' αὖθις εὖ φρονεῖν οὐ δόξο-
μεν.   705

εἰ δ' ἐγὼ ὀρθὸς ἰδεῖν βίον ἀνέρος ἢ τρόπον ὅστις
        ἔτ' οἰμώξεται,
    οὐ πολὺν οὐδ' ὁ πίθηκος οὗτος ὁ νῦν ἐνοχλῶν,
        Κλειγένης ὁ μικρός,
    ὁ πονηρότατος βαλανεὺς ὁπόσοι κρα-   710
    τοῦσι κυκησίτεφροι ψευδολίτρου κονίας
        καὶ Κιμωλίας γῆς,
    χρόνον ἐνδιατρίψει· ἰδὼν δὲ τάδ' οὐκ   713/14
εἰρηνικὸς ἔσθ', ἵνα μή ποτε κἀποδυθῇ μεθύων ἄ- 715
    νευ ξύλου βαδίζων.

πολλάκις γ' ἡμῖν ἔδοξεν ἡ πόλις πεπονθέναι
ταὐτὸν εἴς τε τῶν πολιτῶν τοὺς καλούς τε κἀγα-
        θοὺς
εἴς τε τἀρχαῖον νόμισμα καὶ τὸ καινὸν χρυσίον.   720
οὔτε γὰρ τούτοισιν οὖσιν οὐ κεκιβδηλευμένοις,
ἀλλὰ καλλίστοις ἁπάντων, ὡς δοκεῖ, νομισμάτων
καὶ μόνοις ὀρθῶς κοπεῖσι καὶ κεκωδωνισμένοις
ἔν τε τοῖς Ἕλλησι καὶ τοῖς βαρβάροισι πανταχοῦ
χρώμεθ' οὐδέν, ἀλλὰ τούτοις τοῖς πονηροῖς χαλ-
        κίοις   725

χθές τε καὶ πρώην κοπεῖσι τῷ κακίστῳ κόμ-
   ματι.
τῶν πολιτῶν θ' οὓς μὲν ἴσμεν εὐγενεῖς καὶ σώ-
   φρονας
ἄνδρας ὄντας καὶ δικαίους καὶ καλούς τε κἀγαθοὺς
καὶ τραφέντας ἐν παλαίστραις καὶ χοροῖς καὶ
   μουσικῇ,
προυσελοῦμεν, τοῖς δὲ χαλκοῖς καὶ ξένοις καὶ
   πυρρίαις   730
καὶ πονηροῖς κἀκ πονηρῶν εἰς ἅπαντα χρώμεθα
ὑστάτοις ἀφιγμένοισιν, οἷσιν ἡ πόλις πρὸ τοῦ
οὐδὲ φαρμακοῖσιν εἰκῇ ῥᾳδίως ἐχρήσατ' ἄν.
ἀλλὰ καὶ νῦν, ὠνόητοι, μεταβαλόντες τοὺς τρό-
   πους
χρῆσθε τοῖς χρηστοῖσιν αὖθις· καὶ κατορθώσασι
   γὰρ   735
εὔλογον, κἄν τι σφαλῆτ', ἐξ ἀξίου γοῦν τοῦ ξύ-
   λου,
ἤν τι καὶ πάσχητε, πάσχειν τοῖς σοφοῖς δοκήσετε.

ΟΙΚΕΤΗΣ

νὴ τὸν Δία τὸν σωτῆρα, γεννάδας ἀνὴρ
ὁ δεσπότης σου.

ΞΑ.   πῶς γὰρ οὐχὶ γεννάδας,
ὅστις γε πίνειν οἶδε καὶ βινεῖν μόνον;   740
ΟΙ. τὸ δὲ μὴ πατάξαι σ' ἐξελεγχθέντ' ἄντικρυς,
ὅτι δοῦλος ὢν ἔφασκες εἶναι δεσπότης.
ΞΑ. ᾤμωξε μεντἄν.
ΟΙ.   τοῦτο μέντοι δουλικὸν
εὐθὺς πεπόηκας, ὅπερ ἐγὼ χαίρω ποιῶν.

ΞΑ. χαίρεις, ἱκετεύω;

ΟΙ.   μἀλλ' ἐποπτεύειν δοκῶ,   745
ὅταν καταράσωμαι λάθρα τῷ δεσπότῃ.

ΞΑ. τί δὲ τονθορύζων, ἡνίκ' ἂν πληγὰς λαβὼν
πολλὰς ἀπίῃς θύραζε;

ΟΙ.   καὶ τοῦθ' ἥδομαι.

ΞΑ. τί δὲ πολλὰ πράττων;

ΟΙ.   ὡς μὰ Δί' οὐδὲν οἶδ' ἐγώ.

ΞΑ. ὁμόγνιε Ζεῦ· καὶ παρακούων δεσποτῶν   750
ἅττ' ἂν λαλῶσι;

ΟΙ.   μἀλλὰ πλεῖν ἢ μαίνομαι.

ΞΑ. τί δὲ τοῖς θύραζε ταῦτα καταλαλῶν;

ΟΙ.   ἐγώ;
μὰ Δί' ἀλλ' ὅταν δρῶ τοῦτο, κἀκμιαίνομαι.

ΞΑ. ὦ Φοῖβ' Ἄπολλον, ἔμβαλέ μοι τὴν δεξιάν,
καὶ δὸς κύσαι καὐτὸς κύσον. καί μοι φράσον 755
πρὸς Διός, ὃς ἡμῖν ἐστιν ὁμομαστιγίας —
τίς οὗτος οὕνδον ἐστὶ θόρυβος καὶ βοὴ
χὠ λοιδορησμός;

ΟΙ.   Αἰσχύλου κεὐριπίδου.

ΞΑ. ἆ.

ΟΙ.   πρᾶγμα, πρᾶγμα μέγα κεκίνηται, μέγα
ἐν τοῖς νεκροῖσι καὶ στάσις πολλὴ πάνυ.   760

ΞΑ. ἐκ τοῦ;

ΟΙ.   νόμος τις ἐνθάδ' ἐστὶ κείμενος
ἀπὸ τῶν τεχνῶν, ὅσαι μεγάλαι καὶ δεξιαί,
τὸν ἄριστον ὄντα τῶν ἑαυτοῦ συντέχνων
σίτησιν αὐτὸν ἐν πρυτανείῳ λαμβάνειν
θρόνον τε τοῦ Πλούτωνος ἑξῆς —

ΞΑ.   μανθάνω. 765

ΟΙ. ἕως ἀφίκοιτο τὴν τέχνην σοφώτερος
ἕτερός τις αὐτοῦ· τότε δὲ παραχωρεῖν ἔδει.

ΞΑ. τί δῆτα τουτὶ τεθορύβηκεν Αἰσχύλον;

ΟΙ. ἐκεῖνος εἶχε τὸν τραγῳδικὸν θρόνον,
ὡς ὢν κράτιστος τὴν τέχνην.

ΞΑ.   νυνὶ δὲ τίς;   770

ΟΙ. ὅτε δὴ κατῆλθ᾽ Εὐριπίδης, ἐπεδείκνυτο
τοῖς λωποδύταις καὶ τοῖσι βαλλαντιοτόμοις
καὶ τοῖσι πατραλοίαισι καὶ τοιχωρύχοις,
ὅπερ ἔστ᾽ ἐν Ἅιδου πλῆθος, οἱ δ᾽ ἀκροώμενοι
τῶν ἀντιλογιῶν καὶ λυγισμῶν καὶ στροφῶν   775
ὑπερεμάνησαν κἀνόμισαν σοφώτατον·
κἄπειτ᾽ ἐπαρθεὶς ἀντελάβετο τοῦ θρόνου,
ἵν᾽ Αἰσχύλος καθῆστο.

ΞΑ.   κοὐκ ἐβάλλετο;

ΟΙ. μὰ Δί᾽, ἀλλ᾽ ὁ δῆμος ἀνεβόα κρίσιν ποεῖν
ὁπότερος εἴη τὴν τέχνην σοφώτερος.   780

ΞΑ. ὁ τῶν πανούργων;

ΟΙ.   νὴ Δί᾽, οὐράνιόν γ᾽ ὅσον.

ΞΑ. μετ᾽ Αἰσχύλου δ᾽ οὐκ ἦσαν ἕτεροι σύμμαχοι;

ΟΙ. ὀλίγον τὸ χρηστόν ἐστιν, ὥσπερ ἐνθάδε.

ΞΑ. τί δῆθ᾽ ὁ Πλούτων δρᾶν παρασκευάζεται;

ΟΙ. ἀγῶνα ποιεῖν αὐτίκα μάλα καὶ κρίσιν   785
κἄλεγχον αὐτοῖν τῆς τέχνης.

ΞΑ.   κἄπειτα πῶς
οὐ καὶ Σοφοκλέης ἀντελάβετο τοῦ θρόνου;

ΟΙ. μὰ Δί᾽ οὐκ ἐκεῖνος, ἀλλ᾽ ἔκυσε μὲν Αἰσχύλον,
ὅτε δὴ κατῆλθε, κἀνέβαλε τὴν δεξιάν.
κἀκεῖνος ὑπεχώρησεν αὐτῷ τοῦ θρόνου.   790
νυνὶ δ᾽ ἔμελλεν, ὡς ἔφη Κλειδημίδης,

ἔφεδρος καθεδεῖσθαι· κἂν μὲν Αἰσχύλος κρατῇ,
ἕξειν κατὰ χώραν· εἰ δὲ μή, περὶ τῆς τέχνης
διαγωνιεῖσθ' ἔφασκε πρός γ' Εὐριπίδην.

ΞΑ. τὸ χρῆμ' ἄρ' ἔσται;

ΟΙ.   νὴ Δί' ὀλίγον ὕστερον.   795
κἀνταῦθα δὴ τὰ δεινὰ κινηθήσεται.
καὶ γὰρ ταλάντῳ μουσικὴ σταθμήσεται —

ΞΑ. τί δέ; μειαγωγήσουσι τὴν τραγῳδίαν;

ΟΙ. καὶ κανόνας ἐξοίσουσι καὶ πήχεις ἐπῶν
καὶ πλαίσια ξύμπτυκτα —

ΞΑ.   πλινθεύσουσί τε;   800

ΟΙ. καὶ διαμέτρους καὶ σφῆνας. ὁ γὰρ Εὐριπίδης
κατ' ἔπος βασανιεῖν φησι τὰς τραγῳδίας.

ΞΑ. ἦ που βαρέως οἶμαι τὸν Αἰσχύλον φέρειν.

ΟΙ. ἔβλεψε γοῦν ταυρηδὸν ἐγκύψας κάτω.

ΞΑ. κρινεῖ δὲ δὴ τίς ταῦτα;

ΟΙ.   τοῦτ' ἦν δύσκολον·   805
σοφῶν γὰρ ἀνδρῶν ἀπορίαν ηὑρισκέτην.
οὔτε γὰρ 'Αθηναίοισι συνέβαιν' Αἰσχύλος —

ΞΑ. πολλοὺς ἴσως ἐνόμιζε τοὺς τοιχωρύχους.

ΟΙ. λῆρόν τε τἄλλ' ἡγεῖτο τοῦ γνῶναι πέρι
φύσεις ποιητῶν· εἶτα τῷ σῷ δεσπότῃ   810
ἐπέτρεψαν, ὁτιὴ τῆς τέχνης ἔμπειρος ἦν.
ἀλλ' εἰσίωμεν· ὡς ὅταν γ' οἱ δεσπόται
ἐσπουδάκωσι, κλαύμαθ' ἡμῖν γίγνεται.

ΧΟ. ἦ που δεινὸν ἐριβρεμέτας χόλον ἔνδοθεν ἕξει,
ἡνίκ' ἂν ὀξύλαλόν περ ἴδῃ θήγοντος ὀδόντα   815
ἀντιτέχνου· τότε δὴ μανίας ὑπὸ δεινῆς
ὄμματα στροβήσεται.

ἔσται δ' ἱππολόφων τε λόγων κορυθαίολα νείκη
σκινδαλάμων τε παραξονίων σμιλευματοεργοῦ
φωτὸς ἀμυνομένου φρενοτέκτονος ἀνδρὸς 820
ῥήμαθ' ἱπποβάμονα.
φρίξας δ' αὐτοκόμου λοφιᾶς λασιαύχενα χαίταν,
δεινὸν ἐπισκύνιον ξυνάγων, βρυχώμενος ἥσει
ῥήματα γομφοπαγῆ, πινακηδὸν ἀποσπῶν
γηγενεῖ φυσήματι. 825
ἔνθεν δὴ στοματουργός, ἐπῶν βασανίστρια, λί-
σπη
γλῶσσ', ἀνελισσομένη φθονεροὺς κινοῦσα χαλι-
νούς,
ῥήματα δαιομένη καταλεπτολογήσει
πλευμόνων πολὺν πόνον.

ΕΥΡΙΠΙΔΗΣ

οὐκ ἂν μεθείμην τοῦ θρόνου, μὴ νουθέτει· 830
κρείττων γὰρ εἶναί φημι τούτου τὴν τέχνην.
ΔΙ. Αἰσχύλε, τί σιγᾷς; αἰσθάνει γὰρ τοῦ λόγου.
ΕΥ. ἀποσεμνυνεῖται πρῶτον, ἅπερ ἑκάστοτε
ἐν ταῖς τραγῳδίαισιν ἐτερατεύετο.
ΔΙ. ὦ δαιμόνι' ἀνδρῶν, μὴ μεγάλα λίαν λέγε. 835
ΕΥ. ἐγᾦδα τοῦτον καὶ διέσκεμμαι πάλαι,
ἄνθρωπον ἀγριοποιόν, αὐθαδόστομον,
ἔχοντ' ἀχάλινον, ἀκρατές, ἀθύρωτον στόμα,
ἀπερίλάλητον, κομποφακελορρήμονα.

ΑΙΣΧΥΛΟΣ

ἄληθες, ὦ παῖ τῆς ἀρουραίας θεοῦ; 840
σὺ δὴ 'μὲ ταῦτ', ὦ στωμυλιοσυλλεκτάδη

καὶ πτωχοποιὲ καὶ ῥακιοσυρραπτάδη;
ἀλλ' οὔ τι χαίρων αὔτ' ἐρεῖς.

ΔΙ.   παῦ', Αἰσχύλε,
καὶ μὴ πρὸς ὀργὴν σπλάγχνα θερμήνῃς κότῳ.

ΑΙ. οὐ δῆτα, πρίν γ' ἂν τοῦτον ἀποφήνω σαφῶς   845
τὸν χωλοποιὸν οἷος ὢν θρασύνεται.

ΔΙ. ἄρν' ἄρνα μέλανα, παῖδες, ἐξενέγκατε·
τυφὼς γὰρ ἐκβαίνειν παρασκευάζεται.

ΑΙ. ὦ Κρητικὰς μὲν συλλέγων μονῳδίας,
γάμους δ' ἀνοσίους εἰσφέρων εἰς τὴν τέχ-
νην, —   850

ΔΙ. ἐπίσχες οὗτος, ὦ πολυτίμητ' Αἰσχύλε.
ἀπὸ τῶν χαλαζῶν δ', ὦ πόνηρ' Εὐριπίδη,
ἄναγε σεαυτὸν ἐκποδών, εἰ σωφρονεῖς,
ἵνα μὴ κεφαλαίῳ τὸν κρόταφόν σου ῥήματι
θενὼν ὑπ' ὀργῆς ἐκχέῃ τὸν Τήλεφον.   855
σὺ δὲ μὴ πρὸς ὀργήν, Αἰσχύλ', ἀλλὰ πραόνως
ἔλεγχ', ἐλέγχου· λοιδορεῖσθαι δ' οὐ πρέπει
ἄνδρας ποητὰς ὥσπερ ἀρτοπώλιδας·
σὺ δ' εὐθὺς ὥσπερ πρῖνος ἐμπρησθεὶς βοᾷς.

ΕΥ. ἕτοιμός εἰμ' ἔγωγε, κοὐκ ἀναδύομαι,   860
δάκνειν, δάκνεσθαι, πρότερος, εἰ τούτῳ δοκεῖ,
τἄπη, τὰ μέλη, τὰ νεῦρα τῆς τραγῳδίας,
καὶ νὴ Δία τὸν Πηλέα γε καὶ τὸν Αἴολον
καὶ τὸν Μελέαγρον κἄτι μάλα τὸν Τήλεφον.

ΔΙ. σὺ δὲ δὴ τί βουλεύει ποεῖν; λέγ', Αἰσχύλε.   865

ΑΙ. ἐβουλόμην μὲν οὐκ ἐρίζειν ἐνθάδε·
οὐκ ἐξ ἴσου γάρ ἐστιν ἀγὼν νῷν.

ΔΙ.   τί δαί;

ΑΙ. ὅτι ἡ πόησις οὐχὶ συντέθνηκέ μοι,

τούτῳ δὲ συντέθηκεν, ὥσθ' ἕξει λέγειν.
ὅμως δ' ἐπειδή σοι δοκεῖ, δρᾶν ταῦτα χρή.   870

ΔΙ. ἴθι νυν λιβανωτὸν δεῦρό τις καὶ πῦρ δότω,
ὅπως ἂν εὔξωμαι πρὸ τῶν σοφισμάτων
ἀγῶνα κρῖναι τόνδε μουσικώτατα·
ὑμεῖς δὲ ταῖς Μούσαις τι μέλος ὑπᾴσατε.

ΧΟ. ὦ Διὸς ἐννέα παρθένοι, ἁγναὶ   875
Μοῦσαι, λεπτολόγους ξυνετὰς φρένας αἳ καθο-
ρᾶτε
ἀνδρῶν γνωμοτύπων, ὅταν εἰς ἔριν ὀξυμερίμνοις
ἔλθωσι στρεβλοῖσι παλαίσμασιν ἀντιλογοῦντες,
ἔλθετ' ἐποψόμεναι δύναμιν
δεινοτάτοιν στομάτοιν πορίσασθαι   880
ῥήματα καὶ παραπρίσματ' ἐπῶν.
νῦν γὰρ ἀγὼν σοφίας ὁ μέγας χωρεῖ πρὸς ἔργον
ἤδη.

ΔΙ. εὔχεσθε δὴ καὶ σφώ τι πρὶν τἄπη λέγειν.   885
ΑΙ. Δήμητερ ἡ θρέψασα τὴν ἐμὴν φρένα,
εἶναί με τῶν σῶν ἄξιον μυστηρίων.
ΔΙ. ἐπίθες λιβανωτὸν καὶ σὺ δὴ λαβών.
ΕΥ.   καλῶς·
ἕτεροι γάρ εἰσιν οἷσιν εὔχομαι θεοῖς.
ΔΙ. ἴδιοί τινές σου, κόμμα καινόν;
ΕΥ.   καὶ μάλα.   890
ΔΙ. ἴθι δὴ προσεύχου τοῖσιν ἰδιώταις θεοῖς.
ΕΥ. αἰθήρ, ἐμὸν βόσκημα, καὶ γλώττης στρόφιγξ
καὶ ξύνεσι καὶ μυκτῆρες ὀσφραντήριοι,
ὀρθῶς μ' ἐλέγχειν ὧν ἂν ἅπτωμαι λόγων.

ΧΟ.   καὶ μὴν ἡμεῖς ἐπιθυμοῦμεν   895
      παρὰ σοφοῖν ἀνδροῖν ἀκοῦσαι, τίνα λόγων
            ἔπιτε δαΐαν ὁδόν.
      γλῶσσα μὲν γὰρ ἠγρίωται,
      λῆμα δ' οὐκ ἄτολμον ἀμφοῖν,
      οὐδ' ἀκίνητοι φρένες.
      προσδοκᾶν οὖν εἰκός ἐστι   900
      τὸν μὲν ἀστεῖόν τι λέξειν
            καὶ κατερρινημένον,
      τὸν δ' ἀνασπῶντ' αὐτοπρέμνοις
            τοῖς λόγοισιν ἐμπεσόντα
      συσκεδᾶν πολλὰς ἀλινδήθρας ἐπῶν.   904a

      ἀλλ' ὡς τάχιστα χρὴ λέγειν· οὕτω δ' ὅπως
            ἐρεῖτον,   905
      ἀστεῖα καὶ μήτ' εἰκόνας μήθ' οἷ' ἂν ἄλλος εἴποι.
ΕΥ.   καὶ μὴν ἐμαυτὸν μέν γε, τὴν πόησιν οἷός εἰμι,
      ἐν τοῖσιν ὑστάτοις φράσω· τοῦτον δὲ πρῶτ' ἐ-
            λέγξω,
      ὡς ἦν ἀλαζὼν καὶ φέναξ οἵοις τε τοὺς θεατὰς
      ἐξηπάτα μώρους λαβὼν παρὰ Φρυνίχῳ τραφέν-
            τας.   910
      πρώτιστα μὲν γὰρ ἕνα τιν' ἂν καθῖσεν ἐγκαλύψας,
      Ἀχιλλέα τιν' ἢ Νιόβην, τὸ πρόσωπον οὐχὶ δεικ-
            νύς,
      πρόσχημα τῆς τραγῳδίας, γρύζοντας οὐδὲ τουτί.
ΔΙ.   μὰ τὸν Δί' οὐ δῆθ'.
ΕΥ.   ὁ δὲ χορός γ' ἤρειδεν ὁρμαθοὺς ἂν
      μελῶν ἐφεξῆς· τέτταρας ξυνεχῶς ἄν· οἱ δ' ἐσί-
            γων.   915

ΔΙ. ἐγὼ δ' ἔχαιρον τῇ σιωπῇ, καί με τοῦτ' ἔτερπεν
οὐχ ἧττον ἢ νῦν οἱ λαλοῦντες.

ΕΥ.   ἠλίθιος γὰρ ἦσθα,
σάφ' ἴσθι.

ΔΙ.   κἀμαυτῷ δοκῶ. τί δὲ ταῦτ' ἔδρασ' ὁ δεῖνα;

ΕΥ. ὑπ' ἀλαζονείας, ἵν' ὁ θεατὴς προσδοκῶν καθοῖτο,
ὁπόθ' ἡ Νιόβη τι φθέγξεται· τὸ δρᾶμα δ' ἂν
διῄει.   920

ΔΙ. ὦ παμπόνηρος, οἷ' ἄρ' ἐφενακιζόμην ὑπ' αὐτοῦ.
τί σκορδινᾷ καὶ δυσφορεῖς;

ΕΥ.   ὅτι αὐτὸν ἐξελέγχω.
κἄπειτ' ἐπειδὴ ταῦτα ληρήσειε καὶ τὸ δρᾶμα
ἤδη μεσοίη, ῥήματ' ἂν βόεια δώδεκ' εἶπεν,
ὀφρῦς ἔχοντα καὶ λόφους, δείν' ἄττα μορμορ-
ωπά,   925
ἄγνωτα τοῖς θεωμένοις.

ΑΙ.   οἴμοι τάλας.

ΔΙ.   σιώπα.

ΕΥ. σαφὲς δ' ἂν εἶπεν οὐδὲ ἕν —

ΔΙ.   μὴ πρῖε τοὺς ὀδόντας.

ΕΥ. ἀλλ' ἢ Σκαμάνδρους ἢ τάφρους ἢ 'π' ἀσπίδων
ἐπόντας
γρυπαιέτους χαλκηλάτους καὶ ῥήμαθ' ἱππόκρημνα,
ἃ ξυμβαλεῖν οὐ ῥᾴδι' ἦν.

ΔΙ.   νὴ τοὺς θεούς, ἐγὼ γοῦν   930
ἤδη ποτ' ἐν μακρῷ χρόνῳ νυκτὸς διηγρύπνησα
τὸν ξουθὸν ἱππαλεκτρυόνα ζητῶν τίς ἐστιν ὄρνις.

ΑΙ. σημεῖον ἐν ταῖς ναυσίν, ὠμαθέστατ', ἐνεγέγραπτο.

ΔΙ. ἐγὼ δὲ τὸν Φιλοξένου γ' ᾤμην Ἔρυξιν εἶναι.

ΕΥ. εἶτ' ἐν τραγῳδίαις ἐχρῆν κἀλεκτρυόνα ποῆσαι;   935

ΑΙ. σὺ δ', ὦ θεοῖσιν ἐχθρέ, ποῖ' ἄττ' ἐστὶν ἄττ'
ἐποίεις;

ΕΥ. οὐχ ἱππαλεκτρυόνας μὰ Δί' οὐδὲ τραγελάφους,
ἅπερ σύ,
ἃν τοῖσι παραπετάσμασιν τοῖς Μηδικοῖς γρά-
φουσιν·
ἀλλ' ὡς παρέλαβον τὴν τέχνην παρὰ σοῦ τὸ
πρῶτον εὐθὺς
οἰδοῦσαν ὑπὸ κομπασμάτων καὶ ῥημάτων ἐπ-
αχθῶν,   940
ἴσχνανα μὲν πρώτιστον αὐτὴν καὶ τὸ βάρος
ἀφεῖλον
ἐπυλλίοις καὶ περιπάτοις καὶ τευτλίοισι λευκοῖς,
χυλὸν διδοὺς στωμυλμάτων ἀπὸ βιβλίων ἀπηθῶν·
εἶτ' ἀνέτρεφον μονῳδίαις —

ΔΙ.   Κηφισοφῶντα μειγνύς.

ΕΥ. εἶτ' οὐκ ἐλήρουν ὅ τι τύχοιμ' οὐδ' ἐμπεσὼν
ἔφυρον,   945
ἀλλ' οὑξιὼν πρώτιστα μέν μοι τὸ γένος εἶπ' ἂν
εὐθὺς
τοῦ δράματος.

ΔΙ.   κρεῖττον γὰρ ἦν σοι νὴ Δί' ἢ τὸ σαυτοῦ.

ΕΥ. ἔπειτ' ἀπὸ τῶν πρώτων ἐπῶν οὐδένα παρῆκ' ἂν
ἀργόν,
ἀλλ' ἔλεγεν ἡ γυνή τέ μοι χὠ δοῦλος οὐδὲν ἧττον,
χὠ δεσπότης χἡ παρθένος χἡ γραῦς ἄν.

ΑΙ.   εἶτα δῆτα   950
οὐκ ἀποθανεῖν σε ταῦτ' ἐχρῆν τολμῶντα;

ΕΥ.   μὰ τὸν Ἀπόλλω·
δημοκρατικὸν γὰρ αὖτ' ἔδρων.

ΔΙ.   τοῦτο μὲν ἔασον, ὦ τᾶν.
οὐ σοὶ γάρ ἐστι περίπατος κάλλιστα περί γε
    τούτου.
ΕΥ. ἔπειτα τουτουσὶ λαλεῖν ἐδίδαξα —
ΑΙ.   φημὶ κἀγώ.
ὡς πρὶν διδάξαι γ᾽ ὤφελες μέσος διαρραγῆναι. 955
ΕΥ. λεπτῶν τε κανόνων εἰσβολὰς ἐπῶν τε γωνιασ-
    μούς.
νοεῖν, ὁρᾶν, ξυνιέναι, στρέφειν ἐρᾶν, τεχνάζειν,
κάχ᾽ ὑποτοπεῖσθαι, περινοεῖν ἅπαντα —
ΑΙ.   φημὶ κἀγώ.
ΕΥ. οἰκεῖα πράγματ᾽ εἰσάγων, οἷς χρώμεθ᾽, οἷς ξύνεσ-
    μεν,
ἐξ ὧν γ᾽ ἂν ἐξηλεγχόμην· ξυνειδότες γὰρ οὗτοι 960
ἤλεγχον ἄν μου τὴν τέχνην· ἀλλ᾽ οὐκ ἐκομπολά-
    κουν
ἀπὸ τοῦ φρονεῖν ἀποσπάσας, οὐδ᾽ ἐξέπληττον
    αὐτούς,
Κύκνους ποιῶν καὶ Μέμνονας κωδωνοφαλαρο-
    πώλους.
γνώσει δὲ τοὺς τούτου τε κἀμοὺς ἑκατέρου
    μαθητάς.
τουτουμενὶ Φορμίσιος Μεγαίνετός θ᾽ ὁ Μανῆς, 965
σαλπιγγολογχυπηνάδαι, σαρκασμοπιτυοκάμπται,
οὑμοὶ δὲ Κλειτοφῶν τε καὶ Θηραμένης ὁ κομψός.
ΔΙ. Θηραμένης; σοφός γ᾽ ἀνὴρ καὶ δεινὸς εἰς τὰ
    πάντα,
ὃς ἢν κακοῖς που περιπέσῃ καὶ πλησίον παραστῇ,
πέπτωκεν ἔξω τῶν κακῶν, οὐ Χῖος, ἀλλὰ
Κεῖος.   970

ΕΥ.   τοιαῦτα μέντοὐγὼ φρονεῖν
       τούτοισιν εἰσηγησάμην,
       λογισμὸν ἐνθεὶς τῇ τέχνῃ
       καὶ σκέψιν, ὥστ' ἤδη νοεῖν
       ἅπαντα καὶ διειδέναι   975
       τά τ' ἄλλα καὶ τὰς οἰκίας
       οἰκεῖν ἄμεινον ἢ πρὸ τοῦ
       κἀνασκοπεῖν· ' πῶς τοῦτ' ἔχει;
       ποῦ μοι τοδί; τίς τοῦτ' ἔλαβε; '
ΔΙ.   νὴ τοὺς θεούς, νῦν γοῦν 'Αθη-   980
       ναίων ἅπας τις εἰσιὼν
       κέκραγε πρὸς τοὺς οἰκέτας
       ζητεῖ τε· ' ποῦ 'στιν ἡ χύτρα;
       τίς τὴν κεφαλὴν ἀπεδήδοκεν
       τῆς μαινίδος; τὸ τρύβλιον   985
       τὸ περυσινὸν τέθνηκέ μοι;
       ποῦ τὸ σκόροδον τὸ χθιζινόν;
       τίς τῆς ἐλάας παρέτραγεν; '
       τέως δ' ἀβελτερώτατοι
       κεχηνότες μαμμάκυθοι,   990
       μελιτίδαι καθῆντο.

ΧΟ.   τάδε μὲν λεύσσεις, φαίδιμ' 'Αχιλλεῦ·
       σὺ δὲ τί, φέρε, πρὸς ταῦτα λέξεις; μόνον ὅπως
          μή σ' ὁ θυμὸς ἁρπάσας
          ἐκτὸς οἴσει τῶν ἐλαῶν·   995
       δεινὰ γὰρ κατηγόρηκεν.
          ἀλλ' ὅπως, ὦ γεννάδα,
          μὴ πρὸς ὀργὴν ἀντιλέξεις,
          ἀλλὰ συστείλας ἄκροισι

χρώμενος τοῖς ἱστίοις,　　　　　　　1000
εἶτα μᾶλλον μᾶλλον ἄξεις
καὶ φυλάξεις, ἡνίκ' ἂν τὸ
πνεῦμα λεῖον καὶ καθεστηκὸς λάβῃς.

ἀλλ' ὦ πρῶτος τῶν Ἑλλήνων πυργώσας ῥήματα
σεμνὰ
καὶ κοσμήσας τραγικὸν λῆρον, θαρρῶν τὸν κρου-
νὸν ἀφίει.　　　　　　　　　　　　1005
ΑΙ. θυμοῦμαι μὲν τῇ ξυντυχίᾳ, καί μου τὰ σπλάγχν'
ἀγανακτεῖ,
εἰ πρὸς τοῦτον δεῖ μ' ἀντιλέγειν· ἵνα μὴ φάσκῃ δ'
ἀπορεῖν με, —
ἀπόκριναί μοι, τίνος οὕνεκα χρὴ θαυμάζειν ἄνδρα
ποιητήν;
ΕΥ. δεξιότητος καὶ νουθεσίας, ὅτι βελτίους τε ποιοῦμεν
τοὺς ἀνθρώπους ἐν ταῖς πόλεσιν.
ΑΙ.　　　　　　ταῦτ' οὖν εἰ μὴ πεπόηκας,　1010
ἀλλ' ἐκ χρηστῶν καὶ γενναίων μοχθηροτάτους
ἀπέδειξας,
τί παθεῖν φήσεις ἄξιος εἶναι;
ΔΙ.　　　　　　τεθνάναι· μὴ τοῦτον ἐρώτα.
ΑΙ. σκέψαι τοίνυν οἵους αὐτοὺς παρ' ἐμοῦ παρεδέξατο
πρῶτον,
εἰ γενναίους καὶ τετραπήχεις, καὶ μὴ διαδρασι-
πολίτας,
μηδ' ἀγοραίους μηδὲ κοβάλους, ὥσπερ νῦν, μηδὲ
πανούργους,　　　　　　　　　　1015
ἀλλὰ πνέοντας δόρυ καὶ λόγχας καὶ λευκολόφους
τρυφαλείας

καὶ πήληκας καὶ κνημῖδας καὶ θυμοὺς ἑπταβοεί-
ους.

ΕΥ. καὶ δὴ χωρεῖ τουτὶ τὸ κακόν.

ΔΙ. κρανοποιῶν αὖ μ᾽ ἐπιτρίψει.

ΕΥ. καὶ τί σὺ δράσας οὕτως αὐτοὺς γενναίους ἐξεδί-
δαξας;

ΔΙ. Αἰσχύλε, λέξον, μηδ᾽ αὐθάδως σεμνυνόμενος χα-
λέπαινε. 1020

ΑΙ. δρᾶμα ποήσας Ἄρεως μεστόν.

ΔΙ. ποῖον;

ΑΙ. τοὺς Ἑπτ᾽ ἐπὶ Θήβας·
ὃ θεασάμενος πᾶς ἄν τις ἀνὴρ ἠράσθη δάιος εἶναι.

ΔΙ. τουτὶ μέν σοι κακὸν εἴργασται· Θηβαίους γὰρ
πεπόηκας
ἀνδρειοτέρους εἰς τὸν πόλεμον· καὶ τούτου γ᾽
οὕνεκα τύπτου.

ΑΙ. ἀλλ᾽ ὑμῖν αὔτ᾽ ἐξῆν ἀσκεῖν, ἀλλ᾽ οὐκ ἐπὶ τοῦτ᾽
ἐτράπεσθε. 1025
εἶτα διδάξας Πέρσας μετὰ τοῦτ᾽ ἐπιθυμεῖν ἐξε-
δίδαξα
νικᾶν ἀεὶ τοὺς ἀντιπάλους, κοσμήσας ἔργον ἄρι-
στον.

ΔΙ. ἐχάρην γοῦν, ἡνίκ᾽ ἐκώκυσας, παῖ Δαρείου τεθ-
νεῶτος,
ὁ χορὸς δ᾽ εὐθὺς τὼ χεῖρ᾽ ὡδὶ συγκρούσας εἶπεν·
‘ ἰαυοῖ.’

ΑΙ. ταῦτα γὰρ ἄνδρας χρὴ ποιητὰς ἀσκεῖν. σκέψαι
γὰρ ἀπ᾽ ἀρχῆς 1030
ὡς ὠφέλιμοι τῶν ποιητῶν οἱ γενναῖοι γεγένην-
ται.

Ὀρφεὺς μὲν γὰρ τελετάς θ' ἡμῖν κατέδειξε φόνων
   τ' ἀπέχεσθαι,
Μουσαῖος δ' ἐξακέσεις τε νόσων καὶ χρησμούς,
   Ἡσίοδος δὲ
γῆς ἐργασίας, καρπῶν ὥρας, ἀρότους· ὁ δὲ θεῖος
   Ὅμηρος
ἀπὸ τοῦ τιμὴν καὶ κλέος ἔσχεν πλὴν τοῦδ' ὅτι
   χρήστ' ἐδίδαξεν,   1035
τάξεις, ἀρετάς. ὁπλίσεις ἀνδρῶν;

ΔΙ.   καὶ μὴν οὐ Παντακλέα γε
ἐδίδαξεν ὅμως τὸν σκαιότατον. πρώην γοῦν,
   ἡνίκ' ἔπεμπεν,
τὸ κράνος πρῶτον περιδησάμενος τὸν λόφον ἤμελλ'
   ἐπιδήσειν.

ΑΙ. ἀλλ' ἄλλους τοι πολλοὺς ἀγαθούς, ὧν ἦν καὶ
   Λάμαχος ἥρως·
ὅθεν ἡμὴ φρὴν ἀπομαξαμένη πολλὰς ἀρετὰς ἐπόη-
   σεν,   1040
Πατρόκλων, Τεύκρων θυμολεόντων, ἵν' ἐπαίροιμ'
   ἄνδρα πολίτην
ἀντεκτείνειν αὑτὸν τούτοις, ὁπόταν σάλπιγγος
   ἀκούσῃ.
ἀλλ' οὐ μὰ Δί' οὐ Φαίδρας ἐποίουν πόρνας οὐδὲ
   Σθενεβοίας,
οὐδ' οἶδ' οὐδεὶς ἥντιν' ἐρῶσαν πώποτ' ἐποίησα
   γυναῖκα.

ΕΥ. μὰ Δί', οὐ γὰρ ἐπῆν τῆς Ἀφροδίτης οὐδέν σοι.

ΑΙ.   μηδέ γ' ἐπείη·
ἀλλ' ἐπὶ σοί τοι καὶ τοῖς σοῖσιν πολλὴ πολλοῦ
   'πικαθῆτο,   1046

ὥστε γε καὐτόν σε κατ' οὖν ἔβαλεν.

ΔΙ.   νὴ τὸν Δία τοῦτό γέ τοι δή.
ἃ γὰρ εἰς τὰς ἀλλοτρίας ἐπόεις, αὐτὸς τούτοισιν
   ἐπλήγης.

ΕΥ. καὶ τί βλάπτουσ᾽, ὦ σχέτλι᾽ ἀνδρῶν, τὴν πόλιν
   ἁμαὶ Σθενέβοιαι;

ΑΙ. ὅτι γενναίας καὶ γενναίων ἀνδρῶν ἀλόχους ἀνέ-
   πεισας   1050
   κώνεια πίνειν αἰσχυνθείσας διὰ τοὺς σοὺς Βελ-
   λεροφόντας.

ΕΥ. πότερον δ᾽ οὐκ ὄντα λόγον τοῦτον περὶ τῆς Φαί-
   δρας ξυνέθηκα;

ΑΙ. μὰ Δί᾽, ἀλλ᾽ ὄντ᾽· ἀλλ᾽ ἀποκρύπτειν χρὴ τὸ πονη-
   ρὸν τόν γε ποιητήν,
   καὶ μὴ παράγειν μηδὲ διδάσκειν. τοῖς μὲν γὰρ
   παιδαρίοισιν
   ἐστὶ διδάσκαλος ὅστις φράζει, τοῖσιν δ᾽ ἡβῶσι
   ποηταί.   1055
   πάνυ δὴ δεῖ χρηστὰ λέγειν ἡμᾶς.

ΕΥ.   ἢν οὖν σὺ λέγῃς Λυκαβηττοὺς
   καὶ Παρνασσῶν ἡμῖν μεγέθη, τοῦτ᾽ ἐστὶ τὸ χρηστὰ
   διδάσκειν,
   ὃν χρὴ φράζειν ἀνθρωπείως;

ΑΙ.   ἀλλ᾽, ὦ κακόδαιμον, ἀνάγκη
   μεγάλων γνωμῶν καὶ διανοιῶν ἴσα καὶ τὰ ῥήματα
   τίκτειν.
   κἄλλως εἰκὸς τοὺς ἡμιθέους τοῖς ῥήμασι μείζοσι
   χρῆσθαι·   1060
   καὶ γὰρ τοῖς ἱματίοις ἡμῶν χρῶνται πολὺ σεμνο-
   τέροισιν.

ἀμοῦ χρηστῶς καταδείξαντος διελυμήνω σύ.

ΕΥ.   τί δράσας;

ΑΙ. πρῶτον μὲν τοὺς βασιλεύοντας ῥάκι' ἀμπισχών,
    ἵν' ἐλεινοὶ
τοῖς ἀνθρώποις φαίνοιντ' εἶναι.

ΕΥ.   τοῦτ' οὖν ἔβλαψα τί δράσας;

ΑΙ. οὔκουν ἐθέλει γε τριηραρχεῖν πλουτῶν οὐδεὶς διὰ
    ταῦτα,   1065
ἀλλὰ ῥακίοις περιιλλόμενος κλάει καὶ φησὶ πένε-
    σθαι.

ΔΙ. νὴ τὴν Δήμητρα χιτῶνά γ' ἔχων οὔλων ἐρίων
    ὑπένερθεν.
κἂν ταῦτα λέγων ἐξαπατήσῃ, περὶ τοὺς ἰχθῦς
    ἀνέκυψεν.

ΑΙ. εἶτ' αὖ λαλιὰν ἐπιτηδεῦσαι καὶ στωμυλίαν ἐδί-
    δαξας,
ἣ 'ξεκένωσεν τάς τε παλαίστρας καὶ τὰς πυγὰς
    ἐνέτριψεν   1070
τῶν μειρακίων στωμυλλομένων, καὶ τοὺς Παρά-
    λους ἀνέπεισεν
ἀνταγορεύειν τοῖς ἄρχουσιν. καίτοι τότε γ', ἡνίκ'
    ἐγὼ 'ζων,
οὐκ ἠπίσταντ' ἀλλ' ἢ μᾶζαν καλέσαι καὶ ' ῥυπ-
    παπαῖ ' εἰπεῖν.

ΔΙ. νὴ τὸν Ἀπόλλω, καὶ προσπαρδεῖν γ' εἰς τὸ στόμα
    τῷ θαλάμακι,
καὶ μινθῶσαι τὸν ξύσσιτον κἀκβάς τινα λωπο-
    δυτῆσαι·   1075
νῦν δ' ἀντιλέγει κοὐκέτ' ἐλαύνει· πλεῖ δευρὶ καὖθις
    ἐκεῖσε.

ΑΙ.   ποίων δὲ κακῶν οὐκ αἴτιός ἐστ';
 οὐ προαγωγοὺς κατέδειξ' οὗτος,
καὶ τικτούσας ἐν τοῖς ἱεροῖς,   1080
καὶ μειγνυμένας τοῖσιν ἀδελφοῖς,
καὶ φασκούσας οὐ ζῆν τὸ ζῆν;
κᾆτ' ἐκ τούτων ἡ πόλις ἡμῶν
ὑπογραμματέων ἀνεμεστώθη
καὶ βωμολόχων δημοπιθήκων   1085
ἐξαπατώντων τὸν δῆμον ἀεί,
λαμπάδα δ' οὐδεὶς οἷός τε φέρειν
ὑπ' ἀγυμνασίας ἔτι νυνί.
ΔΙ.   μὰ Δί' οὐ δῆθ', ὥστε γ' ἀφαυάνθην
Παναθηναίοισι γελῶν, ὅτε δὴ   1090
βραδὺς ἄνθρωπός τις ἔθει κύψας
λευκός, πίων, ὑπολειπόμενος
καὶ δεινὰ ποιῶν· κᾆθ' οἱ Κεραμῆς
ἐν ταῖσι πύλαις παίουσ' αὐτοῦ
γαστέρα, πλευράς, λαγόνας, πυγήν,   1095
ὁ δὲ τυπτόμενος ταῖσι πλατείαις
ὑποπερδόμενος
φυσῶν τὴν λαμπάδ' ἔφευγεν.

ΧΟ.   μέγα τὸ πρᾶγμα, πολὺ τὸ νεῖκος, ἁδρὸς ὁ πόλεμος
ἔρχεται.
χαλεπὸν οὖν ἔργον διαιρεῖν,   1100
ὅταν ὁ μὲν τείνῃ βιαίως,
ὁ δ' ἐπαναστρέφειν δύνηται κἀπερείδεσθαι τορῶς.
ἀλλὰ μὴ 'ν ταὐτῷ κάθησθον·
εἰσβολαὶ γάρ εἰσι πολλαὶ χἅτεραι σοφισμάτων.
ὅ τι περ οὖν ἔχετον ἐρίζειν,   1105

λέγετον, ἔπιτον, ἀνὰ ⟨δὲ⟩ φέρετον
τά τε παλαιὰ καὶ τὰ καινά,
κἀποκινδυνεύετον λεπτόν τι καὶ σοφὸν λέγειν
εἰ δὲ τοῦτο καταφοβεῖσθον, μή τις ἀμαθία
προσῇ
τοῖς θεωμένοισιν, ὡς τὰ   1110
λεπτὰ μὴ γνῶναι λεγόντοιν,
μηδὲν ὀρρωδεῖτε τοῦθ'· ὡς οὐκέθ' οὕτω ταῦτ' ἔχει.
ἐστρατευμένοι γάρ εἰσι,
βιβλίον τ' ἔχων ἕκαστος μανθάνει τὰ δεξιά·
αἱ φύσεις τ' ἄλλως κράτισται,   1115
νῦν δὲ καὶ παρηκόνηνται.
μηδὲν οὖν δείσητον, ἀλλὰ
πάντ' ἐπέξιτον, θεατῶν γ' οὕνεχ', ὡς ὄντων σο-
φῶν.

ΕΥ. καὶ μὴν ἐπ' αὐτοὺς τοὺς προλόγους σοι τρέψομαι,
ὅπως τὸ πρῶτον τῆς τραγῳδίας μέρος   1120
πρώτιστον αὐτοῦ βασανιῶ τοῦ δεξιοῦ.
[ἀσαφὴς γὰρ ἦν ἐν τῇ φράσει τῶν πραγμάτων.]
ΔΙ. καὶ ποῖον αὐτοῦ βασανιεῖς;
ΕΥ.   πολλοὺς πάνυ.
πρῶτον δέ μοι τὸν ἐξ Ὀρεστείας λέγε.
ΔΙ. ἄγε δὴ σιώπα πᾶς ἀνήρ. λέγ', Αἰσχύλε.   1125
ΑΙ. ' Ἑρμῆ χθόνιε, πατρῷ' ἐποπτεύων κράτη
σωτὴρ γενοῦ μοι σύμμαχός τ' αἰτουμένῳ.
ἥκω γὰρ εἰς γῆν τήνδε καὶ κατέρχομαι ' —
ΔΙ. τούτων ἔχεις ψέγειν τι;
ΕΥ.   πλεῖν ἢ δώδεκα.
ΔΙ. ἀλλ' οὐδὲ πάντα ταῦτά γ' ἔστ' ἀλλ' ἢ τρία. 1130

ΕΥ. ἔχει δ' ἔκαστον εἴκοσίν γ' ἁμαρτίας.

ΔΙ. Αἰσχύλε, παραινῶ σοι σιωπᾶν· εἰ δὲ μή,
πρὸς τρισὶν ἰαμβείοισι προσοφείλων φανεῖ.

ΑΙ. ἐγὼ σιωπῶ τῷδ';

ΔΙ.   ἐὰν πείθῃ γ' ἐμοί.

ΕΥ. εὐθὺς γὰρ ἡμάρτηκεν οὐράνιον ὅσον.   1135

ΑΙ. ὁρᾷς ὅτι ληρεῖς.

ΕΥ.   ἀλλ' ὀλίγον γέ μοι μέλει.

ΑΙ. πῶς φής μ' ἁμαρτεῖν;

ΕΥ.   αὖθις ἐξ ἀρχῆς λέγε.

ΑΙ. ' Ἑρμῆ χθόνιε, πατρῷ' ἐποπτεύων κράτη.'

ΕΥ. οὔκουν Ὀρέστης τοῦτ' ἐπὶ τῷ τύμβῳ λέγει
τῷ τοῦ πατρὸς τεθνεῶτος;

ΑΙ.   οὐκ ἄλλως λέγω.   1140

ΕΥ. πότερ' οὖν τὸν Ἑρμῆν, ὡς ὁ πατὴρ ἀπώλετο
αὐτοῦ βιαίως ἐκ γυναικείας χερὸς
δόλοις λαθραίοις, ταῦτ' ἐποπτεύειν ἔφη;

ΑΙ. οὐ δῆτ' ἐκείνως, ἀλλὰ τὸν Ἐριούνιον
Ἑρμῆν χθόνιον προσεῖπε, κἀδήλου λέγων   1145
ὅτιὴ πατρῷον τοῦτο κέκτηται γέρας.

ΕΥ. ἔτι μεῖζον ἐξήμαρτες ἢ 'γὼ 'βουλόμην·
εἰ γὰρ πατρῷον τὸ χθόνιον ἔχει γέρας —

ΔΙ. οὕτω γ' ἂν εἴη πρὸς πατρὸς τυμβωρύχος.

ΑΙ. Διόνυσε, πίνεις οἶνον οὐκ ἀνθοσμίαν.   1150

ΔΙ. λέγ' ἕτερον αὐτῷ· σὺ δ' ἐπιτήρει τὸ βλάβος.

ΑΙ. ' σωτὴρ γενοῦ μοι σύμμαχός τ' αἰτουμένῳ.
ἥκω γὰρ εἰς γῆν τήνδε καὶ κατέρχομαι ' —

ΕΥ. δὶς ταὐτὸν ἡμῖν εἶπεν ὁ σοφὸς Αἰσχύλος.

ΔΙ. πῶς δίς;

ΕΥ.   σκόπει τὸ ῥῆμ'· ἐγὼ δέ σοι φράσω.   1155

'ἥκω γὰρ εἰς γῆν,' φησί, 'καὶ κατέρχομαι'·
ἥκειν δὲ ταὐτόν ἐστι τῷ 'κατέρχομαι'.

ΔΙ. νὴ τὸν Δί', ὥσπερ γ' εἴ τις εἴποι γείτονι·
'χρῆσον σὺ μάκτραν, εἰ δὲ βούλει, κάρδοπον.'

ΑΙ. οὐ δῆτα τοῦτό γ', ὦ κατεστωμυλμένε 1160
ἄνθρωπε, ταῦτ' ἔστ' ἀλλ' ἄριστ' ἐπῶν ἔχον.

ΕΥ. πῶς δή; δίδαξον γάρ με καθ' ὅτι δὴ λέγεις.

ΑΙ. ἐλθεῖν μὲν εἰς γῆν ἔσθ' ὅτῳ μετῇ πάτρας·
χωρὶς γὰρ ἄλλης συμφορᾶς ἐλήλυθεν·
φεύγων δ' ἀνὴρ ἥκει τε καὶ κατέρχεται. 1165

ΔΙ. εὖ νὴ τὸν Ἀπόλλω. τί σὺ λέγεις, Εὐριπίδη;

ΕΥ. οὔ φημι τὸν Ὀρέστην κατελθεῖν οἴκαδε·
λάθρα γὰρ ἦλθεν οὐ πιθὼν τοὺς κυρίους.

ΔΙ. εὖ νὴ τὸν Ἑρμῆν· ὅ τι λέγεις δ' οὐ μανθάνω.

ΕΥ. πέραινε τοίνυν ἕτερον.

ΔΙ.   ἴθι πέραινε σύ, 1170
Αἰσχύλ', ἀνύσας· σὺ δ' εἰς τὸ κακὸν ἀπόβλεπε.

ΑΙ. 'τύμβου δ' ἐπ' ὄχθῳ τῷδε κηρύσσω πατρὶ
κλύειν, ἀκοῦσαι' —

ΕΥ.   τοῦθ' ἕτερον αὖθις λέγει,
κλύειν, ἀκοῦσαι, ταὐτὸν ὂν σαφέστατα.

ΔΙ. τεθνηκόσιν γὰρ ἔλεγεν, ὦ μόχθηρε σύ, 1175
οἷς οὐδὲ τρὶς λέγοντες ἐξικνούμεθα.

ΑΙ. σὺ δὲ πῶς ἐποίεις τοὺς προλόγους;

ΕΥ.   ἐγὼ φράσω.
κἄν που δὶς εἴπω ταὐτόν, ἢ στοιβὴν ἴδῃς
ἐνοῦσαν ἔξω τοῦ λόγου, κατάπτυσον.

ΔΙ. ἴθι δὴ λέγ'· οὐ γὰρ μοὐστὶν ἀλλ' ἀκουστέα 1180
τῶν σῶν προλόγων τῆς ὀρθότητος τῶν ἐπῶν.

ΕΥ. 'ἦν Οἰδίπους τὸ πρῶτον εὐδαίμων ἀνήρ' —

ΑΙ. μὰ τὸν Δί' οὐ δῆτ', ἀλλὰ κακοδαίμων φύσει.
    ὅντινά γε, πρὶν φῦναι μέν, Ἀπόλλων ἔφη
    ἀποκτενεῖν τὸν πατέρα, πρὶν καὶ γεγονέναι,   1185
    πῶς οὗτος ἦν τὸ πρῶτον εὐτυχὴς ἀνήρ;
ΕΥ. ' εἶτ' ἐγένετ' αὖθις ἀθλιώτατος βροτῶν.'
ΑΙ. μὰ τὸν Δί' οὐ δῆτ', οὐ μὲν οὖν ἐπαύσατο.
    πῶς γάρ; ὅτε δὴ πρῶτον μὲν αὐτὸν γενόμενον
    χειμῶνος ὄντος ἐξέθεσαν ἐν ὀστράκῳ,   1190
    ἵνα μὴ 'κτραφεὶς γένοιτο τοῦ πατρὸς φονεύς·
    εἶθ' ὡς Πόλυβον ἤρρησεν οἰδῶν τὼ πόδε·
    ἔπειτα γραῦν ἔγημεν αὐτὸς ὢν νέος
    καὶ πρός γε τούτοις τὴν ἑαυτοῦ μητέρα·
    εἶτ' ἐξετύφλωσεν αὐτόν.
ΔΙ.   εὐδαίμων ἄρ' ἦν,   1195
    εἰ κἀστρατήγησέν γε μετ' Ἐρασινίδου.
ΕΥ. ληρεῖς· ἐγὼ δὲ τοὺς προλόγους καλοὺς ποιῶ.
ΑΙ. καὶ μὴν μὰ τὸν Δί' οὐ κατ' ἔπος γέ σου κνίσω
    τὸ ῥῆμ' ἕκαστον, ἀλλὰ σὺν τοῖσιν θεοῖς
    ἀπὸ ληκυθίου σου τοὺς προλόγους διαφθερῶ.   1200
ΕΥ. ἀπὸ ληκυθίου σὺ τοὺς ἐμούς;
ΑΙ.   ἑνὸς μόνου.
    ποεῖς γὰρ οὕτως ὥστ' ἐναρμόζειν ἅπαν,
    καὶ κωδάριον καὶ ληκύθιον καὶ θυλάκιον,
    ἐν τοῖς ἰαμβείοισι. δείξω δ' αὐτίκα.
ΕΥ. ἰδού, σὺ δείξεις;
ΑΙ.   φημί.
ΔΙ.   καὶ δὴ χρὴ λέγειν.   1205
ΕΥ. ' Αἴγυπτος, ὡς ὁ πλεῖστος ἔσπαρται λόγος,
    ξὺν παισὶ πεντήκοντα ναυτίλῳ πλάτῃ
    Ἄργος κατασχών ' —

ΑΙ.   ληκύθιον ἀπώλεσεν.

ΕΥ. τουτὶ τί ἦν τὸ ληκύθιον; οὐ κλαύσεται;

ΔΙ. λέγ' ἕτερον αὐτῷ πρόλογον, ἵνα καὶ γνῶ πάλιν.

ΕΥ. ' Διόνυσος, ὃς θύρσοισι καὶ νεβρῶν δοραῖς   1211
   καθαπτὸς ἐν πεύκῃσι Παρνασσὸν κάτα
   πηδᾷ χορεύων ' —

ΑΙ.   ληκύθιον ἀπώλεσεν.

ΔΙ. οἴμοι πεπλήγμεθ' αὖθις ὑπὸ τῆς ληκύθου.

ΕΥ. ἀλλ' οὐδὲν ἔσται πρᾶγμα· πρὸς γὰρ τουτονὶ   1215
   τὸν πρόλογον οὐχ ἕξει προσάψαι ληκύθιον.
   ' οὐκ ἔστιν ὅστις πάντ' ἀνὴρ εὐδαιμονεῖ·
   ἢ γὰρ πεφυκὼς ἐσθλὸς οὐκ ἔχει βίον,
   ἢ δυσγενὴς ὤν ' —

ΑΙ.   ληκύθιον ἀπώλεσεν.

ΔΙ. Εὐριπίδη, —

ΕΥ.   τί ἐστι;

ΔΙ.   ὑφέσθαι μοι δοκεῖ.   1220
   τὸ ληκύθιον γὰρ τοῦτο πνευσεῖται πολύ.

ΕΥ. οὐδ' ἂν μὰ τὴν Δήμητρα φροντίσαιμί γε·
   νυνὶ γὰρ αὐτοῦ τοῦτό γ' ἐκκεκόψεται.

ΔΙ. ἴθι δὴ λέγ' ἕτερον κἀπέχου τῆς ληκύθου.

ΕΥ. ' Σιδώνιόν ποτ' ἄστυ Κάδμος ἐκλιπὼν   1225
   Ἀγήνορος παῖς ' —

ΑΙ.   ληκύθιον ἀπώλεσεν.

ΔΙ. ὦ δαιμόνι' ἀνδρῶν, ἀποπρίω τὴν λήκυθον,
   ἵνα μὴ διακναίσῃ τοὺς προλόγους ἡμῶν.

ΕΥ.   τὸ τί;
   ἐγὼ πρίωμαι τῷδ';

ΔΙ.   ἐὰν πείθῃ γ' ἐμοί.

ΕΥ. οὐ δῆτ', ἐπεὶ πολλοὺς προλόγους ἔξω λέγειν   1230

ἵν᾽ οὗτος οὐχ ἕξει προσάψαι ληκύθιον.
‘ Πέλοψ ὁ Ταντάλειος εἰς Πῖσαν μολὼν
θοαῖσιν ἵπποις ’ —

ΑΙ. ληκύθιον ἀπώλεσεν.

ΔΙ. ὁρᾷς, προσῆψεν αὖθις αὖ τὴν λήκυθον.
ἀλλ᾽, ὠγάθ᾽, ἔτι καὶ νῦν ἀπόδος πάσῃ τέχνῃ· 1235
λήψει γὰρ ὀβολοῦ, πάνυ καλήν τε κἀγαθήν.

ΕΥ. μὰ τὸν Δι᾽ οὔπω γ᾽· ἔτι γὰρ εἰσί μοι συχνοί.
‘ Οἰνεύς ποτ᾽ ἐκ γῆς ’ —

ΑΙ. ληκύθιον ἀπώλεσεν.

ΕΥ. ἔασον εἰπεῖν πρῶθ᾽ ὅλον με τὸν στίχον.
‘ Οἰνεύς ποτ᾽ ἐκ γῆς πολύμετρον λαβὼν στάχυν
θύων ἀπαρχάς ’ —

ΑΙ. ληκύθιον ἀπώλεσεν. 1241

ΔΙ. μεταξὺ θύων; καὶ τίς αὖθ᾽ ὑφείλετο;

ΕΥ. ἔασον, ὦ τᾶν· πρὸς τοδὶ γὰρ εἰπάτω.
‘ Ζεύς, ὡς λέλεκται τῆς ἀληθείας ὕπο ’ —

ΔΙ. ἀπολεῖς· ἐρεῖ γὰρ ‘ ληκύθιον ἀπώλεσεν.’ 1245
τὸ ληκύθιον γὰρ τοῦτ᾽ ἐπὶ τοῖς προλόγοισί σου
ὥσπερ τὰ σῦκ᾽ ἐπὶ τοῖσιν ὀφθαλμοῖς ἔφυ.
ἀλλ᾽ εἰς τὰ μέλη πρὸς τῶν θεῶν αὐτοῦ τραποῦ.

ΕΥ. καὶ μὴν ἔχω γ᾽ οἷς αὐτὸν ἀποδείξω κακὸν
μελοποιὸν ὄντα καὶ ποιοῦντα ταῦτ᾽ ἀεί. 1250

ΧΟ. τί ποτε πρᾶγμα γενήσεται;
φροντίζειν γὰρ ἔγωγ᾽ ἔχω,
τίν᾽ ἄρα μέμψιν ἐποίσει
ἀνδρὶ τῷ πολὺ πλεῖστα δὴ
καὶ κάλλιστα μέλη ποή- 1255
σαντι τῶν μέχρι νυνί.
[θαυμάζω γὰρ ἔγωγ᾽ ὅπη

μέμψεταί ποτε τοῦτον
τὸν Βακχεῖον ἄνακτα,
καὶ δέδοιχ' ὑπὲρ αὐτοῦ.] 1260
ΕΥ. πάνυ γε μέλη θαυμαστά· δείξει δὴ τάχα.
εἰς ἓν γὰρ αὐτοῦ πάντα τὰ μέλη ξυντεμῶ.
ΔΙ. καὶ μὴν λογιοῦμαι ταῦτα τῶν ψήφων λαβών.
[διαύλιον προσαυλεῖ τις]
ΕΥ. Φθιῶτ' Ἀχιλλεῦ, τί ποτ' ἀνδροδάικτον ἀκούων
ἰὴ κόπον οὐ πελάθεις ἐπ' ἀρωγάν; 1265
Ἑρμᾶν μὲν πρόγονον τίομεν γένος οἱ περὶ λίμναν.
ἰὴ κόπον οὐ πελάθεις ἐπ' ἀρωγάν;
ΔΙ. δύο σοι κόπω, Αἰσχύλε, τούτω.
ΕΥ. κύδιστ' Ἀχαιῶν, Ἀτρέως πολυκοίρανε μάνθανέ
μου παῖ.
ἰὴ κόπον οὐ πελάθεις ἐπ' ἀρωγάν; 1271
ΔΙ. τρίτος, Αἰσχύλε, σοι κόπος οὗτος.
ΕΥ. εὐφαμεῖτε. μελισσονόμοι δόμον Ἀρτέμιδος πέλας
οἴγειν.
ἰὴ κόπον οὐ πελάθεις ἐπ' ἀρωγάν; 1275
κύριός εἰμι θροεῖν ὅδιον κράτος αἴσιον ἀνδρῶν.
ἰὴ κόπον οὐ πελάθεις ἐπ' ἀρωγάν;
ΔΙ. ὦ Ζεῦ βασιλεῦ, τὸ χρῆμα τῶν κόπων ὅσον.
ἐγὼ μὲν οὖν εἰς τὸ βαλανεῖον βούλομαι·
ὑπὸ τῶν κόπων γὰρ τὼ νεφρὼ βουβωνιῶ. 1280
ΕΥ. μή, πρίν γ' ἀκούσῃς χἀτέραν στάσιν μελῶν
ἐκ τῶν κιθαρῳδικῶν νόμων εἰργασμένην.
ΔΙ. ἴθι δὴ πέραινε, καὶ κόπον μὴ προστίθει.
ΕΥ. ὅπως Ἀχαιῶν δίθρονον κράτος, Ἑλλάδος ἥβας,
τοφλαττοθραττοφλαττοθρατ, 1286
Σφίγγα, δυσαμεριᾶν πρύτανιν κύνα, πέμπει,

τοφλαττοθραττοφλαττοθρατ,
ξὺν δορὶ καὶ χερὶ πράκτορι θούριος ὄρνις,
τοφλαττοθραττοφλαττοθρατ, 1290
κυρεῖν παρασχὼν ἰταμαῖς κυσὶν ἀεροφοίτοις,
τοφλαττοθραττοφλαττοθρατ,
τὸ συγκλινές τ' ἐπ' Αἴαντι,
τοφλαττοθραττοφλαττοθρατ. 1295

ΔΙ. τί τὸ φλαττοθρατ τοῦτ' ἐστίν; ἐκ Μαραθῶνος ἢ
πόθεν συνέλεξας ἱμονιοστρόφου μέλη;
ΑΙ. ἀλλ' οὖν ἐγὼ μὲν εἰς τὸ καλὸν ἐκ τοῦ καλοῦ
ἤνεγκον αὔθ', ἵνα μὴ τὸν αὐτὸν Φρυνίχῳ
λειμῶνα Μουσῶν ἱερὸν ὀφθείην δρέπων· 1300
οὗτος δ' ἀπὸ πάντων μέλι φέρει, πορνῳδιῶν,
σκολίων Μελήτου, Καρικῶν αὐλημάτων,
θρήνων, χορειῶν. τάχα δὲ δηλωθήσεται.
ἐνεγκάτω τις τὸ λύριον. καίτοι τί δεῖ
λύρας ἐπὶ τούτου; ποῦ 'στιν ἡ τοῖς ὀστρά-
κοις 1305
αὕτη κροτοῦσα; δεῦρο, Μοῦσ' Εὐριπίδου,
πρὸς ἥνπερ ἐπιτήδεια τάδ' ἔστ' ᾄδειν μέλη.
ΔΙ. αὕτη ποθ' ἡ Μοῦσ' οὐκ ἐλεσβίαζεν, οὔ.
ΑΙ. ἀλκυόνες, αἳ παρ' ἀενάοις θαλάσσης
κύμασι στωμύλλετε, 1310
τέγγουσαι νοτίοις πτερῶν
ῥανίσι χρόα δροσιζόμεναι·
αἵ θ' ὑπωρόφιοι κατὰ γωνίας
εἰειειειειλίσσετε δακτύλοις φάλαγγες
ἱστότονα πηνίσματα, 1315
κερκίδος ἀοιδοῦ μελέτας,
ἵν' ὁ φίλαυλος ἔπαλλε δελ-

φὶς πρώραις κυανεμβόλοις.
μαντεῖα καὶ σταδίους.
οἰνάνθας γάνος ἀμπέλου,   1320
βότρυος ἕλικα παυσίπονον
περίβαλλ', ὦ τέκνον, ὠλένας.
ὁρᾷς τὸν πόδα τοῦτον;

ΔΙ.   ὁρῶ.

ΑΙ.   τί δαί; τοῦτον ὁρᾷς;

ΔΙ.   ὁρῶ.

ΑΙ.   τοιαυτὶ μέντοι σὺ ποιῶν   1325
τολμᾷς τἀμὰ μέλη ψέγειν,
ἀνὰ τὸ δωδεκαμήχανον
Κυρήνης μελοποιῶν;

τὰ μὲν μέλη σου ταῦτα· βούλομαι δ' ἔτι
τὸν τῶν μονῳδιῶν διεξελθεῖν τρόπον.   1330

ὦ Νυκτὸς κελαινοφαὴς
ὄρφνα, τίνα μοι δύστανον ὄνει-
ρον πέμπεις ἐξ ἀφανοῦς Ἀίδα
πρόπολον, ψυχὰν
ἄψυχον ἔχοντα, μελαίνας   1334a
νυκτὸς παῖδα, φρικώδη δεινὰν ὄ-   1335
ψιν, μελανονεκυείμονα, φόνια φόνια
δερκόμενον, μεγάλους ὄνυχας ἔχοντα;

ἀλλά μοι, ἀμφίπολοι, λύχνον ἅψατε
κάλπισί τ' ἐκ ποταμῶν δρόσον ἄρατε, θέρμετε δ'
ὕδωρ,
ὡς ἂν θεῖον ὄνειρον ἀποκλύσω —   1340
ἰὼ πόντιε δαῖμον.

τοῦτ᾽ ἐκεῖν᾽· ἰὼ ξύνοικοι,
τάδε τέρα θεάσασθε.
τὸν ἀλεκτρυόνα μου ξυναρπάσασα
φρούδη Γλύκη.　1344a
Νύμφαι ὀρεσσίγονοι,　1344b
ὦ Μανία, ξύλλαβε.　1345

ἐγὼ δ᾽ ἁ τάλαινα
προσέχουσ᾽ ἔτυχον ἐμαυτῆς
ἔργοισι, λίνου μεστὸν ἄτρακτον
εἰειειλίσσουσα χεροῖν
κλωστῆρα ποιοῦσ᾽, ὅπως　1349a
κνεφαῖος εἰς ἀγορὰν　1350
φέρουσ᾽ ἀποδοίμαν.

ὁ δ᾽ ἀνέπτατ᾽ ἀνέπτατ᾽ ἐς αἰθέρα
κουφοτάταις πτερύγων ἀκμαῖς,
ἐμοὶ δ᾽ ἄχε᾽ ἄχεα κατέλιπε,
δάκρυα δάκρυά τ᾽ ἀπ᾽ ὀμμάτων　1354a
ἔβαλον ἔβαλον ἁ τλάμων.　1355

ἀλλ᾽, ὦ Κρῆτες, Ἴδας τέκνα, τὰ
τόξα ⟨τε⟩ λαβόντες ἐπαμύνατε, τὰ
κῶλά τ᾽ ἀμπάλλετε κυκλούμενοι τὴν οἰκίαν.
ἅμα δὲ Δίκτυννα παῖς, ἁ καλά,
τὰς κυνίσκας ἔχουσ᾽ ἐλθέτω διὰ δόμων παν-
ταχῇ.　1360

σὺ δ᾽, ὦ Διός, διπύρους ἀνέχου-
σα λαμπάδας ὀξυτάτας χεροῖν,
Ἑκάτα, παράφηνον εἰς Γλύκης,
ὅπως ἂν εἰσελθοῦσα φωράσω.

ΔΙ. παύσασθον ἤδη τῶν μελῶν. 1364a

ΑΙ. κἄμοιγ' ἅλις.

ἐπὶ τὸν σταθμὸν γὰρ αὐτὸν ἀγαγεῖν βού-
λομαι, 1365

ὅπερ ἐξελέγξει τὴν πόησιν νῷν μόνον·

τὸ γὰρ βάρος νὼ βασανιεῖ τῶν ῥημάτων.

ΔΙ. ἴτε δεῦρό νυν, εἴπερ γε δεῖ καὶ τοῦτό με,

ἀνδρῶν ποητῶν τυροπωλῆσαι τέχνην.

ΧΟ. ἐπίπονοί γ' οἱ δεξιοί. 1370

τόδε γὰρ ἕτερον αὖ τέρας

νεοχμόν, ἀτοπίας πλέων,

ὃ τίς ἂν ἐπενόησεν ἄλλος;

μὰ τόν, ἐγὼ μέν — οὐκ ἂν εἴ τις

ἔλεγέ μοι τῶν ἐπιτυχόντων — 1375

ἐπιθόμην, ἀλλ' ᾠόμην ἂν

αὐτὸν αὐτὰ ληρεῖν.

ΔΙ. ἴθι δή. παρίστασθον παρὰ τὼ πλάστιγγ'.

ΑΙ. κ. ΕΥ. ἰδού.

ΔΙ. καὶ λαβομένω τὸ ῥῆμ' ἑκάτερος εἴπατον,

καὶ μὴ μεθῆσθον, πρὶν ἂν ἐγὼ σφῷν κοκ-
κύσω. 1380

ΑΙ. κ. ΕΥ. ἐχόμεθα.

ΔΙ. τοὔπος νυν λέγετον εἰς τὸν σταθμόν.

ΕΥ. ' εἴθ' ὤφελ' Ἀργοῦς μὴ διαπτάσθαι σκάφος.'

ΑΙ. ' Σπερχειὲ ποταμὲ βούνομοί τ' ἐπιστροφαί.'

ΔΙ. κόκκυ.

ΑΙ. κ. ΕΥ. μεθεῖται.

ΔΙ. καὶ πολύ γε κατωτέρω

χωρεῖ τὸ τοῦδε.

ΕΥ.   καὶ τί ποτ' ἐστὶ ταἴτιον;   1385

ΔΙ.   ὅ τι; εἰσέθηκε ποταμόν, ἐριοπωλικῶς
ὑγρὸν ποήσας τοὔπος ὥσπερ τἄρια,
σὺ δ' εἰσέθηκας τοὔπος ἐπτερωμένον.

ΕΥ.   ἀλλ' ἕτερον εἰπάτω τι κἀντιστησάτω.

ΔΙ.   λάβεσθε τοίνυν αὖθις.

ΑΙ. κ. ΕΥ.   ἢν ἰδού.

ΔΙ.   λέγε.   1390

ΕΥ.   'οὐκ ἔστι Πειθοῦς ἱερὸν ἄλλο πλὴν Λόγος.'

ΑΙ.   ' μόνος θεῶν γὰρ Θάνατος οὐ δώρων ἐρᾷ.'

ΔΙ.   μέθετε.

ΑΙ. κ. ΕΥ.   μεθεῖται.

ΔΙ.   καὶ τὸ τοῦδέ γ' αὖ ῥέπει·
θάνατον γὰρ εἰσέθηκε, βαρύτατον κακόν.

ΕΥ.   ἐγὼ δὲ πειθώ γ', ἔπος ἄριστ' εἰρημένον.   1395

ΔΙ.   Πειθὼ δὲ κοῦφόν ἐστι καὶ νοῦν οὐκ ἔχον.
ἀλλ' ἕτερον αὖ ζήτει τι τῶν βαρυστάθμων,
ὅ τι σοι καθέλξει, καρτερόν τι καὶ μέγα.

ΕΥ.   φέρε ποῦ τοιοῦτον δῆτα μουστί; ποῦ;

ΔΙ.   φράσω·

' βέβληκ' Ἀχιλλεὺς δύο κύβω καὶ τέτταρα.'   1400
λέγοιτ' ἄν, ὡς αὕτη 'στὶ λοιπὴ σφῶν στάσις.

ΕΥ.   ' σιδηροβριθές τ' ἔλαβε δεξιᾷ ξύλον.'

ΑΙ.   ' ἐφ' ἅρματος γὰρ ἅρμα καὶ νεκρῷ νεκρός.'

ΔΙ.   ἐξηπάτηκεν αὖ σε καὶ νῦν.

ΕΥ.   τῷ τρόπῳ;

ΔΙ.   δύ' ἅρματ' εἰσέθηκε καὶ νεκρὼ δύο,   1405
οὓς οὐκ ἂν ἄραιντ' οὐδ' ἑκατὸν Αἰγύπτιοι.

ΑΙ.   καὶ μηκέτ' ἔμοιγε κατ' ἔπος, ἀλλ' εἰς τὸν σταθμὸν
αὐτός, τὰ παιδία χἠ γυνή, Κηφισοφῶν,

ΤΟΙΟΥΤΟΝ – of what type
ΤΟΣΟΥΤΟΝ – how great

ἐμβὰς καθήσθω, ξυλλαβὼν τὰ βιβλία·
ἐγὼ δὲ δύ' ἔπη τῶν ἐμῶν ἐρῶ μόνον —   1410
ΔΙ. ἄνδρες φίλοι, κἀγὼ μὲν αὐτοὺς οὐ κρινῶ.
οὐ γὰρ δι' ἔχθρας οὐδετέρῳ γενήσομαι·
τὸν μὲν γὰρ ἡγοῦμαι σοφόν, τῷ δ' ἥδομαι.

ΠΛΟΥΤΩΝ
οὐδὲν ἄρα πράξεις ὧνπερ ἦλθες οὕνεκα;
ΔΙ. ἐὰν δὲ κρίνω τὸν ἕτερον;
ΠΛ.   λαβὼν ἄπει   1415
ὁπότερον ἂν κρίνῃς, ἵν' ἔλθῃς μὴ μάτην.
ΔΙ. εὐδαιμονοίης. φέρε, πύθεσθέ μου ταδί.
ἐγὼ κατῆλθον ἐπὶ ποητήν.
ΕΥ.   τοῦ χάριν;
ΔΙ. ἵν' ἡ πόλις σωθεῖσα τοὺς χοροὺς ἄγῃ.
ὁπότερος οὖν ἂν τῇ πόλει παραινέσειν   1420
μέλλῃ τι χρηστόν, τοῦτον ἄξειν μοι δοκῶ.
πρῶτον μὲν οὖν περὶ Ἀλκιβιάδου τίν' ἔχετον
γνώμην ἑκάτερος; ἡ πόλις γὰρ δυστοκεῖ.
ΕΥ. ἔχει δὲ περὶ αὐτοῦ τίνα γνώμην;
ΔΙ.   τίνα;
ποθεῖ μέν, ἐχθαίρει δέ, βούλεται δ' ἔχειν.   1425
ἀλλ' ὅ τι νοεῖτον εἴπατον τούτου πέρι.
ΕΥ. μισῶ πολίτην, ὅστις ὠφελεῖν πάτραν
βραδὺς φανεῖται, μεγάλα δὲ βλάπτειν ταχύς,
καὶ πόριμον αὑτῷ, τῇ πόλει δ' ἀμήχανον.
ΔΙ. εὖ γ', ὦ Πόσειδον. σὺ δὲ τίνα γνώμην ἔχεις;   1430
ΑΙ. [οὐ χρὴ λέοντος σκύμνον ἐν πόλει τρέφειν.]   1431a
μάλιστα μὲν λέοντα μὴ 'ν πόλει τρέφειν·   1431b
ἣν δ' ἐκτραφῇ τις, τοῖς τρόποις ὑπηρετεῖν.

ΔΙ. νὴ τὸν Δία τὸν σωτῆρα, δυσκρίτως γ᾽ ἔχω·
ὁ μὲν σοφῶς γὰρ εἶπεν, ὁ δ᾽ ἕτερος σαφῶς. *clearly*

one more? ἀλλ᾽ ἔτι μίαν γνώμην ἑκάτερος εἴπατον 1435
περὶ τῆς πόλεως ἥντιν᾽ ἔχετον σωτηρίαν.

ΕΥ. [εἴ τις πτερώσας Κλεόκριτον Κινησίᾳ,
αἴροιεν αὖραι πελαγίαν ὑπὲρ πλάκα —

ΔΙ. γέλοιον ἂν φαίνοιτο. νοῦν δ᾽ ἔχει τίνα; *but what's the point*

ΕΥ. εἰ ναυμαχοῖεν, κᾆτ᾽ ἔχοντες ὀξίδας 1440
ῥαίνοιεν εἰς τὰ βλέφαρα τῶν ἐναντίων.]
ἐγὼ μὲν οἶδα καὶ θέλω φράζειν. *wish to tell*

ΔΙ.   λέγε.

whenever we put ΕΥ. ὅταν τὰ νῦν ἄπιστα πίσθ᾽ ἡγώμεθα,
our trust in what's   τὰ δ᾽ ὄντα πίστ᾽ ἄπιστα —
untrusted, and what's
trustworthy yes ΔΙ.   πῶς; οὐ μανθάνω.
untrusted   ἀμαθέστερόν (πως) εἰπὲ καὶ σαφέστερον. 1445

ΕΥ. εἰ τῶν πολιτῶν οἷσι νῦν πιστεύομεν,
τούτοις ἀπιστήσαιμεν, οἷς δ᾽ οὐ χρώμεθα,
why wouldn't we be τούτοισι χρησαίμεσθα, σωθεῖμεν ἄν. *we might save (it)*
saved by doing the εἰ νῦν γε δυστυχοῦμεν ἐν τούτοισι, πῶς
opposite? τἀναντί᾽ ἂν πράξαντες οὐ σωζοίμεθ᾽ ἄν; 1450

ΔΙ. εὖ γ᾽, ὦ Παλάμηδες, ὦ σοφωτάτη φύσις.
[ταυτὶ πότερ᾽ αὐτὸς ηὗρες ἢ Κηφισοφῶν;

ΕΥ. ἐγὼ μόνος· τὰς δ᾽ ὀξίδας Κηφισοφῶν.]

ΔΙ. τί δαὶ σύ; τί λέγεις; *added*

ΑΙ.   τὴν πόλιν νῦν μοι φράσον
πρῶτον τίσι χρῆται· πότερα τοῖς χρηστοῖς;

ΔΙ.   (πόθεν;) *whence (did you get it)?*

μισεῖ κάκιστα *worst of all*

ΑΙ.   τοῖς πονηροῖς δ᾽ ἥδεται; 1456

ΔΙ. οὐ (δῆτ᾽) ἐκείνη γ᾽, ἀλλὰ χρῆται πρὸς βίαν.

*of course
she does not*

ΑΙ. πῶς οὖν τις ἂν σώσειε τοιαύτην πόλιν,
ᾗ μήτε χλαῖνα μήτε σισύρα ξυμφέρει;

ΔΙ. εὕρισκε νὴ Δί', εἴπερ ἀναδύσει πάλιν.　　1460

ΑΙ. ἐκεῖ φράσαιμ' ἄν, ἐνθαδὶ δ' οὐ βούλομαι.

ΔΙ. μὴ δῆτα σύ γ', ἀλλ' ἐνθένδ' ἀνίει τἀγαθά.

ΑΙ. τὴν γῆν ὅταν νομίσωσι τὴν |τῶν πολεμίων|
εἶναι σφετέραν, τὴν δὲ σφετέραν τῶν πολεμίων,
πόρον δὲ τὰς ναῦς, ἀπορίαν δὲ τὸν πόρον.　　1465

ΔΙ. εὖ, πλήν γ' ὁ δικαστὴς αὐτὰ καταπίνει μόνος.

ΠΛ. κρίνοις ἄν.

ΔΙ.　　　　αὕτη σφῷν κρίσις γενήσεται.
αἱρήσομαι γὰρ ὅνπερ ἡ ψυχὴ θέλει.

ΕΥ. μεμνημένος νυν τῶν θεῶν |οὓς ὤμοσας|
ἦ μὴν ἀπάξειν μ' οἴκαδ', αἱροῦ τοὺς φίλους,　　1470

ΔΙ. ἡ γλῶττ' ὀμώμοκ' . . . Αἰσχύλον δ' αἱρήσομαι.

ΕΥ. τί δέδρακας, ὦ μιαρώτατ' ἀνθρώπων;

ΔΙ.　　　　　　　　ἐγώ;

ἔκρινα νικᾶν Αἰσχύλον. τίη γὰρ οὔ;

ΕΥ. αἴσχιστον ἔργον |προσβλέπεις μ'| εἰργασμένος;

ΔΙ. τί δ' αἰσχρόν, ἢν μὴ τοῖς θεωμένοις δοκῇ;　　1475

ΕΥ. ὦ σχέτλιε, περιόψει με δὴ τεθνηκότα;

ΔΙ. τίς δ' οἶδεν εἰ τὸ ζῆν μέν ἐστι κατθανεῖν,
τὸ πνεῖν δὲ δειπνεῖν, τὸ δὲ καθεύδειν κῴδιον;

ΠΛ. χωρεῖτε τοίνυν, ὦ Διόνυσ' εἴσω.

ΔΙ.　　　　　　　　τί δαί;

ΠΛ. ἵνα ξενίζω σφὼ πρὶν ἀποπλεῖν.

ΔΙ.　　　　　　　　εὖ λέγεις　　1480
νὴ τὸν Δί'· οὐ γὰρ ἄχθομαι τῷ πράγματι.

ΧΟ.　　　μακάριός γ' ἀνὴρ ἔχων

ΑΡΙΣΤΟΦΑΝΟΥΣ

ξύνεσιν ἠκριβωμένην.
πάρα δὲ πολλοῖσιν μαθεῖν.
ὅδε γὰρ εὖ φρονεῖν δοκήσας   1485
πάλιν ἄπεισιν οἴκαδ' αὖθις,
ἐπ' ἀγαθῷ μὲν τοῖς πολίταις,
ἐπ' ἀγαθῷ δὲ τοῖς ἑαυτοῦ
ξυγγενέσι τε καὶ φίλοισι,
διὰ τὸ συνετὸς εἶναι.   1490

χαρίεν οὖν μὴ Σωκράτει
παρακαθήμενον λαλεῖν,
ἀποβαλόντα μουσικὴν
τά τε μέγιστα παραλιπόντα
τῆς τραγῳδικῆς τέχνης.   1495
τὸ δ' ἐπὶ σεμνοῖσιν λόγοισι
καὶ σκαριφησμοῖσι λήρων
διατριβὴν ἀργὸν ποιεῖσθαι,
παραφρονοῦντος ἀνδρός.

ΠΛ. ἄγε δὴ χαίρων, Αἰσχύλε, χώρει,   1500
καὶ σῷζε πόλιν τὴν ἡμετέραν
γνώμαις ἀγαθαῖς, καὶ παίδευσον
τοὺς ἀνοήτους· πολλοὶ δ' εἰσίν·
καὶ δὸς τουτὶ Κλεοφῶντι φέρων
καὶ τουτουσὶ τοῖσι πορισταῖς,   1505
Μύρμηκί θ' ὁμοῦ καὶ Νικομάχῳ
τόδε δ' Ἀρχενόμῳ· καὶ φράζ' αὐτοῖς
ταχέως ἥκειν ὡς ἐμὲ δευρὶ
καὶ μὴ μέλλειν· κἂν μὴ ταχέως
ἥκωσ', ἐγὼ νὴ τὸν Ἀπόλλω   1510
στίξας αὐτοὺς καὶ ξυμποδίσας

μετ' Ἀδειμάντου τοῦ Λευκολόφου
κατὰ γῆς ταχέως ἀποπέμψω. 1513/14

ΑΙ. ταῦτα ποήσω· σὺ δὲ τὸν θᾶκον 1515
τὸν ἐμὸν παράδος Σοφοκλεῖ τηρεῖν
καὶ διασώζειν, ἢν ἄρ' ἐγώ ποτε
δεῦρ' ἀφίκωμαι. τοῦτον γὰρ ἐγὼ
σοφίᾳ κρίνω δεύτερον εἶναι.
μέμνησο δ' ὅπως ὁ πανοῦργος ἀνὴρ 1520
καὶ ψευδολόγος καὶ βωμολόχος
μηδέποτ' εἰς τὸν θᾶκον τὸν ἐμὸν
μηδ' ἄκων ἐγκαθεδεῖται.

ΠΛ. φαίνετε τοίνυν ὑμεῖς τούτῳ
λαμπάδας ἱεράς, χἄμα προπέμπετε 1525
τοῖσιν τούτου τοῦτον μέλεσιν
καὶ μολπαῖσιν κελαδοῦντες.

ΧΟ. πρῶτα μὲν εὐοδίαν ἀγαθὴν ἀπιόντι ποητῇ
εἰς φάος ὀρνυμένῳ δότε, δαίμονες οἱ κατὰ γαίας,
τῇ δὲ πόλει μεγάλων ἀγαθῶν ἀγαθὰς ἐπι-
νοίας.
1530
πάγχυ γὰρ ἐκ μεγάλων ἀχέων παυσαίμεθ' ἂν
οὕτως
ἀργαλέων τ' ἐν ὅπλοις ξυνόδων. Κλεοφῶν δὲ
μαχέσθω
κἄλλος ὁ βουλόμενος τούτων πατρίοις ἐν ἀρούραις.

NOTES

[PRELIMINARY NOTE. Full titles of works cited by their authors' names will be found in the Book List. Further references to terms printed with capital letters and in italics—*e.g. Coined Words, Cleophon, Orchestra*—are given in the Index.

The following abbreviations have been used : L.-S.-J.= Liddell and Scott, *Greek-English Lexicon*, 9th edn. ed. by H. Stuart Jones; Ar.= Aristophanes ; MS. or MSS.= manuscript(s) ; R, V, etc.= the MS. from Ravenna, Venice, etc. (as described in Introduction § 14) ; Σ= information in the *Scholia*. Capital letters are occasionally used for the names of characters under discussion. References like § 8 refer to the Introduction.

In the notes on metre the sign ∧ marks catalexis (the omission of a syllable at the end of a line) and · (as in ∪ − · −) marks syncopation, *i.e.* the omission of a syllable within a metrical unit.]

For uncertainties in the numbering of the lines see § 14 n. 75 (at end).

1-34. ACTION. A comical pair enter the *Orchestra*. *Dionysos,* the god, is an ungodly sight, for over his own usual, rather effeminate yellow tunic (see on **46-7** and in **§ 10**) he wears the formidable lion-skin of Heracles, and he holds a Herculean club in his delicate hands. His slave, Xanthias, carries a heavy load of baggage over his shoulder (see on **8**) and is riding on a donkey. They are clearly prepared for a long journey. But Ar. leaves the audience to wonder for a while where these two are going. Meanwhile he exploits some well-seasoned jokes about porters carrying baggage (**1-20**) and introduces a short parody of sophistic argument (**21-32**).

METRE. 1-207 is in the usual metre for dialogue in comedy (except in the *Agon*), *i.e.* iambic trimeters of the free comic type. As in tragedy the basic pattern of this metre is :

$$\overset{\vee}{-} \; - \; \cup \; - \; \overset{\vee}{-} \; - \; \cup \; - \; \overset{\vee}{-} \; - \; \cup \overset{\vee}{}$$

The following variations were allowed in comedy. Tribrachs (∪ ∪ ∪) and anapaests (∪ ∪ −) occur in the first five feet, and

dactyls ($-\cup\cup$) in the first, third, and fifth. The normal varia-
tions, then, are (for further possibilities see on **76** and **1203**) :

$$\underset{\smile}{-}\, - \qquad \cup\, - \qquad \underset{\smile}{-}\, - \qquad \cup\, - \qquad \underset{\smile}{-}\, - \qquad \cup\, \underset{\smile}{-}$$

$$\cup\cup\cup \qquad \cup\cup\cup \qquad \cup\cup\cup \qquad \cup\cup\cup \qquad \cup\cup\cup$$

$$\cup\cup\, - \qquad \cup\cup\, - \qquad \cup\cup\, - \qquad \cup\cup\, - \qquad \cup\cup\, -$$

$$-\cup\cup \qquad\qquad -\cup\cup \qquad\qquad -\cup\cup$$

(White 38 ff. gives statistics of the frequency of each variation and
discusses caesura, etc. He takes a less rigorous view than Bern-
hardi on the division of the anapaests.)

Porson's law does not hold in comic trimeters ; caesura is often
neglected ; greater freedom is allowed in *Elision, Crasis, Hiatus,
Aphaeresis* and *Synizesis*, than in tragic trimeters. For details see
White and Descroix.

1-2. 'Master, am I to say one of the usual things that the
spectators always laugh at ?' εἴπω : this is the regular use of the
subjunctive ('deliberative ') in asking for guidance in uncertainty.
τι τῶν εἰωθότων : one of the constantly repeated, stale jokes
which inferior comedians kept on using (and at which, as Ar. notes
with a sly dig at his audience, the theatre-goers kept on, ἀεί,
laughing). οἱ θεώμενοι : 'the spectators'. This word, like θεατής
and θέατρον (all connected with θεάομαι 'see'), indicates the im-
portance of the visual elements in Greek drama.

3-4. Tucker takes γε as giving 'an intonation' to βούλει ('what-
ever you like'). Goligher more convincingly takes it as 'yes', an
indication of the omission of εἰπέ : 'By Heaven, yes, (say) what
you like except . . .' : *cf.* γε in 7. With Dionysos's 'except'
Ar. introduces a subtle use of comic technique. It allows him by
referring to some well-seasoned jests to get a series of easy laughs
from the cruder members of the *Audience* and at the same time to
guard himself from incurring the more critical spectators' scorn
for poets who used stale jokes. So Dionysos is made to play the
part of a man of some discrimination in his choice of jokes—in
contrast with Xanthias, who is ready to provide any cheap
buffoonery. (Thus Philip the buffoon in Xenophon, *Symposium*
1, 11, uses the word πιέζομαι, the word forbidden by Dionysos as
disgusting here.) In fact, as soon as Dionysos utters (in dis-
approval) the words which he forbids Xanthias to say, many of the
audience will laugh at them anyway (by that kind of automatic
response, or 'conditioned reflex' to old, favourite jokes which no
professional comedian can afford to neglect). This technique is
similar in method and effect to the oratorical device of saying 'I
shall omit the cowardice, dishonesty, ignorance (etc., etc.) of
so-and-so', when in fact one is *not* omitting them. The 'forbidden'
words are πιέζομαι 'I'm hard pressed', θλίβομαι 'I'm tight squeezed'

(5), χεζητιậς 'You want to ease yourself' (8). In 10 Xanthias slips in another objectionable term, ἀποπαρδήσομαι, 'I'll burst out', and in 20 he repeats θλίβεται. All these vulgar terms perhaps refer directly (as in 8 and 10) or indirectly to the effect on the stomach and bowels of carrying a heavy weight (Xanthias exaggerates his burden, of course) : *cf. Kn.* 998, 1057, fr. 323. See § 10 n. 40.

4. φύλαξαι, as the accent shows, is 1st aor. mid. imperative : 'be on your guard against, beware of'. **τοῦτο** : broadly speaking, ὅδε indicates something close to the speaker or within his direct range of interest (*e.g.* 308), ἐκεῖνος something at a distance from the speaker (*cf.* 69) or of only remote interest to him, or not previously referred to (*cf.* 7), and οὗτος something just mentioned as here, or at a middling distance from the speaker (*e.g.* 181), or of some interest to the person he is speaking to (*e.g.* 183). **πάνυ . . . χολή** : 'utterly disgusting'. χολή (the root of *melancholic*) literally means 'bile, gall' : an excess of it in the stomach causes nausea and vomiting.

5. μηδ' : we must supply a verb of saying, in the deliberative subjunctive (as also in 7 and 9): 'Am I not even to make some other smart remark'. **ἀστεῖον** : literally 'such as townsmen [ἀστοί] use', in contrast with ἄγροικον 'boorish, rude', *i.e.* such as country yokels might use. Ar. is being sarcastic here and in 6, for obviously what Xanthias thinks 'smart' and 'amusing' is low and cheap.

6. δαί : this mainly colloquial particle, rare in serious poetry, occurs only in questions, often giving a tinge of half-humorous surprise or impatience : here 'Oh, all right : well . . .'.

7. γε : as in 3. **ἐκεῖν'** : 'that famous one', or else almost = 'the following', as in *Wasps* 784. **ὅπως μὴ <ἐ>ρεῖς** : 'Take care you don't say' : this construction without a preceding verb in the imperative is rare outside colloquial writers like Plato and Ar. **τὸ τί;** : 'What one?' An idiomatic use of the article in demanding further details, paralleled in the French *lequel?* *Cf.* on 40.

8. '<Saying> as you change over your carrying-pole that *you want to ease yourself* ' (*cf.* on 3). Slaves carried baggage on the end of a short pole (ἀνάφορον) resting on the shoulder (see Ehrenberg 177 and plate xiv b).

9-10. Ar. distorts the natural order of the words (which would begin 'Not even that I'll burst out from carrying . . .') so as to keep the low word to the end.

11. μὴ δῆθ', ἱκετεύω : 'Oh, *please* don't . . .'. The particle emphasizes the urgency of his request. πλήν γ' : here γε emphasizes the single exception : 'At any rate only whenever I'm going to be sick' (*i.e.* such a disgusting remark is only fit to act as an emetic).

12. Xanthias asks why then (δῆτ') was he made (by Ar. himself in this case : note this ironical self-criticism on the poet's part) to carry the baggage if he couldn't make any of the stock porters' jokes. (The answer was, so that Ar. could make jokes about porters' jokes and about the comedians who used them.) τὰ σκεύη : see on 165.

13-14. ποήσω, ποιεῖν : the spelling without iota is preferable in Attic when the first syllable is scanned short : it has the (erratic) support of the better MSS. and 5th-century inscriptions : but see L.-S.-J. μηδὲν ὧνπερ, a condensed phrase = 'nothing of what . . .' for 'none of the things which'. For the comic poet Phrynichus see § 1. Ameipsias's *Revellers* beat Ar.'s *Birds* in 414, and his *Konnos* beat the first version of *Clouds* in 423. Lycis was another comic poet : his name occurs elsewhere only in an inscription (*Inscriptiones Graecae*, ed. min. ii/iii 2325, 65) and (with the alternative Lycos) in the *Scholia* on this line.

15. The construction of this line has been much disputed since ancient times. Variant readings go back to Σ, and many modern editors have offered emendations : others prefer to delete the line as an interpolation, or to mark a lacuna after **14** (so Radermacher). Good sense can be made if it can have the force of a relative clause, and many emendations have aimed at this. I have suggested in *Hermathena* lxxxix (1957) that ἑκάστοτ' might be taken here as = 'each time' in a relative sense (as in English 'each time you come, I'm glad'), which would make the line mean 'each time they carry baggage [*i.e.* introduce baggage-carriers] in comedy'. ἑκάστοτε seems to have a similar relative force in *Kn.* 1070 : cf. the use of words like ἔνθα, τώς, τόθι, as relatives (see also L.-S.-J. τότε ii for its use as a relative in later Greek).

16-17. θεώμενος : 'when I'm a spectator' (see on 2) : ἴδω carries on the same idea. σοφισμάτων : 'wise-cracks', with a side-blow at the *Sophists*.

18. πλεῖν : apparently a shortened form of πλεῖον (Kühner-Blass 1, 216 ; Schwyzer 1, 249). The following *Metaphor* (cf. 'It puts years on me') is frequent (as Tucker and Kock exemplify) in Greek literature, beginning with *Odyssey* 19, 360.

19-20. 'O thrice, then, unfortunate this shoulder here . . .' : Xanthias rants like a tragedian. τράχηλος = 'neck and shoulders' as elsewhere (like χείρ = 'hand and arm'). οὑτοσί : the 'deictic' iota (*iota demonstrativum*), attached to pronouns, demonstrative adjectives, and a few other adjectives, in comedy and oratory. It indicates something visible and near (like Latin -ce and French -ci). It is always long, always takes the accent, shortens a preceding long vowel or diphthong, and absorbs a preceding short : e.g. 26, 39, 98, 99, 139. ἐρεῖ : personification of a part of the body as in 237.

21 ff. The 'pressure' joke having been thoroughly exhausted, Ar. now introduces a parody of contemporary *Sophists*' arguments about the meanings of words. Should a slave who carries a load while seated on a donkey be described as 'carrying' or 'being carried'? (For a serious argument about the active and passive voices of a verb—this was an epoch when grammar was an exciting new science—see Plato, *Euthyphron* 10 A ff.) Here the fallacy is that of the exclusive either/or : in fact Xanthias is both 'carrying' and 'being carried'.

21-2. εἶτα regularly introduces an indignant question : ' Now . . .'. ὅτ'= ὅτε as the iota of ὅτι is never elided in Attic : cf. on 520. υἱὸς Σταμνίου : 'son of Jar', a παρὰ προσδοκίαν joke (§ 10) : hearers would expect something like 'son of Zeus'. Σταμνίου may, as Peppler suggests, imply a nominative Σταμνίας formed hypocoristically as a personal name (like Xanthias, Καπνίας). The stamnos-type of jar had a special connexion with the Lenaean rites (see Pickard-Cambridge, *Dramatic Festivals* 28 ff. and figs. 11 ff.).

23-4. ὀχῶ . . . ἵνα μὴ ταλαιπωροῖτο : the optative after a primary tense may be rendered 'my intention being [when I let him ride] that he should not suffer . . .': cf. on 766.

25-6. Note the force of the particles. 'Do you mean to say [γάρ] I'm not carrying ? Yes I do [γάρ], because how can you be carrying when, as you must admit [γε], you are being carried ?'

26-7. βαρέως πάνυ : 'very hardly' (lit. 'heavily'). To add to the comic confusion Ar. makes X. answer D.'s τίνα τρόπον as if it was an enquiry about his personal condition and not about the possibility of carrying something when one is being carried. Then, for further confusion, Dionysos takes βαρέως as referring to X.'s physical burden and not to his grievances.

28. 'Certainly not what I'm holding and carrying, at any rate [γ'], by Heavens *no*.' Note the triple emphasis in the particles, the oath, and the accented οὔ.

30. πιέζεται : Ar. has no scruples against working in this stale jest once more—and doubtless he got another laugh with it.

31-2. σὺ δ' οὖν : 'All right, then, since you . . . .': οὖν 'permissive'. ἐν τῷ μέρει : 'in turn, as your share'. ἀράμενος (for the ᾱ *cf.* 377, 525), etc. : 'take up the donkey and carry it yourself ' (σύ repeated). A pleasant *reductio ad absurdum* of X.'s argument.

33. 'Why wasn't I in the sea-fight ?' Slaves who had fought in the Athenian victory at *Arginusae* were set free, and so could curse their former masters with impunity, if (like X. here) they wanted to. The γάρ is hardly translatable in English : it explains the preceding exclamation. ἐγὼ οὐκ = ◡ — by *Synizesis.* Peppler discusses the use of the imperfect, ἐναυμάχουν, in *American Journal of Philology* liv (1933), 47-53, taking it as 'conative', 'Why was I unwilling to fight ?'

34. ἦ τἄν (= τοι ἄν) . . . ἄν : emphatic, 'Then, I can certainly tell you' (τοι was perhaps originally an 'ethical' dative of σύ). The repetition of ἄν is common. κωκύειν . . . ἐκέλευον μακρά : 'would have given you my *worst* wishes'. The phrase is a comic distortion of the normal χαίρειν κελεύω πολλά (as in *Ach.* 200 and elsewhere). The imperfect implies that the effect of the command depends on someone else's reaction (Schwyzer 2, 277).

35. πανοῦργος (by etymology 'working at everything') means an unscrupulous ruffian *capable de tout* (*cf.* Rabelais's *Panurge*), in contrast with the honourable man who will do only what is right and fitting.

35 ff. ACTION. The comical pair, who have probably been going slowly forward during their argument, now come to a door in the scene-building (§ 9), and stop. The audience do not know whose house it is meant to be until Heracles appears (after 37). (For conjectural plans of D.'s movements in these opening scenes contrast Bieber and Flickinger.)

37. ἔδει : 'my purpose was' : the imperfect as in 12 : *cf.* on 1209. παιδίον : D. assumes that a door-keeper will answer.

38-9. *Heracles* answers the door himself, not, I think, as a sign of boorishness (*cf.* Theophrastus 4, 9) but probably to save an extra actor. ὡς κενταυρικῶς : 'How savagely . . .': H. had fought the Centaurs and knew their outrageous violence. ἐνήλαθ' [ἐνάλλομαι] ὅστις . . .: 'he leaped at it, whoever he . . .'. Here, I take it, H. breaks off his sentence in astonishment at D.'s costume. τουτὶ τί ἦν : 'What's the idea of *this* ?' The imperfect of intention (*cf.* 37, 12), I think, rather than of discovery or of 'sudden appreciation of the real state of affairs' (Tucker) : *cf.* 438.

40. ὁ παῖς : to X. The nominative form of address is more haughty than the vocative. D. is standing on his dignity. Note the quadruple ἀντιλαβή (division between different speakers) here : *cf.* 56, etc. τὸ τί : 'just what ?' or 'what precisely ?' (as in 7) : impatiently (see Humbert, § 52).

41. μή . . . γε: 'Yes, for fear . . .'. For this use of the particle where a preceding verb is understood cf. on **3.**

42–3. 'By Demeter': surprisingly this form of oath is confined to men in Ar.'s plays. It was (with those by Zeus and by Apollo) an official oath in Athens. See Werres 45. καίτοι δάκνω γ᾽: 'Even though I *am* biting myself ' (*i.e.* 'my lips' in an effort to stop laughing).

44. δαιμόνιε sometimes implies a touch of pained surprise or sudden wonder (perhaps retaining a hint of δαίμων : see further in E. Brunius-Nilsson, *Daimonie*, Uppsala, 1955). Murray translates : ' Don't be absurd '.

45. ἀποσοβῆσαι : the word normally refers to 'shooing' away birds or flies (see L.-S.-J. and cf. Plato, *Letter* 7, 348 A). Here it is used as a *Comic Distortion* of ἀποσβέσαι 'quench' (cf. the ἄσβεστος γέλως of Homer's gods). Translate : ' I can't squelch my laughing '.

46–7. 'A lion-skin on top of a yellow tunic.' The κροκωτὸς χιτών was worn by participants in Dionysiac festivals, by women, by effeminate men, and by members of royal houses (see Fraenkel on *Agamemnon* 239 and Knox-Headlam on Herodas 8, 28). Heracles himself wore one when in servitude to Omphale (acc. to Lucian, *On Writing History* 10). The κόθορνος was a loose boot worn by women and travellers (as it protected the foot better than a sandal) and by Dionysos (on vases : see Pickard-Cambridge, *Dramatic Festivals* 232-3). ῥόπαλον : the large club characteristically carried by Heracles. The contrast (§ 10) is ultimately between the soft, luxurious costume of D. and that of the rugged, arduous H. (A hint that D. is abnormally effeminate is not certain, though D.'s effeminacy is suggested in *Bacchae* 455 ff., Lucian, *Bacch.* 3 and *Dial. deorum* 18 : but on the other hand see Diodorus Siculus **4, 4, 4**, on D., the warrior with his panther-skin uniform.) For νοῦς= 'idea' cf. on 580 ff.

48. ἀπεδήμεις : '. . . were you off to ?', lit. 'going abroad', *sc.* before you arrived here. ἐπεβάτευον Κλεισθένει : 'I was serving [as a marine, ἐπιβάτης] under Cleisthenes' : cf. Thucydides 8, 61, and on **422.** For a possible second meaning here see L.-S.-J. at ἐπιβαίνω A iii 3.

50. ἢ δώδεκ᾽ ἢ τρισκαίδεκα : round numbers : 'a dozen or more' (cf. Fraenkel on *Agamemnon* 1605). But Denniston (MS.) takes the repeated ἢ as being intended to convey an impression of meticulous accuracy.

51–2. σφώ : 'The pair of you ?', *i.e.* D. and Cleisthenes (but Radermacher thinks D. and X.). X. sarcastically completes D.'s brag with 'And then I woke up !' D. ignores this and continues his romance with the lively connective particles καὶ δῆτα, 'And further'.

52-3. ἀναγιγνώσκοντί . . . πρὸς ἐμαυτὸν : 'reading aloud to myself' : silent reading is not mentioned before the 4th cent. A.D. τὴν 'Ανδρομέδαν : 'the *Andromeda*', Euripides's popular romantic play (now lost) produced in 412, a favourite target for Ar.'s mockery (*cf. Thesm.* 1012 ff.). It apparently expressed much nostalgic yearning (πόθος : *cf.* the extraordinary account of its effect on the Abderites given by Lucian, *On Writing History* 1).

54. πῶς οἴει was originally a parenthetical question, but became a kind of lively interjection= 'You can't think how', as here. πῶς δοκεῖς is similarly used.

55. πόθος ; πόσος τις ; 'A yearning ? What size ?' The Greek contains comic *Assonance.* σμικρός [always ῐ] ἡλίκος Μόλων : 'Small : the size of big Molon'—which Frere justly calls 'the irony of imbecility' (but for *some* of the audience it may also have seemed an amusing παρὰ προσδοκίαν). The evidence on Molon is confused (see Blaydes and Σ), but probably this Molon was a leading actor in Euripides's plays and a very large man. Possibly an allusion to the gigantic Molions in *Iliad* 11, 709, is also intended. For the construction of ἡλίκος see F. E. Robbins in *Classical Philology* xxv (1930), 344-5 : *cf.* ὅσος in 781 and 1135.

56. γυναικός : genitive of object of desire as normally. οὐ δῆτ'. . . . ἀλλὰ : 'Certainly not. Well, then . . .' For the elision between different speakers see on 1134.

57. ἀπαπαῖ (this is Fritzsche's emendation of the unmetrical ἀππ- of R and V : other MSS. have ἀττ- : *cf.* on 649) : an inarticulate expression of grief or pain. A good actor would make much of this opportunity of expressing unspeakable emotion : *cf.* in 63. ξυνεγένου τῷ Κλ. : 'Did you get in touch with your Cleisthenes ?' For ξυν- see § 14 n. 75.

58. 'Brother' : D. and Heracles were both sons of Zeus. οὐ γὰρ ἀλλ' : for this colloquial idiom *cf.* 498, 1180 : 'For I really *am* in a bad way'.

59. The metre and language are in the tragic style. D. probably declaimed the line with some exaggeration of tone and gesture : *cf.* § 12.

60. ὠδελφίδιον : 'little brother' (*cf.* on 58) : probably an affectionate rather than a contemptuous *Diminutive* here. Note the double accent in these forms of *Crasis* : but some MSS. have ὦ 'δελφίδιον with *Aphaeresis* : *cf.* in 64.

61 ff. ὅμως γε μέντοι : 'Yet all the same . . .'. δι' αἰνιγμῶν :

'by riddles', 'symbolically'. D. chooses his analogy to suit Heracles's notorious fondness for food (see § 8 n. 27). ἔτνος, 'soup', was generally made from vegetables.

64. Part of this line is, according to Σ, from Euripides's *Hypsipyle*. For **'τέρᾳ** = 'in another way', *cf. Kn.* 35, *Clouds* 813. The MSS. have τέρα (R), τερα (VAM), *τερα (U), which Coulon thinks indicates a reading πέρα 'further' : but against this see Radermacher and Erbse.

66-7. δαρδάπτει : 'devours' : an epic word, used of ravenous beasts.

67. 'For Euripides' : the surprise is kept to the end of the sentence. **καὶ ταῦτα τοῦ τεθνηκότος :** usually **καὶ ταῦτα** with the participle means 'especially when', as in **704.** The use of the article here has also been questioned : and Blaydes suggests it is used to distinguish the dead poet from his living son also called Euripides. Palmer suggested **καὶ ταῦτ' ἔτος τεθνηκότος** 'even though he's dead a year' (*cf. Wasps* 1058). The evidence for the date of E.'s death is contradictory, but the beginning of 406 seems the likeliest time (*cf.* Schmid-Stählin 1, 3, 1, 314). But the text may be sound, and we may translate : 'Even when he's dead'.

69. ἐπ' ἐκεῖνον : 'in search of, to get him back' (see on 4) : ἐπί is often so used. **εἰς Ἅιδου :** according to Humbert (§ 517) this is a survival from a primitive use of εἰς (like ἐν) with a partitive genitive 'limiting a portion of space'. The older view of grammarians was that some word like 'house, dwelling-place' had dropped out before the genitive.

70. 'Yes and even lower, by Heaven, if there *is* [γ'] anywhere lower' : a reference to Tartarus is not necessarily intended.

72. A direct quotation from Euripides's *Oineus*, where it is spoken in reply to the question 'Are you perishing abandoned by your allies thus ?'

73. Iophon, Sophocles's son, is said to have written 50 plays. He competed against Euripides's *Hippolytus* in 428. See further on **79. καὶ μόνον :** 'just the only thing' : *cf.* on 170.

74-5. εἰ καὶ τοῦτ' ἄρα : 'if, on second thoughts [ἄρα], that actually [καὶ] is so'. οὐ γὰρ : 'I say that because I don't . . .'. This dithering uncertainty about Iophon's dramatic powers is explained in **78-9.**

76. εἶτ' οὐχὶ Σοφοκλέα πρότερον ὄντ' Εὐριπίδου : this is the MS. reading. As it stands we must either scan **οὐχὶ Σοφοκλέα** as — ∪ ∪ ∪ ∪ — or (by *Synizesis*) — ∪ ∪ ∪ —. The first alternative gives ∪ ∪ ∪ ∪ (a 'proceleusmatic') in the second foot, which

Coulon defends (*Revue des Études Grecques* lxvi, 1953, 36-8) citing three other possible examples in the MSS. (*Ach.* 78, *Kn.* 676, *W.* 967 : cf. Starkie, *Wasps* p. 418). (But H. J. Newiger, *Hermes* :xxxix, 1961,175 ff. has now questioned all such proceleusmatics.) The second alternative, to treat the final -έα as a single syllable by synizesis, is unlikely, as trisyllabic proper names in -ῆς (or quadrisyllables in -έης : cf. 787) with their first syllable short are not so treated elsewhere. *Bentley* preferred to emend οὐχὶ to οὐ (cf. Blaydes's apparatus criticus for parallels). I have accepted Coulon's view and retained the MS. reading. Secondly, some editors have objected to ὄντ' and have emended it to give the meaning 'instead of Euripides' (Palmer's ἀντ' being widely accepted). But if we take πρότερον = 'superior' (to the references in L.-S.-J. A iii add Aristotle, *Poetics* 1453 b 3 ὅπερ ἐστὶ πρότερον καὶ ποιητοῦ ἀμείνονος), the phrase makes good sense : 'as he's superior to Euripides'. (Mitchell thinks that Ar. deliberately used πρότερον in an ambiguous sense, capable of meaning 'prior to' or 'superior to' here.) Sophocles had died in 406, some months at least after Euripides (if we can trust the story in the *Life of Euripides* that he dressed his chorus in black at the City Dionysia in March 406, in mourning for Euripides's death). On the question whether Ar. had originally drafted the *Frogs* before Sophocles's death and then altered it here and elsewhere see § 7 n. 25.

77. μέλλεις ἀναγαγεῖν : this is the reading of the inferior MSS. (R. and V. have ἀνάγειν which will not scan). Objections to the division of the anapaest (πέρ|έκεῖ) in the fourth foot (see W. G. Arnott, *Classical Quarterly* n.s. vii, 1957, 188 ff. on Bernhardi's over-strict views) cannot be conclusively sustained : so *Bentley's* emendation εἴπερ γ' (with ἀνάγειν) need not be adopted.

79. ὅ τι ποεῖ κωδωνίσω : 'until I test the metal of his poetry'. κωδωνίζω (cf. κώδων 'a bell') refers to the testing of metal objects, especially coins, by striking them on a hard surface and listening to their 'ring', or else to the testing of the courage of horses and fighting quails by ringing bells at them (see Σ and A. S. Pease in *Harvard Studies in Classical Philology* xv, 1904, 56). (The Σ offer other less likely explanations.) The implication is that Iophon was helped by his father Sophocles and might be incapable of producing good plays without him.

80-1. 'And further, Euripides being, in contrast [γ' emphasizes the μέν : cf. 290, 907], a versatile rogue [see on 35] would be fit to try [potential optative with ἄν] escaping back here [sc. from Hades] for me' [μοι: see on 986]. ἀποδιδράσκω may have a derogatory implication here, being used elsewhere of deserters and runaway slaves.

82. εὔκολος : not an easy word to render exactly in English. Aristotle (*Rhetoric* 1381 a 30 ff.) contrasts people who are εὔκολοι with the censorious (ἐλεγκτικοί) and the quarrelsome (φιλόνεικοι). If, as L.-S.-J. suggests, it is derived from κόλον ' the large intestine ', its primary meaning would be 'eupeptic', hence 'having the good temper of those who enjoy a good digestion'. Perhaps 'contented' or 'easy-going' expresses it best. (For this quality in Sophocles see F. J. H. Letters, *Life and Work of Sophocles*, London, 1953, chap. 2 : he quotes Mahaffy's remark that Sophocles was 'perhaps the only distinguished Athenian now known who lived and died without a single enemy'.) For other references to Sophocles in Ar. see *Peace* 531, 695-9, and fr. 581 ; and *cf.* 787 ff. below. Phrynichus in his *Muses* (§ 1) described him as μάκαρ, εὐδαίμων (*cf. Peace* 696), and δεξιός. Ar.'s single superbly chosen epithet shows his finer taste and style. What was the real reason why Ar. did not make Sophocles a leading figure in his play ? Some say because he had not died when Ar. first planned his plot (see § 7 n. 25). But the more likely explanation is that Sophocles's personality and plays did not offer such good material for caricature and parody as did Euripides's and Aeschylus's.

83-5. Agathon is generally ranked as fourth in ability to the Big Three of Greek tragedy : see Schmid-Stählin 1, 3, 1, 845-6. Born about 450 B.C., he won his first victory in 416 (the supposed occasion of Plato's *Symposium* in which he figures prominently with Aristophanes). His personality and poetry are ridiculed by Ar. in *Thesm.* He went, like Euripides, to the court of Archelaos in Macedonia c. 407 : hence ἀποίχεται 'has departed' (with, perhaps, a suggestion of being 'as good as dead' : also 84, as Wecklein notes, resembles an epitaph). μακάρων is probably a *Pun* on Μακεδόνων (with a further hint again of the 'blessed departed', *cf. W.* 639). εὐωχίαν : the Macedonians were renowned for lavish meals.

86-7. Xenocles is ridiculed elsewhere in comedy (*e.g. Thesm.* 169) as an inferior tragic poet ; but he won first prize against Euripides's *Troades* in 415. Before D. replies to Heracles's question about Pythangelos—presumably another inferior tragedian— Xanthias breaks in with a complaint about having to keep on carrying the baggage. This becomes a kind of refrain during the rest of the scene : *cf.* 107, 115.

89. μειρακύλλια : contemptuous *Diminutive* of μεῖραξ 'a girl or effeminate youth,' : 'Namby-pamby lads', 'sissies'.

91. 'And miles verboser than Euripides' (Murray).

92. The meaning of ἐπιφυλλίδες (*sc.* σταφυλαί) has been much disputed by ancient and modern commentators. The likeliest meaning is 'stunted grapes', *i.e.* grapes growing in an unnatural position at or near (ἐπι-) the leaves, in contrast with the separate and fully developed bunches. But Fritzsche argues that vines with too much foliage are meant : 'mere leaf-growth'. The general sense is : 'Words are like leaves, and where they most abound, Much fruit of sense beneath is rarely found' (Pope, *Essay on Criticism* 2, 109). The *Metaphor* is apt for a festival of Dionysos and an *Audience* composed partly of vineyard-keepers. στωμύλματα : 'chatterations', probably a *Coined Word* : *cf.* 943.

93. χελιδόνων μουσεῖα : 'music-halls of swallows', a parody of ἀηδόνων μουσεῖα in Euripides's *Alcmene*. The Greeks thought the twitter of the swallow barbarous, confused, and garrulous (*cf.* in 681) in contrast with the nightingale's song. See further in van Leeuwen's note on this line and also passages cited by Fraenkel on *Agam.* 1050.

94-5. 'Who if they achieve a single production vanish at once, after one feeble assault on [or 'defilement of'] tragedy.' θᾶττον : 'quicker than you'd expect', 'double quick' (Merry). ἢν . . . χορὸν λάβῃ : 'receive a chorus', *i.e.* be selected by the Eponymous Archon as worthy of being granted actors and a chorus for a production of their play. Only five authors (or three during the Peloponnesian War) were chosen for this, out of, probably, many competitors. A feeble poet, D. implies, would be satisfied with this preliminary honour and never try again.

96-7. γόνιμον : 'fertile, creative' : probably a *Medical Term* : and *cf.* Denniston, *Technical Terms.* ὅστις ῥῆμα γενναῖον λάκοι : 'one who [*cf.* 98] could utter a gallant phrase'. γενναῖον : 'generous-hearted, worthy of a nobleman, gentlemanly' (connected with γέννα, poetic for γένος from which comes εὐγενής referring more to ancestry, pedigree) : perhaps like the Confucian concept of *jên* and the Latin *gentilis* it primarily means 'possessing the good qualities of one's clan' (see Arthur Waley, *Analects of Confucius*, London, 1938, 27). λάσκω is a word of tragic and epic associations : see Björck 280-4. For the absence of ἄν see Humbert § 204.

99 ff. τοιουτονί τι παρακεκινδυνευμένον : 'something adventurous [or 'audacious'] like this' (*Deictic Iota*). D.'s first example, 'sky, the bungalow of Zeus', is a distortion of the phrase in Euripides's *Melanippe* αἰθέρ' οἴκησιν Διός (*cf. Thesm.* 272), by substitution of the prosaic, *Diminutive* δωμάτιον : *cf.* Plautus, *Amphit.* 3, 1, 3 *in superiore qui habito cenaculo* (Jupiter) : his second example, 'the foot of Time' (for Χρόνου, personified, with a capital χ see on 335), apparently suggested a ludicrous figure : *cf.* 1323 below and Dodds on *Bacchae* 888. 'A mind unwilling to

swear an oath by the sacred victims [at a sacrifice], but a
tongue that perjures itself independently of the mind' alludes
to the notorious line in Euripides's *Hippolytus* 612 (see on **1471**) :
the language is deliberately prosaic in style (especially ἰδίᾳ).

103. σὲ δέ : note the emphatic position and accentuation of
the pronoun : ' *You* like these, do you ?' ἀρέσκω more usually
governs the dative. μάλλὰ : the μή seems to imply that originally
some verb in the imperative was understood, lit. ' Don't say that
but . . .' (see Denniston, 4-5). Translate : 'Please *me* ? Why
I'm more than crazy about them.'

104. ἦ μὴν : particles used in oaths and solemn affirmations :
'I'll swear they're . . .'. κόβᾱλά γ' : 'downright humbug'.
κόβᾱλος (see Björck 46), used in *Kn*. 635 of mischievous, deceiving
imps, is possibly cognate with 'goblin' and 'cobalt' (from goblin-
guarded mines), hence implying such grotesque trickery or im-
posture as lepracauns or gremlins are still sometimes blamed for.
ὡς καὶ σοὶ δοκεῖ : 'And you think so, too'. Heracles accuses
D. of hypocrisy in pretending to like such phrases : he assumes
that everyone must scorn them as much as he does himself.

105-6. According to the Σ this line as far as νοῦν comes from
Euripides's *Andromache*, but these precise words do not occur in
that play (though *cf.* l. 581): perhaps the *Andromeda* (*cf.* **53**) was
meant. For a possible proverbial source see Schmid 337 n. 1.
Translate : ' Don't try to manage my views. You have a *ménage*
of your own ' (adapted from Merry) : in other words, ' Leave
literary criticism to me : your *métier* is food [*cf.* **107**] not art '.
Heracles replies : ' Yes, I'll even go further and say [καὶ μὴν . . .
γε] it's absolutely villainous stuff '.

108. σκευήν : 'costume, get-up'. Distinguish this from σκεύη,
neut. pl. in **15**. ἔχων here, as often, may be translated 'with'
(like φέρων, ἄγων).

109-10. κατὰ σὴν μίμησιν : 'impersonating you', not just
'copying' here. The construction of the optatives after ἵνα has
been variously explained (see, *e.g.*, Radermacher who takes it as
equal to an imperative). I have punctuated to indicate ana-
colouthon after μίμησιν and would translate : 'Well the reason
why I've come with this costume, impersonating you—it was
[*cf.* on **23**] so that you . . .'. ξένους : this word can mean either
those who give hospitality (hosts) or those who receive it (guests)
or, in general, those who are bound and obliged to each other by
giving and receiving hospitality. In a time when hotels and inns
were few and frugal a strict etiquette of private hospitality was
a necessity for comfortable travelling. εἰ δεοίμην : 'in case of
need '.

111. 'To fetch [ἐπὶ] Cerberus' (the watch-dog of Hades) : this was one of Heracles's twelve labours.

112-15. A comic rigmarole of places a traveller would like to know about. ἐκτροπάς : either 'by-paths' or 'branches in the road'. κόρεις : 'bed-bugs', *cf*. on 439.

116. ὦ σχέτλιε : probably mock-heroic as the phrase is frequent in Homer in the sense of 'audacious, headstrong, stubborn'. σχέτλιος is connected with ἔχω, ἔσχον 'hold on'. Translate : 'Oh valiant heart'. γὰρ explains the exclamation. καὶ σύ γε : 'even *you*' (Seidler, followed by Tucker and Coulon, gives this to Dionysos).

119-20. 'And don't tell me one that's too hot or too cold'. ἄγαν goes (by the ἀπὸ κοινοῦ construction) with both adjectives. Ar. makes D. say this to lead up to some macabre humour from Heracles, who takes a moment (in 120) to make up his mind (*Mystification*). φράσω : deliberative subjunctive (*cf*. on 1). For the reflective repetition in τίνα . . . τίνα *cf*. 460, 1399.

121 ff. ἀπὸ κάλω καὶ θρανίου : 'by means of rope and bench'. For ἀπό in this sense *cf*. 1201. The words might primarily suggest a voyage, 'by reef [or 'cable'] and rower's bench'. But the next words make the intention clear—'by hanging yourself' (*i.e.* by jumping off a bench with a rope round your neck). When D. finds this 'stifling' πνῖγηρὰν (πνίγω 'throttle'), Heracles suggests two other ways to the Land of the Dead : by crushing hemlock κώνειον, 124) with a pestle and mortar (θυείας) to make a poisonous drink ; or by jumping off a high tower (131 ff.). For the proverbial 'three ways of suicide' see E. Fraenkel in *Philologus* lxxxvii (1932), 470-3.

123-4. σύντομος τετριμμένη : the words are chosen so as both to describe a path as 'a short cut, well trodden' and also to describe hemlock when 'chopped up and crushed' in a mortar. The general meaning is 'a quick, well-smoothed short cut'.

125-6. μάλιστά γε : 'Yes, certainly' (μάλιστα is still used in this sense in modern Greek). D. describes this route, by 'Hemlock Street', as cold and wintry, because the first effect of hemlock poison is to paralyse and chill the lower limbs (*cf*. Socrates's death in *Phaedo* 117 E). He expresses this in terms also applicable to travelling over frozen ground : 'For your shins begin freezing right away'.

128. 'As I'm not so very walkative' (Cope's translation) : βαδιστικοῦ seems to be a *Coined Word* (*cf*. Cratinus's βαδισματίας) intended to mock the *Sophists*' fondness for terms in -ικός as in *Kn*. 1378-81. (So Peppler : but K. J. Dover in *Classical*

Review lxix (1955), 207 thinks the -ικός ending is more typical of 5th-century administrative language.) For μή (instead of οὐ) with a causal (or descriptive) participle, as here, see A. F. Braunlich in *American Journal of Philology* lxxvii (1956), 417.

129-31. 'Well stroll down to the Kerameikos': a district N.W. of the Acropolis and Agora, described in Thucydides 2, 34 as the most beautiful suburb of Athens : named after either the deme Κεραμῆς (*cf.* 1093) or the potters (κεραμεῖς) in general. The 'lofty tower' (130) is probably that of Timon the misanthrope whose hatred of his fellow men was the subject of a play by the comic *Phrynichus* (and of later writings by Plutarch, Lucian, and Shakespeare). Visible from this tower, apparently, was the starting-place of a torch-race (λαμπάδ') : *cf.* Pausanias 1, 30, 2, with Frazer's notes, and 1090 ff. below. Ritual torch-races were held at Athens in honour of Athena and other divinities. (For conflicting views on their rules see van Leeuwen on this passage and Fraenkel on *Agamemnon* 314.) ἀφιεμένην : 'being started' : *cf.* ἡ ἀφετηρία 'the starting-line'. ἐντεῦθεν goes with θεῶ (imperative of θεάομαι) : 'watch from there'.

133. εἶναι (ἵημι): infinitive for imperative, as elsewhere (*cf.* on 169) : 'Let them [the runners] go'. Apparently at these ritual races the spectators (perhaps at an agreed signal) started the race. Some editors (see Radermacher) have thought this unlikely : Seidler conjectured εἶνται, 'They're off', which Radermacher adopts (*cf.* the curious εἴητε in Σ). But·this weakens the force of the second εἶναι, etc. : 'Then *you* let *yourself* go'. Note ἵημι here for the more precise ἀφίημι (131) : perhaps it was the traditional word in these ceremonies.

134. 'But I'd destroy two rissole-wrappers of my brain (if I did that).' ἐγκεφάλου θρίω δύο refers to the fact known to 5th-century physicians (see, *e.g.* Hippocrates, *On the Holy Disease* 6, 4-5) that the brain was in two sections and was contained in a wrinkled membrane. This membrane resembled the fig-leaf (θρῖον) used to contain the meat rissoles (also called θρῖα and sometimes composed of animals' brains) which the Athenians enjoyed eating then (and still enjoy now). It is hardly worth trying to decide whether Ar. is referring to the outside or the inside (*cf.* Fritzsche and van Leeuwen) of the brain and rissole.

136. τότε: *cf.* on 111. ὁ πλοῦς πολύς : note the *Assonance* which would be specially effective in a deep Herculean voice (*cf.* 55) : 'Well, it's a hu-u-ge cru-uise'.

137 ff. In the next 26 lines we have a comic parody of what may be called Hades-geography. Before the time of Ar. there had been much speculation about the topography of the Land of the Dead, in poetry (notably *Odyssey* 11), myth (*e.g.* in the descents into Hades of Heracles, Theseus, Orpheus), and in religious thought (both Orphic and Eleusinian). Ar. had already used the theme of a descent into Hades in his *Gerytades*. (Later poets developed the theme : *e.g.* Virgil, Dante, Milton : and *cf.* the gruesome late Greek fragment in Page, *Greek Lit. Pap.* 416-421.) See further in Pauly-Wissowa at κατάβασις, and 'Orpheus' fr. 17 (Diels-Kranz).

137-8. 'A lake, a big one—very much so—, bottomless' : Heracles piles on the alarming adjectives to frighten D. πάνυ (which usually comes after its adjective) can hardly go with the absolute term ἄβυσσον (whence is derived 'abyss', 'abysmal'). The lake is not named : perhaps Acheron is intended : see on 471. πῶς γε is the reading of R. Radermacher defends the γε and Coulon retains it, but Denniston 124 thinks the stress is inappropriate and that V is right in omitting it.

139-40. ἐν πλοιαρίῳ τυννουτῳί : 'In a little boat [*Diminutive*]· such a wee one, like this'. Heracles, to frighten D. more, emphasizes the smallness of the boat in contrast with the vastness of the lake. τυννοῦτος : a lengthened form of the *Doric* word τυννός 'small' : first found in *Ach.* 367. (Perhaps Dorisms like this and γεννάδας in 179 are 'war slang' taken from the Peloponnesian enemy, like blitz, flak, strafe in English. It is hardly an indication of Heracles's own Doric origins.) In τυννουτῳί the *Deictic Iota* indicates a gesture by Heracles appropriate to a *very* small boat. The old sailor is Charon : see **183.** δύ' ὀβολώ : a sly allusion to various contemporary payments or doles given by the State to Athenian citizens, *e.g. Cleophon's* wartime dole (the διωβελία) introduced in 410, the daily pay for soldiers and sailors, and the theoric fund (see Ehrenberg 227-8). It was also, according to Plato (*Gorgias* 511 D), the fare from the Peiraeus to Aegina. Charon's charge elsewhere is usually one obol (but we need not, with Hilberg and van Leeuwen, introduce the notion of a return ticket here). Perhaps wartime inflation was also in Ar.'s mind.

141. φεῦ : an *extra metrum* exclamation, as elsewhere : not 'Alas' here, but expressing either disgust (as in *Agamemnon* 1307)—'Ugh !'—or a whistle of admiration (*cf.* the modern 'wolf' whistle) as in *Birds* 1724.

142. κἀκεῖσε : 'even to Hades' : *cf.* ἐκεῖ in 82 and the German *Jenseits*, English 'the Other World'. Θησεύς : because he was the mythical founder of the Athenian State and had himself gone down to Hades.

144. μή μ' ἔκπληττε etc. : note the force of the *Present*

Imperative, 'Don't keep on trying to terrify me'. Heracles has overdone his terrorization, and D. sees through his little game.

145 ff. 'Then ⟨you'll see⟩ a mass of foul mire and ever-flowing sewage, and lying in it . . .'. This curious feature of Hades is probably Orphic. *Cf.* the grotesque διαρροίας ποταμός in Ar.'s *Gerytades* (*cf.* on **137** ff. above), and Dante, *Inferno* **18**, 113-14 *in uno sterco | Che dalli uman privadi parea mosso*.

150. 'Or swore a perjured oath': for ἐπίορκον see M. Leumann, *Homerische Wörter* (Basle, 1950), 87 ff.

151. 'Or anyone who had a messenger's speech by Morsimos copied out for himself', ἐξεγράψατο: Tucker notes: 'an author γράφει; his amanuensis ἐκγράφει; but a person who makes or gets made a copy for his own use ἐκγράφεται'. Morsimos, an incompetent tragic poet (but a grand-nephew of Aeschylus), is mocked by Ar. also in *Kn.* 401, *P.* 801. Coulon prints **151** after **153** (and there is evidence in Σ for early objection to the position of **152-3**). This re-arrangement makes a tidier thought-sequence and confines the literary references to D. But Heracles had *some* interest in literary matters (*cf.* **73, 76**), and the incongruity of **151** has greater comic force coming immediately after **150**. See further in Erbse, who accepts the traditional order.

153. 'Learnt a war-dance by Cinesias': for possible origins of πυρρίχην see L.-S.-J. Note its meaning 'strange contortions' in Euripides, *Andr.* 1135 and 'fierceness' in *Birds* 1169; and *cf.* 'rock 'n' roll' in A.D. 1957. Cinesias (an extraordinarily thin dithyrambic poet) is often mocked by Ar.: *cf.* **1437** below and see Lilian B. Lawler in *Transactions of the American Phil. Assocn.* lxxxi (1950), 78-88.

154 ff. Heracles now describes the pleasanter parts of Hades. Here, too, Ar. is probably drawing on Orphic or Eleusinian beliefs: *cf.* Pindar, fr. 114 and Virgil, *Aen.* 6, 638 ff. φῶς κάλλιστον: an often emphasized feature of Elysium and Heaven. ὥσπερ ἐνθάδε: the Athenians were specially proud of the luminosity of the atmosphere in Attica: *cf.* Euripides, *Medea* 828 f. αἰεὶ διὰ λαμπροτάτου βαίνοντες ἁβρῶς αἰθέρος. The 'plentiful hand-clapping' in **157** primarily refers to those in Hades who clap their hands to keep time for the happy mystical groups (θιάσους) of dancers; but it also hints at the applause that Ar. hopes his play will win in the theatre. μυρρινῶνας, 'groves of myrtle', a plant associated with religious festivals: *cf.* on **328**. ἀνδρῶν γυναικῶν: for similar omission of 'and' (*Asyndeton*) *cf.* **114, 857, 861**. Radermacher suggests that it has a solemn effect here.

158-60. οἱ μεμυημένοι: 'those who have been initiated',

sc. into a Mystery Cult (see § 8) in which the first stage of initiation was called μύησις : see further on 336. At this reference Xanthias interrupts—'By Heaven, then *I'*m [γοῦν= γε emphatic + οὖν] the ass at the Mysteries'. ἄγω (*v.l.* ἄγων) has been taken by some editors as= φέρω here, giving the translation 'carrying the equipment for the Mysteries' (*cf.* L.-S.-J. on μυστήριον) : but there seems to be little authority for using ἄγω for 'carry (inanimate objects)'. Other editors translate 'celebrating [a regular use of ἄγω] the mysteries' : but it is hard to see how a donkey could do that (outside the conditions of Apuleius's *Golden Ass*) in any literal sense. Tierney in *Mélanges Navarre* (Toulouse, 1935), 395-403 suggests that ὄνος here means a low grade of membership in the Dionysiac cult. No interpretation seems to me to have conclusively established, so I have translated loosely. For donkey proverbs see van Leeuwen, and now add Page 314 l. 9 and *Dyskolos* 550-1. Xanthias's real donkey is forgotten after 32. τὸν πλείω χρόνον : 'for any longer time' : the article is found with similar phrases in, *e.g.*, Thucydides 4, 117 ; 5, 15. X.'s grumbles and threats are ignored by D. and H.

164-5. 'Well, a hearty farewell to you, brother.' The emphatic πόλλ' hints that D.'s journey is a perilous one. D. tries to make his answer sound confident—'Well, by Heaven, good health to you, too'. After this Heracles goes back into his house. τὰ στρώματα : 'the bedding'. Innkeepers until recently in parts of Eastern Europe and the Levant provided only a room with little, if any, furniture : travellers brought their own bed-clothes, as here.

166. πρὶν καὶ καταθέσθαι : 'before I've even put them down': presumably X. was slowly and cautiously beginning to put down his load after 160. D. replies, 'Yes and mighty fast, too'.

167 ff. ACTION. Here Ar. introduces a brilliantly conceived incidental scene which helps to make the audience understand that D. and X. are now really on their way to Hades. Some mourners enter carrying a corpse on a funeral bier (170). X. suggests that the dead man (as he, too, is obviously going to Hades) might be hired to carry the baggage. An amusing piece of bargaining follows.

168. ἐκφερομένων : the regular word for carrying out a corpse for burial. ὅστις ἐπὶ τοῦτ' ἔρχεται : ὅστις, not ὅς, because the antecedent τινα is vague. ἐπὶ τοῦτ' 'for this purpose' (*cf. Bacchae* 967) has been taken to mean (*a*) to go to Hades ; (*b*) to be buried ; (*c*) to carry the baggage. The last is, perhaps, likeliest.

169. μηὔρω (for μὴ εὔρω : how exactly this contraction should be marked is uncertain) : 'But what if I don't find ⟨someone⟩ ?'

τότ' ἔμ' [Krüger's re-arrangement of the MSS. τότε μ'] ἄγειν : 'then take me' : infinitive for imperative as in 133 and 388.

170. καὶ γάρ : 'for here, you see, . . .'. γάρ explains why D. thinks X.'s suggestion good : καὶ is either the 'motivating' use, emphasizing D.'s reason for approval, or the 'specifying' use, giving reality to X.'s τινα in 167. For these and other uses of καὶ not='and' see W. J. Verdenius's supplements to Denniston in *Mnemosyne* iv, ix (1956), 248 ff. and S. Trenkner, *Le style* KAI etc. (Brussels, 1948) and on 67, 74. 509, 715-16.

172. σκευάρι' : 'some little pieces of baggage'. The *Diminutive* is used as a preliminary to offering a low wage for carrying them. The Greeks were, and are, adroit bargainers.

173 ff. To the delight of the audience the Corpse sits up and takes an interest in D.'s offer. **πόσ' ἄττα** : 'About how many'. ἄττα is Attic for τινά (formed from the -a of the preceding word +ττα for τya=τινα). When D. replies, 'These here', the Corpse inquires, 'Will you pay [τελεῖς] two drachmas as my wages ?' A drachma was worth 6 obols. In 177 D. tries to beat him down by 25%, but fails.

174. ὑμεῖς : the bier-bearers (rather than D. and X. as some suggest). **τῆς ὁδοῦ** : for the genitive 'along the road' *cf.* Thucydides 4, 47.

175. δαιμόνι' : see on 44. **ἐὰν**, etc. : 'In case I am willing to come to some agreement with you'. For the use of ξυμβαίνω (= συμ- : *cf.* § 14 n. 75) *cf.* 807.

177. ἀναβιοίην νῦν πάλιν : 'Strike me alive again if . . .' : a delightful comic reversal of the imprecation 'Strike me dead if . . .'. The sardonic implications of the phrase (the opposite of Achilles's affirmation in *Odyssey* 11, 489 ff. that any form of living is better than being dead) may reflect current pessimism in Athens. The MSS. read the form ἀναβιῴην : but this is generally regarded as a late form in 2nd aor. optatives of this kind. See Kühner-Blass 2, 384.

178. D. (see end of this n.) finds the Corpse's arrogance intolerable. X. loyally intervenes on his master's side (a genial touch, this) and volunteers to go on carrying the baggage. **οὐκ οἰμώξεται** : 'Let him go hang' (lit. 'Will he not go and groan ?'), a variation òn the imperative (*cf.* 257). The MSS. are uncertain about· the speakers in this line (*cf.* § 14 n. 86). Most editors give the whole line to X. It seems to me more lively to divide it as in the text.

179-80. 'You're a loyal fellow and a decent chap.' **χρηστὸς** (conn. w. χράομαι 'use') implies (*cf.* on 735) serviceability, hence (in war or necessity) reliability, honesty, loyalty. **γεννάδας** suggests something of the 'gentleman' (*cf.* on the cognate **γενναῖος** in 97.): it is a *Doric* form (*cf.* on 139), occurring first in *Ach.* 1230 : see Björck 51-4. **ἐπὶ τὸ πλοῖον** : 'in search of the boat' (which Heracles told us about : *cf.* 139) : *cf.* on 69.

180 ff. ACTION. The Corpse and his carriers have now passed on. D. and X. trudge in silence round the *Orchestra*. Charon, the ferryman of the Dead, appears in his boat, indicating that D. and X. have reached the bank of Acheron. A dialogue (with some arguing, as usual) follows. (Just how Charon's boat was brought in is entirely a matter of speculation : ropes, rollers, and/or stage-hands may have been used : see Tucker, Radermacher, and A. L. M. Cary in *Classical Review* li, 1937, 52-3.)

180. Charon (probably so named from his glaring eyes, *cf.* **χαροπός**) was a familiar figure in classical literature (first in the *Minyad* according to Pausanias) and art (notably in Polygnotos's *Lesche* of the Cnidians at Delphi) ; so, too, in Etruscan art, and in later European literature (*e.g.* Dante, *Inferno* 3, 98-9 'the pilot of the livid swamp with eyes like wheels of flame', and Shakespeare, *Troilus and Cressida* 3, 2, 10-11, 'O ! be thou my Charon, and give me swift transportance . . .'), also in modern Greek folklore (see F. A. Sullivan in *Classical Journal* xlvi, 1950, 11-17). **ὤόπ** : here apparently 'Easy there' or 'Avast', *i.e.* stop rowing (as in Σ on *Birds* 1395 : but see on 208 below). **παραβαλοῦ** : 'Lay her alongside'. Is this spoken to a crew (so Radermacher, who argues that the singular is permissible in such a case), to a scene-shifter (so Cary, *loc. cit.* on 180 ff. above : he compares *Peace* 174), or to Charon himself (Tucker) ? Each of these is possible. My own view is that these nautical phrases are not addressed to anyone in particular but simply introduced by Ar. to help to identify Charon (instead of crudely making him say 'I am a typical sailor such as you may see and hear any day at the Peiraeus'). In vase-paintings Charon sometimes rows (or punts) his own boat, sometimes not : see Cary, *loc. cit.* and J. D. Beazley's translation of Pfuhl's *Masterpieces of Greek Drawing* (London, 1926), p. 72 and fig. 97.

182-3. Denniston (MS.) draws attention to 'the eager, excited **γε**'s '.

184. χαῖρ' ὦ Χάρων etc. : according to the Σ the line is a quotation from *Aithon*, a satyr play by Achaeus. Radermacher considers it solemn (comparing Pindar, *Pythians* 4, 61) ; but it is more likely (with its *Assonance*) to be intended as comic. Some editors (following a suggestion by the Σ) divide the three greetings between D. and X. (see, *e.g.*, van Leeuwen), and suggest that

Charon was rather deaf, being an old man.   For other triple
salutations *cf.* 271, 369, 1176.

185-7.   A parody of a ferryman's announcement of his stopping-
places.   The first phrase, however, 'Respite from work and woes',
would poignantly touch the hearts of war-weary Athenians in
405 B.C.   The 'Plain of Forgetfulness' was a feature of esoteric
Greek doctrine about the scenery of Hades (*cf.* on 137, 154):
cf. Plato, *Repub.* 621 A.   Later Lethe came to be regarded as a
river, *e.g.* in Virgil, *Aen.* 6, 705.   'Ονουπόκαs, written thus as a
single word and a proper name, is Radermacher's improvement
of the MSS. ὄνου πόκαs (I ignore the unnecessary conjecture
'Οκνου πλόκαs).   It literally means 'Ass-shearings', hence (since
nobody would be fool enough to waste time shearing a donkey
for its useless hair), 'Never-never-land'.   A hint at the place
called 'Ονου γνάθος in Laconia is possibly intended.   's 'Ον.:
normally in Ar. εἰς is found before a vowel : see Starkie's *Wasps*,
p. 404 and Coulon i, xxviii.   Κερβερίους : 'the Cerberians',
referring primarily to Hades's watchdog (*cf.* 111) and perhaps
to the Κιμμέριοι (*v.l.* Κερβέριοι) of Homer's description of the
approach to Hades in *Odyssey* 11, 14.   's Κόρακας : 'to the Ravens':
an allusion to the curse βάλλ' ἐς κόρακας (*cf.* σκορακίζω in L.-S.-J.),
i.e. 'may the ravens pick your bones'.   Ταίναρον is rather surpris-
ing in this comic list, as Tainaros (or -on : see L.-S.-J.) was an
actual place, the southern promontory of Laconia.   But Ar.
often surprises us, and this may be a passing allusion to the
hellishness of the Peloponnesian War (with further allusion to
the fact that there was said to be an entrance to Hades at Tainaros).
ἐπὶ is regularly used of ports of call.

188.   ποῦ : 'where' : it is hardly necessary, as Fritzsche shows,
to adopt ποῖ the reading of U.   But Radermacher prefers to
read ἔμβαινέ που as part of Charon's order to D.   σχήσειν : 'put
in' : note this 'momentary' future form of ἔχω, formed from the
2nd aorist (in contrast with the 'continuous' ἕξω) : *cf.* Neil on
Kn. 130.

189.   σοῦ γ' εἵνεκα : 'just for *your* sake', in sardonic parody
of an obliging ferryman.

191.   εἰ μὴ νεναυμάχηκε τὴν [*sc.* μάχην] περὶ τῶν κρεῶν :
'unless he has fought in the neck-or-nothing sea-fight' (Tyrrell).
A much disputed line (see, *e.g.*, Fritzsche).   It apparently com-
bines two allusions : first to the Athenian life-and-death struggle
and victory at *Arginusae* (at which slaves helped to man the
ships, and were afterwards freed : *cf.* § 4), and secondly to a
proverb, ὁ λαγὼς τὸν περὶ τῶν κρεῶν (*sc.* δρόμον) τρέχει 'the hare
runs the race to "save his bacon"' : *cf.* Herodotus 7, 57 and

Wasps 375 τὸν περὶ ψυχῆς δρόμον δραμεῖν. The variant νεκρῶν in U (presumably with reference to the corpses which the Generals failed to recover after Arginusae) is inept : there was no battle for the corpses.

192. 'No, by Heaven, not me—I happened to have eye-disease' : I follow Denniston in placing a comma after γάρ. Diseases of the eyes are, and were, common in the Eastern Mediterranean. But probably Ar. is specially mocking a prevalent excuse for evading military service : *cf.* Herodotus 7, 229.

193. οὔκουν : the use of this word is a mannerism of Charon's here, *cf.* 200, 201. (The MSS. mostly have οὐκοῦν : the editors and L.-S.-J. reject that accentuation in impatient or sharp questions. But is a sardonically polite Charon impossible here ?) περιθρέξει : a continuous future (*cf.* on 188) perhaps implying (Humbert, § 255) 'make a tour round' in contrast with περιδραμοῦμαι simply 'run round'.

194. τὸν Αὐαίνου [Kock emends to Αὐ- as this seems to be the usual Attic form : *cf.* 1089] λίθον : 'the Stone of Withering' ('Withering Heights'). It is unknown whether Ar. invented this alarming landmark in Hades or took it from mystic doctrine (for parallels see Radermacher, especially the Ἀγέλαστος Πέτρα). Perhaps some allusion to dry and shrunken corpses, αὖοι νεκροί and ἀλίβαντες, is intended (*cf.* Σ, and J. C. Lawson in *Classical Review* xl, 1926, 56). The adjectival form is not found elsewhere, but the words αὐαντή and αὐασμός are Hippocratic. (The suggestion that it is an imperative, 'The Stone of "Be shrivelled"', is hardly admissible.) Denniston (MS.) notes that in an Orphic phrase the soul is δίψῃ αὖη (see L.-S.-J. at αὖος), and in modern Greek folksongs the dead are 'the thirsty ones', 'the dry ones'.

195. ἐπὶ ταῖς ἀναπαύλαις : 'the resting-places' : *cf.* 113 and 185 : probably a familiar term in the mystic topography of Hades.

196. τῷ (= τίνι) : 'what thing' (*sc.* 'of ill omen'). The Greeks believed that one should be particularly careful about ominous encounters when starting out on a journey (*cf.* Theophrastos 16 on the Superstitious Man, Horace, *Odes* 3, 27, and modern regard for black cats and magpies). 'What crossed my path when I was setting out ?'

197 ff. ACTION. Xanthias sets out on his lonely tour round the infernal lake. Charon orders Dionysos aboard. D., being unused to boats, makes a stupid mistake in 199. Doubtless, in the actual production, the actor took this opportunity for much comic '*Business*'. Eventually the boat moves (or is imagined to move) off.

197-8. κάθιζ' ἐπὶ κώπην : 'Sit to your oar', *i.e.* in the right position for rowing. D. idiotically takes it (199) as 'Sit on your oar'. **εἴ τις ἔτι πλεῖ** (Kuster's emendation of ἐπιπλεῖ, which is a dubious use of that verb) : 'If there is anyone further who wants to make the voyage' (lit. 'is for sailing', present tense expressing intention as often). **οὗτος** : 'Here, you', to D.

200. οὔκουν (see on 193) . . . **δῆτ'** : 'Then will you kindly . . .'. **γάστρων** : 'fatty, pot-belly', a *Comic Name* formed from γαστήρ (like Πλάτων from πλατύς, 'broad-shouldered', Στράβων, στραβός 'squinting'; and Latin names like Cicero, Naso) : see further in Knox-Headlam on Herodas 5, 1, and on 588 below. **ἰδού** : from ἰδοῦ, the aor. mid. imperative of ὁράω; but, as the sharper accent indicates, an exclamation = 'There you are' (*cf.* French *voilà*).

202-3. οὐ μὴ φλυαρήσεις ἔχων : 'Stop playing the fool' : φλυαρῶ can hardly refer to *words* here as the harassed D. has been unusually laconic. Note **οὐ μὴ** with the 2nd pers. fut. here (and in 298, 462, 524) expressing negative command. Originally it was probably a pressing question (Humbert, § 656) : còntrast on 508. **ἔχων** = 'keeping on', as often. **ἀντιβὰς** : 'setting your foot against the stretcher'.

204. 'Unpractised, unseaworthy, unsalaminian.' The sonorous Greek with its triple negatives in ἀ- and spacious three-word structure (*cf.* Descroix, *Le Trimètre iambique* 75-82 and *cf.* on 838-9) is a *Parody* of the tragic style (*cf.* Tucker, who compares Milton, *P.L.* 2, 185 'unrespited, unpitied, unreprieved' : so, too, *Hamlet* 1, 5, 77 'unhousel'd, disappointed, unanel'd'). **ἀσαλαμίνιος** could refer to the Greek sea-victory over the Greeks at Salamis in 480 B.C., or to the *Salaminia*, one of the two (*cf.* on 1071) sacred Athenian warships (its crew would be specially well trained), or to the island itself (its natives being specially good seamen). The general sense is 'with no naval training' : all three words in the line are almost synonymous (*cf.* on 1154).

205. εἶτα repeating the κᾆτα of 203 implies (as Denniston, MS., observes) an almost weeping tone : 'how *can* I row?'

205-6. Charon takes D. as meaning that he will find it hard to keep time in his rowing, so he explains that there will be music to help him with this. Greek crews were accustomed to have a boatswain (κελευστής : *cf.* **κατακέλευε** in 207) who gave orders for the rowing and a piper (τριηραύλης) who marked the pace with music (the Frog chorus takes his place in what follows). **ἐμβάλῃς** : 'lay to', *i.e.* lean forward for the stroke : ἐμβάλλω is perhaps intransitive here as in *Od.* 9, 489 ff.

207-8. βατράχων κύκνων θαυμαστά : 'songs [μέλη is understood

from 205] of swan-frogs—wonderful songs'. 'Swan-frogs' (a con-
tradiction, as swans were considered superb singers and frogs ugly
croakers) is perhaps a phrase from country humour. (For parallels
see L. Deubner and W. Kranz in *Hermes* lxii, 1927, 128 and 256,
and Cantarella : for the *Asyndeton* see Radermacher.) κατακέλευε
δή : 'Then give the rowing-speed'. ὦ ὄποπ : here apparently =
'Yo-heave-ho' or something similar, not an order to stop as in
180 : the accentuation and spelling vary in the mss. (I follow VM :
but A.'s ὦ ὄπ· ὄπ ὦ deserves attention), and ὦ ὄποπ is written
three times in V. The rhythm is dactylic, and as the phrase is *extra
metrum,* it may have been repeated several times in the original
production to make the Frogs' sudden trochaic interruption more
effective. Higham, following MacGregor, thinks that the ὦ re-
presents the pulling of the oarblade through the water, the first
ὄπ the lifting of it clear, and the second ὄπ the recovery of position :
hence ὦόπ in 180 indicates that position is not recovered and the
rowing has ceased : *cf.* Σ on *Birds* 1395.

209 ff. ACTION. The famous Frog Chorus (which though lasting
only 60 lines gave the play its title : see § 7) begins. The singers
are heard only, not seen (see ἀκούσει in 205, and on 227). To
compensate for their invisibility Ar. exploits some skilful rhyth-
mical effects in the dispute between the Frogs and D. Charon in
208 has set the rowing-time for D. in dactyls (*i.e.* 4/4 time in
musical terms), and we may suppose him to begin rowing as best
he can to that rhythm. Then the Frogs break in with trochaic
and iambic rhythms (*i.e.* 3/4 time): this doubtless confuses D.
greatly. To make matters worse, when D. has adapted his rowing
to the trochees and iambs, the Frogs begin singing in dactyls.
Then in the argument that follows (221 ff.) D. preserves his inde-
pendence and dignity for a while by shouting in iambs against
the Frogs' trochees. In 250 ff. he carries the battle into the
enemies' camp by using their own trochees against them ; and
he varies his rhythms until he finally triumphs in 268. Besides
the variations in rhythm (musical 'time') we should also probably
assume that the speed (musical 'tempo') and volume (*crescendo*
and *diminuendo*) of this passage varied considerably in the
original production. The surviving text contains no indications
of this, but we may surmise that the speed and loudness rose to a
climax round about 242 ff. (241-9 metrically suggests a trochaic
Pnigos). For a detailed scheme see Zielinski in *Eos* xxxvii, 1936,
105-8. During all this D. presumably does some very irregular
and comical feats of oarsmanship in Charon's boat.

METRE. The rhythms are mainly trochaic and iambic with
lyrical dactyls in 218-19. For detailed discussion see White,
Wilamowitz, Radermacher, Dale.

209-10 (the frog's croak): ⏑⏑⏑ –⏑ –⏑ – ⋀ : trochaic dimeter catalectic with resolution in 1st foot (*Lecythion*).

211-12 : ⋎– ⏑– . – ⏑⋎ : iambic dimeter with *Syncopation* in 3rd foot.

213 : –– ⏑– –⏑⏑– : iambic metron + choriambic (=2 iambs by 'interior' anaclasis : see White 24).

214 : ⏑– . – ⏑– ⏑– : iambic dimeter with syncopation in 2nd foot.

215-16 (reading Διώνυσον for Διόνυσον with G. Hermann) = 211-212.

217 : –– ⏑– –– ⏑– (but the quantity of *ia-* is uncertain : *cf.* L.-S.-J., Schroeder, and Radermacher).

218 : –⏑⏑ –⏑⏑ –– : dactylic.

219-219a : –⏑⏑–⏑⏑–⏑| ––⏑⏑–⏑⏑–––⏑– : uncertain but probably dactylo-epitritic (Radermacher reads Χύτροις for Χύτροισι which gives an easier rhythm).

From **220** to **268** the rhythms are iambic or trochaic (with anapaestic variations in 230).

221-2= 224, 226-7, 236-8, 251, 257, 262 : ⋎– ⏑– ⋎– ⏑– : regular iambic dimeters.

228= 232, 243-4a, 246-8, 252, 253/4, 258-9, 263, 264a : trochaic dimeters : regular pattern –⏑ –⋎ –⏑ –⋎, but ⏑⏑⏑ is allowed in any foot : note especially ⏑⏑⏑ ⏑⏑⏑ ⏑⏑⏑ ⏑⏑⏑ in 232.

229 : ⏑⏑⏑ – . –⏑ –⏑ –– : trochaic trimeter with syncopation in 2nd foot.

230 : –⏑ ⏑⏑– –⏑ ⏑⏑– –⏑ –– : trochaic trimeter with anapaestic variations (see Dale 89).

231 : ⏑⏑⏑ –⏑ –⏑ –– –⏑ –– : trochaic trimeter.

233= 242, 249, 255, 260, 265 : trochaic dimeters catalectic (*cf.* 209).

240-1= 211-12 above.

245 : ⏑⏑⏑ – . –⏑ ⏑⏑⏑ : trochaic dimeter with syncopation.

266 : regular iambic trimeter (as in dialogue) : as this is surprising among all the trochees, Wilamowitz and Radermacher rearrange 265-6 to give trochees in 266. But the iambic trimeter may foreshadow the return to comparatively tranquil dialogue in 269 ff.

209. Βρεκεκεκὲξ κοὰξ κοάξ (accentuation varies considerably in the MSS.: Coulon, following Wilamowitz, omits all accents): an imitation of the croaking of frogs (English *croak* was originally more like *cro-ak*, disyllabically, as pronounced still by countryfolk : *cf.* the similar *Onomatopoeia* in the French *coasser*, and Ovid's ingenious *sub aqua, sub aqua, maledicere tentant* in *Metamorphoses* 6, 376). Ar.'s imitation of the bull-frogs' cry (which is as loud as a duck's quack) is lifelike, but I have not been able to detect an initial β in any Greek croaking that I have heard : however, even frog-language may change in 23 centuries. *Cf.* J. B. S. Haldane in *Journal of Hellenic Studies* lxxv (1955), 25, and E. S. Smith in *The Times*, 23 May 1956.

210 ff. The song begins in Ar.'s pure lyric style (*cf.* § 11), but shows a touch of coarseness in 218 with κραιπαλόκωμος 'tipsy-revelling'. Note the picturesque compound adjectives in 212, 213, 229 ff., and 245 ff., which are typical of choral lyric. There is no need to imagine (with Tucker) that any special parody is intended.

215-16. ἀμφὶ Νυσήιον . . . Διώνυσον : 'for the sake of [a common lyric use] D. of Nysa' (a name applied to various places in Greece, Asia, and Libya, connected with D.). For the reading Διώνυσον see on the metre of 216 above.

216 ff. ἐν Λίμναισιν etc. : at Athens every year during the month Anthesterion (approximately February) the festival of the Anthesteria was celebrated in the precinct of Dionysos 'in the marshes' (the exact site of this is much disputed : see Pickard-Cambridge, *Dramatic Festivals* 19 ff. and Gomme on Thucydides 2, 15, 4). The Anthesterian festival was mainly concerned with the previous season's wine but included certain cults of the dead (see especially Pickard-Cambridge, *loc. cit.*). It lasted for three days : on the first was the opening of the wine-casks (Πιθοιγία) ; on the second the pouring of libations and lavish sampling of the wine (Χόες), on the third the sealing of the wine in jars (Χύτροι as in 219) with offerings and prayers to the dead. A general mood of revelling and tipsiness (κραιπαλόκωμος) seems to have prevailed, as at mid-lenten carnivals (*mi-carême*) in Latin countries. τέμενος in 219a = ἐν Λίμναις (wherever that was : perhaps near the S.W. slope of the Acropolis). Pickard-Cambridge denies that there was any direct connexion between this precinct and the Lenaean festival (§ 2).

222. τὸν ὄρρον : 'my rump' : as amateur oarsmen soon learn, it is not only the hands that get sore in rowing : *cf.* **236-7** and on 1070. Experienced Greek oarsmen sat on a cushion (*cf.* Hermippus, fr. 54). ὦ κοὰξ κοάξ : ὦ with this accent usually

implies that a vocative follows : hence 'O you Koax-koaxers' not
'Oh koax, koax' (but see L.-S.-J. at ὤ).

226-7. αὐτῷ κοάξ : 'with your koax included' : for other
examples of this, the 'sociative' dative (more commonly plural) in
Ar. *cf*. 476, 560, Humbert, § 483 ff. and Starkie on *Wasps* 119. **γάρ
ἐστ'** : 'for I see you're . . .'. **οὐδὲν** . . . **ἀλλ' ἤ** : Denniston 24 ff.
prefers to take ἀλλ' here as representing ἄλλο (the accent having
been dropped by 'fusion' with ἀλλά) : in any case the meaning is
'nothing else but' : *cf*. 1073, 1130. In 227, 'You are nothing else
but koax', Ar. takes advantage of the fact that the Frog Chorus
was not visible, to make D. score a point in the slanging match.

228. 'Yes, and quite reasonably so, you busy-body.' The
Frogs accuse D. of being over-officious in complaining about their
insistent koaxing, and go on in the next line to say that, whatever
D. may think, both the Muses *and* Pan *and* Apollo like it. For
Greek dislike of meddlesomeness, πολυπραγμοσύνη (apparently a
common feature of public life in 5th-century Athens), see V.
Ehrenberg in *Journal of Hellenic Studies* lxvii (1947), 46-67.

229 ff. Since the croaking of frogs was generally considered
harsh and unmusical by the Greeks (*cf*. on 207), we need not take
their claim to high patronage too seriously. **ἔστερξαν** : the aorist
is not past in sense, but *Gnomic* : 'naturally love'. **κεροβάτας** :
this is explained by Σ as 'he who walks on the mountain-tops' or
'he who goes with horns on his head' or 'goat-hoofed'. The last
is most likely right : *cf*. Pan's description elsewhere as τραγόπους
and αἰγίπους. **καλαμόφθογγα παίζων** : 'playing on the tuneful
reeds', *i.e.* on the pan-pipes (σῦριγξ). **φορμικτὰς** : 'player on the
lyre' : the φόρμιγξ was a stringed instrument, with structural
differences from the λύρα (which is referred to in 229 and 232).
The **δόναξ**, which is mentioned here as serving as a base or support
for the lyre (**ὑπολύριος** : apparently either as a kind of bridge or
else to hold the lower ends of the strings), was a more slender
kind of reed than the large pole-reed, κάλαμος mentioned in 230.
ἔνυδρον : here 'growing in the water' : in 247 'water-laden'.

233/4. For the anomalous numbering of the lines here and in
240-5, and elsewhere, see § 14 n. 75.

236-8. 'Well anyway [notice the self-assertive use of **γε** here
and in 221, 228, 253/4, 258, 264, and the similar γάρ (= γε ἄρ
originally) in 229, 257, 264a] I've got blisters, and my tail-end has
been sweating for some time, and, what's more, in a minute when
it bends it'll say . . .' D. apparently intends to refer to the kind
of rude posterior noise mentioned by Xanthias in 10 (a constant
source of amusement, apparently, to some of the comedian's
hearers) : but the Frogs comically intervene. ἰδίω was probably

originally σΕιδίω, connected with *sweat* and Latin *sudo*. For the personification of the πρωκτός *cf.* 308. The *Papyrus* has ἐκκύψας (*i.e.* 'peeping out', *sc,* below D.'s chiton) for the MSS. ἐγκύψας 'bending down'. Both forms occur elsewhere in Ar., and confusion between γ and κ in such a position is easy (and indeed may here be merely variants in the *Spelling* of the same word). Physiologically 'bending down' (*i.e.* as D. rows) better prepares the way for ἐρεῖ: but as a crude comic touch 'peeping out' is perhaps preferable.

241 ff. μᾶλλον μὲν οὖν : the frequent corrective or adversative use of μὲν οὖν : 'On the contrary, all the more shall we give voice'. Note the poetic ending -μεσθα for -μεθα in 242, 248, 252, 258 : see Schwyzer 1, 670. εἰ δή ποτ' etc. : 'If indeed we have ever hopped on fine sunny days through the galingale and the reeds . . .'. εἰ δή is used here and in *Wasps* 86 (see Starkie's note) in a condition which the speaker knows to be true 'if, as is the fact' : elsewhere it usually implies scepticism (*cf.* Denniston 223).

247-9. χορείαν αἰόλαν : 'our changeful dance-song'. πομφολυγοπαφλάσμασιν : this wondrous *Polysyllable* and *Coined Word* (from πομφόλυξ 'a bubble' and παφλάζω 'splutter, splash') amusingly mimics the sound (*Onomatopoeia*) of a bubble swelling up (πομφ-) and bursting (παφ-) with a splash (φλασ-) : *cf.* Homer's πολυφλοίσβοιο θαλάσσης. Translate : 'with bubblosplashifications'. But Denniston (MS.) prefers to take it as referring to splashing raindrops in answer to which the frogs croak. Higham, however, notes that παφλάζω in Ar. fr. 498 means 'bubbling *up*' (of boiling soup) and explains the expression used here as a modal dative describing the way in which the frogs' song comes up from under the water.

250-5. D. now launches a counter-attack on the Frogs by shouting their own cry back at them. λαμβάνω='I am going to take' (not, I think, 'I am beginning to catch', like an infectious illness). The Frogs reply 'If you *do* [ἄρα] it will be an outrage on us' (*i.e.* if you take over our cry). D.'s δεινότερα mockingly echoes the Frog's δεινὰ τάρα.

258. ἀλλὰ μὴν : the 'assentient' use : 'All right then, [if you don't care] we *will* [or 'we will' : γ'] yell [note perfect form here and in 264a, as regularly with verbs of utterance] as loudly as our throat can stretch [I take χανδάνῃ as suggesting χανδόν here, not simply 'hold, contain'] all day . . .'. With δι' ἡμέρας *cf.* 265, *Peace* 56, and διὰ νυκτός in fr. 13. The separation of ἄν from the relative pronoun is unusual (but see L.-S.-J. and add Herodas 5, 43). Before the Frogs can add their Koax, D. breaks in with it himself (if my punctuation and division of speakers is right).

263, σύ is put after ἡμᾶς for scornful emphasis : 'Well us *you*
certainly [μήν] will not conquer, either—no doubt about that'
(πάντως).

265. κἄν με δῇ: this is the reading of V (R has δῇ : other
MSS. have δεῖ or δέῃ) : Vahlen and Radermacher doubt that such
a contraction of δέω in the sense of 'it is necessary' is permissible;
but see L.-S.-J. and Wilamowitz, *G.V.* 594. Erbse prefers δέῃ
with *Synizesis.*

267-8. After D.'s shout of Brekekekex in **267**, he probably
pauses for a reply. But the Frogs have fallen silent for ever :
the god of comedy has prevailed over his opponents. Then he
triumphantly announces 'So, you can see [ἄρα], I *was* going to
make you stop [*cf.* 241] sooner or later [ποθ'] from your "Koax"'.
The imperfect ἔμελλον may be taken as showing that the action
was predestined (as the speaker knew all along) : *cf. Acharnians*
347 (after a similar slanging-match) ἐμέλλετ᾽ ἄρα πάντως ἀνήσειν τῆς
βοῆς. For a different view see Tucker. See on metre above.

269. For παραβαλοῦ see on 180. Blass's conjecture τὼ κωπίω
'your oars' for τῷ κωπίῳ is ingenious but unnecessary (since
rowers often use a single oar for bringing a boat alongside a
landing-stage). Note the *Diminutive* form of κώπη (*cf.* 197)
found only here in classical Greek (and probably used only for
metrical convenience : see Peppler).

271 ff. SCENE and ACTION. Charon and his boat now go off
the scene, and, as indicated in **273 ff.**, we are to imagine that D.
and X. are entering the fearsome realms of Hades. X. amusingly
exhibits D.'s cowardice by pretending that a horrible spectre is
in sight (**285 ff.**).

271-2. For the triple call *cf.* 184. Here, perhaps, it indicates
D.'s increasing alarm. Translate : 'Xanthias [rather formally :
cf. on 40]. Where's Xanthias ? Hey [note ἤ exclamatory here],
Xanthias.' X. calls back 'Coo-ee' (ἰαῦ, *cf.* 1029).

273. τἀνταυθοῖ (= τὰ ἐντ.) etc. : literally 'as regards things in
the place you've [or 'we've'] come to', as distinct from τἀνταῦθα.
For the βόρβορος, 'filthy muck', see on 145.

274-6. Here Ar. exploits a favourite comic device. When
D. asks X. whether he saw (on his way round the lake) the father-
beaters and perjurers that Heracles 'was telling [ἔλεγεν] us
about', X. asks D., 'Well, don't *you* see them ?' and points towards
the *Audience*. *Cf.* 783 : for other direct references to the audience
by Ar. see Pickard-Cambridge, *Dramatic Festivals* 268 ff. and
Schmid 47 n. 2.

278-9. οὖ τὰ θηρία τὰ δείν᾽ ἔφασκ': 'where that fellow

kept saying the wild beasts were'. Some editors have con-
sidered the Greek untranslatable. Hamaker and von Velsen
insert εἶναι before τὰ δεἰν' (the repeated -ειν- perhaps causing
the omission) and delete ἐκεῖνος as a later addition. I have
followed Tucker in putting a dash after ἐκεῖνος to show that D.
interrupts before X. finishes. ὡς οἰμώξεται: 'how sorry he'll
be' (see L.-S.-J. at ὡς, D. 1, 2), hardly a hope or wish here, as
some editors take it. Cf. 257.

280-1. ἠλαζονεύεθ' etc. : 'he was exaggerating [cf. on 909] so
as to make me frightened, knowing I was a valiant chap—out of
jealousy'. The meaning of φιλοτιμία and its cognates varies
from 'love of honour' in the good sense to 'ambition, rivalry'
and hence 'jealousy' as here : cf. on 679.

282-4 are in tragic style and metre (showing D.'s rising self-
conceit). 282 is a Parody of a line, οὐδὲν . . . ὡς ἀνὴρ ἔφυ, from
Euripides's Philoctetes (fr. 786). ἐγὼ δέ γ': 'But I' (being truly
valiant, and not merely a conceited fellow, γαῦρος). ἀγώνισμ':
'contest, feat, exploit'.

285-6. X. ironically agrees. Then (καὶ μὴν here draws
attention to a new development, something just heard or seen :
cf. 288) he proceeds to show how little courage D. really has. In
what follows the trembling D. (note the terrified repetition of
ποῦ) tries to get X. to stand between him and the imaginary
monster.

289-95. Here Ar. caricatures the average Athenian's fear of
ghosts. The best known bogies were Lamia (subject of a comedy
by Crates : she could take her eyes out and put them back
again), Ephialtes (the demon of nightmares), Epialos (demon of
cold shivering), Mormo (cf. on 925), and Empousa, who, as
described here, could change her appearance and traditionally
had a donkey's leg (hence the foolery in 294-5, where some
comparison with a χαλκόπους Erinys may also be intended). Her
shining face (293-4) shows the usual phosphorescence of night-
ghosts. Waser (in P.-W. v, 2540-3) gives much curious information
from later literature about her : see also Radermacher.

295-6. βολίτινον θἄτερον: 'the other leg made of cow-dung'
(or, acc. to Σ, 'ass-dung'): a crudity to amuse the more bucolic
members of the audience. See previous note. In Crasis ἕτερος
keeps its older form ἅτερος : see L.-S.-J. X.'s 'And where am
I (to turn to) ?' is spoken in scornful mimicry of D.'s anxious
cry.

297. ἱερεῦ: in panic D. turns to the Priest of Dionysos
Eleuthereus who customarily sat in the centre seat of the front
row at the Dionysiac dramatic festivals (§ 3). ἵν' ὦ σοι ξυμπότης:

'so that I may drink with you at the wine-party' (*i.e.* at the symposium after the play, in honour of the victorious playwright) : *cf. Acharnians* 1085.

298. 'O Lord Heracles' : X. slyly reminds D. of the part he is supposed to be playing, perhaps with a hint at the cult of 'Heracles Who Wards Off Evil' (ἀλεξίκακος). For οὐ μὴ with the future καλεῖς, equivalent to a command, see on 202. μ' : note the elision at the end of a line before a vowel at the beginning of the next, the only example of με so treated in comedy according to Maas 31. The device is called the 'Sophoclean type' (εἶδος Σοφόκλειον) from Sophocles's use of it : *cf.* δ' in *Birds* 1716, *Eccl.* 351 and see further in Descroix, *Trimètre* 292-4. But the better MSS. here place the μ' at the beginning of line 299. Porson preferred to delete μ' entirely.

300. Why does D. not want his own name to be spoken ? Radermacher explains this as being due to a widespread belief that if a demon or ghost knows your name he has greater power over you (*cf.* Lucian, *Menippus* 8). In parts of Africa people for a similar reason have a public name for general use and a private name which they are careful to keep secret from any possible enemy.

301. ἴθ' ᾗπερ ἔρχει : 'go upon thy path', a ritual formula used to send away an evil spirit or an angry divinity (the 'apotropaic' use) : *cf. Lysis.* 834, and Radermacher. X.'s δεῦρο δεῦρ' indicates that D. has retreated as far as he can from the imaginary spectre.

302. πεπράγαμεν : πράττω here as elsewhere means 'to fare (well or ill)' : translate here 'everything has turned out well for us'.

303-4. ὥσπερ Ἡγέλοχος . . . γαλῆν ὁρῶ : Hegelochos was protagonist in the first production of Euripides's *Orestes* (408 B.C.). Unfortunately when he had to say the line (*Orestes* 279) ἐκ κυμάτων γὰρ αὖθις αὖ γαλήν' [= γαληνά 'calm things'] ὁρῶ, he said γαλῆν ὁρῶ. As the γαλῆ (probably a ferret. *i.e.* the domesticated variety of the polecat or marten) was a familiar vermin-killing house-pet of the 5th-century Athenians (the cat, αἴλουρος being then a rare luxury except in Egypt), the Athenians laughed mightily at this ludicrous lapse (which may have helped to make Euripides leave Athens in 408/7). Commentators explain the difference in pronunciation either as a failure to mark the elision (but I have seen no evidence that Greek elision was perceptible in pronunciation) or as a slip in pronouncing the acute accent as a circumflex (like French ê instead of é), which seems the more likely explanation. Suggested English versions are : 'After the

storm the sea(l) looks calm again' or '. . . there comes a calm
along (camel long)'. Greek audiences were quick to notice
lapses in pronunciation : see Merry, Tucker, Blaydes, and
Radermacher ; and *cf.* the story of Demosthenes's deliberate
mispronunciation of μισθωτός as μίσθωτος in *De corona* 52.

307 ff.: ὠχρίασ'[α]: 'I went pale': compare the English
ochre. ὁδὶ δὲ in 308 has been explained by Σ and some later
editors as referring to the Priest of Dionysos (*cf.* on 297). But
ὑπερεπυρρίασέ σου, 'has grown orange-red, tawny, for you',
could hardly mean 'blush': a blush is a different colour (not
πυρρός but ἐρυθρός : L.-S.-J. misinterprets πυρρός in *Kn.*
900 : *cf.* Hippocrates, *Prognostic* 11, 15). Others suggest that
X. points to some notorious red-headed person in the audience,
which is possible. Van Leeuwen, followed by Radermacher and
van Daele, takes it (rightly I think) as referring to the colour
of D.'s clothes after the effects of his panic on his evacuatory
system : if so, ὁδὶ refers to ὁ κροκωτός (see 46 : *cf. Eccl.* 329 ff.)
or possibly to ὁ πρωκτός (see Süss in *Rhein. Museum* lxiii, 1908,
17, and *cf.* on 237 and 482 ff.). For the general notion *cf. Kn.*
899-900 (as Κόπρειος there indicates); *Eccl.* 329-30 (note reference
to κροκωτίδιον in 332) and 1061-2 (note ὑπὸ τοῦ δέους there).
For σου (R) other MSS. have που and μου.

309-11. D. rants in tragic style (but the metre is not strict
enough to be tragic : note the dactyls in **309** and the absence of
caesura in **310**). In **311** X. mocks D.'s remark in 100 (see note
there).

312 ff. ACTION. X. now hears the sound of a flute (note the
stage direction, παρεπιγραφή: 'Someone plays the flute from
inside', *i.e.* in the *Scene-building*: a similar direction occurs after
1263 below) ; and (313-14) D. smells the smoke of torches.
They assume that these indicate the coming of the Mystic
Initiates (see § 8 and on **336**) whom Heracles mentioned (154-8).
The sound of the Iacchos cry in 316-17 confirms this. They
crouch down (315) out of the way while the Chorus (see on **316**)
enters in the *Parodos*.

313-14. X. 'A breath of flutes' (*cf.* 154 and Euripides, *Bacchae*
128 αὐλῶν πνεύματι). D. replies 'Yes I do [hear it], and, what's
more, a kind of whiff [αὖρα elsewhere='breeze, steam', etc.] of
torches [a regular accompaniment of mystic ceremonies, *cf.* 1525],
most mystical'.

315. ἠρεμεὶ : 'quietly': a unique adverbial form in classical
Greek for the usual ἠρέμα : see Schwyzer 1, 623.

316-17. For the Chorus of Initiates see § 8 and on **158**. For
Iacchos see on **324**. For metre see on **325**.

318-19. τοῦτ' ἔστ' ἐκεῖν': 'This is it' (*i.e.* what Heracles described : *cf.* **154** ff.) : see on **4.** που : 'I suppose' : X. hasn't actually seen the Chorus.

320. γοῦν : 'at any rate', *i.e.* 'even though we can't see them yet'. τὸν Ἴακχον ὅνπερ Διαγόρας (*v.l.* δι' ἀγορᾶς) : if the first reading (which the better MSS. support) is correct, we can translate 'the Iacchos-song which Diagoras sang'. This would be a παρὰ προσδοκίαν reference to a notorious atheist who (according to the Σ here and on *Birds* 1073) used to mock the mysteries, *cf. Birds* 1073 and Lysias, *Against Andocides* 17 : he is probably also referred to in *Clouds* 830. (See Schmid 493.) Σ also suggests a reference to a dithyrambic poet called Diagoras who used the refrain 'Iacchos, Iacchos' continually. But some editors (with support in Σ) prefer the other reading and explain 'through the Agora' as alluding to the route of the mystic procession (see especially Tierney).

324-36. METRE. This strophe corresponds to the antistrophe in **340-53.** The rhythm is predominantly ionic a minore (∪ ∪ − −), which was associated with Dionysiac rites (*cf.* Dodds on *Bacchae* 65 ff.). It also contains bacchiac feet (∪ − − : in the Iacchos cry only), cretics (− ∪ −), epitrites (− ∪ − −), and 'anaclastic' (see below) variations. See further in White, Radermacher, and Dale.

324= **340** (see n.) : ∪ − − ∪ ∪ − − ∪ ∪ − − ∪ ∪ − − : bacchiac +3 ionies a minore.

325= **341** (Iacchos cry) : ∪ − − ∪ − ⌣ : bacchiac dimeter (the final ∪ being anceps at end of metron).

326= **342** : − ∪ − ∪ ∪ − − ∪ ∪ − − : cretic + 2 ionics.

327 : ∪ ∪ − − ∪ ∪ − −. The corresponding **343/4** shows the variation ∪ ∪ − ∪ − ∪ − − in which the 4th and 5th syllables of the ionics are interchanged by 'anaclasis' : *cf.* on **329.**

328 : ∪ ∪ − − − ∪ − − : ionic + epitrite. The corresponding **345** shows the same variation as **343.**

329= **346** : ∪ ∪ − ∪ − ∪ − − : 2 anaclastic ionics (as in **343, 345**) : the 'anacreontic' metre, so called from its use by Anacreon.

330/1 : ∪ ∪ − − − ∪ − − ∪ ∪ − − : ionic + epitrite + ionic. The corresponding **347** begins ∪ ∪ − ∪ − ∪ − − with anaclasis.

332 and **333/4**= **349, 350** : ∪ ∪ − · ∪ ∪ − − : syncopated ionic + ionic.

335= **351/2** : ∪ ∪ − − ∪ ∪ − − ∪ ∪ − − ∪ ∪ − ∧ : catalectic ionic sequence.

336: anacreontic as in **329:** the corresponding **353** returns to 2 regular ionics.

324. Iacchos was a minor divinity associated with the Athenian Dionysiac processions. His name was originally, perhaps, derived from the verb 'to shout' ἰαχέω (a κ being inserted to match Βάκχος) : cf. τὸν μυστικὸν ἴακχον 'the mystic cry' in Herodotus 8, 65. According to legend he was a son of Demeter or of Persephone. Others regard Iacchos as a mystic name for Dionysos (see L.-S.-J., Tierney, and Guthrie). ἐν ἕδραις ἐνθάδε ναίων : presumably referring to the Iaccheion in the Kerameikos (see on 129) in Athens (hardly, as some have taken it, in Hades). Other allusions in the following lyrics could refer either to Attica or to Hades : e.g. the meadow (326, 343, 352, 373-4) and the brightness of the atmosphere (343). For possible Orphic-Dionysiac allusions throughout this *Parodos* see Tierney. πολυτίμητ' 'highly honoured' is Reisig's emendation for the unmetrical πολυτιμήτοις : cf. in 397.

327. ὁσίους εἰς θιασώτας : 'to the partners of your holy band'. By using reverential terms in the opening songs of this chorus Ar. makes it clear that he is not mocking the Mysteries (see § 6). Note the three words used : ὅσιος generally means (of persons) 'pious, devout, scrupulous in observing religious duties' and (of things) 'divinely sanctioned'; ἁγνός (335) 'pure' is used of purificatory ceremonies or of persons who have become ritually pure as a result of such ceremonies ; ἱερός (335) 'holy' (perhaps connected with ἴς, vis, 'strength' : cf. the Polynesian *mana*) means 'endowed with supernatural power, consecrated, or sacrosanct'. (For qualifications of these broad definitions see, e.g., J. C. Bolkestein, Ὅσιος en Εὐσεβής, Amsterdam, 1936, and A. D. Nock, *Classical Review* lii, 1938, 38.) A θίασος was a cult-association, generally Orphic-Dionysiac (see Tierney).

328-36. Rogers translates : 'Come whilst round thy forehead hurtles | Many a wreath of fruitful myrtles, | Come with wild and saucy paces | Mingling in our joyous dance, | Pure and holy, which embraces all the charms of all the Graces, | When the mystic choirs advance'. τινάσσων : vigorous movements of the head are a feature of 5th-century vase-paintings of Bacchic followers. For the Dionysiac dances see E. R. Dodds's introduction to Euripides's *Bacchae* (Oxford, 1944), x ff. μύρτων : wreaths of evergreens, especially myrtle (πολύκαρπον here because of its abundant berries), ivy, and smilax, were worn at Dionysiac festivals (perhaps primarily as a winter substitute for flowers). Athenaeus 15, 675 a ff. gives some curious lore about these wreaths and their medicinal value : he mentions one called ἴακχα for the Iacchos festival. Ar. has over 50 references to the wearing of garlands, of wild olive, violets, lilies, roses, bay, etc. ἀκόλαστον : 'unrestrained, uninhibited'. τιμήν : here 'worship, rite' : the fact that this noble word came to mean 'price, monetary value' in the 5th century indicates a decline in ideals. Note the Attic ending in -ην here (there is no MSS. authority here for the editors' *Doric* -αν, though ἀγνάν has some support in 335 and ἥβαν has good authority in 353). To introduce consistency against the MSS. begs a large question : see § 14 n. 75.

335. Χαρίτων : I take this (against most editors) as a personification and print it with a capital χ : cf. 100. (There was no distinction between capitals and minuscule letters in Ar.'s time : see § 14 n. 75.) A personification seems more apt for a religious hymn ; cf. Bacchylides 3, 71 μέρος ἔχοντα Μουσᾶν. The Charites (see Hesiod, *Theogony* 907-11) personified charm, attractiveness, gracefulness : they are introduced, says van Daele, 'où sont célébrés les jeux, la nature en fleurs, le plaisir de vivre, les danses, les festins, la musique et les chants : toutes choses qui sont du domaine de Dionysos'. ἀγνήν : see on 327.

336. μύσταις : this word, like μυστήριον, may derive from μύω 'to keep one's mouth shut' (hence μυέω : cf. μεμνημένοι in 158). 'Mystery' to us implies something hard to understand, but μυστήριον to the Greeks primarily meant something revealed only to those who had gone through special initiatory rites. If we translate μύσται as 'mystics' we must be careful not to associate modern notions of mysticism with it : 'initiates' is a safer rendering.

337-8. For the 'daughter of Demeter', Persephone, cf. on 378, 504, 671. χοιρείων κρεῶν : 'pig meat', 'pork' : pigs were the regular sacrificial victims to Demeter (perhaps as being the worst enemies to corn-fields, as goats to the vines of Dionysos) : cf. *Peace* 374-5. (Radermacher suggests that χοῖρος in its 'Corinthian usage' [L.-S.-J. i 2] is hinted at here.) μοι προσέπνευσε : 'I got a smell of . . .' : for the impersonal use with genitive of source cf. *Plutus* 1020.

339. ἤν. τι καὶ etc. : 'in case you may get some sausage as well [as a smell of pork]'. The *Assonance* in χορείαν, χοιρείων, χορδῆς, hardly amounts to a pun.

340 ff. ACTION. The Chorus now appears, carrying torches. It seems to have represented women and girls (who were apparently led by the torch-bearer : see 445-6) as well as men (who were presumably led by the *Coryphaios*, representing the Hierophant of the Mysteries). *Aristarchus* (see Σ) has stated that the Chorus was divided at 354. Just how the singing of the lyrics was apportioned is quite uncertain. Denniston (MS.) thinks that a double *Chorus* of 48 members was perhaps employed, the female half leaving after 446 (since the subsequent literary and political discussions would not concern them). But this hardly squares with the current economizing in theatre expenses (see on 404 ff.).

340. The MSS. vary greatly here, and the punctuation is uncertain. A very complex problem in textual criticism and metre (since the line should correspond to 324) arises : see especially Blaydes, Tucker, Radermacher, Coulon, and Erbse. My text follows a suggestion by Goligher : that the metrically superfluous τινάσσων of the MSS. was inserted by some copyist who took the ἔγειρε intransitively as 'awake' (referring to Iacchos), leaving λαμπάδας without a governing verb, or else it was inserted as an explanatory gloss on ἔγειρε ἐν χερσί. For the use of παρήκω='advance, come forward' see Sophocles, *Ajax* 742. We may then translate this text as : 'rouse the flaming torches in your hands [ἔγειρε being an order specially addressed to the ritual torch-bearer, δᾳδοῦχος]. Thou comest, Iacchos, O Iacchos.' ἔγειρε must have final ε̄ (before φλ) to correspond with 324 : see on metre of 680. But many other suggested emendations (based on deleting λαμπάδας or γὰρ ἥκεις) are possible. Σ notes that τινάσσων was absent in some ancient versions : which favours Goligher's line of approach.

342. φωσφόρος ἀστήρ : 'light-bearing star of our nocturnal rite' : a beautiful symbolism found also in Jewish and Christian imagery, *e.g.* in 'Lucifer, son of the morning' (Isaiah 14, 12), and in the words of Christ ἐγώ εἰμι . . . ὁ ἀστὴρ ὁ λαμπρὸς ὁ πρωϊνός (Revelation 22, 16) : see further on this star emblem in Radermacher and Tierney.

343/4. 'Now [for δὲ 'consecutive' see W. J. Verdenius in *Mnemosyne* ser. iv, ix (1956), 248] the meadow gleams with flame [*sc.* of the torches].' For φέγγεται *cf.* on 446, for λειμών *cf.* on 324.

345-50. A feeling of rejuvenation and of liberation from anxiety is often mentioned as a feature of Dionysiac influence, whether mystical (*cf. Bacchae* 187-9, 381) or simply as a result of wine-drinking (as in Horace, *Odes* 3, 21, 13-20). With 345 *cf.* Isaiah 35, 6, 'Then shall the lame man leap as an hart'. χρονίους τ' ἐτῶν παλαιῶν ἐνιαυτούς (R's reading) : 'and they [the old men] shake off the lengthy cycles of their ancient years' : a repetition of the idea of rejuvenation. The pleonastic phrase has been much challenged and emended ; but (as Radermacher notes, citing A. Wilhelm, *Wiener Sitzungsberichte* 124, 4) it can be paralleled. ἐνιαυτός (? from ἐνί and αὐτός implying 'anniversaries') perhaps means the twelve-month period of the solar year, as distinct from ἔτος, the official (archon's) year, here : *cf.* Gomme's Thucydides, vol. i (see index). For a popular definition of ἐνιαυτός see Hermippus fr. 4 ; see also Wilhelm as cited above.

350-3. The MSS. φλέγων will not fit the metrical correspondence. In 343 φλέγεται is found as a variant for the metrical φέγγεται, so Voss was doubtless right in emending φλέγων to φέγγων here. Translate 'making a radiance [see on 446] with your torch'. μάκαρ 'blessèd one' in 353 shows that Iacchos is the subject here. προβάδην : 'with forward march'. The 'flowery, marshy ground' could refer to the precinct of Dionysos ἐν Λίμναις (*cf.* on 216 ff.), or to the Thriasian Plain near Eleusis, or to the happier parts of Hades.

354-71. These anapaestic lines are probably spoken by the leader of the Chorus (*Coryphaios*) in half-serious, half-jesting imitation of the proclamation made before the beginning of mystic ceremonies to warn all who were uninitiated or impure to keep out of the way (*cf.* *Bacchae* 68 ff.). They show some resemblance to a *Parabasis*.

METRE. Catalectic anapaestic tetrameters, called τὸ Ἀριστο-φάνειον μέτρον from Ar.'s skill in using it :

∪∪ _ ∪∪ _ ∪∪ _ ∪∪ _ | ∪∪ _ ∪∪ _ ∪∪ _ _ ∧

Dactyls are allowed in the 1st, 2nd, 3rd, and 5th feet, but not preceding an anapaest (to avoid ∪∪∪∪). There is usually diaeresis after the 4th foot, as marked. See White 121 ff.

354. εὐφημεῖν : lit. 'speak well', *i.e.* avoid ill-omened words. This is often most safely achieved by saying nothing at all : so, like Horace's *favete linguis* (*Odes* 3, 1, 2), it often meant simply 'preserve a reverential silence'. Ar. frequently introduces parts of his choruses with this word (see Todd). **κἀξίστασθαι** : 'stand apart from' : *cf.* Virgil, *Aen.* 6, 258 *procul, O procul este profani*, Callimachus, *Hymn to Apollo* 2 ἑκὰς ἑκὰς ὅστις ἀλιτρός, and *Bacchae* 69-70.

356. ὄργια is governed by ἐχόρευσεν as well as by εἶδεν : 'has neither seen nor danced in the rites of the noble Muses' : *cf.* παν-νυχίοις χοροῖς in *Bacchae* 862. This Dionysiac play of Euripides has many similarities with the present chorus : *cf.* on 324 (metre), 328 ff., 345 ff., 354, 396, 400-2.

357. 'In the Bacchic tongue-rites of Cratinos, the bull-devourer' : a compliment to the greatest Athenian comic poet before Ar. Cratinos defeated Ar.'s *Clouds* in 423 and died in 422. **ταυροφάγου** probably refers to the ceremonial devouring of the raw flesh of a bull in the rites of Dionysos-Zagreus (hence one of Dionysos's cult titles was ταυροφάγος) : from it the worshippers were supposed to derive divine strength : hence the word as applied to Cratinos also implies 'vigorous', with perhaps a hint at some crudity in his work. A reference to success in winning the prize of an ox at the dithyrambic contests may also be intended.

358. βωμολόχοις : 'fit for buffoons'. Aristotle, *Nic. Ethics* 1128 a 4 ff., defines βωμολόχοι as people who are eager to be funny at all costs and who value raising a laugh above all considerations of seemliness or kindness. In this they contrast with the εὐτράπελοι who are witty, graceful, and polite. Ar. implies that he and his Chorus belong to the εὐτράπελοι. **μὴ 'ν καιρῷ τοῦτο ποιοῦσιν :** if the text is sound this presumably means 'buffoonish words [or 'verses' : see on 862] which produce their buffooneries at an unsuitable time' (*i.e.* **ποιοῦσιν**= βωμολοχευομένοις) : *cf.* the vague uses of τοῦτο in **168** and of δρᾷς in **584**. Van Leeuwen with some reason denies the possibility of this interpretation, but attempts at emendation have been unconvincing.

359. στάσις here and in **760** means 'faction, party quarrelling', the prevailing political fault of the keen-witted Greeks (in contrast with the more cohesive, blunter-minded Romans). Note other uses of the word : in **1281** it means 'a set, group, of lyrics' ; in **1401**, 'a weighing'. All are derived from various meanings of ἵστημι, transitive and intransitive. For **εὔκολος** see on **82**.

361. χειμαζομένης : 'in a storm' : for the *Metaphor* (from a ship) see on **704**. **ἄρχων :** 'while in office'. **καταδωροδοκεῖται :** 'is corrupted by bribes'. Cobet, followed by Blaydes and van Leeuwen, considered this passive form a solecism : but *cf.* the parallels in L.-S.-J. on this word and on δωροδοκῶ.

362-3. '. . . or if he exports contraband [ἀπόρρητα] from Aegina, when he's a Thorycion [reference unknown : presumably an unpopular or contemptible person] and a wretched five-per-center' (*i.e.* a customs official whose duty was to collect the special war tax put on imports and exports in **413** : see Thucydides 7, 28). It was particularly odious that a customs man should be a smuggler. Aegina, lying between the coasts of Attica and the Peloponnese, was a convenient *entrepôt* for illicit trade during the Peloponnesian War.

364. 'Oar-pads [leather bags put round oars in the rowing-ports to keep out the seas], canvas [for sails : λίνα, Latin *linum* : *cf.* 'linen'], and pitch [for caulking ships], to Epidauros' (in Argolis across the Saronic Gulf from Aegina). The naval emphasis in this passage shows how much Athens's fate in the war now depended on her ships.

366. 'Or defiles Hecate's shrines [at the cross roads, or her statues standing at the street-doors of Athenian houses] while singing in accompaniment to the dithyrambic choruses.' The details are unknown, but a crack at the incompetent and incontinent *Cinesias* is (as Σ suggests) probably intended : *cf. Eccl.* 330. For variations in the spelling of Ἑκατείων see L.-S.-J.

367. 'Or the person who when he is a politician [or 'party leader' : ῥήτωρ] proceeds to [this is the force of εἶτ'] nibble away [ἀποτρώγει is a *Metaphor* from goats or some rodent : *cf.* 988] the rewards of the poets' : or possibly (since demagogic politicians were generally advocates of higher pay for everyone then, as now) '*though* he is a party-leader, *yet* nibbles away . . .'. These rewards were given to the poets chosen to compete at the dramatic festivals (see Pickard-Cambridge, *Dramatic Festivals* 84).

368. κωμῳδηθείς : 'once he is mocked [*i.e.* in pique at being mocked] in the ancestral rites of Dionysos' (*i.e.* the comic festivals). Ar. emphasizes that the mockery on these occasions (*cf.* on 375) was not personal and malicious, but a traditional and essential part of venerable ceremonies.

369-70. τοῖς μὲν ἀπαυδῶ : 'to these I proclaim'. The chief MSS. have τούτοις ἀπαυδῶ (RUM) and τούτοις μὲν ἀπαυδῶ (A), τούτοις αὐδῶ (V). I print Blaydes's τοῖς μὲν because it explains the reading in A and gives a desirable antithesis to ὑμεῖς δ' in 370. ἀπαυδῶ elsewhere governs the accusative and takes μή with the infinitive, in the sense of 'forbid' (see L.-S.-J.). I take the use of the dative here to imply a slightly different meaning. (For the absence of μή with the infinitive Erbse refers to the similar idioms cited in Kühner-Gerth 2, 566k.) Similar proclamations in connexion with mystic processions are found elsewhere (*e.g. Bacchae* 68-9). μύσταισι here =μυστικαῖς.

372-82. Now comes a solemn processional song, to which the chorus slowly marches round the orchestra.

METRE. Entirely spondaic, except for an anapaest (to admit a proper name) in 382 (otherwise 372-6 exactly correspond with 377-82).

374-6. ἐγκρούων : 'stamping on the ground' as in 330. 'With jeers and pranks and mockery' : editors generally refer this to the ritual abuse and mockery (γεφυρισμός) exchanged by pilgrims and bystanders at the bridge (or causeway) over the river Kephisos on the Sacred Way from Athens to Eleusis. But (as Pickard-Cambridge, *Dramatic Festivals* 12, points out) similar jests and taunts were a feature of the Lenaea and Anthesteria, and were perhaps a general apotropaic rite in popular processions (as in the Roman Triumph).

376. ἠρίστηται δ' ἐξαρκούντως : 'for there has been sufficient breakfast' or, if Radermacher is right in taking **ἐξαρκούντως** as meaning 'with restraint' (as perhaps in Plato, *Gorgias* 493 c), 'our breakfasting has been with abstinence' (*i.e.* with some religious restraints, as a preparation for the mystical ceremonies). There may also be a reference to the meal given by the *Choregos* to the members of the Chorus before the performance (*cf. Acharnians* 1153), and possibly also to the spectators' breakfast (*cf. Birds* 788-9). ἀριστάω and ἄριστον (connected with ἠρι- and *early*) originally referred to the first meal of the day (later called ἀκράτισμα : see further in Wecklein 18-19 : he argues that the difference between the two was a matter of menu rather than of time).

377-8. χὦπως [= καὶ ὅπως] . . . **ἀρεῖς** etc. : 'see that you extol the Saving Goddess' (Persephone presumably : but Tierney thinks Demeter here). **γενναίως :** 'in gallant style' : see on 97.

381-2. εἰς τὰς ὥρας : 'from season to season', *i.e.* constantly and for ever. *Cf.* Gow on Theocritus 15, 74. For **Θωρυκίων** *cf.* 363.

383-4. Two catalectic anapaestic tetrameters (*cf.* on 354), probably spoken by the leader of the Chorus (*Coryphaios*). **ἰδέαν** (governed by **κελαδεῖτε**) : 'form', 'type'.

384a-93. A short hymn to Demeter in two corresponding stanzas.

METRE. (384a-88 = 389-93) 4 iambic dimeters ($\asymp - \cup - \asymp - \cup -$) + a catalectic iambic dimeter ($\asymp - \cup - \asymp - - \wedge$).

387 ff. The following infinitives may be imperatival (as in 169) or we may understand some phrase suitable for a prayer, like 'grant that . . .'.

389 ff. Here the prayer becomes more apt for the Chorus's (and author's) desire to win the comic competition than for any mystical intention. Note **γέλοια** and **σπουδαῖα** together : Ar. made this mixture of the gay and the grave the essence of his plays : *cf.* Plato, *Laws* 816 E, 'without the comic [γελοίων] it is impossible to understand the serious' (τὰ σπουδαῖα) : *cf.* § 10 n. 53.

393. ταινιοῦσθαι : 'to wear the victor's bands' : the victor in athletic or dramatic contests was decorated both with a garland of leaves and with a ribbon or headband (ταινία), which floated down like a streamer. *Cf.* Thucydides 4, 121.

394-6. METRE. 394: ∪–∪: *extra metrum*, a rhythmical echo of the Iacchos cry in 316 etc.

395-6: – – ∪– ⵜ– ∪– ⵜⵜ∪ –∪ – ⵜ: iambo-trochaic = an iambic dimeter + a trochaic 'ithyphallic': this long line was called the 'Euripidean fourteen-syllable': see Radermacher and White.

395. ὡραῖον: 'lovely', used especially of something in its finest season (ὥρα), hence often of youthful beauty. *Cf. florens Iacchus* in Catullus 64, 251.

396. ξυνέμπορον: 'fellow pilgrim': here ἔμπορος retains its primary meaning of 'traveller' as in *Odyssey* 2, 319, not 'merchant' (*cf.* on τιμήν in 334). In *Bacchae* 57 the Bacchanals are described as ξυνεμπόρους of Dionysos : *cf.* 'fellow-travellers'.

397-413. METRE. Three corresponding stanzas ending with a refrain (403 = 408 = 413), which Murray translates 'Iacchus, happy dancer, be our guide'. The rhythm is iambic.   397: ⵜ– ∪ⵜⵜ ⵜ– ∪ⵜⵜ ∪– ⵜ ∧ : catalectic iambic trimeter. 398/9 : a similar rhythm (but note the dactylic correspondence in the 3rd foot of 405). 400 : – – ∪– : iambic metron. 401 : iambic dimeter. 402 : – – ∪– ∪– – ∧ : catalectic iambic dimeter. 403 : iambic trimeter.

400-2. τὴν θεὸν: Demeter. When Ar. omits the article he uses θεά for 'goddess', *e.g.* in 384. **ἄνευ πόνου:** 'without tiredness', a feature of mystical and Bacchic exertions, mentioned in *Bacchae* 67 and 194.

404 ff. Both text and general meaning are disputed. I have adopted an eclectic version from R and V (following Tucker and Coulon), and take σὺ to refer to Iacchos as representing the festival in general. ῥάκος, then, refers to the custom of wearing old clothes (perhaps those worn at one's first initiation, see Guthrie 167 and *Plutus* 842-5) in the mystic processions. But, as a secondary meaning (as so often in Ar.), we may also probably understand that σὺ etc. hints at the stinginess of the provider of the Chorus, the *Choregos*, since owing to war-time stringencies these formerly rich citizens were finding it hard to dress the Choruses well : hence a method of sharing the expenses had to be introduced (see Σ on 404, and Pickard-Cambridge, *Dramatic Festivals* 54). Translate : 'For you have torn my little sandal and my tattered dress for the sake of laughter and economy, and have discovered the means for us to sport and dance without loss to our pockets' (ἀζημίους). Note μὲν in 404 followed by καὶ (κἀξ-) in 407 = 'both . . . and . . .': see Denniston 374.

(For objections to this general interpretation—but I still think it the best one—see especially Kock, van Leeuwen, Radermacher.)

405. σανδαλίσκον: depreciatory *Diminutive* of σάνδαλον: *cf.* in 409, 412. τόδε τὸ is Bergk's emendation of the unmetrical τόνδε τὸν of the mss. and τὸν of the Σ.

409-11. 'Yes and what's more when I glanced aside I caught a glimpse just now [νῦν δὴ: Coulon prefers νυνδὴ] of a girleen [μειρακίσκης: affectionate *Diminutive*], a specially pretty one, a partner in our sportive dance, and, through a tear in her little dress [χιτωνίου: another diminutive], her pretty breast bobbing out.' τιτθίον adds a third appreciative diminutive: Peppler notes that the men singers here use this form but a woman speaker in *Thesm.* 640 uses the matter-of-fact τιτθός. (*Cf.* Herodas 6, 71, for a feminine usage in similar circumstances.) Admiration of a shapely bosom is often expressed in Greek literature and art.

414-15. As a result of the last remark Xanthias, always interested in girls (*cf.* 515 ff.), now decides to join in the procession, and Dionysos, no misogynist either, agrees.

METRE. 414 : ∪− ∪− −∪∪ ∪− ∪− ∪− ∪− − ∧ : catalectic iambic tetrameter (or a full iambic dimeter + a catalectic iambic dimeter : *i.e.*= 401 + 402) : see on 905. 415 : an iambic trimeter.

416-39. The Chorus, having referred to mockery and jesting, now produce some. Then (431) D. breaks in, using the same metrical form, to ask the way to Pluto's house. (On this whole interlude see Wüst, and Cornford, p. 40.)

METRE. Eight corresponding three-line stanzas consisting of two catalectic iambic dimeters + an iambic trimeter (*cf.* second half of 414 + 415).

417. Archedemos, the blear-eyed (*cf.* 588), was a demagogue who came into power in 406/5. He was prominent in the indictment of the generals after *Arginusae*. For his bad character see Lysias 14, 25. If he is the same as the Archedemos described in Xenophon, *Memorabilia* 2, 9, 4 ff., we see him there in a more favourable light. See § 5.

418. Literally : 'who though seven years old has not grown his fraternity-teeth'. At the age of seven an Athenian child, if entitled by his parentage to full citizenship, was enrolled in one of the ancient Athenian tribal divisions, the φρατρίαι (cognate with Latin *frater*, and *brother*): see further on 798. Only children whose right to citizenship could be clearly proved (in 405 B.C. both parents had to be Athenians for their child to qualify) were admitted. That is one half of the pun in **φράτερας**: the other half is that a normal child of seven would have grown the kind of teeth called φραστῆρες (lit. 'tellers', because they indicate age): *cf.* Solon 25, 1. The gibe is primarily intended as a reflection on Archedemos's (alleged) non-Athenian parentage. Accusations of alien parentage were apparently rife during the anxious closing years of the War. See further in Ehrenberg, 160-1. Text: all MSS. give φράτορας, but the Σ and ancient grammarians agree that the form in -ερας is 5th-century Attic: see L.-S.-J.

420-1. 'Among the dead above': humorous (or mystical) for the normal phrase, 'the dead below'. A reference to Arginusae or to the line cited in 1477 is unlikely. τὰ πρῶτα: as in modern slang, 'he's the tops': *cf.* Lucretius 1, 86 *prima virorum*. **τῆς ἐκεῖ μοχθηρίας**: 'of the villainy there' (on earth): a παρὰ προσδοκίαν joke, since normally after τὰ πρῶτα one would expect a reference to virtue or (in the case of a politician) politics (which Ar. implicitly equates with villainy here). ⁱ

422-30. The Chorus mocks two notorious Athenians. Rogers gives the general sense as follows: 'And Cleisthenes, they say, | Is among the tombs all day, | Bewailing for his lover with a lamentable whine. | And Callias, I'm told, | Has become a sailor bold, | And casts a lion's hide o'er his members feminine.' Cleisthenes (*cf.* 48) was an effeminate person, previously mocked by Ar. in seven plays. Callias, son of Hipponikos (here comically distorted to Hippobinos: *cf. Birds* 283-6), a profligate γυναικομανής, who squandered his hereditary riches and died in poverty. 'Sebinos, the Anaphlystian' (*cf. Eccl.* 979-80), is obviously a *Comic Name* (for its etymology see 740 and L.-S.-J. at φλάω ii), like 'Hippobinos'. **πρωκτὸν τίλλειν** is a comic perversion of the phrase τρίχας τίλλειν 'to tear the hair' (as a sign of grief), with perhaps a hint of τίλλειν ἑαυτόν as a gesture of idleness (as in *Peace* 546) and effeminacy (*cf.* 516).

431-3. Dionysos interrupts in the metre of the chorus: a kind of metrical joke. **ἔχοιτ' ἄν**: 'could you': the potential optative in a question, as here, is polite: compare the non-interrogatory use (if the punctuation adopted is correct) in 437 ('Kindly take it up again'). **Πλούτων'**, the more idiomatic accusative of respect after φράσαι, is preserved only in M: the other MSS. have the nominative Πλούτων. **ὅπου 'νθάδ'**: 'whereabouts here'.

438-9. Ar. reverts for the last time in this play to the comic porter motif (*cf.* 1 ff. and on 12-15). **τουτὶ τί ἦν τὸ πρᾶγμα ἀλλ' ἤ** (R ἤ, Σ ἤ): note the interlinear *Hiatus*: I follow Neil on *Kn.* 780 and Denniston 581 in taking ἀλλ(ο) with τί and translate : 'Does this carry-on (πρᾶγμα) mean anything else after all but our old friend "Corinth child of Zeus" as far as the bedding [see on 165] is concerned ?' With 'after all' and 'our old friend' I have emphasized the force of the imperfect which I take (with Tucker) to indicate discovery of a pre-existing fact (cf. on 39). Coulon and others prefer to put a question-mark after πρᾶγμα and read ἀλλ'⟨ὰ⟩ ἢ in 439, giving the meaning 'What's this carry on here ? It's just "Corinth child of Zeus" in the baggage.' Humbert, § 239, adopting this version, explains the imperfect as 'affective', as in a phrase like 'What a nice little boy it was'. Διὸς Κόρινθος : a well-known cant-phrase (like 'Rule, Britannia' or 'the Emerald Isle') here implying 'it's always the same old story'. Apparently the Corinthians were never tired of boasting that their founder Corinthos was Zeus's son (see Σ here and on Pindar, Nemeans 7, 105 : cf. Eccl. 828). Probably a punning reference to bed-bugs (κόρεις, called 'Corinthians' in Clouds 710 : cf. 115 above) is also intended (and perhaps a reference to the fact that Corinth manufactured bedding for export). Corinth had been one of Athens's bitterest enemies for many years before this.

440 ff. ACTION. As D. and X. move forward to the door of Pluto's house (§ 9), the Chorus sings.

METRE. χωρεῖτε (extra metrum : cf. **394**). **441-6 :** iambic dimeter + ithyphallic as in **395-6**. **448-69 :** two corresponding stanzas consisting of 1 iambic dimeter + 1 catalectic iambic dimeter + 3 lines (**451-3**) of the form ⌣ − ⌣ ⌣ − ⌣ −, a choriambic rhythm (= acephalous glyconic) called 'telesillean' + 1 line of the form − − ⌣ ⌣ − ⌣, another choriambic rhythm (= acephalous pherecratean) called 'reizianum'.

441. ἱερὸν ἀνὰ κύκλον θεᾶς : 'along the sacred circular precinct of the Goddess' (Demeter). Or possibly κύκλον here means a 'dance-in-a-ring' (cf. εὐκύκλου χορείας in Thesm. 968) : θεᾶς then goes with ἄλσος.

446. φέγγος : in distinction from φῶς this word seems often to denote mystic, 'glamorous' light, as in **455**. (See Neil on Kn. 1319 and L. W. Lyde, Contexts in Pindar, Manchester, 1935.) Here it primarily refers to the gleam from the torch of the Coryphaios who speaks these lines : cf. on 343/4 above.

452-3. ὃν (understand χορὸν from καλλιχορώτατον) ὄλβιαι Μοῖραι ξυνάγουσιν : 'in the dance which the Moirai, bringers of prosperity, assemble'. For the connexion of the Moirai ('Apportioners', goddesses of fate) with Demeter and Persephone see Radermacher.

454-9. The text of these lines has been found in a Rhodian inscription (1st cent. B.C.), which agrees with the readings of R (except ἡμεῖν for ἡμῖν in 454) : see G. P. Carratelli, *Dionysos* viii (1940), 119, and *cf. Revue des Études Grecques* lix/lx (1946/7), 335-6. **μόνοις . . . ἡμῖν** : 'to us alone', *i.e.* only the Initiates enjoy a radiant, happy life after death : *cf.* Pindar, fr. 114 and Sophocles, fr. 753. But initiation alone is not considered here to be a guarantee of these blisses : a life of reverence and respect to one's neighbours is also necessary. **φέγγος ἱερόν** : so RV and the Rhodian inscription as in 446 : other MSS. have ἱλαρόν, which was perhaps inserted by a Christian scribe from the phrase φῶς ἱλαρὸν ἁγίας δόξης in the beautiful and popular early-Christian vesper hymn. **εὐσεβῆ τε διήγομεν τρόπον περὶ** : 'were faithful [*i.e.* when we were alive] in showing respect towards' or 'used to preserve a habit of respect towards'. εὐσεβής approximates to ὅσιος 'pious' (*cf.* on 327) here. **ξένους . . . ἰδιώτας** : 'strangers and unpolitical people' : these were the two most vulnerable kinds of people in Athens, those with no civic rights at all and those who had no political 'pull'. **ἰδιώτας** : literally men who through diffidence, or slackness, or self-centredness, took little or no part in political affairs : see further on 891. (Possibly, as Tierney suggests, it means non-initiated people, 'laity', here.) Ar. also, perhaps, hints at his practice of not allowing his Choruses to attack humble, defenceless 'men-in-the-street' (ἰδιώτας ἀνθρωπίσκους, *Peace* 751).

460 ff. ACTION. D. and X. have now arrived at the door of Pluto's house (§ 9), where an alarming encounter with Aeacus (see on 465) awaits them. D., who has lost his confidence in knocking at doors (contrast 37 ff.), hesitates and wonders how he can best imitate the local custom (461). X., always quick to detect any failure of nerve in his master, brusquely advises him to knock without delay.

461. ἐνθάδ' : in Hades. **ἄρα** adds liveliness to the question and forecasts the effect of learning the answer : translate : 'If I only knew how the local people knock here'. **οὐπιχώριοι** : Crasis for οἱ ἐπι- ; *cf.* οὑμοί in *Kn.* 1003).

462-3. οὐ μή : *cf.* on 202-3. **γεῦσαι** (so *Hesychius* : -ση R : γεῦσαι V, etc.) : 'take a bite of'. **σχῆμα . . . λῆμα** : *Assonance.* Merry translates 'fashion and passion'. Mr. B. K. Wilson has suggested 'figure and vigour'. **καθ'** : 'according to, like' : not often so used with proper names.

464 ff. Here a characteristically irascible door-keeper (like a college porter) comes out and abuses D. In all MSS. except V this character is called Aeacus. But V (and Σ) calls him 'a servant' θεράπων. Perhaps this was due to a reluctance to have

a great hero and one of the three great judges of the dead acting
a menial part. But this objection is not valid for comic bur-
lesque : Hermes plays a similar role and uses some identical
language in *Peace* 180 ff. : so, too, St. Peter in Christian humour.
Besides, some parody of Euripides's (or Critias's) *Peirithous* (in
which Aeacus met Heracles in Hades) may be intended in this
scene. (*Cf.* Lucian, *Menippus* 1 and *Dialogues of Dead* 20, 1 :
also Radermacher, Schmid 340, 7, and Pauly-Wissowa at *Janitor*.)

465 ff. Aeacus, deceived by D.'s lion-skin and club, takes him
for Heracles (who had once stolen his watch-dog Cerberus, **467-8**),
and pours out a wonderful flood of picturesque abuse (perhaps
spoken at high speed in a grim, rasping voice : *cf.* § **10** n. **44**).
His tirade begins in mainly comic style (vocabulary, metre, and
imagery). It develops into tragic parody in **470 ff.** (see below).
Cf. Hermes's language in *Peace* 180 ff.

468. ἀπῆξας (ἀπάσσω : a word of elevated diction) . . . κάπο-
δράς (2 aor. part. ἀποδιδράσκω): note the regular -άς in the first
form and -ᾱς in the second : *cf.* **130**. This line, as Merry notes, is
entirely composed of verb-forms, showing Aeacus's furious energy.

469. ἐγώ : emphatic, '*I* was responsible for guarding it'
(Cerberus). ἔχει μέσος : lit. 'You are held by the middle', *i.e.*
'You are firmly gripped' (*cf. Clouds* 1047) : a *Metaphor* from
wrestling (but not quite= English 'I have you on the hip', which
refers more to throwing than to gripping).

470-8. With τοία (tragic or epic style for τοιαύτη) Aristophanes
begins a choice passage of tragic *Parody*. Although Σ refers
some of it to the *Theseus* of Euripides, in general it more closely
resembles some of Aeschylus's more bombastic moments (*e.g.*
fr. 281, *cf.* Stanford, *Aeschylus* 9 ff.) : note especially the long
compounds (*cf.* Earp 6-38) : 'black-hearted' (**470**), 'blood-
dripping' (**471**), 'round-racing' (**472**), 'hundred-headed' (**473**) ;
the three-word lines (see on **204**) in **471, 474, 476, 477** ; the
impressive use of geographical adjectives in **471, 475, 477**, and
the gory references to blood and entrails. But the fulsome
phrase in **478** 'I shall launch the speeding foot' (for 'I shall
hasten ') rather parodies the style of Sophocles (as, *e.g.*, *Ajax* 40,
369) and Euripides (*e.g. Orestes* 45). Into this pseudo-solemn
farrago Ar. inserts some comically incongruous elements : see
on **475, 477**. It would probably be fatuous to enquire what
exactly Ar. meant by the 'Acherontian peak' (**471** : *cf.* on **137**),
'the dogs of Cocytus' (**472**), and 'the hundred-headed viper'
(**473** : *cf.* Hesiod, *Theog.* 297) : they are picturesque mouthfuls
rather than precise descriptions. For the earliest references to
the rivers of Hades see *Od.* 10, 512 ff. For the parody in general
see further in Radermacher and *cf. Birds* 1706-19.

474 looks like an echo of Sophocles, *Trach.* 778 σπαραγμὸς αὐτοῦ πλευμόνων ἀνθήψατο.

475. Ταρτησσία (the MSS. have -ησία) μύραινα : 'the Tartessian eel' : a brilliant Aristophanic medley of terror and triviality. 'Tartessian' literally means 'from Tartessos' (a town in Spain, at first more or less fabulous, then localized at Cadiz : good eels, a delicacy for Athenian tables, came from there). But in this context the word also suggests Tartaros (and possibly Τιταρήσιος, a river associated with the Styx in *Iliad* 2, 751 ff.). So, too, μύραινα combines delectable with terrifying associations. As food it was considered a delicacy ; but in the water it was known to be a dangerous, greedy creature, quick to attack divers : *cf.* Aeschylus, *Choëph.* 994 and the many references in D'A. W. Thompson's *Glossary of Greek Fishes* 162-5. Thompson identifies it with the murry (or moray) eel, *Muraena helena*, an evil-looking fish with wicked temper and poisonous bite, as modern undersea explorers have found to their cost.

477. Γοργόνες Τειθράσιαι : another mixture of the terrible and the trivial. The hideous and dreadful Gorgon-sisters of Greek legend are ludicrously called Teithrasian, from the Attic deme celebrated for dried figs (*cf.* Athenaeus 652 f) and perhaps (to guess from Ar.'s phrase here) for ugly, scolding old women.

479 ff. Aeacus's abuse alarms D. so much that his already disturbed bowels (*cf.* 308) again react to his terror. Some comic *Business* follows with a sponge (normally used for cleansing but also for relieving pain : see Hippocrates, *Reg. Acut.* 21, 8). What is especially astonishing for modern readers in this Rabelaisian passage is that Ar. comically distorts two religious phrases to fit this context. First, ἐγκέχοδα (perf. ἐγ-χέζω)· κάλει θεόν, translatable as 'I have done my order : summon the god', parodies the formula used after pouring a libation, ἐκκέχυται· κάλει θεόν. (If, as Σ says, this formula was specially used by the Torchbearer at the Lenaea, it would have special aptness here in a Lenaean comedy.) Secondly, ὦ χρυσοῖ θεοί (for the colour *cf.* on 308), 'Ye golden gods', deliberately misappropriates a religious phrase. (For the popular belief that the actual substance of the gods was gold see H. L. Lorimer in *Greek Poetry and Life : Essays presented to Gilbert Murray*, Oxford, 1936, 14-33). No blasphemous or malicious intention towards Greek religion need be inferred from such usages : see § 6.

482. οἶσε : this imperative of φέρω is found only in epic and comedy. (For these imperatives formed from futures see M. Leumann in *Glotta* xxxii, 1952, 204 ff.) πρὸς τὴν καρδίαν : D. pretends it is his heart that is affected by the shock ; but he does not deceive Xanthias, or anyone else, in what follows. Apparently a damp sponge was applied to the heart as a restorative at times.

483. ἰδού: see on **200.** The division of this line between X. and D. is uncertain : the MSS. disagree. But προσθοῦ, middle, 'apply it for yourself' must be said to D. I follow Coulon. ποῦ 'στιν (Aphaeresis) : 'Where have you put it ?'

485. τὴν κάτω . . . κοιλίαν : the Hippocratic physicians distinguished upper and lower sections of the greater intestine : cf. Hippocrates, Reg. Acut. 50, 10-11.

486-91. The style and metre of 486-7 imply tragic parody. ὅστις : lit. 'being the sort of man who . . .'. The kind of thing the other sort of man (i.e. the coward, as D. sees it) would do is described in **489.** X.'s γε in **491** is 'exclamatory-sarcastic' (Denniston 128).

493 ff. ACTION. When X. has proclaimed his scorn for Aeacus's threats, D. thinks of a plan to save himself from the threatened catastrophes. He suggests that X. should change costumes and roles with him. This appeals to X.'s love of trickery. He accepts (and at the same time Ar. prepares the way for a nice reversal in 503 ff.).

494. ληματιᾷς : 'have passion for boldness' (cf. λῆμα in **463** and **500**) : verbs in -ιάω generally imply a morbid craving or condition (cf. in **192**).

495. Note τὸ before ῥόπαλον : this lengthening of a short vowel before ρ is regular in Ar. (cf. **406, 1059, 1066**), the only exception (according to White 366) being Wasps 1067.

496. ἀφοβόσπλαγχνος : 'unfearful-hearted'. The compound occurs only here : probably a Coined Word for mock-heroic effect.

498. φέρε δή : best taken (cf. φέρε νῦν in **502**) as 'Well, come on . . .' (like ἄγε δή), understanding δός with αὔτ' (= club and lion-skin). For οὐ γὰρ ἀλλά see on **58.**

499. καί = 'now' : there would be a moment or two of silence before this, for the exchange of costume. τὸν Ἡρακλειοξανθίαν : 'your Xanthiheracles' : for the pompous compound cf. Aristotle, Poetics 1457 a 36.

501. 'By heaven, I'm sure you won't be that, but genuinely the scoundrel from Melite ' : a deme lying S.W. of the Agora containing a very renowned shrine of Heracles. Instead of saving ' genuinely the hero ', Ar. substitutes μαστιγίας, lit. ' one who needs a whipping ' (Latin verbero : cf. **756**), as a comic surprise. (But a scholiast sees here a reference to Callias, whom

Cratinos called ὁ ἐκ Μελίτης στιγματίας : cf. 428 and see further in Radermacher.)

503 ff. ACTION. Now comes a surprise. Instead of the furious Aeacus, as expected, a friendly manservant (see next note) enters, welcomes Xanthiheracles, and invites him to a banquet with Persephone (ἡ θεός in 504)—much to Dionysoxanthias's chagrin.

503. θεράπων : I follow a scholiast and Werres 44 in rejecting the θεράπαινα of the MSS. here. As Werres notes, women do not normally swear by Apollo (see 508) in Ar. (note the masculine imputation in *Eccl.* 155-160 and in *Lys.* 917) : also 513-14 and 516 come better from a man.

505 ff. Note the different methods of cooking mentioned here : πέττω (also πέπτω)='bake' (also 'soften, ripen, digest') ; ἕψω= 'boil, seethe' ; ἀπανθρακίζω='broil, roast' (on a wood fire or charcoal) ; ὀπτῶ='bake, roast', ἀναβράττω (510) 'stew' ; φρύγω (511) 'toast' (cf. φρύγανα 'dry sticks'). All these verbs are used causatively here in the sense 'made the cook bake' etc., as 517 shows. Artistic cooking was always done by a man in ancient Greece : and, besides, Persephone was Queen of Hades. As was fitting for the feasts of Dionysos, the Greek comedians often described lavish feasts. Cooking was already a fine art in the time of Ar. Notable contemporary writers on the subject were Archestratos of Sicily (famous for its chefs and cuisines) and Philoxenos of Leucadia (some fragments of his *Banquet*, with a menu and cooking instructions, survive).

507. I have punctuated to indicate an uncompleted sentence, as otherwise the *Asyndeton* is rather awkward here. For descriptions of πλακοῦντες, 'honey-cakes', see Athenaeus 643 e.

508. κάλλιστ' [understand some word like ἔχει], ἐπαινῶ : 'It's all right, thanks' : a formula for polite refusal, like πάνυ καλῶς in 512. X.'s reason for declining the invitation is not clear. Perhaps he fears his master's wrath (cf. 522 ff.) ; perhaps he anticipates detection by Persephone. But when he hears about the flute-girl and the dancing-girls (513-14) he cannot resist. Note the *Synizesis* in 'Απόλλω_οὐ. Compare the *Crasis* in 509 (for περιόψομαι ἀπ. : *Porson's* emendation of the unmetrical elision in MSS.), 511 κῷνον (καὶ οἶνον), and 518 χἡ (καὶ ἡ) : in each case what looks like a breathing is a 'coronis' marking crasis (as an apostrophe marks elision). οὐ μὴ with the 1st person future here in denial (a mixture of affirmation and apprehension : Humbert, § 655).

509-10. ἐπεί τοι καί : 'especially when she is actually' [καί, in climax to what has been described in 505-7] : cf. Denniston 297.

515. ἕτεραι : 'as well', implying 'to complete the party' since music and dancing naturally went together. Illustrations of flute-girls and dancers at banquets often occur on 5th-century vases.

516. 'Nicely in the bloom of youth [ἡβυλλιῶ is a comic form, based on an affectionate *Diminutive* of ἥβη] and freshly plucked' (παρατίλλω='remove superfluous hair').

517-18. See on 505 ff.   **τεμάχη** (*cf.* τέμνω)='slices of fish' : *cf.* on 1041.   **ἔμελλ'**='was just going to' (*i.e.* when the speaker left the kitchen).   **ἀφαιρεῖν**='take off [the fire]'.   **εἰσήρετο** : small tables were brought to each guest.   **τράπεζα** : originally 'the piece of furniture with four feet', from *τετρά-πεζος.

519-20. X. shows lack of manners in addressing his acceptance to the dancing-girls and not to Persephone.   **αὐτός** : here in its special sense of 'the master', 'boss', as in *Clouds* 218, fr. 268, and in the Pythagorean αὐτὸς ἔφα, 'The Master said'. Note *Hiatus* in ὅτι εἰσέρχομαι, as regularly after τι, ὅτι, and περί in comedy : *cf.* on 22 and see Descroix 28-9.

521-3. ὁ παῖς : in a lordly tone, followed by a verb in the 2nd person as elsewhere : see on 40. How joyfully X., after all his earlier tribulations with the baggage, gives this order to D.! But D., ever fickle, refuses to bear the consequences of his change of role.   **οὔ τί που** etc. : 'Surely you are not taking the fact that I jokingly dressed you up as Heracles seriously?' For οὔ τί που in this kind of incredulous or reluctant question *cf.* 526. RAM have ποεῖς (see on 13) not ποεῖ here : but the middle form seems necessary in this periphrasis for σπουδάζειν='take it seriously that . . .' (*cf.* Plato, *Phaedrus* 236 B).

527. οὐ τάχ', ἀλλ' etc. : 'There's no perhaps about it : I'm doing it here and now'. τάχα is almost a noun here as in Ar. fr. 869 τάχας 'perhapses'.

528-9. ταῦτ' ἐγὼ μαρτύρομαι : 'Well I, for my part, call for witnesses to this (outrage)'. Athenians were quick to take legal action. X. (who speaks as if he were a free citizen here) would need a witness to prove his case against D.   **ἐπιτρέπω** 'I entrust my cause to', *i.e.* he leaves it to the god to see that justice is done : *cf.* the title of Menander's play Ἐπιτρέποντες, *People seeking arbitration.*

529. ποίοις θεοῖς : not just 'what kind of gods', but, as similar uses elsewhere show, contemptuously 'gods, indeed'. D. as a god himself feels he needn't worry about them. *Cf.* πόθεν in 1455, and further in van Leeuwen.

530. The punctuation (which I take from Tucker's note) im-plies a mixture of an exclamatory accusative and infinitive (as in

741) and a parenthetical question : 'To think that you—isn't
it silly and senseless ?—should expect that though you're a slave
and a mortal you would be Alcmene's son [Heracles] !' Lenting
(whom Coulon follows) thinks it necessary to read Ἀλκμήνης
(= ὁ 'Αλκ.), perhaps rightly. The line (like 533) is in tragic style.

532. X. (in a tone of resignation) : 'Never mind. It's all
right. Keep them' (the lion-skin and club).

534 ff. The Chorus, impressed by D.'s quick changes of policy
and costume, sing an ode in praise of the versatile man (but Ar.,
of course, is being ironical), leading up to a crack at the turn-
coat *Theramenes*.

METRE. Trochaic dimeters with catalectic trochaic dimeters
in **535, 538, 539b, 541, 544b, 547, 548b.** This strophe corresponds
to **589a** ff. Note the symmetrical arrangement of 2 full dimeters
+ 1 catalectic dimeter in 3 groups, concluded by 1 group of 1 full
dim. + 1 catalectic dim. (an 'epodic tetrad' : see Dale 187).

535 ff. A *Metaphor* from the navy in which so many Athenian
citizens had to serve during the War. For figurative references
to ships *cf.* **361, 704-5.** μετακυλίνδειν : 'roll over', μετα-
indicating change as in **538.** τὸν εὖ πράττοντα τοῖχον : 'the
comfortable side (of the ship)'. 'Rather than stay fixed like a
graven image' : *cf.* Coleridge, *Ancient Mariner,* 'As idle as a
painted ship | Upon a painted ocean'.

540-1 : 'is the way of a dexterous fellow and a born Thera-
menes', *i.e.* naturally endowed with Theramenes's adaptability
(*cf.* **967** below). Opinions differ greatly on this adroit politician
(§ 5). Against Lysias's indictment (12, 62-80) stands Aristotle's
praise in *Ath. Pol.* 28, 5. But whatever the rightness or wrongness
of his principles and methods, all agree on his agility as a politician:
hence his nickname ὁ κόθορνος, the boot that will fit either foot
(*cf.* on **47**).

543-5. στρώμασιν Μιλησίοις : 'on Milesian bed-clothes'.
Miletos, chief city of Ionia, was renowned for the softness of its
wool : *cf.* Theocritus 15, 125 ff. ἀνατετραμμένος : 'lying on his
back '. With these lines *cf.* Hermippos, fr. 82.

542-8. Rogers renders : 'Truly an exquisite joke 'twould be, |
Him with a dancing girl to see, | Lolling at ease on Milesian rugs ; |
Me, like a slave, beside him standing, | Aught that he wants to
his lordship handing ; | Then as the damsel fair he hugs, | Seeing me
all on fire to embrace her, | He would perchance (for there's no
man baser), | Turning him round like a lazy lout, | Straight on my
mouth deliver a facer, | Knocking my ivory choirmen out '. τοὺς
χοροὺς τοὺς προσθίους : lit. 'my rows [of teeth], the front ones '.

χορός is used in this way for 'row' elsewhere. The notion of 'teeth' would be suggested by the previous mention of a 'bash on the jaw'. The emendation τοῦ χοροῦ (= 'out of their row') makes smoother Greek, but is superfluous.

549 ff. ACTION. Now Ar. introduces a further reversal. D., having resumed the garb of Heracles, is just about to go in to Persephone's feast, when an irate female innkeeper rushes out and denounces him (as Heracles) for fraud and damages to her inn during his previous visit. She is accompanied by another innkeeper called Plathane (coined from πλάθανον, a mould for baking cakes or bread in : hence Tucker aptly renders 'Patty' : see on 551-2). Each of these women is probably followed by a maidservant : see on 570. Note that four actors (with silent attendants) take part in this scene as in 1411 ff. The three-actor rule of tragedy does not hold for comedy.

551. 'Sixteen' : a round number here as elsewhere (see Radermacher) : *cf.* on 50.

551-2. I follow Coulon (and MU) in calling this character 'Second Innkeeper' : RVA call her Plathane (from 549). Some editors think that there is only one innkeeper (549) with a maidservant named Plathane (here) : but against this view see on 570.

552. κακὸν ἥκει : 'trouble has arrived' (not 'is coming'). Naturally X. is delighted (as in 554) that D. will have cause to regret his change of policy.

553-4. ἀνάβραστ' : from ἀναβράττω (see on 505 ff.). **ἀν' ἡμιωβολιαῖα,** 'at the rate of half-an-obol apiece', is the reading suggested by Kuster from Pollux 9, 64, for RVA's ἀνημιωβολιαῖα and MVU's ἀνημιωβολιμαῖα. The grammatical correctness of these terms has been much disputed : but perhaps the speaker here is not a pure-bred Athenian (Plathane looks like a metic's name). ἀνά= 'at the rate of' is regular (but it normally goes with a noun or a number, not an adjective as here : see L.-S.-J.). For the value of the loaves *cf.* Eupolis, fr. 154 ἡμιωβολίου κρέα. See further in Radermacher.

556. μὲν οὖν : these particles with οὐ, as here, indicate a negative deduction from a preceding statement : ' On the contrary you didn't expect . . .', as in 1188. Contrast on 612.

557. κοθόρνους : see on 47. **ἂν γνῶναι :** Elmsley's emendation of ἀναγνῶναι.

559. ' Yes, by heaven, and you haven't yet mentioned the *cheese* [γ'], the fresh stuff.' **τάλαν :** best taken as '(you) poor thing ' : this neuter form is only used by women in Ar. : see

Wilamowitz, *Das Schiedsgericht* 74. Contrast the feminine in 565.

560. αὐτοῖς τοῖς ταλάροις : 'with even the baskets as well' : for the sociative dative see on 226-7. Fresh cheese was hung in baskets to dry (*cf. Od.* 9, 247). In Ion's *Omphale* Heracles the glutton (§ 8) devoured the fire-wood and coals as well as the roasting meat. Note the vivid imperfects here and in **561, 562** (with ἔβλεψεν as a contrasting aorist 'He gave me a fierce look, and kept on roaring'), **564** ('he set about drawing his sword') : the speaker is revisualizing each process as it happened. Contrast the 'factual' aorist in **551** and the 'instantaneous' aorists in the climax **566-7** : and *cf.* W. B. Sedgwick, *Classical Quarterly* xxxiv (1940), 122.

562-4. Note καὶ . . . γε here and in **564** : 'Yes, and what's more . . .'. It is varied with δὲ . . . γε (565, 567) : 'Yes, and then . . .'. Tucker suggests (and Denniston agrees) that these particles indicate 'feminine emphasis' : *cf.* Queen Victoria's fondness for underlining words in her letters.

564-5. μαίνεσθαι δοκῶν : 'looking like a madman'. (Not 'pretending to be mad' : δοκῶ in that sense is usually found in a negative sentence, and Heracles was not given to pretence.) *Cf.* the madness of the hero in Euripides's *Heracles*. δεισάσᾱ : a rare feminine dual form. που : 'somehow' : her memory of the alarming affair is confused. Or perhaps, as van Leeuwen suggests, she cannot understand how they could have been frightened at a Heracles like *this* one (D.). R's reading, πω, hardly makes sense, unless it is 'metic Greek' as in **554**.

566-7. The κατῆλιψ was, apparently, a broad beam or shelf running from wall to wall, near the ceiling in the main room of a house (*cf.* the Homeric μεσόδμη) : it was used mainly for storage (as in West of Ireland cottages today). ψίαθοι were rush-mats supplied in inns as foundations for travellers' bed-clothes (see on 165).

568 ff. The division of the following dialogue among the various speakers has been much disputed since ancient times. Possibly the text is interpolated in places. I follow Coulon's arrangement except in **571, 574, 577** (see notes).

568. ἀλλ' ἐχρῆν etc. : 'Well, we should have been doing something (about it)' : imperfect of neglected duty (or of delayed recognition).

569-70. ἴθι δὴ . . . σὺ δ' . . .: it seems best to take these commands as addressed to the two innkeepers' attendants. προστάτην : the word has two possible meanings here : (a) 'official protector', *i.e.* an influential Athenian citizen chosen by a resident alien (who would not have full political rights) to protect his interests, like a Roman *patronus* or an undergraduate's tutor ; (*b*) 'leader of the people', a kind of unofficial *tribunus plebis* (as *Cleon* and *Hyperbolos* were, in succession, during their lifetime : both are now dead). Ehrenberg 151 and 353 thinks both meanings are intended here and in *Peace* 684. But only the first meaning seems necessary in the present context.

570-1. The better mss., except V, indicate no change of speaker for this line. V indicates Plathane, presumably intending the Second Innkeeper. Tucker argues strongly, but, I think, wrongly, for Dionysos as the speaker. Some editors delete this line and 574. I follow V and Coulon. σὺ δ', then, refers to Plathane's maidservant (such as normally accompanied respectable women out-of-doors : see Radermacher). In dividing 571 between the two Innkeepers I follow what seems to be the implication of RUAM. φάρυξ (the spelling of the better mss. here and in 259 for more common φάρυγξ) : 'throat, gullet', here='glutton, greedy gut'. As Professor L. J. D. Richardson (to whom I also owe many other helpful comments) points out, the genitive form φάρυγος supports the better mss. tradition here, while the contrasting λάρυγγος attests the nominative λάρυγξ (see on 575).

572-3. τοὺς γομφίους κόπτοιμ' ἄν : 'could bash your molars' (lit. wedge-shaped teeth : from γόμφος).

574. I follow the 'τινές' mentioned by Σ, in giving this line to D. Ar. dislikes leaving an actor silent for long in a scene like this. The optative here expresses a wish, while those with ἄν in 573 and 575 mean 'I would if I could'. The βάραθρον was a ravine outside the S.-W. walls of Athens into which the bodies of criminals were thrown.

575. The λάρυγξ in strict medical usage was the upper part of the windpipe, the larynx, but here it may be merely a synonym for φάρυξ 'gullet' (571).

577-8. αὐτοῦ . . . ἐκπηνιεῖται ταῦτα : a horrifying expression : 'will wind these things out of him'. ἐκπηνίζομαι is derived from πηνίον 'spool of thread' (*cf.* on 1315). Perhaps the Innkeeper is thinking of something like the vengeance taken (according to the *Burnt Njal Saga*) on the slayer of King Brian Boru at Clontarf : 'Wolf the quarrelsome . . . wound all the entrails out of him'. (And *cf.* the song of the witches after the battle : 'The woof is y-woven | With entrails of men'.) προσκαλούμενος : 'with a summons to court' (*cf.* *Wasps* 1406, with a similar reference to theft of φορτία).

579 ff. Action. The two Innkeepers now go out. D. shame-

lessly tries to coax X. into undertaking the role of Heracles
again. X., after some sarcastic references to D.'s earlier remarks
(with 582-3 *cf.* 530-1), agrees.

580-1. Note X.'s emphatic repetitions here. In 581 the second
ἅν ironically emphasizes the impossibility of his becoming a
Heracles, *cf.* 530-1. τὸν νοῦν : 'your idea' or 'scheme' as in 47.

581-2. μηδαμῶς : 'Don't' (understand 'say that'). Ξανθίδιον :
'dear Xanthy-wanthy' : an affectionate *Diminutive*. One would
expect the first ι to be long (from Ξανθι-ίδιον), but perhaps
it is shortened by analogy with forms like Σωκρατίδιον, Εὐριπίδιον
(or else we could delete ὦ with Meineke).

587-8. With the exception of the παρὰ προσδοκίαν ending 'and
the blear-eyed Archedemos' (see on 417), these lines more or less
follow the usual formula for imprecatory oaths of this kind (for
examples see Blaydes). For the tree *Metaphor* in πρόρριζος
('by the root', 'root and branch') *cf.* 902. *Asyndeton* seems to
be regular in this kind of phrase : *cf.* 157, 1408. γλάμων (probably
cognate with English 'clammy') 'blear-eyed' (*cf.* γλαμός 'mucus,
slime'). Note the *Comic Termination* in -ων (like others in
-ιων, -ω, -ιας, -ᾶς, -ᾶξ : *cf.* on 200, 909, and in 1074, and see
Peppler).

589a ff. The Chorus and X. sing in turn on the need for
courage and caution in playing the role of Heracles.

METRE.   Corresponding to 533-48 (but see on 592 below).

591-2. It is uncertain whether ἐξ ἀρχῆς πάλιν lit. 'from the
beginning again' should go with εἴληφας or ἀνανεάζειν. On the
whole the second seems preferable and I have so punctuated.
(The phrase should not be divided : *cf. Peace* 1327, *Plutus* 221.)
ἀνανεάζειν : 'recover your youthful [*i.e.* bold and vigorous]
spirit' : *cf.* νεάζειν in *Agamemnon* 764 (with Fraenkel's note).
If the line is to correspond strictly with 536, words scanning
‒ ◡ ‒ ◡ must have originally followed this word : but against
this see Dale 197 ; and the sense does not require any addition.

594b. I have printed Radermacher's ἀλῶς ἤ for ἁλώσῃ (or -ει)
in RVM.

595. κἀκβάλῃς τι μαλθακόν : 'you even let fall some faint-
hearted word' : *cf. Wasps* 1289. (RAU have καὶ βάλῃς.)

597. Dawes's 'σται for V's 'στί is metrically necessary : the
other chief MSS. omit the word.

599b-601. 'What's more [μὲν οὖν here is perhaps not quite
so 'corrective' as in 241], if anything good [for χρηστὸν see on

735] comes [*sc.* out of the following events : X. knows that D. is an out-and-out opportunist], he will try to take this gear back from me—I know it well.' The double ὅτι does not seem to be impossible here, especially after συννοούμενος at the end of the previous sentence : but Coulon may be right in adopting Blaydes's ὅδε for the first ὅτι. For εὖ οἶδ' ὅτι at the end of a sentence like this *cf. Lysis.* 154. Note colloquial *Hiatus.*

604. βλέποντ' ὀρίγανον : 'with a mustardy look' : a comic version of phrases like βλέπειν δριμύ (562), τὸ δεινόν (593) : for variations see *Kn.* 631, *Wasps* 455, *Peace* **1184** (*cf.* 'of such vinegar aspect' in Shakespeare, *Merchant of Venice* **1**, 1, 54). The comic compound βλεπεδαίμων 'with the look of a ghost' shows a further development. ὀρίγανον is marjoram, a pungent herb used in cooking (*cf. Ach.* 874).

604b. καὶ δή : 'just as I expected'. For this use *cf.* **1018**, and contrast that in **647**. (I follow Denniston, MS., here.)

605 ff. ACTION. Aeacus returns accompanied by at least two (dual in **606, 607**) personal attendants. He orders them to bind 'Heracles'. X. first shows fight (**607**). But when Aeacus calls up some police as reinforcements (**608-9**), X. tries to deny that he ever came to Hades before or stole Cerberus (**612-14**, *cf.* **605**). To prove his innocence he makes a 'gentlemanly offer' (see on **615**). There is uncertainty about the speakers in this dialogue. I mainly follow Coulon.

606. D. gleefully repeats (with slight variation for metrical reasons) X.'s phrase in **552**.

607. I have printed the usual punctuation. A. Y. Campbell in *Classical Review* lvii (1943), 58-61 supports Verrall's suggestion (followed by Tucker) that one should take οὐκ with μὴ πρόσιτον (the verb then being future dual, not imperative as in the usual punctuation) as an emphatic prohibition (*cf.* on **202**), with ἐς κόρακας (*cf.* on **187**) as an interjection (*cf.* English 'What the devil are you doing ?'). Tucker quotes good parallels for this ; and it may be right. εἰέν : 'O-ho !' : note the curious internal aspiration as in the Bacchic cry εὐοῖ (acc. to Apollonius Dyscolus : Latin *euhoe*). καὶ μάχει : 'you're even offering resistance, are you ?' For καὶ *cf.* on **170**.

608. Ditýlas (*cf.* τύλη 'a thickening of the skin', 'a callus'), Skeblyas (*cf.* κέβλος 'baboon'), Pardokas (*cf.* πορδή and Strabo **13**, 2, 6 : V has a *v.l.* Σπαρδόκας, which Blaydes compares with Spartacus), are probably parodies of Scythian or Thracian names (*cf. Wasps* 433, and further in Radermacher). In 5th-century Athens Scythian archers were employed as police.

610-11. τουτονί (see on 19), meaning X., is the subj. of τύπτειν (here='strike a policeman'). μάλλ' [see on 103] ὑπερφυᾶ : 'Shocking ? I call it monstrous.'

612. μὲν οὖν : 'I'd go further and say it's stubborn and . . . shocking' : cf. on 241 and on 116. If the text is sound, D. is so much overcome by indignation (or pretends to be so) that he can't think of a stronger word to describe X.'s outrageous conduct, and falls back on his original δεινά (Bathos).

615 ff. ACTION. With the words καί σοι etc., 'What's more [καί : cf. on 170], I'll make you a very gentlemanly [for γενναῖον see on 97] offer', X. introduces a masterpiece of roguery. Making use of the Attic law that a master might allow his slave to be tortured to determine the truth of an accusation (the πρόκλησις εἰς βάσανον, a sombre aspect of 5th-century society in Athens), X. handsomely offers his 'slave' D. for torture. If he (X.) is proved in this way to have done any injustice (**617**), he consents to be executed at once. We can imagine how D. squirms at this development.

618 ff. A list of permissible tortures (with a comic diversion in **621-2**) : (a) tying the victim to a ladder and letting him hang from it (but some take this as only a preliminary to whipping, which, perhaps, the aorist participles indicate here : some think the κλῖμαξ was not an ordinary ladder but a framework specially made for torture : see L.-S.-J.) ; (b) whipping with a ὑστριχίς (conn. w. ὑστριξ 'porcupine'), i.e. a lash with bristles (for its effect on the victim's back see Peace 747) ; (c) 'flaying', perhaps a synonym for (b), or else literally 'skinning' ; (d) twisting or stretching the limbs presumably on some kind of 'rack' ; (e) pouring vinegar into the nostrils, which is not a comic touch, as some have thought : see A. D. Nock in Classical Review xli (1927), 58 ; (f) 'putting on bricks' : in this it is uncertain whether the pain resulted from the increasing weight on the body (the medieval peine forte et dure) or from the fact that the bricks were heated first.

621-2. 'All the other tortures—except you're not to beat this fellow with leek-stalks or young onions' : a parody of the reservations which a merciful master would make. Here the excepted 'tortures' would not, of course, be painful at all. These exceptions may be sheer fancy ; but some editors (see especially Radermacher) see a reference to kathartic rites (as, e.g., in Hipponax 5 and Theocritus 7, 106).

623-5. 'That's a fair offer, and if I cripple your slave in any way . . .' : Aeacus recognizing the generosity of X.'s offer makes an equally generous reply. τἀργύριον : money lodged by the

accuser with the court officials in a legal action of this kind :
cf. Knox-Headlam on Herodas 2, 89. **κείσεται** : 'will be lodged,
deposited' (*i.e.* to pay for the damages). X. with princely
magnanimity waives this offer.

628-9. D. now asserts that he is not really the slave he appears
to be. **ἀγορεύω τινὶ** 'I proclaim to anyone (whom it may con-
cern)' : a formula for giving warning that an impending act is
illegal (*cf.* on 528)—in this case the torture of a citizen (as Tucker
notes **ἀθάνατον** here takes the place of 'Αθηναῖον). *Cf.* St. Paul's
protest at being flogged, though a Roman citizen (Acts 16, 37).
For the proclamation see Fraenkel, *Agamemnon* 1317.

630. 'Blame your own self', *i.e.* having heard my warning
that I'm a citizen not a slave, you won't be able to plead ignorance
when you're punished (by the gods or the Athenians) for it.
Aeacus, rather shaken by D.'s warning, replies : '*What* [τί is
emphatic by its position] are you saying ?'

634-6. The argument and counter-argument are perhaps pure
Aristophanic wit, or perhaps a parody of *Sophists'* legal quibbles
in the Corax and Teisias tradition. **εἴπερ . . . γάρ**: 'if, in
fact' : sceptically, as often.

638. **κλαύσαντα** : 'bursting into tears' : κλαίω indicates more
violent weeping than δακρύω. **προτιμήσαντά τι** : 'noticing any-
thing'. **εἶναι τοῦτον ἡγοῦ μὴ θεόν** : 'you may take it he's not
a god'.

640-1. **γεννάδας** : see on 179. **χωρεῖς γὰρ εἰς . . .**: 'for you
come to meet', *i.e.* you don't try to avoid.

643 ff. ACTION. It is now decided that both X. and D. shall
be beaten, turn about. Superficially it seems a fair arrangement.
But in fact D. will be at a big disadvantage : he is definitely *not*
the kind of god who feels no pain (even less so than Homer's gods
who are often physically hurt: *e.g. Iliad* 5, 352 ff. ; 21, 417 ff.);
on the contrary he is highly sensitive and nervous. X., on the
other hand, has a skin toughened by many a beating already
(*cf.* 501, 756), and will be able to endure the lash much better
than D. In this scene one must imagine much comic *Business*
on the part of Aeacus and the other two. Aeacus gradually gets
crosser and crueller with his whip, D. and X. gradually lose their
assumed indifference.

644. It is best to assume that Aeacus strikes X. as soon as X.
says 'There' (for ἰδού see on 200). But X. craftily speaks as if
nothing has happened : 'Watch now and see if I flinch'.

645. **ἤδη 'πάταξά σ'** : the text, punctuation, and speaker are
uncertain in the MSS., perhaps owing to confusion with 647.

The main alternatives are : (a) a statement by Aeacus, as printed in my text (Meineke preferred a question, which Coulon accepts) ; or (b) a question by X. : ἤδη 'πάταξας ; ; similarly the speaker of οὐ μὰ Δί' etc. is variously given in the mss. as Xanthias or Aeacus (and some divide it between X. and Aeacus). It seems best to give it to X. and instead of οὐδ' ἐμοὶ to accept Erbse's οὐδέπω 'not yet'. Coulon reads Radermacher's οὐδαμοῖ 'nowhere', i.e. on no part of my body. Note the personal construction οὐ δοκεῖς (where we say 'it doesn't seem') as usual in Greek.

646. πηνίκα : 'Exactly when ?' Aeacus has in fact already struck D. before he says this. D. is trying to be as cunning as X.

647. καὶ δὴ etc. : 'Actually I've hit you already' (cf. on 604b). κᾆτα (Crasis for καὶ εἶτα) : in pretended surprise : 'Well then ...?' πῶς οὐκ ἔπταρον : 'Why didn't I sneeze?' : D. apparently wishes to imply that he might have felt some draught of air or tickling sensation from the whip, which might have made him sneeze. Some think this is too far-fetched. Tucker surmises that there was a current phrase at Athens like 'It didn't even make me sneeze' : others try to emend (e.g. Rogers suggests ἔπτακον 'flinched'; but this 2nd aor. of uncompounded πτήσσω is not attested).

649-51. This time Aeacus hits X. harder. X. tries to be as nonchalant as before, but cannot restrain a yell of 'A-a-ah !' (Variants in the mss. seem to indicate that the exclamatory ἰατταταῖ may have been prolonged : I follow Dindorf's arrangement here.) When Aeacus asks 'You didn't feel pain, did you ?', X. pretends it was just an exclamation at a sudden thought (aorist ἐφρόντισα) of Heracles's festival held in the Athenian deme called Diomeia. γίγνεται : 'takes place'.

652. ἄνθρωπος ἱερός : 'A holy man !' (or if we adopt Dindorf's emendation, ἄνθρωπος : 'The man's a saint') : like a martyr in the flames X. thinks only of holy things and disregards the agony. Or else perhaps ἱερός (cf. on 327) here implies supernaturally immune to pain, like a Hindu fakir on his bed of spikes. δεῦρο πάλιν : Aeacus grimly strides back towards D. (then back to X. in 656 ; then back to D. in 658).

653-5. After 652 Aeacus silently strikes D. D. screams, and then (imitating X.) pretends his exclamation was caused by seeing some horsemen in the distance. ἰού could, in fact, be used as an exclamation of sorrow or joy : here perhaps in view of the equestrian reference we may translate: 'Gee! Gee !' (Note ἱππέας, as regularly.) But D. has also begun to cry, as Aeacus notices in 654. D. explains this as the result of a smell of onions (possibly because they were part of the standard rations for the cavalry : *cf. Kn.* 600).

655. ἐπεί . . . γ' . . . : 'for you noticed nothing, of course' (sarcastically). 'No,' replies D., 'it means nothing to me.' (This is a modification of Merry's view : others prefer to emend : the mss. show variations.)

657. X. certainly feels something this time, for οἴμοι is unambiguously a cry of pain. He quickly pretends he has stepped on a thorn. (This is a poor excuse in the circumstances, since it implies he *does* feel some kinds of pain : but we need not press the logic or follow Tucker's ingenuities : in such a rollicking scene few would worry about inconsistencies like this ; and the critical main question is whether D. feels pain or not.)

658-9. After 658 Aeacus lashes D. savagely. D. screams to Apollo, and then tries to cover up his self-betrayal by adding some words from an iambic poet to make a familiar quotation. (In English he might have used the line from Wordsworth's sonnet: 'Great God ! . . . I'd rather be | A pagan . . .'.) Πυθών (the form Πυθώ is commoner) is an old name for Delphi.

661. Hippōnax : the satirist of the sixth century B.C. But Σ says that the line is by another poet of the same time, Ananios. Probably Ar. himself has made a slip (*cf.* Erbse). Or else perhaps Ar. wishes to suggest that D. was greatly confused by his pains and fears.

662-3. X., seeing that D. will not be able to take much more punishment, urges Aeacus on with : 'The fact is you're getting nowhere [lit. 'doing nothing']. You'd better give his sides [which would be more tender than his back : for beating in this way *cf.* Knox-Headlam on Herodas 5, 33] a dusting.' Aeacus cruelly goes further and says to D. 'Here, stomach forward now' (*cf.* D.'s pot belly in 200). Editors have noticed the injustice of this. X. is missing a turn at being whipped. Some think D.'s second blow and quotation (663-5) should be deleted. Others try to adapt 663-5 to the view that X. is struck again here (with support from V). I diffidently retain the traditional text : neither Ar. nor his audience would worry much about the injustice here (and D. is a *funnier* victim than X.) ; and as for the repetition of the quotation-joke, comedians like to use a good, new joke twice over. Possibly, too, as Higham suggests, X. may have received a blow after **661** without making any direct comment on it.

665. According to Σ the quotation is from Sophocles's *Laocoon* : but he quotes a different version. I follow van Leeuwen's rearrangement (as in Coulon) : but the metre of **665** (which Kock

deletes) remains dubious, and the whole quotation uncertain.
See further in Radermacher. Translate : 'who dost rule over the
Aegean promontory [perhaps Sounion or Geraistos, if Scaliger's
emendation πρωνὸs for πρῶναs is correct : Radermacher thinks
not] and the grey-green . . .' (the quotation breaks off). For the
irregular numbering of the lines see § 14 end of n. 75.

668 ff. ACTION. Baffled, Aeacus ends the inquisition, leaving
it to Pluto (ὁ δεσπότηs in **670**) and Persephone ('as they are both
gods, too' : **671**) to decide which is the god.

671. Note the Attic name of Persephone here (but the MSS.
vary greatly) : Latin *Proserpina*, in Homer Persephoneia. There
are many other forms (see A. Carnoy in *Mélanges Bidez*, Brussels,
1934, 71-7).

673. ἐβουλόμην δ' ἄν : 'I would have preferred'. For the
imperfect see Schwyzer 2, 347, Humbert, § 277. Compare the
colloquial use of 'I wished you had . . .' for 'I wish . . .'.

674-737. ACTION. All the actors now leave the scene. The
Chorus remain to sing, dance, and recite, in the Parabasis (see
§ 13).

METRE. **674-85** (the *Ode* or *Strophe* of this Parabasis) corre-
sponds to the *Antode* or *Antistrophe* in **706-16**. The rhythm is
mainly dactylic (with anapaestic variations) and trochaic : see
White 224-5, and Fraenkel, *Lyrische Daktylen* 182-3 for complica-
tions ignored in the following analysis :

674 = 706 : $- \cup \cup ~ - \cup \cup ~ - \cup \cup ~ - \cup \cup ~ - \cup \cup ~ - ⌣$: dactylic
hexameter.

675 = 707 : $\cup - - \cup -$: apparently a dochmiac.

676 = 708 : $- \cup \cup ~ - \cup \cup ~ - - ~ - \cup \cup ~ - \cup \cup ~ - \wedge$: catalectic
form of **674** (but the lengthened πίθηκὄs in **708** implies a rhyth-
mical break after the third foot).

677 = 681 = 685 = 709, 712, 716 : $- \cup ~ - \cup ~ - ⌣$: three trochees
(an ithyphallic : *cf.* 395-6).

679 = 710 : $\cup \cup - ~ \cup \cup - ~ \cup \cup - ~ \cup \cup - ~ -$: anapaests (or
'ascending dactyls' ?).

680 = 711 : $- \cup \cup ~ - \cup \cup ~ - \wedge ~ - \cup \cup ~ - \cup \cup ~ - \wedge$: two cata-
lectic dactylic tripodies. For the lengthening in ἐπιβρέμεται *cf.* on
814 and see White 365 ff. and Descroix 11 ff.

682 = 713/14 : $\cup \cup - ~ \cup \cup - ~ \cup \cup - ~ \cup \cup -$: anapaestic dimeter.

683/4 = 714 : $⌣ - ~ \cup \cup - ~ \cup \cup - ~ \cup \cup - ~ \cup \cup - ~ -$:
anapaests (or 'ascending dactyls') : *cf.* 679, 682.

674. χορῶν ἱερῶν (*cf.* 335 and 686) is best taken as the object of ἐπίβηθι 'enter upon'. The special Muse of dancing was Terpsichore (cf. τέρψιν ἀοιδᾶς here).

679. φιλοτιμότεραι: here in a good sense (cf. on 281), 'more devoted to honour', as in official Attic inscriptions. *Cleophon* the lyre-maker followed *Hyperbolos* as chief demagogue in 410. A persistent opponent of peace-making and an expert in finance, he is abused by Ar. in *Thesm.* 805 and *Frogs* 1504, 1532, as well as here, and also by Plato Comicus (who, acc. to Σ on 681, said Cleophon's mother was a Thracian ; see next note) in his *Cleophon* (see § 1). But Lysias defends him (13, 8-12 ; 30, 12-13). An ostrakon found in the Athenian Agora (see E. Vanderpool in *Hesperia* xxi, 1952, 114-15) inscribed 'Cleophon son of Cleippides' (415 B.C.) seems to show that his father, at least, was a respectable Athenian (against the usual interpretation of Aelian, *Varia Historia* 12, 43).

679 ff. 'On whose lips of mongrel speech a Thracian swallow makes horrible din as it sits on a foreign leaf' : this is a lyrical way of alleging that Cleophon talked in a way that suggested Thracian origins (hence impugning his citizenship : cf. previous note). I have adopted Merry's translation of ἀμφιλάλοις : other possibilities are 'bilingual' or 'ambiguous' (cf. ἀμφίλογος). For the significance of the swallow symbol here see on 93, and for the imagery cf. *Odyssey* 19, 520 and *Peace* 800-1. There may be an allusion to the tradition that Tereus, husband of the woman who was turned into a swallow in the myth, was a Thracian. Cf. *Birds* 774.

683-5. κελαδεῖ: this is the reading of V and can be retained (since κἔλᾰ- can correspond to εἶ in 715 : see Maas § 39): cf. the similar language in *Peace* 800 ff. R's κελαρύζει spoils the metrical correspondence. (Dindorf emended to ῥύζει 'snarls', Fritzsche to τρύζει 'murmurs', et alii alia.) ὡς ἀπολεῖται : 'since [or 'on the ground that' : not, I think, a wish as in 279] he will perish'. ἴσαι : what feminine noun is intended ? Tucker thinks σπονδαί, with reference to the making of an equitable peace in spite of Cleophon's militarism. Radermacher thinks σοφίαι (from 676). But ψῆφοι, as suggested by Σ, still seems despite difficulties the likeliest (the Athenians were quick to think of litigation : cf. on 528). The phrase will then mean 'even if the votes [of the jurymen] turn out to be equal'. This would normally lead to an acquittal, but Ar. says that Cleophon, for some unspecified reason, was doomed to perish anyway. Denniston (MS.) thinks that Ar. here is distorting the proverb cited by Hesychius, σώζεσθαι κἂν ἴσαι γένωνται (='to be saved although the votes are equal', i.e. even though at first sight the matter is left undecided : cf. Aeschylus, *Eum.* 741), the notion being that

Cleophon 'will get the *dis*advantage of the doubt'. Ar.'s prophecy came true a year later when Cleophon was condemned to death and executed under a law specially enacted for the purpose.

686 ff. Action. The Chorus now (as usual in a *Parabasis*) expresses Ar.'s personal opinion on current political matters. Here he pleads for those Athenians who had been deprived of civic rights as a result of the oligarchical revolution in 411 (see § 5). Apparently many of them had been kept in constant fear of indictment (*cf.* 688) and had been excluded from public office (*cf.* Andocides, *On the Mysteries* 75). Ar. pleads for a general amnesty, so that a united front can be formed to meet the problems of the War. For this advice the *Frogs* was (according to Dicaearchus as cited in the first Hypothesis to the play) honoured with a second performance. This is the last parabasis in extant Greek comedy.

Metre. Catalectic trochaic tetrameters (see White 99 ff.) :

$$- \cup - \breve{} - \cup - \breve{} \, || - \cup - \breve{} - \cup \, \breve{} \, \wedge.$$

Tribrachs are permissible in all feet ; anapaests in the 2nd, 4th, and 6th ; dactyls (rarely) in 1st. 4th, and 5th. There is generally diaeresis (as marked) after the 4th foot.

686. 'The holy chorus' (*cf.* 674) : not 'holy' here, I think, simply because it consists of Initiates but also because it deserves veneration for its Dionysiac function. Ar. wants to enlist the greatest possible respect for his following suggestions : for a similar reason he repeats his reference (676, 700) to the wisdom of the Athenians and refrains from any touches of comedy or vulgarity here (and in 718-37). Perhaps some of his own friends were among those he pleads for.

688. ἐξισῶσαι τοὺς πολίτας : 'free the citizens from inequalities'. Apparently there were some citizens who, without having been entirely deprived of civil rights, had been subjected to disabilities of various kinds. The question of the re-enfranchisement of the disfranchised is not introduced until 692 (εἶτ' marking a new suggestion there). I follow Denniston (ms.) in this note.

689. 'The manœuvres [lit. 'wrestling-tricks'] of Phrynichus' : he (contrast in 13 and 910) was a leader in the revolution of 411.

690-1. 'I say that it should be permitted to those who made a slip then to state a case and purge their former errors.' αἰτίαν ἐκθεῖσι might also mean 'when they have expounded their reason' (but hardly van Daele's 'après s'être mis hors d'inculpation').

692. εἶτ' : 'then', *i.e.* 'secondly' in succession to πρῶτον in 687 : *cf.* on 810.

693-4. μίαν : *sc. ναυμαχίαν.* After *Arginusae* the Athenians freed all slaves who had fought in this victory, and gave them 'Plataean' rights of citizenship. The Plataeans, traditional allies of Athens, had been made citizens of Athens after the destruction of Plataea by the Peloponnesians in 427 : but certain religious privileges and official positions were not permitted to them (see Demosthenes 59, 104).

695-6. After τοὺς μὲν in 693 one would expect an immediate reference (with δέ) to the disfranchised citizens whom Ar. wants to be forgiven. But for fear of being misunderstood as wishing to object to the enfranchisement of the heroes of Arginusae, he breaks off to emphasize his approval of it. The μή before οὐ is due to the preceding negation of the main verb. κοὐδὲ . . . ἔχοιμ' ἂν etc. : 'could not deny that these things were well arranged'.

697 ff. It seems best to take πρὸς δὲ by itself adverbially as 'but besides this', and τούτοις as governed by παρεῖναι (2 aor. infin. act. παρίημι 'overlook, forgive' : *cf.* in 948) with ὑμᾶς as its subject and συμφορὰν as direct object. εἰκὸς : 'reasonable', a favourite word in Greek rhetoric. αἰτουμένοις is middle : note the force of the present tense : 'at their constant request'. The *v.l.* αἰτουμένους, passive agreeing with ὑμᾶς, means the same. συμφοράν (the newer Attic form is given here and in 701 by the better MSS., but in 702 all have ξυν- : see § 14 n. 75) : 'misfortune'. Ar. minimizes their fault, as in 690, 691.

700. σοφώτατοι : *cf.* on 686 : Ar. tactfully suggests that the natural (φύσει) wisdom of the Athenians was overcome by uncharacteristic anger.

701-2. πάντας . . . ὅστις ἂν ξυνναυμαχῇ : 'every man who fights in the navy with us', *i.e.* every loyal and able citizen, not (in this context) 'all men' ; but it perhaps also implied resident aliens : see Hugill 86. κτησώμεθα : 'let us acquire, get', implying a definite gain : note the tactful 'us' with the hortatory subjunctive instead of 'you' with the imperative (which he entirely avoids in this passage). συγγενεῖς : 'as kinsmen' : compare the construction in 523.

704-5. As punctuated in this text τὴν πόλιν is object of ἔχοντες : this gives a better parallel to the line from Archilochus which, according to Σ, is half-quoted here, namely, ψυχὰς ἔχοντες κυμάτων ἐν ἀγκάλαις. (For the political *Metaphor* of the storm at sea *cf.* 361.) Parallels to the unusual position of καὶ ταῦτα 'and this, too' or 'especially when' (which usually comes at the beginning of the clause) are quoted by Blaydes : *cf.* on 67.

705. αὖθις perhaps only strengthens ὑστέρῳ χρόνῳ : see

L.-S.-J. Or perhaps it indicates à contrast with the Athenians' good sense after *Arginusae* (695-6).

706-15. METRE= 674-85. These lines contain much *Parody*: *cf.* on 710 ff. According to Σ, 706 is from Ion of Chios.

708-9. πολὺν goes with χρόνον in 713. πίθηκος: 'ape, monkey': here, as elsewhere, an emblem of shameless flattery and vulgar exhibitionism (*cf.* in 1085). Apes were kept as pets by Athenians (Theophrastus, *Char.* 5, 9 : *cf.* Knox-Headlam on Herodas 3, 41). Cleigenes, a supporter of *Cleophon*, was one of the demagogues most active in securing the disfranchisement of citizens after the oligarchical revolution and in blackmailing them with threats of legal proceedings (*cf.* Andocides, *On the Mysteries* 73). For the contemptuous tone of μικρός see A. C. Moorhouse in *Classical Quarterly* xli (1947), 41.

710-12. Ar. attacks Cleigenes in his profession as a keeper of a public bath and laundry. (Athenian bath-keepers were distrusted : *cf.* Jebb-Sandys, *Theophrastus* p. 127.) Ar. accuses him of cheating his customers by using (or supplying for use, if the customers did their own washing) adulterated (ψευδο-) detergents. κυκησίτεφροι (I have adopted this emendation by Radermacher for the MS. -ου) refers to a method of making a washing-powder from 'lye' or 'pearl ash' (κονίας here) by mixing wood-ash (τέφρα) with water (*i.e.* by 'lixiviation'). ψευδο-λίτρου refers to another active ingredient in washing-powders, sodium carbonate ('washing soda', λίτρον here : also spelled νίτρον, hence 'nitre'). Κιμωλίας γῆς introduces a third kind of detergent, 'fuller's earth' : the island Kimolos in the Cyclades produced a specially good variety of this cleansing clay (see Pliny, *Natural History* 35, 57). Ar. is parodying elevated diction with these compound adjectives and the lordly phrase ὁπόσοι [a poetic form] κρατοῦσι . . . γῆς. Translate : 'as many as be ash-watering lords of the impure detergents and the Cimolian earth'.

713. ἐνδιατρίψει (*cf.* on 1498) has its last syllable shortened by *Correption* to correspond with 683. ἰδὼν is *Bentley's* emendation for the unmetrical εἰδὼς of the MSS. : the corruption was doubtless due to the preceding -ει. τάδ': out of several possibilities I take this to refer to the political advice given by Ar. in this parabasis.

715-16. οὐκ εἰρηνικὸς : 'bellicose', presumably referring to both his politics and his personal conduct. The ξύλον mentioned is probably not just a walking-stick, such as fashionable Athenians carried (Jebb-Sandys, *Theophrastus* p. 64), but a staff of office which would give him immunity from assault even when he was drunk.

The force of the καί in κἀποδυθῇ is apparently 'in addition to losing
his office he may be stripped of his clothes'. According to this
view Ar. is hoping that his advice to restore the disfranchised
citizens will be taken, and, as a result, worthless war-loving
demagogues like Cleigenes will lose their political power and be
personally assaulted by their victims.

718 ff. Metre as in 686 ff. Now Ar. uses his famous analogy
between the Athenian citizens and the coinage. The historical
background is this : after the occupation of Decelea by the Spar-
tans in 413 the Laureion silvermines ceased to be worked by the
Athenians and the good old silver coinage (τἀρχαῖον νόμισμα in
720) could no longer be coined. In 407 the Athenians produced a
gold coinage by melting down the gold plating on the statues of
Victory in the Acropolis (for the discovery of what may be a head
of one of these see H. A. Thompson, *Harvard Studies in Classical
Philology*, suppl. vol. i (1940), 183-210) : this is the καινὸν χρυσίον
of 720. These coins were worth more as metal than the silver
coins of the same face value, and so (by Gresham's law that
bad coinage always displaces any better coinage) disappeared
from circulation. In 406 the Athenian Treasury minted coins
of silver-plated copper (τοῖς πονηροῖς χαλκίοις in 725 : *cf.
Eccl.* 815 ff.). It led to higher prices and had a bad psychological
effect on the Athenians, who took a pride in their silver 'owls'.
(See Ehrenberg 220 ff. for illustrations of the various coins and
further discussion.) Ar. argues in what follows here that just as
the Athenians have been suffering economically from the recent
introduction of a spurious coinage (copper with a coating of silver),
so they have been suffering from base politicians, many of them
aliens and 'red-heads' (730) masquerading as true Athenian
citizens, who have driven out the silver and the gold coinage of
true-born and true-hearted citizens. (Actually after 720 Ar.
does not explicitly refer again to the temporary gold coinage,
having hinted there, I take it, that the temporary rule of the
oligarchs in 411 resembled it in some ways.) The cure, Ar.
suggests, is to go back to the political ascendancy of the older
type of 'well-born, moderate, just, handsome, and good citizens'
(727-8). καλούς τε κἀγαθοὺς (*cf.* 728) : this is a complex term
difficult to translate (but *cf.* French *honnêtes hommes*). Primarily
it referred to aesthetic and moral excellence : 'the fair and brave'.
But it also generally implied nobility of birth in the sense of 'the
fine gentlemen'. In 5th-century Athens the conservative and
oligarchical parties tried to monopolize the term for themselves.
See especially A. W. Gomme, *Classical Quarterly*, n.s. iii (1953),
65-8. Ar. probably wishes to exploit both its ethical and its
political implications here. *Cf.* his use of σώφρονας in 727 : it

also, as Gomme notes, was a propagandist term of the conservatives, in the sense of 'the Moderate Party'.

721-5. οὐ κεκιβδηλευμένοις : 'not counterfeited', *i.e.* of sterling quality, unlike the silver-plated copper coins mentioned in **725**. **κοπεῖσι** : 'struck', *sc.* stamped with the Athenian emblems, the owl and Athena's head : from the same verb (κόπτω) comes κόμμα 'minting' (**726**). **κεκωδωνισμένοις** : see on **79**. For further uses of coinage terms in an ethical sense see Radermacher, and Neil 204. **724** refers to the fact that the silver Athenian coins were 'hard currency' throughout Greece and the Mediterranean. **725** : χαλκία is a contemptuous *Diminutive*.

729. A reference to the two main branches of 5th-century Greek education, μουσική and γυμναστική.

730. προυσελοῦμεν : a word of mysterious form and origin, occurring only here and in Aeschylus, *P.V.* 438 in classical Greek (see Fritzsche and L.-S.-J.). It apparently means 'maltreat, outrage'. **πυρρίαις** (from πυρρίας : for the *Comic Termination* see on **22**): 'red-heads', *i.e.* foreigners, perhaps especially Thracians (*cf.* **681**) or slaves. Radermacher suggests it also implies bad character. Mr. E. S. G. Robinson has pointed out to me that the place where the thin silver plating would most quickly get worn away and show the reddish copper underneath was the area of highest relief, in this case the forehead of Athena on the Athenian drachms and tetradrachms : hence there is a special aptness in the term 'red-heads' in connexion with these plated 'coppers'.

732-3. πρὸ τοῦ (*sc.* χρόνου) : 'before this', apparently a survival of the demonstrative use of the article, as in **977**. **οὐδὲ φαρμακοῖσιν** : 'not even as scapegoats'. Every year at Athens during the festival of Thargelia in May two condemned criminals, a man and a woman, were beaten out of the city and put to death as a rite of purification. They were believed to take with them the collective guilt and ill-luck of the community. For parallels to Ar.'s phrase see Blaydes. Distinguish φαρμακός here from φάρμακον 'drug'. **εἰκῇ ῥᾳδίως** : lit. 'at random readily', *i.e.* in your most thoughtless mood. Goligher finds this pleonastic and suggests that parenthetical οἶμαι was ousted by εἰκῇ (a gloss on ῥᾳδίως) : hence he conjectures οἶμαι ῥᾳδίως.

734. ἀνόητοι (= ὦ ἀνόητοι, *cf.* in **530**) : 'silly ones' : contrast the praises of the audience's intelligence in **676** and **700**. Ar. is confident now that his arguments have convinced them and ventures to criticize them a little.

735-7. χρῆσθε τοῖς χρηστοῖσιν : *Assonance*, with some *Paronomasia* (χρηστός originally meant 'usable, usefully good' : see on **179**). Note the particles in what follows : **καὶ . . . γὰρ**

. . . **κᾶν** . . . **γοῦν** : Ar. is trying to make his argument valid
even if his plan fails to achieve success (presumably in the War).
Translate : 'Then, you see, if you succeed it will be laudable,
and if you trip up a bit [a litotes for 'fail']—well at any rate
. . .'. **ἐξ ἀξίου τοῦ ξύλου** : apparently there was a proverbial
phrase to the effect that if you were going to be hanged it was
some small comfort to be hanged from a good tree (*cf.* the Latin
ex infelici arbore). **ἤν τι** etc. : Ar. rather nervously repeats his
reference to possible failure. Continue the translation : '. . . if
you do suffer any reverse, the wise will think "worthy the tree"'.
It is true that the last line is awkward and repetitive ; but any
suggestion that it should be deleted is prevented by the line-
equivalence between the two trochaic parts of the *Parabasis* :
also the sentiment closely balances that in the corresponding
705. Its awkwardness is perhaps an indication of Ar.'s anxiety
that even if the Athenians do take his advice they may possibly
have further troubles. He is too honest to imitate the dema-
gogues who promise unalloyed bliss if their advice is taken.

738 ff. ACTION. Enter Xanthias and—who ? Here the
uncertainty of the MSS. in indicating which character is speaking
is sadly exemplified. The main MSS. say that X.'s companion
here is 'A servant', or 'A servant of Pluto', or 'A servant of
Aeacus', or 'Aeacus'. I have followed Coulon in printing simply
Οἰκέτης, 'A servant' (most likely of Pluto). Against R's indica-
tion that Aeacus returns here I find it hard to believe that the
genial character portrayed in this scene can be the same as the
grim Aeacus of the previous scenes (but such vagaries are not
entirely impossible in Aristophanic comedy). This conversation
between slaves (*cf. Wasps* 1 ff.) acts as a kind of prologue to the
following contest (*Agon*) between Euripides and Aeschylus.

740. 'Seeing that he's the kind who only knows about fuddling
and cuddling' or 'guzzling and nuzzling' (Fitts's translation) :
note *Assonance*. X. offers a cynical slave's-eye view of what
constitutes a γεννάδας ἀνήρ (*cf.* on **179**).

741. Exclamatory infinitive : *cf.* on **530**.

743-4. **ᾤμωξε** is Brunck's emendation for the nonsensical
οἴμωζε of the MSS. **μέντἄν** : μέντοι is emphatic here : 'he certainly
would have regretted it [if he had beaten me]'. This is sheer
brag on X.'s part. **δουλικὸν** : elsewhere used as a term of con-
tempt 'slavish' : here amusingly used (among servants) as a
eulogistic word : 'slaveworthy' (*cf.* Ehrenberg 166). **εὐθὺς** :
here used of the first thing that comes into one's mind (*cf.*
εὐθύγλωσσος) : 'for example'.

745. **χαίρεις, ἱκετεύω** : 'Excuse me [*cf.* the use of ἀντιβολῶ

in *Eccl.* 1071], what do you mean by "which you *enjoy* doing"?'
X. repeats only the term that puzzles him most. (This seems to
me the best explanation of this highly condensed phrase.) μᾶλλ':
'more than that': see on 103. ἐποπτεύειν δοκῶ: 'I feel the
utmost bliss': ἐποπτεύω refers to initiation into the highest
degree of the Mysteries (*cf.* 454-9).

747. τονθορύζων: 'muttering your grumbles': note the
Onomatopoeia. For the word *cf. Wasps* 614 and Knox-Headlam
on Herodas 7, 77.

749. πολλὰ πράττων: 'playing the busybody': *cf.* on 228.
ὡς μὰ Δί' οὐδὲν οἶδ' ἐγώ: Merry gets good sense by taking οἶδ' ἐγώ
as an asseverative addition as in *Medea* 948 (*cf. Clouds* 1175)
and rendering 'Nothing like it, I'm quite sure'.

750. ὁμόγνιε (ὁμό-γνιος: *cf.* γένος) 'of kinship', *i.e.* presiding
over the interests of people belonging to the same clan. Possibly
some parody of a typical recognition scene in tragedy is intended
in this passage as Roemer (followed by Tucker) suggested.
παρακούων: lit. 'hear from the side': we say 'overhear'.

753-5. κἀκμιαίνομαι: 'I can't contain myself': a *Comic
Distortion* of the previous μαίνομαι. In 754-5 the feeling is that
of 'Shake hands brother, | You're a rogue and I'm another'.

755 ff. It is uncertain when exactly X. begins to notice the
'din inside' (757); and the punctuation depends on this. One
may mark the change of attention (*a*) after κύσον (but then the
following καί is hardly abrupt enough); (*b*) after φράσον (but
ὁμομαστιγίας would seem to be apter for a continuation of their
'slaveworthy' discussion); (*c*) after ὁμομαστιγίας (which Σ
prefers). I have, diffidently, accepted (*c*), assuming that X.
breaks off just as he is going to exchange some more servant-
gossip. Perhaps before this the audience could hear the sound of
loud arguing from within the *Scene-building*.

756. ὁμομαστιγίας: coined by Ar. as a comic distortion of
ὁμόγνιος in 750 with μαστιγίας (*cf.* 501): lit. 'patron of the
flogged slaves' fraternity'.

758. 'Of Aeschylus and Euripides': this introduces the
second main theme of the *Frogs*, the literary contest (see § 7).

759-60. ἆ probably expresses a long-drawn-out exclamation
of interest and awakened expectancy on X.'s part: 'A-ha!'
(with a rising intonation). (For an isolated ἆ like this at an
important transition in a play *cf. Bacchae* 810.) Note the mock-
solemn emphasis in the repeated πρᾶγμα and μέγα, and in πάνυ at
the end of 760. πρᾶγμα perhaps has its legalistic meaning 'law-

suit, action' here (as in **1099** and elsewhere). στάσις: see on **359**.

762. ἀπὸ τῶν τεχνῶν: apparently ἀπὸ means 'referring to' here : for the nearest analogies (Herodotus only) see L.-S.-J. at ἀπό iii, 7. (Compare the English parliamentary phrase 'arising out of' as an equivalent for 'referring to': in *Lysistrata* 138, ἀφ' ἡμῶν . . . αἱ τραγῳδίαι, we can perhaps see an intermediate stage in this semantic development.) ὅσαι μεγάλαι καὶ δεξιαί: 'the great and skilful ones', 'the fine arts'. By τέχνη the Greeks meant both arts and crafts.

764-5. 'Food in the Prytaneion', *i.e.* in the City Hall (at the public expense), an honour reserved for Athenian citizens who had done the State special honour or service (including Olympic victors) : *cf. Kn.* 535, 575 etc., and Plato, *Apology* 36 D. θρόνον: 'chair of honour', not a 'throne' for a citizen of democratic Athens.

766. ἀφίκοιτο: for the optative after the primary tense *cf.* on **24**. σοφώτερος: 'more highly skilled': see on **1118**.

768. 'Tell me [δῆτα], how has this come to disturb Aeschylus ?' Apparently X., being a slave with more old-fashioned literary tastes than his master (who adores Euripides, according to 66 ff.), assumes that Aeschylus has no reason to fear any rival in literary skill. (Or has Ar. inadvertently allowed X. to know more than he could in the circumstances have known about Aeschylus's feelings ?)

771. ὅτε δή: 'You see, when . . .'. But Denniston 220 renders 'just when' and compares **789, 1090**. κατῆλθ': 'came down': the preposition implies the belief that Hades was underground, which is not referred to in D.'s journey from Athens. (For similar uncertainties on the position of Hades *cf.* my note on *Odyssey* 11, 65.) ἐπεδείκνυτο: 'he began showing off his oratory': 'display' oratory (ἐπιδεικτική) was a genre much exploited by the *Sophists*. Note how E. is presented as a sophist and popular agitator in what follows here.

773-4. τοιχωρύχοις: see on **1149**. ὅπερ ἔστ' ἐν Ἅιδου πλῆθος: I prefer the rendering 'who [ὅπερ for οἵπερ, attracted to gender and number of πλῆθος] are the majority in Hades' to 'of whom [ὅπερ for ὧνπερ] there is a large number'. ἀκροάομαι is the proper word (not ἀκούω) for listening to a lecture or speech (*cf.* ἀκροατής).

775. ἀντιλογίαι are 'counter-arguments', examples of sophistic skill in arguing either side of a case (rather than simply 'controversies' here). λυγισμοί: 'twists', probably a metaphor from wrestling, like στροφαί 'turns'. (Murray, *Aristophanes* 122, thinks that musical implications, 'changing tones of voice' and 'strophes', are also intended in the last two. Radermacher cites Sophocles, *Philoctetes* 431 and Plato, *Repub.* 405 c for other *Metaphors* from wrestling applied to oratory.)

778. ἵνα: 'where' as frequently in poetry and occasionally in Attic prose. ἐβάλλετο: 'pelted', *i.e.* had things thrown at him by the audience (not *necessarily* stones).

779. μὰ Δί' ἀλλ': 'on the contrary, by Heaven . . .'. κρίσιν ποεῖν: 'to arrange a trial'.

781. With ὁ understand δῆμος from **779**; with οὐράνιόν γ' ὅσον ('Yes, heaven-high') understand ἀνεβόα from **779.** *Cf.* *Clouds* 357, *Wasps* 1492, and **1135** below. This use of ὅσος to indicate unusual size or force is found elsewhere: *cf.* Latin *immane quantum*.

782-3. ἕτεροι σύμμαχοι: 'others, as his allies'. ἐνθάδε: with a gesture towards the *Audience*.

788-90. A much disputed passage : for a study of 20 interpretations from Callistratos to Kock see S. G. Oliphant in *Transactions of the American Philological Association* xl (1909), 93 ff., and for more recent views, P. T. Stevens in *The Classical Review* lxix (1955), 235-7. The main difficulty is κἀκεῖνος in **790**: is it Aeschylus or *Sophocles* ? The sense seems to demand Sophocles : for even if ὑπεχώρησεν could bear the meaning 'made room for', two people cannot share a θρόνος with any comfort. But many editors hold that ἐκεῖνος here must denote a change of subject (especially after anaphoric καί, as Denniston asserts) and so cannot refer to Sophocles. Some (including Wilamowitz in *Hermes* lxiv, 1929) delete **790** entirely : others emend (Coulon's κἄνεικος= καὶ ἄνεικος, being nearest to the text : he compares *Wasps* 471 and 818, 1099 below). On the other hand, a few (Rogers, Oliphant, Tucker, Stevens) hold that κἀκεῖνος can refer to Sophocles in further contrast with Euripides. Stevens translates from **789** : 'Not *he* ; when he arrived he kissed Aeschylus and clasped his hand [as a pledge of co-operation : see Oliphant] and *he* [Sophocles : in contrast again with Euripides] stood back from the θρόνος . . .'. I think this interpretation is best (see further in Stevens's article for reasonable answers to the difficulties involved ; for another example of ἐκεῖνος used in reference to last person mentioned see **69**).

791-2. The subject is still Sophocles. νυνὶ δ': 'just now', *i.e.* when I left them. ὡς ἔφη Κλειδημίδης : this person is unknown (Σ gives contradictory guesses): apparently on some notorious occasion he said he would 'sit by as odd-man-out', as is Sophocles's intention here. An ἔφεδρος sat and watched a conflict, intending to challenge the winner. Possibly Cleidemides used it, in a political sense, to mean 'sitting on the fence'. (The view of Radermacher and others that we should punctuate after ἔφη and take Cleidemides as subject of ἔμελλεν seems less probable.)

794. διαγωνιεῖσθ': 'will fight to the finish' (δια-). πρός γ' Εὐριπίδην : the particle (omitted in some MSS.) is necessary for the metre. Its force is probably limitative : ' at any rate, against Euripides '. As Stevens notes, the possibility that E. may beat Aeschylus is not thought absurd.

796. κἀνταῦθα δὴ etc. : 'And on this very spot, let me tell you, will its wonders be set going'.

797 ff. 'There'll even be a measuring of the poetic art on a weighing-scales' (Beare suggested σταθήσεται 'will be weighed', for σταθμήσεται). X., astonished at this curious announcement —and Ar. doubtless hopes the audience is equally surprised— replies 'What ? Will they treat tragedy like a sacrificial lamb ?' In the following lines Ar. adds to the *Mystification*. In fact the weighing-scales is not used until 1379 ff. and the other instruments of measurement are never used in the play. Some mockery of contemporary materialism may be intended. μειαγωγήσουσι : the word occurs only here. It is derived from μεῖον, the sacrificial lamb offered by an Athenian father at the festival of Apaturia when sons were enrolled in the φρατρίαι (see on 418). Possibly the μεῖον part of the compound comes from the cry of 'Too small, too small ' of the congregation (who got a share of the sacrificial meat) as each victim was presented : hence, presumably, each lamb had to be weighed in the presence of the brotherhood. *Cf.* Eupolis 116.

799-802. κανόνας : 'measuring-rules'. πήχεις : 'cubit-measures'. πλαίσια ξύμπτυκτα (the MSS. offer many variants for the adjective) : 'folding rectangular frames' (there seems to have been some current joke about ξύμπτυκτος : cf. Pherecrates 79). The last-named object was most frequently, it seems, used for brick-making. Hence X.'s interjection 'Will they be making bricks, too ?' διαμέτρους : here apparently (from its meaning 'diagonal') 'mitre-squares' or 'bevels', used for measuring angles (for another suggestion see Rutherford 1, 362). σφῆνας : normally 'wedges' (here, perhaps, to be used for splitting up the tragedies κατ' ἔπος, or perhaps with a hint of torture as in Aeschylus, *P.V.* 64 : cf. βασανιεῖν in 802 and see on 616 ff.). Radermacher suggests some kind of measuring instrument is intended (but items in an Aristophanic list are not always strictly homogeneous). For the need for accuracy of measurement in joinery *cf.* Plato, *Philebus* 56 B.

803. ἦ που : 'Well, I suppose . . .'. **τὸν Αἰσχύλον :** 'your Aeschylus', *i.e.* being the kind of man he is. (But Ranke conjectured τόδ' for τὸν, giving a direct object for the verb and supplying a suitably tragic caesura.)

804. 'He glared, at least, like a bull, with lowered head.' **ταυρηδὸν :** probably in parody of Aeschylus's use of forms in -ηδόν, *cf.* 824 below and Aeschylus, *Supp.* 431, *Septem* 328, fr. 39. This kind of glance from under lowered brows could be quizzical (as when Socrates uses it in *Phaedo* 117 B) or angry (as here). *Cf.* Homer's use of ὑπόδρα, and see Pfeiffer on Callimachus 194, 101. Perhaps the adverb also implies the inflamed eyes of an angry bull (*cf. Medea* 92) : we have the bellowing in 814 below.

805. δὲ δή : in a crucial question as elsewhere : see Denniston 259 : he renders : 'And who's the *judge* to be ? '

807. For the causes of Aeschylus's disagreement with the Athenians *cf.* Stanford, *Aeschylus* 141·2 (and see further on 886 below). He died in Sicily in 456 B.C.

808. 'Perhaps he thought the blackguards were in the majority' : *cf.* 772-3.

809-10. Ignoring X.'s remark, the Servant continues with τε (as often after οὔτε) : 'and he considered the .rest of mankind mere trash for discerning poetic genius'. **πέρι,** as its accent shows, governs **τοῦ γνῶναι :** for similar 'anastrophe' *cf.* 1212, 1244, and Starkie on *Wasps* 1118. **ποιητῶν :** for the spelling see on 13. **εἶτα :** 'so at last'.

813. ACTION. Xanthias and the Servant leave the scene and do not appear again. Their actors presumably now adopt the roles of Euripides and Aeschylus.

814-29. METRE. Four corresponding stanzas consisting of two dactylic hexameters (note the self-contained spondee at the beginning of each couplet and the caesura 2½ feet from end of dactyls : see Wilamowitz 352) + one dactylic pentameter (spondees only in the final foot) + a catalectic trochaic dimeter (the 'lecythion') :

```
– – – ∪ ∪ – ∪ ∪ –‖∪ ∪ – ∪ ∪ – –
– ∪ ∪ – ∪ ∪ – ∪ ∪ –‖– – ∪ ∪ – –
    – ∪ ∪ – ∪ ∪ –‖∪ ∪ – ∪ ∪ – –
      – ∪ – ∪ – ∪ – ∧
```

Probably the dactyls are intended to suggest a heroic mood (or perhaps Aeschylean : see Dale 44, and on 1264 ff.), while the sudden change to the catalectic trochaic dimeter provides an anticlimax (the trochee being a much less dignified foot than the dactyl and spondee).

STYLE. This is a brilliant piece of pseudo-elevated diction (*Parody* of any particular piece is unlikely), superbly contrived to make the spectators view the coming contest between Aeschylus and Euripides as a mock-epic conflict of savage beasts or of heroes in chariots. (Compare the duel of Tweedledum and Tweedledee in Lewis Carroll's *Through the Looking Glass*.) Subtleties of metre, vocabulary, and imagery contribute to the general effect. The metre, as we have seen, lurches in the fourth line from lofty dactyls into common trochees. The vocabulary is a mixture of epico-Aeschylean words (Aeschylus consciously derived much of his style and material from Homer : see on 1041) and sophistic terms (implying Euripides's strong sophistic traits, as emphasized by Ar. in 771 and elsewhere) : for examples see in the following notes. The imagery suggests a similar contrast : Aeschylus appears (by implication) as a bull, or a boar, or a lion, or a titan, huge, ponderous, and violent : Euripides emerges (see further on 815) as an agile, deft, light-weight creature. There is also a psychological contrast : Aeschylus is maddened by deep-felt passion (814, 816-17, 822-5) : Euripides is cool and subtle (826-829). Phonetics, too, are enlisted to help in exaggerating the grotesque contrast : 822-3 have a high percentage of double consonants as well as guttural κ and χ, to represent Aeschylean αὐστηρία, which (according to Dionysius, *On Composition* 22) 'does not in the least shrink from using frequently harsh sound-clashings which jar on the ear' (see further in Stanford, *Aeschylus* 6 ff.) : in contrast the smooth sigma (favoured by Euripides) dominates 826-7. Doubtless the music and dancing also heightened the mock-heroic humour. Probably the alternate verses were sung by half-choruses.

814. ἤ που : as in 803. ἐριβρεμέτας 'the loud-roarer', used in epic (with -ης for Doric -ας) and lyric of Zeus and a lion ; but here (in view of 804) perhaps intended to suggest a bull. Note ῐ in ἐριβρ- here but ἒ in ἀντιτεχν- in 816 (see White 365 ff., Descroix 11 ff.).

815. The text, syntax, and imagery are uncertain. Variants are περιίδῃ, παρίδῃ for περ ῐδῃ, and ὀδόντας for ὀδόντα. ὀξύλαλον apparently agrees with ὀδόντα ; but the syntax of θήγοντος etc. is dubious : it can hardly be either a genitive absolute or an objective genitive after ὁρῶ (while παρ- or περι-ορῶ in the sense of 'ignore, neglect' is inept here). And what kind of creature is the 'loud-roarer's' rival in art (ἀντιτέχνου 816) supposed to be ? Since θήγειν ὀδόντα (or ὀδόντας) is used of a wild boar in epic and

tragedy (*Iliad* 11, 416 ; 13, 474 ; Hesiod, *Shield* 388 ; *cf.* Euripides, *Phoen.* 1380, Ar. *Lys.* 1255), editors generally take it that Euripides is imagined as a wild boar here. In so far as a boar is lighter on its feet than a bull, and strikes with an oblique blow, the analogy is perhaps justified. But for another suggestion see end of note on 826-9.

817. 'His eyes will roll around.' (Note -τᾰ as usual before στ-, σκ- etc. ; *cf.* 878, 987. Rolling of the eyes was a well-known sign of madness or fury (see, *e.g.*, Hippocrates, *Prognostic* 7, 9) : here perhaps with special reference to the bull (*cf.* on 804). For Aeschylus as poet of μανία see Stanford, *Aeschylus* 13-14 and 129-31.

818-21. Now the opponents are represented as heroes fighting from chariots. ἱππολόφων : 'horse-crested' (like Homer's ἱππόκομος) or perhaps in a general sense 'huge-crested' (*cf.* on 929) : there is a variant ὑψιλόφων : 'high-crested'. κορυθαίολα : 'with glancing helmet', a favourite epic description of Hector, here transferred to quarrels (perhaps with a hint at Solon's phrase ἔπος αἰόλον).

819-21. The text and meaning of 819 are uncertain. Except for substituting παραξονίων for -ια, I have followed Coulon's text, accepting Heiberg's σμιλευματοεργοῦ (a conjectural form, *cf.* Knox-Headlam on Herodas 5, 42, meaning 'worker in carving') for RV's σμιλεύματα τ' ἔργων. (Though Coulon has withdrawn his support for this conjecture in *Revue des Études Grecques* lxvi, 1953, 47 f., I think φωτὸς needs an epithet : see end of this note.) σκινδάλαμοι (probably connected with σχίζω, *scindo*, 'split') : 'splinterings', with reference both to the breaking of chariots and (as in *Clouds* 130) to sophistic hair-splitting arguments (*cf.* Plato, *Greater Hippias* 304 A κνήσματα . . . καὶ περιτμήματα τῶν λόγων . . . κατὰ βραχὺ διῃρημένα). παραξόνια literally means 'things beside the axles' : the precise meaning is much disputed (see Radermacher for possible rhetorical implications), and many emendations have been offered. (Coulon, *loc. cit.*, now prefers van Herwerden's παραξόανα : see also J. Taillardat in *Revue des Études Grecques* lxi, 1948, 367-72, and A. Y. Campbell in *Classical Review* lxvii, 1953, 137-8.) If παραξονίων is accepted we can translate : 'helmet-glancing quarrellings consisting of horse-crested arguments and splinterings near the axle' (*sc.* when the axles of opposing chariots crash into each other as they sweep past in conflict). What follows is a genitive absolute : 'when the worker-in-fine-carving [σμίλη is a chisel or knife] strives to ward off the horse-prancing words of the mind-builder'. φρενοτέκτονος refers to the deep emotionalism of Aeschylus's style : see Stanford, *Aeschylus* 4 and 129-30 (five out of the six compounds in φρενο-in tragedy are confined to Aeschylus : and for the ending -τέκτων see *P.V.* 714). This deep-felt, creative genius is contrasted here with the superficial cleverness of the σμιλευματοεργὸς φώς (*cf.* the 'mouth-worker' in 826), who is Euripides. For φώς and ἀνήρ in one epic phrase *cf. Iliad* 17, 377-8.

ADDENDUM. If the internal hiatus in σμιλευματο-εργοῦ (contrast στοματουργός in 826) is too harsh, the best remedy would perhaps be to amend the ἔργων of the text to give an epithet for φωτός. Von Velsen suggests ἀτειροῦς 'stubborn' : possibly (σμιλεύματ') ἐνεργοῦ (in the sense of 'busy' or 'productive') might be read.

821. 'Horse-prancing phrases', *i.e.* high-stepping, lofty. ἱπποβάμων is applied by Aeschylus to an army (*P.V.* 805) and (if Turnebus's conjecture is correct) in *Supp.* 284 to a camel. Sophocles (*Trach.* 1095) uses it of the Centaurs. Ar. comically transfers it to Aeschylus's own language. *Cf.* Björck 39 and 336-9 for the ᾱ.

822. φρίξας . . . λασιαύχενα χαίταν : 'raising the bristling hair on his shaggy neck', a characteristic of the wild boar (*cf. Iliad* 13, 473 ; *Odyssey* 19, 446) : but here the boar is Aeschylus not Euripides (see on 815). αὐτοκόμου λοφιᾶς : lit. 'of self-haired crest', *i.e.* with a crest of natural hair. The epithet has a double force : in style it parodies Aeschylus's fondness for compounds in αὐτο- (*cf.* on 837) : in meaning it suggests that Aeschylus was a more sincere and genuine poet than Euripides. So, too, λασιαύχενα 'shaggy-necked' implies heroic strength (in an epic context : but see further in L.-S.-J.) in contrast with the smooth Euripides (826).

823. ἐπισκύνιον : the flesh over the eyes, which is drawn together (ξυνάγων) in a ferocious frown (by a lion in *Iliad* 17, 136). βρυχώμενος : 'bellowing', used of men and animals (especially of the bull in tragedy).

824. γομφοπαγῆ : 'fastened with bolts', perhaps a parody of Aeschylus's γομφόδετος (of a ship) in *Supplices* 846. These are the only two compounds in γομφο-in Greek. πινακηδὸν : more Aeschylean parody (*cf.* on 804) : not simply 'plankwise' here but 'like ship's-timber' : *cf. Odyssey* 12, 67 πίνακάς τε νεῶν.

825. γηγενεῖ φυσήματι : 'with titanic blast', or 'with the puff of a giant's lungs' (*cf.* the possible reference in 848 to Τυφώς, one of the Earth-born). There is perhaps a hint at Aeschylus's bombast in the *Oreithyia* (see 'Longinus', Περὶ ὕψους 3) : *cf.* the description of Cratinus's style in *Kn.* 527-9.

826-9. A highly metaphorical description of Euripides. στο-

ματουργός (lit. 'mouth-worker') may be an adaptation of Aeschylus's στόμαργος in *Septem* 447 (*cf. γλώσσαργος* in L.-S.-J.) : for its implication see on 820. **ἐπῶν βασανίστρια** 'tester [or possibly 'torturer' : *cf.* on 618 ff.] of phrases' (see on 862). **λίσπη γλῶσσ'** : 'smooth tongue' (*cf. Agamemnon* 1228). 'Unrolling itself, shaking the bridle of envy [*i.e.* urging on his envy as a driver urges on a horse], will dissect and splinter [for λεπτολογεῖν= 'split hairs' *cf. Clouds* 320 ; and see further in Radermacher for the use of λεπτός as 'subtle, refined' in literary criticism] the phrases [of Aeschylus], the large labour of his [Aeschylus's] lungs.' Mitchell (whose translation I have adapted in the last phrase) notes the alliteration of the π's in 829, and compares Aeschylus, *Persians* 751 πολὺς πλούτου πόρος (*cf.* on 136).

(This follows the traditional renderings. For a tentative reinterpretation, which takes into account the variant γλῶσσαν ἐλισσομένη in 827 and Callistratus's curious explanation of λίσπη in 826 as 'a very small little animal', see further in *Hermathena* lxxxix (1957). Briefly, my suggestion there is that in 815 and 825-6 Ar. intends us to see Euripides as some kind of fly with a high-pitched buzz (ὀξύλαλον) and long, probing proboscis (reading γλῶσσαν ἐλισσομένη), which vexes and bites the huge and unwieldy Aeschylus, as the gad-fly persecutes Io in *Prometheus Vinctus*. But clear proof is lacking ; and it is uncertain whether in this phantasmagoria of emblematic animals any clear emblem is intended for Euripides.)

830 ff. ACTION. After the Chorus's fantastic introduction (which favours Aeschylus, though he is not presented as flawless by any means) the rival poets enter, accompanied by Dionysos, and possibly Pluto (see on 1414).

830. οὐκ ἄν μεθείμην τοῦ θρόνου : 'I won't give up my claim to [lit. 'let go my hold on' : the 2 aor. opt. mid. is potential or quasi-conditional, *sc.* 'whatever you do', here] the chair of honour' (*cf.* on 765). **μὴ νουθέτει :** the *Present Imperative* implies 'don't keep on advising me to'. Euripides is presumably addressing Dionysos or Pluto.

833-4. 'He'll be putting on a high-and-mighty pose [*cf.* in 703] at the beginning—the kind of hocus-pocus he used to produce every time in his tragedies.' E. means A.'s use of the silent actor, as described in 911 ff. Ar. uses τερατεία and its cognates elsewhere of pretentious humbug (see *Clouds* 318, *Kn.* 627, *Lysis.* 762, and fr. 198, 9).

837. ἀγριοποιόν : 'a poet of boors', *i.e.* producing boorish characters in his plays (prolonged silence in company being regarded as a mark of the ἄγριος καὶ ἀπαίδευτος). For the compound

in -ποιός (note the regular accent for the transitive force) cf. in
842 and 846. αὐθαδόστομον : 'stubborn-mouthed', i.e. obstinately
refusing at first to speak (cf. 1020) and then, when he does deign
to speak, speaking in a self-willed way without accommodating
his manner to his hearers. αὐθαδία comes from αὐτός and ἥδομαι,
'self-pleasing' : it occurs first in Aeschylus's P.V. 79, 1034. For
Aeschylus's fondness for αὐτο- compounds see Stanford, Aeschylus
7-8 : Ar. parodies it also in 822 and 903.

838-9. The three negative compounds (cf. 204) parody Euri-
pides's own style. He uses ἀχαλίνων στομάτων in Bacchae 386,
and cf. fr. 492 and Heracles 382. ἀθύρωτος (v.l. ἀπύλωτος) is
perhaps a variation on his remarkable ἀθυρόγλωσσος in Orestes
903 (but cf. Theognis 421). The two long compound words in
839 probably mock Aeschylus's fondness for grandiose epithets :
see Earp 6 ff. They also form a grotesque two-word trimeter,
perhaps to parody A.'s frequent use of three-word trimeters (see
on 204). The negative prefix in ἀπεριλάλητον probably implies
here, as sometimes elsewhere (e.g. 898, 1443), deficiency rather
than complete deprivation—hence 'lacking in discursive babble'
(Denniston) rather than 'unperiphrastic' (Rogers) : cf. the use
of περίλεξις in Clouds 318, and see frs. 376, 667. λαλιά is Euripides's
strong point : cf. 91, 954, and Radermacher. κομποφακελορρή-
μονα : lit. 'boast-bundle-phrased' : for κομπο- cf. in 940, 961, and
Acharnians 589, 1182. Translate : 'with mouth unbridled, un-
controlled, undoored : subperiphrastic, bombastiloquent' (adapted
from Rogers).

840. ἄληθες : 'Is that so ?', with heavy irony. Note the reces-
sive accent in this use of ἀληθής. 'Child of the agricultural
goddess' : a parody of a phrase from Euripides (fr. 878), by
substituting ἀρουραίας for E.'s θαλασσίας. It refers to the accusa-
tion made elsewhere by Ar. (cf. 946-7, Acharnians 478 etc.) that
E.'s mother, Cleito, was a greengrocer. The evidence for this is
dubious : Theopompus says it is true, Philochoros that Cleito
was of noble birth. Perhaps, as Denniston (MS.) suggests, she was
an aristocrat reduced by poverty to selling vegetables, for the
joke needs some basis in fact.

841-2. More of Ar.'s comic polysyllabic Coined Words, two of
them having patronymic endings as elsewhere : 'Do you (δή) say
this about me, Mactwaddlegleaner, poet of beggars [see on 837],
Fitzragpatcher ?' Note the rhyme at the end of each line. E.
introduced ragged characters into at least nine of his plays (in-
cluding Telephus) : cf. 1063 ff. and Ach. 415 ff.

844. 'And do not angrily inflame your heart with rancour.'
πρὸς ὀργὴν : adverbially : cf. in 856, 998, and 855. The line is

tragic in metre and style : **σπλάγχνα**, lit. 'bowels', hence 'deep feelings, heart', and **κότος** 'rancour' (cf. Eustathius on *Iliad* 1, 81-2 : χόλος γὰρ καταπεφθεὶς κότος γίνεται), are favourite words of Aeschylus. R. Goossens in *Mélanges Navarre* (Toulouse, 1935) 225-30 argues that this line and the similar line in Euripides, *Cyclops* 424, are both parodies of a lost Aeschylean line.

846. χωλοποιὸν : 'poet of cripples' (cf. on **837**), e.g. Bellerophon, Philoctetes, Telephus.

847-8. D. in mockery of A.'s stormy vehemence (cf. **825**) calls for a victim suitable to placate the wrath of an angry storm-god, i.e. a black (as for a chthonic divinity) male (for a male divinity : **μέλανα** is the reading of R and the *Papyrus* here) lamb. **τυφὼς** 'whirlwind' : personified as Typhos, son of Gaia and Tartaros (Earth and Hell), who in turn was often confused with Typhon, Lord of the Winds : see L.-S.-J. Note the excited repetition, **ἄρν' ἄρνα**. **παῖδες** : either attendant slaves (as in **571**), or else (more probably, I think) stage-hands (cf. *Peace* 174).

849-50. 'Cretan monodies' (cf. **1330** ff.) : the objection to these was partly because they involved drastic innovations in music and dancing, and partly because they were considered immoral (since Aërope, Phaedra, and Pasiphaë were Cretans). 'Unholy marriages' : **γάμους** is apparently used loosely here (as in Eur. *Hel.* 190, *Troades* 932) to describe such relationships as those between Canace and Macareus in *Aeolus* (cf. *Clouds* 1371-2 and **1081** below).

851-2. D. begins abruptly (as Denniston notes) with 'Hold on, you there (**οὗτος**)' to A. But the change of tone in the next phrase, 'much-honoured Aeschylus' (cf. **324, 337**), contrasts with the advice to 'my poor Euripides', and is an omen for the result of the contest. On the proparoxytone **πόνηρ** here and **μόχθηρε** in **1175** see L.-S.-J. at μοχθηρός : the former accentuation is attested in RVUM here.

854. κεφαλαίῳ . . ῥήματι : as the adjective has widely varying meanings, the translation is much disputed here. I take it that two ideas, rhetorical and anatomical, are uppermost : (a) 'summing up', i.e. giving the chief 'heads' of an argument ; (b) having to do with the head : hence a 'heady' (or 'crowning') phrase. An architectural association may also be intended as κεφάλαιος occurs in 5th-century building inscriptions : cf. the other architectural terms in -αιος in *Inscr. Gr.* (ed. minor) 1, 372, and also the phrase, ἐπικρανίτιδες πλίνθοι (referring to the top course in a wall), used there and elsewhere.

855. τὸν Τήλεφον : is a παρὰ προσδοκίαν joke (see Index) : Ar. substitutes the name of E.'s notorious beggar-hero for some similar-

sounding word like ἐγκέφαλος (cf. 134) : cf. Ach. 555-6. The line
begins in tragic style.

856. πραόνως : 'with gentle spirit', 'mildly' : an adverb formed
from πρᾶος, cf. Peace 936, 998, and νοῦς. πρᾶος is the word used in
the Beatitudes (St. Matthew 5, 5) in 'Blessed are the meek'. It
means a kind and courteous person. Aristotle (Nicomachean
Ethics 1125 b 26 ff.) describes the quality as lying between
quick-temperedness and lack of spirit. Xenophon (Eq. 9, 10)
uses τὰ πραέα for 'caresses'.

859. ὥσπερ πρῖνος ἐμπρησθείς : 'like a holm oak set ablaze' (the
v.l. ἐμπρισθείς 'sawn into' of VA is less effective). The holm oak,
quercus ilex, when dry burns with a mighty roar (like our gorse
or furze: cf. Plutarch, Quaest. de Arati signis 5). The aptness
of this Metaphor for Aeschylus's mind and style is discussed in
Stanford, Aeschylus 11-12.

861. 'To bite, be bitten, first' : i.e. to begin the fierce contest,
like some fierce animal : a scholiast says that a cock-fight is
meant. The phrase almost parodies the beginning of 857. Note
Asyndeton.

862. τἄπη : 'the words', i.e. the phrasing, diction (or possibly
the dialogue as opposed to the lyrical parts). In my opinion ἔπος
never clearly means 'lines, verses' in Aristophanes (see Herma-
thena lxxxix, 1957). μέλη : 'songs, lyrics' (less likely 'tunes', as
music without words was of little importance in 5th-century
drama) : Plato (Repub. 398 D) defines μέλος as consisting of
verbal content, melody, and rhythm. νεῦρα : 'sinews', i.e. the
plot or construction which controls the movement of the play
(see Schmid 347 n. 2). Since μέλη can also mean limbs, perhaps
a personification of Tragedy is intended : cf. 1323. These are
accusatives of respect after δάκνεσθαι.

863-4. 'And, by Heaven, with regard to . . .' : γε in enumera-
tion as elsewhere. The heroes named in what follows are all
from E.'s plays. Πηλέα may be scanned as a spondee by Synizesis
(cf. in 76) as -α is generally long in accusatives from -ευς ; but
since Euripides himself occasionally shortens the α (see Denniston
on Electra 599 and Descroix 25), Ar. may be subtly mocking that
licence here. κἄτι μάλα points to a strong climax, which Ar.
turns into an anti-climax by adding the always-to-be-laughed-at
Telephus.

866. ἐβουλόμην : the tense implies 'my attitude was (and is)
that I don't want . . .' : so Goligher citing Wyse on Isaeus 10, 1 :
cf. Schwyzer 2, 354. οὐκ ἐρίζειν : one would expect μή if the
negative goes with the infinitive. Mr. A. C. Moorhouse has sug-

gested to me that the οὐ goes with ἐβουλόμην, being postponed to
avoid οὐ μέν (as in *Medea* 83, Sophocles, *Electra* 905, Herodotus
3, 115). So, too, οὐ δέ is avoided in *Medea* 74 (where Page cites
a different explanation by A. S. Owen). Mr. Moorhouse thinks
this line may be a quotation from, or a parody of, Aeschylus. *Cf.*
on 1392.

868-9. Despite Aeschylus's quarrels with the Athenians (*cf.*
on 807), his plays were highly esteemed and were honoured by a
public decree allowing their re-performance after his death (see
Σ on *Acharnians* 10, and Quintilian 10, 1, 66). But when A. says
here that Euripides's plays have died with their author, he is
a false prophet : in the 4th century B.C. and later Euripides's
popularity far surpassed Aeschylus's (and Sophocles's).

872. The incense (see on 888), and the fire for burning it are
required for a rite of solemn invocation to the gods (not a sacrifice)
as in *Wasps* 861-2.

874. ὑμεῖς : the Chorus. ὑπᾴσατε : 'sing in accompaniment'
(to the rite of igniting and wafting the incense) : for the same
use of ὑπο- see 366.

875-82. A dactylic hymn of invocation (ὕμνος κλητικός : for
structural analogies with serious hymns of this genre see Rader-
macher).

METRE.   **875** : – ∪∪ – ∪∪ – ∪∪ – – : dactylic tetrameter.
876-8 : 3 dactylic hexameters.   **879** : – ∪∪ – ∪∪ – ∪∪ – ∧ :
dactylic tetrameter catalectic.   **880** = 875.   **881** = 879.   **882** =
875 + ithyphallic (– ∪ – ∪ – –). This last sudden change of
metre may be for comic effect—the trochees making a kind of
metrical *Bathos* after the lordly dactyls, as in **814** ff.

876. λεπτολόγους : 'subtle' : *cf.* on 828. ξυνετὰς : 'intelli-
gent' : see on 893. γνωμοτύπων : 'coiners of maxims' (γνῶμαι) :
cf. Clouds 950, *Kn.* 1379.

877-8. 'When they come to the contest, offering counter-
arguments with keenly studied, crooked wrestling tricks' : *cf.* 775.

879. Note ἐφορῶ here = 'supervise, look upon' from near at
hand, while καθορῶ in 876 = 'look down from above' (while they
are still in the celestial sphere).

880-1. 'A pair of mouths most skilled to provide phrases and
sawdust of words.' Many editors have considered 'phrases',
ῥήματα, too colourless to stand beside the vivid παραπρίσματ᾽, and
emend (*e.g.* Kock πρέμνα τε, Thiersch ῥεύματα, Bergk ῥήγματα :
see Blaydes for others).

886. With θρέψασα 'nursed' here *cf. Clouds* 519. Aeschylus was born at Eleusis, the centre of Demeter's Mysteries. Apart from this, the invocation of Demeter is not particularly apt for Aeschylus, since he does not seem to have shown much interest in her cult: see H. Lebrun, 'Eschyle et Déméter', *Revue des Études Grecques* lix-lx (1946-7), 28 ff. According to Aristotle, *Nicomachean Ethics* 1111 a 9 ff., he was accused of divulging forbidden mysteries in his plays: but this does not prove he was an Eleusinian initiate (see Rose 148 n. 1, Schmid-Stählin 1, 2, 106 n. 2).

887. εἶναι: either infinitive as imperative (*cf.* on **169**), or else some word meaning 'grant' must be understood. *Cf.* **894**.

888. The word-order in this line varies greatly in the MSS. and *Papyrus*. I follow Fritzsche's arrangement: *cf.* Erbse 272. ἐπίθες . . . λαβών: 'take and put on the fire'. λιβανωτόν: 'incense'. (The word comes from a Semitic source: *cf.* Hebrew *lebona*.) Euripides politely refuses this traditional aid to prayer, with καλῶς ('It's all right, thanks': *cf.* on **508**): *cf.* the similar refusal in *Clouds* **426**.

890. ἴδιοι: 'private' or 'personal'. κόμμα καινόν: 'a new minting': for the coinage *Metaphor cf.* **720** ff. καὶ μάλα: 'actually, very much so' (καὶ 'expressing the reality of an idea': *cf.* Verdenius as cited on **170**).

891. τοῖσιν ἰδιώταις θεοῖς: *cf.* on ἰδιώτης in **459**: here it seems to mean 'unofficial' or 'unprofessional' (see L.-S.-J. iii): Ar. here as elsewhere assumes the widespread (but misleading) view that Euripides (like *Socrates*) did not believe at all in the traditional gods of Greece (§ 6): *cf.* Socrates's similar views in *Clouds* 247-8, 264-5.

892-4. 'O air, my food, O pivot of my tongue, | O mother-wit, O nostrils keen of scent' (Cope's translation). With these expressions (Blaydes quotes many parallels) Ar. mocks at Euripides's materialism. Like Socrates (in *Clouds* 264-5: *cf.* 424), he is represented as believing in αἰθήρ, the upper air, as the first principle of life (see Euripides, frs. 839, 877, 941), volubility (*cf.* 826-7), hyper-intelligence (Euripides often uses the term ξύνεσις, Aeschylus and Sophocles never), and over-fastidious criticism. For sophistic 5th-century uses of the main words in **894** see Schmid 347-8. E.'s prayer is much less modest than A.'s.

895-904. An Ode with corresponding Antode in **992-1003** (but with interchange of ◡ ◡ for −). See § 13 n. 72. Its dramatic purpose is to stimulate interest in the coming contest.

METRE. **895**: −− −− ◡◡− −−: spondaic-anapaestic dimeter. **896=904a**: ⏓◡ −− −◡ −− ⏓◡ − ∧: catalectic

trochaic trimeter. 897 = 902 : ⏑⏑ ⏑ – ⏑ – ⏑ – ⋏ : catalectic
trochaic dimeter. 898 = 900-1 = 903-4 : trochaic dimeters.

896-7. All the better MSS. read ἀκοῦσαί τινα (with -σαι τινὰ,
perhaps for -σαι τίνα, in VMU) λόγων ἐμμέλειαν. This does not
scan in trochees and does not correspond with 992. I have
followed Dindorf and others in deleting ἐμμέλειαν (which could
have come in as a gloss—an early one, since the Σ had it in his
text—on δαίαν ὁδόν) and reading the interrogative τίνα. This
gives the translation : 'Hear from men of poetic skill what war-
like literary path [perhaps a quotation from some serious poet]
you will enter upon'. But many other emendations have been
offered, and correction still remains very uncertain. ἐμμέλεια
means 'dance' in *Wasps* 1503 and in Plato, *Laws* 816 B, but in
later authors 'harmony, gracefulness' : see Pickard-Cambridge,
Dramatic Festivals 258-9. Denniston suggests 'euphony' here.

898-9. ἄτολμον . . . ἀκίνητοι : 'deficient in boldness . . . lack-
ing in agility' : see on 839.

901-2. τὸν μὲν : Euripides. ἀστεῖον : see on 5. κατερρινη-
μένον : connected with ῥίνη, a 'file' or 'rasp' : hence implying
'with superfluous matter removed' rather than 'polished' : *cf.*
Dionysius Halicarnassus, *Thucydides* 24, 18 καθ' ἐν ἕκαστον τῶν
τῆς φράσεως μορίων ῥινῶν καὶ τορεύων. Translate 'well trimmed' :
κατα- often means 'thoroughly', as here.

903-4. τὸν δ' : Aeschylus. ἀνασπῶντ' αὐτοπρέμνοις τοῖς λόγοι-
σιν ἐμπεσόντα : the difficulty in rendering this phrase lies in the
dative. One would expect an accusative after ἀνασπῶντ' (*cf.*
Sophocles, *Ajax* 302 λόγους ἀνέσπα) ; G. W. Mooney's emendation
αὐτοπρέμνους (to go with ἀλινδήθρας in 904a) supplies this, but the
adjective would be rather far from its noun. Radermacher com-
pares Philo, *De plant.* 24 τυφῶσι μὲν . . . αὐτόπρεμνα δένδρα πρὸς
ἀέρα ἀνασπᾶται. The general picture seems to be that Aeschylus
is like a furious storm or storm-demon (*cf.* 825, 848), which
sweeps everything away with it. Tucker suggests, as one possi-
bility, that we should understand 'him' (Euripides) as object of
ἀνασπῶντ' and, taking the dative as sociative (*cf.* on 560), translate
'snatching *him* up with his arguments root and all, he will fall
upon him . . .'. Green takes λόγοισιν as an instrumental dative
'with uprooted words'. Radermacher understands αὐτοπρέμνους
τοὺς λόγους ⸾from the dative (he compares the construction in
999-1000 ; and see his n. on 815), which gives a rendering 'snatch-
ing up his arguments root and branch [λόγοισιν metaphorically=
δένδροις as in the quotation from Philo] he will fall upon them . . .'.
This last seems best. αὐτόπρεμνος first occurs in Aeschylus,
Eumenides 401 : it literally means 'with the trunk itself', hence
'completely, utterly'. For possible parody in αὐτο- see on 837.

904a. συσκεδᾶν (fut. of συ(ν)σκεδάννυμι : found here only) :
'scatter completely' (*cf.* Humbert, § 607). **ἀλινδήθρας** : 'rolling-
place' (from ἀλινδέω) either for wrestlers (in the on-the-ground
struggle called ἀλίνδησις) or for horses (see *Clouds* 32, Xenophon,
Oeconomicus 11, 18). Goligher translates : 'scatter many a
passage of wordy wallowing'.

905-70. ACTION. The first round of the Aeschylus *v.* Euripides
contest : the *Agon*.

METRE. Catalectic iambic tetrameters (see White 62 ff.) :

$$\leftmoon - \smile - \leftmoon - \smile - \leftmoon - \smile - \leftmoon - \leftmoon \wedge$$

Tribrachs and anapaests occur in the 1st-6th feet in Ar., dactyls
in 1st, 3rd, 5th. There is usually diaeresis after the 4th foot.
For English metrical equivalents *cf.* 'A captain bold of Halifax
who lived in country quarters', and W. S. Gilbert in *The Gondo-
liers*, 'With admirals the ocean teemed all round his wide do-
minions'. This metre is used elsewhere by Ar. in debates where
feeling runs high and language is violent (White 63). The Unjust
Argument uses it in *Clouds* 1036 ff. When Aeschylus leads his
counter-attack in 1004 ff. he uses the weightier and more dignified
anapaests (like the Just Argument in *Clouds* 961 ff.).

905-6. The *Coryphaios*, speaking for the Chorus, introduces the
Agon (*cf.* 1004-5, and regularly elsewhere in Ar.). **οὕτω δ' ὅπως
ἐρεῖτον** : 'But see that you talk in this way . . .'. For other
possible renderings see Tucker. For the future as used here *cf.*
627. μήτ' εἰκόνας : 'not (using) comparisons', *i.e.* avoiding the
far-fetched analogies (*cf.* Aristotle, *Rhetoric* 1407 a 10 ff.) which
were fashionable among would-be wits in Athens at this time :
cf. the efforts of Philip the buffoon in Xenophon, *Symposium* 6,
8, and further in Radermacher. In fact Ar. himself uses them
copiously (*e.g.* 62, 718 ff., *Wasps* 1308 ff.). In the next phrase
'and not the kind of thing someone else would say', the Coryphaios
emphasizes the note of originality and exemplifies the typical
Athenian's love of novelty : *cf. Clouds* 547-8 and Gomme on
Thucydides 3, 38, 5.

907. καὶ μὴν : 'Very well' : a regular use when someone accepts
an invitation (Denniston 355) : *cf.* 1249. As in **830**, Euripides
speaks before Aeschylus—a bad omen for his success, for, as Neil
notes on *Kn.* 338-9, the first to speak is usually the loser in an
Aristophanic contest. **μέν γε** : as in **290**.

908. ἐν τοῖσιν ὑστάτοις : 'in my final remarks' : an orator's
phrase.

909. ἀλαζὼν καὶ φέναξ : 'an impostor and a cheat'. The first
word has the special sense 'one who boasts and exaggerates his

own merits': *cf.* Starkie on *Acharnians* 63. For the *Comic Termination* of φίναξ see Björck 47-8, 61 ff. and 260 ff.; and *cf.* on **587-8** : E.'s accusation is that A. presents appearances and not realities and is a pretentious showman not a sincere dramatist. **οἴοις τε . . . ἐξηπάτα** : 'and by what means he used to deceive . . .'. Perhaps a reference to *Gorgias's* doctrine of rhetorical ἀπάτη is intended : see T. C. Rosenmeyer, 'Gorgias and Aeschylus and Apate', *American Journal of Philology* lxxvi (1955), 256-60.

910. παρὰ Φρυνίχῳ : 'in the school of Phrynichus'. This was Aeschylus's most famous predecessor as a tragedian. Ar. seems to have especially admired his lyrics (see on **1299** below ; also *Birds* **749,** *Thesm.* 164-5, *Wasps* 220, 269). Distinguish the other Phrynichuses in **13** and **689.**

911-13. 'He would wrap up some individual [**ἕνα τιν'**] and have him seated ⟨on the scene⟩ . . . not showing his face—a mere façade of tragedy—they'd not even grunt *this* much' (for **τουτί,** indicating a gesture here, see on **19**). E. is attacking A.'s use of the silent figure in his tragedies. Despite E.'s mockery it probably was a highly effective and quite legitimate dramatic device (as, for example, in Pirandello's *As You Desire Me*) : hence Dionysos's remark in **916.** These figures were 'wrapped up' because to cover the head and face was a traditional sign of grief (*cf. Odyssey* **8,** 92, etc., and 'the mobled queen', Hecuba, in *Hamlet* 2, 2, 523). E. unscrupulously suggests that it was mainly for *Mystification* (*cf.* **918-19**). Actually E. sometimes employs silent figures himself. **Ἀχιλλέα τιν'** : 'someone like Achilles' (*cf.* Aeschylus, *Agamemnon* 55 ἤ τις Ἀπόλλων) : Achilles was a silent figure in A.'s *Phrygians* (*cf.* Ar., fr. 678), Niobe in his *Niobe*. **πρόσχημα** : lit. 'something held in front of something else' (προέχω), hence an outward show with little of value behind, pretentious 'window-dressing'. For **ἂν καθῖσεν** denoting customary action in past time (more commonly with the imperfect as in **914** and **920**) *cf.* **924.**

914-15. 'Yes and then the Chorus would thump down strings of lyrics four in a row, without a break.' **ἐρείδω** is used in Homer and later of various kinds of vigorous pressure. Ar. uses it as here in *Clouds* 1375 and *Kn.* 627 (*cf.* τερατευόμενος there with **834**). **ὁρμαθοὺς** (cognate with ὅρμος 'chain', from εἴρω 'string together') suggests monotony and length (*cf.* **1296-7**). **τέτταρας** : particular for general, as in 'A stitch in time saves *nine*'. **ἐστίγων** : 'continued their silence'.

918. κἀμαυτῷ δοκῶ : 'And so it seems to me (now)' : for the personal construction see on **645** and *cf.* ῥάδια in **930**. Note how

154   ARISTOPHANES: FROGS

fickle and susceptible D. is. **ὁ δεῖνα**: 'Mr. So-and-so' or 'our friend here'. See L.-S.-J. for this curious pronoun (not to be confused with the adjective δεινός). D. avoids mentioning Aeschylus by name presumably because he fears his anger.

920. ἂν διῄει (δίειμι) : 'would go on and on' (without any word from Niobe).

921. ὦ παμπόνηρος: 'Oh, the utter wretch'. This seems a better rendering than 'Oh, how unfortunate I was'.

922. As in *Acharnians* 30, **σκορδινῶμαι** here seems to mean 'stretch oneself' as a sign of weariness or boredom. Miller thinks **δυσφορεῖς** (*cf. Thesm.* 73) has a *Medical* nuance 'show signs of discomfort'. Translate : 'fidget and fret'. The object of D.'s question (to which he knows the answer) is to direct the audience's attention to A.'s silent fury.

924-5. 'A dozen ox-like [*i.e.* huge and lumbering] words with eyebrows and crests, terrible sorts of things, with bogy faces' : these are vague terms half-terrible, half-comic, perhaps not intended to portray anything very precise. **μορμορωπά** (there is a variant μορμυρωπά 'terrible-faced', which Radermacher prefers) : from μορμώ (cognate with *formido*), the name of a Greek bogywoman with huge ears and a changeable face (*cf.* Erinna, *Distaff* 12-15, and see on 289 ff.).

926. ἄγνωτα: either 'unknown' or 'unintelligible'. **σιώπα**: *Present Imperative:* 'stay quiet', rather than ' be [*i.e.* become] silent'. **οἴμοι τάλας**: A. groans to express his misery in having to endure such unfair criticism.

927. σαφές: clarity of meaning was highly valued by the 5th-century *Sophists* : see further in Radermacher and *cf.* 1434. Aeschylus's obscurity of style in general is discussed in Stanford, *Aeschylus* 131-7. **οὐδὲ ἕν** : a regular *Hiatus* : see L.-S.-J. at οὐδείς. **μὴ πρῖε τοὺς ὀδόντας** : lit. ' Don't keep on sawing your teeth ', a more vivid *Metaphor* than our ' grind '.

928-9. Here E. produces a miscellaneous jumble of references to Aeschylus's vocabulary and stage-effects. 'Scamanders' perhaps mocks his Miltonic liking for lordly geographical names. The ' bronze-wrought griffon-eagles on shields' recalls the emblems mentioned by Ar. in *Seven against Thebes* 478, 540-2. **ἱππόκρημνα** : 'horse-cliffed' or 'huge-cliffed' (*cf.* on 818). Ar. had already mocked A.'s fondness for cliffs and steep rocks in *Clouds* 1366-7, where he is described by the Euripides-loving Pheidippides as 'first among poets for noise, incoherence, rant, and cliff-producing' (κρημνοποιόν): *cf.* ὑψηλόκρημνος and ὑψίκρημνος in *Prometheus Vinctus* 5 and 421 (and also Aeschylus, fr. 32).

931. Ironically Ar. makes D.'s first phrase recall Euripides's
Hippolytus 375 : ἤδη ποτ'... νυκτὸς ἐν μακρῷ χρόνῳ.

932-3. τὸν ξουθὸν ἱππαλεκτρυόνα : 'the tawny [or possibly
'clear-voiced'] horse-cock'. According to the Σ on *Peace* 1177
(where the same phrase occurs, as in *Birds* 800) Aeschylus men-
tioned this creature (an emblem on ships, as he says in 933) in
his *Myrmidons*. It was a familiar figure : a horse with the wings
and tail of a cock (see further in P. Perdrizet, 'L'Hippalectryon',
Revue des Études Anciennes vi, 1904, 7-30). ὠμαθέστατ' (ὦ ἀμ.) :
'you great ignoramus'. ἐνεγέγραπτο : 'was depicted' : the
pluperfect because the making of the emblem was prior to the
composition of A.'s play, which in turn was prior to the discussion
here.

934. D. flippantly introduces a crack at a contemporary figure.
Nothing is known of Eryxis himself, so we cannot say what the
point of the comparison is. (W. Schmidt in *Philologus* lxxvi,
1920, 222-5, guesses that it was not his appearance but a fondness
for fighting-cocks that Ar. had in mind.) His father Philoxenos
(son of another Eryxis) was presumably the notorious glutton
(Athenaeus 6 b : *cf.* Sir Thomas Browne, *Pseudodoxia epidemica*
7, 14).

935-6. εἶτ'⟨α⟩ : 'Tell me then' : indignantly. κἀλεκτρυόνα :
'even a cock', as mentioned by Aeschylus in *Agam.* 1671, *Eum.*
861, but not by Euripides in his works as now extant : but A.
introduces one in the parody of E. in 1344. Note the Attic ἄττα
for τινά and ἅττα for ἅτινα here (*cf.* on 173) : 'what kinds of things
were the kind of thing you used to make poetry about ?'

937-8. 'Goat-stags' : E. implies that these also were entirely
fabulous creatures (*cf.* Plato, *Republic* 488 ᴀ). But the original
may have been a kind of antelope : *cf.* Diodorus Siculus 2, 51, 2.
ἅν = ἅ ἐν. The παραπετάσματα (derived from πετάννυμι 'spread
out') were 'hangings' (for walls) or 'curtains'. Μηδικοῖς : Persian
art was renowned for its fanciful animal-figures. Possibly anti-
Persian sentiment is being evoked by E. here.

940-4. Euripides describes tragedy as if she were a medical
patient suffering from some kind of swelling (οἰδοῦσαν : for
κομπασμάτων see on 839). He, then, like a good doctor reduced
(ἰσχναίνω : used by Hippocratic writers : *cf.* the ἰσχνὸς χαρακτήρ
of style, discussed by Radermacher) her weight (βάρος) with
versicles (ἐπύλλιον, Diminutive of ἔπος, used of E.'s style in
Acharnians 398, *Peace* 532 : Kock suggests that a pun on ἑρπύλ-
λιον 'wild thyme', *cf.* *Peace* 168, is intended : see Radermacher)
and with exercises (περιπάτοις : lit. 'walkings about' : much
recommended as a means to health by Greek doctors : *cf.* Hippo-

156 ARISTOPHANES: FROGS

crates, *Reg.* 2, 62, 953 below, and Astydamas, fr. 7) and white beet (τευτλίον : *Diminutive:* recommended as a laxative by Greek physicians). He continued this treatment by giving an infusion (χυλός : obtained by cutting up a herb, pounding the pieces in a mortar, and steeping them in water) of babblings (*cf.* 92), having strained it (the infusion) off from books (*i.e.* books were E.'s *materia medica* : for E. as an early collector of books see Athenaeus 3 a, and for possible mockery of E.'s bookishness here see further in Mitchell). E. then nourished tragedy up again (ἀνατρέφειν is a *Medical Term*) with monodies (*cf.* on 849).

944. As E.'s speech is running on rather too long, Ar. now makes D. interject a cheap gibe about Cephisophon. He was an Athenian who lived in E.'s house and was alleged to have had something to do with E.'s plays and with his wife (*cf.* 1046-8, 1408, 1452, *Acharnians* 395 ff., and fr. 580). I follow von Velsen in giving this interjection to Dionysos. It seems incredible that E. himself could have been portrayed as mentioning this damaging scandal : and *cf.* D.'s interruptions in **934, 947** : he is acting the βωμολόχος (see § 8 n. 26) in this and the following scenes.

946-7. 'But the person who first of all came out [of the scene building : *cf.* § 9] customarily explained at once on my behalf [μοι] the nature [or genealogy : γένος] of the play.' E. is referring to his formal prologues : *cf.* 1200 ff. D. seizes on the ambiguity in γένος to disparage E.'s own genealogy : see on **840**.

948. ἔπειτα responds to μέν in **946** : 'and then'. οὐδένα παρῆκ' [*cf.* in 699] ἀν ἀργόν : 'I allowed no one to stay idle'. I have adopted (with Blaydes) Lenting's emendation of οὐδέν in the mss. here.

952-3. δημοκρατικὸν γὰρ αὖτ' ἔδρων : 'for my action was truly democratic'. E. uses this catch-word from contemporary politics to excuse his readiness to allow every kind of person equal rights of speech in his plays. The word is similarly used for political whitewash in modern times ; but in the late 5th-century Athens the δῆμος which held the κράτος was composed exclusively of adult, male, pure-bred citizens. Here E. probably refers especially to ἰσηγορία, 'equal rights of public speaking', or παρρησία, 'freedom of speech': *cf. Thesm.* 541. D. interrupts with a mocking insinuation that E. was no true democrat himself, but, rather, inclined to favour the oligarchs (he was friendly with Critias, Plato, and Xenophon) and aristocrats (he spent his last years at the court of the king of Macedonia) 'Drop *that* [μὲν = μήν for emphasis], old chap [for τᾶν see on **1243**], for *you* [emphatic by position] haven't the best line of argument [περίπατος : see on **942**] on *that* particular [γε limitative] point'.

954. τουτουσί : 'the spectators here'. **λαλεῖν** : E. uses this as an appreciative word meaning 'to talk freely'. Ar. in his sardonic 'I say so, too', takes the word in its bad sense of 'to be garrulous, to talk too much' (*cf.* the description of the garrulous man in Theophrastus **7** where λαλιά is defined as ἀκρασία τοῦ λόγου ; and see Index).

955. ὡς πρὶν διδάξαι γ' ὤφελες μέσος διαρραγῆναι : best taken as a wish (*cf.* **1382**, and L.-S.-J. at ὀφείλω, ii, 3, and ὡς, D ii 2). The **γε** 'retains little force' in ὡς . . . γε (Denniston 143). With 'burst in the middle' as a term for a violent death *cf.* Judas's death as described in Acts of the Apostles **1**, 18.

957. στρέφειν ἐρᾶν : 'to love to twist' (a *Metaphor* from wrestling). Many editors have found ἐρᾶν in the sense of 'to love' here, either by itself or taken with στρέφειν, awkward ; and many emendations have been offered (see Blaydes). Recently L. J. D. Richardson has suggested (*Hermathena* lxxii, 1948, 80-1) that ἐρᾶν should be taken here in the sense of 'to pour out' hence, rhetorically, 'to spout' : but this meaning is confined to compounds like ἀπερᾶν (though found in tmesis in *Agamemnon* 1599) and the notion seems more apt for Aeschylus's style than for Euripides's (*cf.* **1005**). R. G. Ussher in *Hermathena* lxxxv (1955), 57 notes that στρέφειν in the sense of 'twist (oneself)' is in the middle voice elsewhere ; so he conjectures στρέφειν ἕδραν 'to turn the buttocks' (a wrestling term for 'cross-buttocking' : *cf.* Theocritus **24**, 111, with Gow's note), hence 'to' wriggle' with perhaps a reference to dancing (*cf.* Euripides's *Electra* 737 ff.). Since Aristophanes's lists of single terms are often rather jumbled, I agree with Radermacher (who takes ἐρᾶν ἀπὸ κοινοῦ with both στρέφειν and τεχνάζειν) that the ms. reading may stand : *cf.* Starkie on *Ach.* 385-6, and *cf.* Sophocles, fr. 314, 362 (Pearson).

958. 'To suspect evil, to be over-clever in everything.' The verb περινοεῖν does not recur in the 5th or 4th centuries, but *cf.* περίνοια in Thucydides **3**, 43, 3. (Van Leeuwen is hardly justified in objecting to it as coming too soon after νοεῖν.) Ar. is mocking the suspicious and hypercritical temper of contemporary Athenians : *cf.* **971** ff.

958. 'Introductions [for this use of εἰσβολή see Euripides, *Ion* 677 : but *cf.* on **1104** and L.-S.-J.] of subtle [for λεπτός *cf.* 828] rules and verbal angulations' [or 'squarings-off of verses' : *cf.* on **862** and γωνιαῖον ῥῆμα in Plato Comicus 67]. For the *Metaphors* from joinery or building *cf.* **799** ff.

959. 'Introducing domestic affairs both useful and familiar to us.' (Goligher compares Isaeus **1**, 4 : χρώμενοι δὲ ἐκείνῳ πάντων οἰκειότατα.) This is in contrast with Aeschylus's heroic and fabulous themes, as 961-3 indicates. *Cf. Wasps* 1179 ff.

960. ἂν ἐξηλεγχόμην : 'I would have been open to refutation' : *sc.* 'if I had made any mistakes'. *Cf.* **857.**

963. 'By portraying people like Cycnus and Memnon [allies of the Trojans, killed by Achilles : they appeared in plays by Aeschylus] with bells [κώδωνες were attached to shields or to horses' harness : less likely 'trumpets' here : see L.-S.-J.] and cheek-pieces [φάλαρα] on their steeds' : *i.e.* fabulous heroes with archaic equipment.

965-6. Rogers renders : 'Uncouth Megaenetus is his [τουτου-μεν-ὶ], and rough Phormisius too ; | Great long-beard-lance-and-trumpet [see on **963**] men, flesh-tearers with the pine'. For the shaggy Phormisius (the name suggests φορμός 'a mat or rug' : *cf.* Shakespeare's reference to Irish soldiers as 'rug-headed kerns' in *Richard II*, 2, 1, 157) *cf. Eccl.* 97 : he was associated with Cleitophon (see **967**) in politics. *Cf.* Aeschylus, fr. 27. Megaenetus is not mentioned elsewhere. Σ says he was self-willed and ambitious. ὁ Μάνῆς : the precise meaning is doubtful, and A has a variant Μάγνης. Manes was the name of Phrygian slaves (*cf.* Μᾱνία in **1345**), a bad throw at dice (*cf.* the metaphor in **970**), and the bronze figure aimed at in the game of κότταβος. The variant in A, 'the Magnesian', might refer to the proverbial insolence of the people of that region. Note the wondrous two-word tetrameter (*cf.* on **204**) and the *Coined Words* in **966**. Into these two *Polysyllabic Terms* are telescoped : (*a*) a reference to heroic accoutrements ; (*b*) a reference to the alarming beards of soldiers (*cf.* Shakespeare, *As You like It*, 2, 7, 149-50 'a soldier . . . bearded like the pard') ; (*c*) a comic *Patronymic* ; (*d*) a reference to Sinis the legendary brigand of the Isthmus who used to tie his victims between two bent-down pine-trees and then release the trees to tear the victim's flesh asunder (σαρκάζω, *cf. Peace* 482 : a reference to σαρκασμός 'mockery, sarcasm' is possible, but not, I think, the primary implication here).

967. Cleitophon is probably the member of the Socratic circle after whom a Platonic dialogue is named. He helped *Theramenes* in establishing the Four Hundred in 411. κομψός : 'smart, ingenious' : P. Chantraine in *Revue des Études Grecques* lviii (1945), 90-6 connects it with κομέω 'tend, take care of' and translates *chic, bien soigné*. Euripides was apparently the first to use the word in serious literature : hence κομψευριπικῶς in *Kn.* 18.

969-70. 'Who, if he encounters [a frequent use of περιπίπτω] trouble anywhere, and gets close beside it [παραστῇ]' : Radermacher quotes parallels to the verbs here : *cf.* especially Strattis, fr. 23 Χῖος παραστὰς Κῷον οὐκ ἐᾷ λέγειν (with Kock's note). **970** is desperately disputed. A reference to *Theramenes's* political adroitness in changing sides is presumably intended. Rogers takes πέπτωκεν etc. as a simple reference to a change of citizenship and translates : 'A Kian with a kappa, sir, not Chian with a chi', and rejects further subtleties. But the term ὁ χῖος (*sc.* βόλος) was used for the lowest throw in playing with dice (*cf.* Strattis as quoted above), and the verb πέπτωκεν could refer to the fall of dice. Hence, since the best throw was called ὁ κῷος, Ar. may have intended a *Pun* and a παρὰ προσδοκίαν joke in Κεῖος 'not the Chian but the Keian [instead of Koän]'. Possibly, too, there is a reference to the misfortunes of Chios (note Χῖος is the name of the island, Χῖος, from Χίιος, for an inhabitant) during the Peloponnesian War, and to the fact that the Sophist Prodicus was born in Keos. (Theramenes was in fact a thoroughbred Athenian : Plutarch's remark in *Nicias* 2 that he was from Keos probably comes from Aristophanes's sneer here.) For other possible innuendoes and for many editorial conjectural emendations of the text (including *Aristarchus's* Κῷος for Κεῖος which removes a joke) see Radermacher (whose Χεῖος Coulon has now rejected), Tucker, Blaydes, and van Leeuwen. The problem is complicated by the fact that in Aristophanes's time there was no distinction between capital and 'lower-case' letters (*cf.* § 14 n. 75). The perfect tense of πέπτωκεν implies entry into a stable condition from an uncertain and temporary one : see Humbert, § 250. I translate (after Rogers) : '. . . there you'll find him safely out of danger, like a lucky throv of the dice—a Keian with a *kappa*, not a Chian with a *chi*'.

971–91. METRE : iambic dimeters with a final (991) catalectic iambic dimeter. The absence of any rhythmical cadence until the end is perhaps an indication that the lines were gabbled at high speed, *i.e.* as a πνῖγος : see § 13 n. 72.

ACTION. In turn E. and D. sing (and perhaps dance) in a short lively passage which embroiders the theme of domestic realism in E.'s plays (*cf.* 959).

971–9. E. (absurdly) argues that his plays have taught Athenian householders to be clever and careful in the management of their households. τούτοισιν : the Athenians in the theatre. εἰσηγησάμην : 'instructed'. For the rhetorical implications of questions beginning πῶς, ποῦ, τίς (978–9), *i.e.* what manner, what place, what person, see Radermacher (and *cf.*, *e.g.*, Euripides, fr. 277).

975–6. διειδέναι τά τ' ἄλλα καὶ etc. : I take τά τ' ἄλλα καὶ here as a variant of ἄλλως τε καί, and translate 'have a thorough knowledge especially of progressive [ἄμεινον ἢ πρὸ τοῦ] household management'. Other renderings are possible.

980-91. D. caricatures E.'s claims by describing absurd details of this domestic realism, which, it is implied, has turned Athenians into busybodies (see on 228) and skinflints (*cf.* what Theophrastus 10 and 30 says about the μικρολόγος and αἰσχροκερδής) : Tucker believes that this kind of parsimony and suspicion 'did prevail at Athens then, but that the cause was the War not Euripides.

981. εἰσιὼν : understand 'his house', as οἰκέτας in 982 indicates.

983 : χύτρα : 'pot' : not to be mentioned in dignified conversation according to Plato, *Greater Hippias* 288 D.

984. ἀπεδήδοκεν : 'has eaten off' (-εσθίω) rather than 'has bitten off' (which would be ἀποδέδηχε, -δάκνω) : *cf.* παρέτραγεν 'nibbled off' (-τρώγω) in 988. These are cautious thieves.

986. τέθνηκε : 'has perished', an amusing touch of tragic style in this homely context of pots and sprats (*cf. inutiles maenae* in Martial 12, 32, 15 : μαινίς is a *Diminutive*). μοι : dative of the person interested : the Hiberno-English 'on me' (*e.g.* 'He lost a book on me') gives a better rendering than any idiom in standard English.

988. ἐλάα (Attic for ἐλαία) means the olive-fruit here, but the olive tree in 995.

989-91. 'Hitherto full of stupidity they used to sit gaping [κεχηνότες : χάσκω/χαίνω : *cf.* the Κεχηναῖοι in *Kn.* 1263 and the French *gobe-mouche* 'idiot'], mammy's darlings [μαμμάκυθοι : perhaps conn. w. κεύθω, *i.e.* hiding their heads in their mother's lap : *cf.* βλιτομάμμας in *Clouds* 1001], silly fools.' See Björck 157-8. The origin of μελιτίδαι (for other instances see Blaydes) is uncertain. It possibly is connected with the deme Melite (*cf.* 501) where there was (*cf.* Athenaeus 614 d) a Fool's Club, a *Confrérie des Sots.* Kock connects it with μέλι 'honey', and compares *Honigpüppchen* and βλιτομάμμας above (and Tucker adds 'Sugar-Baby') : Radermacher connects it with Maltese lap-dogs, Μελῖταῖοι (*cf.* Theophrastus 21, 9). The variation ι/ῑ renders these explanations dubious, but see H. Langerbeck in *Harvard Studies in Classical Philology* lxiii (1958), 47-9, who scans μελῖτίδαι here.

992-1003. In this antistrophe to 895-904a the Chorus sings an ode to introduce Aeschylus's counter-attack (which begins in 1006). The metre corresponds to 895 ff. with interchanges of ◡ ◡ for —, and vice versa. For the irrational anapaest for trochee in the 2nd foot of 993 (φέρε πρὸς) see Platnauer, *Antistrophic Variations.*

992. A quotation from Aeschylus's *Myrmidons* (*cf. Oxyrhynchus Papyri* xviii, 2163), implying that A. in his haughty and angry reserve towards Euripides in the last scene resembled Achilles in his sulky fury after Briseis had been taken from him.

993. For μόνον introducing a reservation see Knox-Headlam on Herodas 2, 89. ὅπως : 'see that'.

995. ἐκτὸς . . . τῶν ἐλαῶν : 'off the course' : olive trees were planted on each side of race-courses : this view (cf. Wecklein) seems better than 'beyond the winning-post' (Blaydes and others). For the general notion cf. Aeschylus, Choëph. 1022-4, P.V. 883.

997-8. γεννάδα : see on 179. πρὸς ὀργὴν : see on 844.

999-1003. The Metaphor has changed. A. is no longer a charioteer. He is now a mariner in a storm (which is his anger : cf. 825, 829). Translate : 'But take in a reef and use only the tips of your sails, then gradually [lit. 'more and more'] bring on [ἄξεις] your ship and watch out for whenever you may get a smooth and settled breeze'. For the construction of συστείλας (which assumes an accusative ἱστία from ἱστίοις) see on 903 ff. ἄξεις is unexpected but, as Tucker observes, does not demand emendation. Cf. the use of προσάγω in Medea 523-4.

1004 ff. METRE : catalectic anapaestic tetrameters as in 354 ff. This metrical identity with the ritual warning of the Mystics there would lend solemnity to the opening lines here.

1004-5. Spoken, like the similar admonition in 905-6, by the Coryphaios on behalf of the Chorus. Frere renders : 'Now for your answer, illustrious architect, Founder of lofty theatrical lays! Patron in chief of our tragical trumperies! Open the floodgate of figure and phrase!' For the architectural Metaphor in πυργώσας, lit. 'build like a tower', cf. Peace 749 where Ar. uses it of his own 'ennoblement' of comedy (see further in Blaydes). Ar. introduces a grotesque anticlimax (Bathos) with λῆρον (cf. 809) 'boloney, twaddle' (instead of something like τέχνη or λέξις : cf. in 923, 945). Radermacher's emendation ληρόν 'gold ornament' spoils a joke : so, too, the suggestion that λῆρος refers to the inferiority of tragedy before A. improved it. τὸν κρουνὸν : 'the spout', sc. of eloquence, cf. Kn. 89 κρουνοχυτρολήραιον εἶ (note the combination with λῆρος there, too).

1009-10. 'For dexterity and advice, and because we make the citizens better.' Whether Euripides in real life would have agreed with the moral purpose implied in the last two terms is far from certain. In what follows Aeschylus, ignoring the technical quality of δεξιότης (in which E. might well have been judged the victor : cf. 71 ff.), concentrates his attack on the moral effect of E.'s plays.

1012. The Σ sees a joke in τεθνάναι, since A. and E. are already

dead. μὴ τοῦτον ἐρώτα : 'You needn't ask him', rather than 'Don't ask him' : *cf.* on 1020.

1014-15. τετραπήχεις : 'six-footers' here in a good sense (*cf. Wasps* 553 : contrast Theocritus 15, 17). μὴ διαδρασιπολίτας : 'not citizens of Runaway-town', *cf.* χαυνοπολίτας in *Acharnians* 635 and μικροπολίτας in *Kn.* 817. ἀγοραίους : 'loafers in the Agora' (which is *not* primarily the 'market-place'). For κοβάλους and πανούργους see on 104 and on 35.

1016-17. πνέοντας : 'breathing forth' : Aeschylus (following Homer) is fond of using this word in the sense of 'passionately exhibiting' (see L.-S.-J. and Blaydes). πήληκας : 'casques', an epic word. θυμοὺς ἑπταβοείους : 'sevenfold-oxhide passions' : the epithet is comically transferred from Homer's description of the shield of Ajax in *Iliad* 7, 219 ff. and elsewhere. Aeschylus is made to parody his own style here.

1018. καὶ δή : 'already, you see', καὶ here implying 'as we might have expected' (*cf.* on 170). χωρεῖ : 'is advancing' (*cf.* 884). The phrase is repeated from *Wasps* 1483. κρανοποιῶν : 'with his helmet-making' (a noisy process in real life). αὖ : 'further, what's more'. The division of speakers is uncertain here and in 1019-20. I agree with Erbse.

1020. 'Speak, Aeschylus, and don't keep on with your stubborn pride and anger' : a good example of the difference between the aorist imperative (used of a non-continuous or new action) and the *Present Imperative* (of a continuing action), though this is not always strictly observed. αὐθάδως : see on 837.

1021-2. 'By composing a play brim-full of the War God.' This description of Aeschylus's *Seven against Thebes* was first used by the Sophist *Gorgias* (Plutarch, *Moralia* 715 E : *cf.* Kraus, *Testimonia* and Schmid-Stählin 1, 3, 77 n. 4 on this line). ἄν . . . ἡράσθη : 'might well have felt a desire' : see Schwyzer 2, 347.

1024. τύπτου : 'take a beating for that at any rate' (γ'), *i.e.* you deserve to be beaten for that if for nothing else. *Cf.* on 1020. The Thebans were enemies of the Athenians for most of the 5th century and had defeated them at Coronea in 447 and Delion in 424. For evidence that the Athenians felt some martial inferiority to the Thebans at this time see Xenophon, *Memor.* 3, 5, 4 ff.

1026. εἶτα . . . μετὰ τοῦτ' : in fact A.'s *Persians* was produced in 472, five years before *Seven against Thebes*. Ar. has probably made a mistake in his dates. Tucker's and Radermacher's arguments that the words refer only to rhetorical sequence are unconvincing. *Cf. Birds* 810-11. διδάξας : 'by producing . . .'. ἐξεδίδαξα (Bentley's emendation for the unmetrical ἐδίδαξα): 'I taught fully' (but Radermacher thinks that the ἐξ- is merely due to the repetition of the verb : cf. his note on 369).

1028-9. The better MSS. have ἡνίκ' ἤκουσα περὶ Δαρείου, in which ἤκουσα gives – – ◡ where ◡ – ◡◡ – is required by the metre. Also περὶ makes poor sense, as Darius (whose ghost appears in the play) had died long before the actions described there : this fact is also against the reading ἀπηγγέλθη in some minor MSS. Many emendations have been suggested (see Blaydes, van Leeuwen, and Radermacher), none entirely convincing. I have provisionally adopted Tyrrell's ἐκώκυσας, παῖ Δαρείου 'when you cried out in grief, O child of dead Darius' (i.e. Xerxes, who begins crying out in grief in v. 908 of the play and continues to do so to the end : 'dead' Darius I take to be a reference to the ghost). This fits in with δ' εὐθὺς in 1029, for the Chorus does immediately begin to lament violently with Xerxes in *Persians* 918 ff. They do not actually say ἰαυοῖ in any part of the play as we now have it : but they do say ἰωά twice at the end of the last scene (1070-1 : cf. ὀᾶ in 117, 122). Possibly Ar. has deliberately distorted this cry to give a barbaric effect (cf. βάρβαρα βάγματα in *Persians* 634-6) : cf. his use of Ἰαοναῦ in *Ach.* 104 and κόραυννα, βασιλιναῦ in *Birds* 1678. Or else possibly the Chorus in *Persians* did in fact pronounce ἰωά very like ἰαυοῖ. At any rate it seems best to take both 1028 and 1029 to refer to the lamentation scene at the end of *Persians*, which when well performed must have been very impressive but, if badly done, very ludicrous.

1030. A. ignores D.'s remark. His next statement is ambiguous : either 'these are the things that men of poetry [ἄνδρας ποιητὰς : cf. 1008] should practise' (so Tucker) or 'poets should train men in these things' (so Merry : cf. *Plutus* 47). I prefer the first.

1031-4. ὠφέλιμοι : 'of practical use, helpful'. In what follows A. extends his moral criterion (of 1009 ff.) of good poetry to include religious and social improvements. Orpheus is a shadowy and controversial figure (see Guthrie, chap. 15), the reputed founder of the Orphic cult (τελετάς). φόνων τ' ἀπέχεσθαι : probably the prohibition was specially directed against the slaughter of animals for food : cf. Euripides, *Hippolytus* 952, Horace, *Ars Poetica* 391-2. The poet Musaeus is an even dimmer figure : Herodotus (7, 6) says that his oracles were edited by Onomacritos in Athens in the late 6th century B.C. Cf. Plato, *Rep.* 363 c ff., and see Guthrie 307 ff. Hesiod, the early Boeotian poet, gives advice on agriculture in his *Works and Days* (Ἔργα καὶ ἡμέραι : paraphrased here by ἐργασίας and ὥρας). Note the special epithet, 'divine', for Homer, as in Plato, *Phaedo* 95 A.

164   ARISTOPHANES: FROGS

1035. ἀπὸ τοῦ=ἀπὸ τίνος. τοῦδ' is *Bentley's* necessary correction of the MS. τοῦθ'.

1036-9. 'Well I can tell you he certainly didn't teach Pantacles, at any rate, that clumsy clown : because the other day [πρώην can also mean 'the day before yesterday'] when he was acting as escort to a procession [ἔπεμπεν sc. πομπήν, as often : perhaps the Panathenaia] he was going to fasten his helmet on his head first and then tie on the crest': an obviously idiotic procedure. Nothing else is known of Pantacles, unless he was the lyric poet of that name.

1039-42. ἀλλ' . . . τοι: 'well, anyhow'. We must understand 'Homer taught . . .'. Lamachos was mocked by Ar. during his life in *Acharnians* and *Peace* but now, after his death in the Sicilian Expedition (§ 4 n. 12), he is cited with respect (ἥρως). Plutarch, *Nicias* 18, describes his heroic death. ὅθεν: 'whence', from Homer : according to Athenaeus 347 e Aeschylus himself described his plays as 'slices from the great banquets of Homer' (τεμάχη τῶν Ὁμήρου μεγάλων δείπνων, cf. on 517). ἀπομαξαμένη: 'taking its shape': ἀπομάσσω literally means 'take an impression' by pressing a soft substance into a mould : cf. αὐτέκμαγμα σόν 'the very image of you' in *Thesm.* 514. Πατρόκλων, Τεύκρων: 'warriors like P. and T.' (Homeric heroes): for the plural cf. 963, 1043. ἀντεκτείνειν: lit. 'stretch himself out against': *i.e.* straining to equal someone else in size : 'to measure up to'.

1043. ' Phaedras as harlots [*i.e.* in E.'s *Hippolytus*] nor Stheneboias ' : for new evidence of the *Stheneboia* see Page 126-9 and Pickard-Cambridge in Powell, *New Chapters* 3. *Cf.* on 1051. For the omission of ὡς in this comparison see on 701-2. The description of Phaedra is not justified by her noble conduct in the *Hippolytus* as we now have it : perhaps A. is referring to the lost earlier version (the *Hippolytus Crowned* which according to the *Life of Euripides* shocked the Athenians with its display of feminine shamelessness) ; or perhaps the description is only another of Aristophanes's ruthless exaggerations (*cf. Thesm.* 386 ff. and 547-8). Stheneboia, wife of Proitos, king of Tiryns, appears as Anteia in *Iliad* 6, 150 ff. ; so Euripides was not the first to use this theme in poetry. Against Ar.'s strictures here van Leeuwen notes that E. portrayed many noble women in his plays, *e.g.* Alcestis, Macaria, Polyxena, Iphigeneia, and compares Lycurgus's eulogy of E. (*Against Leocrates* 100).

1044. Aeschylus's boast holds for all his plays as now known, if it is agreed that Clytaemnestra in *Agamemnon* is not in love with Aegisthus. Plato, *Republic* 395 D, also condemns the presentation in poetry of women in love.

1045-6. In E.'s retort Aphrodite symbolizes sensual beauty and loveliness (like the Latin Venus). In A.'s reply she represents passionate love, and he adds a mocking reference to E.'s domestic unhappiness (according to Suidas he divorced his first wife and found his second unfaithful): *cf.* on **944.** For R's οὐδὲ γὰρ ἦν I have adopted AU's οὐ γὰρ ἐπῆν: 'For there was nothing of Aphrodite in your possession'. The second meaning of ἔπειμι 'be upon' leads to the grotesque exaggeration ἐπικαθῆτο 'sat upon' (*cf.* the play on ἐπί in **197** ff.). πολλὴ πολλοῦ: 'very much': the emphatic genitive recurs in *Kn.* 822 and *Clouds* 915 (see further in Poultney).

1047. κατ' οὖν ἔβαλεν: for κατέβαλεν οὖν: Denniston 430 thinks this remarkable *Tmesis* is an Ionism or Dorism in parody of E. who uses it freely. Radermacher compares Epicharmus **35,** 6 κἀπ' ὧν ἠχθόμαν. τοῦτό γέ τοι δή: 'yes, she certainly did that'. For the unusual grouping of particles see Denniston 551: he thinks that perhaps σοι should be read for τοι, meaning 'That's one for you' (*cf.* Merry).

1051. 'To drink hemlock': *cf.* on **124-5.** κώνεια must have εἰ (by internal *Correption*) to scan before πίνειν: *cf.* Radermacher who prefers to print κώνεα. Otherwise we must read πιεῖν with AU. διὰ τοὺς σοὺς Βελλεροφόντας: 'because of people like your Bellerophon' (*cf.* on **1042**): hardly 'plays like your *Bellerophon*'. B. appeared in E.'s *Stheneboia* (*cf.* on **1043**), and caused the death of the love-distracted Stheneboia in that play. Women were probably present at the tragic performances: see § 2 n. 7. On suicide by women see the remarkable passage in Euripides, *Ion* 843-7.

1052. 'Tell me, was it an untrue [οὐκ ὄντα] story this I composed about Phaedra?': *cf.* τὸν ἐόντα λόγον in Herodotus **1, 95** and **116.** See end of next note.

1053-4. τόν γε ποιητήν: *i.e.* whatever others may do 'the poet, at any rate, should . . .'. (In actual fact Aeschylus himself displays a formidable amount of πονηρά in his plays, to say nothing of the πονηρά of a poet called Aristophanes.) Plato (especially in *Republic* 378 A ff.) supports A.'s view here that such 'evil things' should be passed over in silence even though true. Plato goes on from it to suggest literary censorship.

1054-5. 'For little boys have a teacher who gives them advice, while young men have the poets': *cf.* Plato, *Protagoras* 325 E. A. emphasizes the didactic function of poetry (one must remember that university education and church sermons did not exist then). He ignores the claims of the *Sophists* to instruct youths and adults. I follow Richards in taking ὅστις after ἐστί as=ὅς : cf. in 427.

1056-7. Lycabettus is a small but prominent hill N.E. of the Acropolis. Parnassus is 8,038 feet high. With these grotesque exaggerations E. returns to his attack on A.'s grandiosity (cf. 940) and perhaps also alludes to his love of mentioning mountain peaks.

1058-9. 'But, you perverse fellow, it is the destiny of great thoughts and concepts to bring forth phrases on an equal magnitude.' For this lofty view cf. Sallust, *Catiline* 3, 2. For κακοδαίμων in this sense, lit. 'possessed by an evil genius', cf. the description of Socrates in *Clouds* 104. For τᾶ before ῥήμ. cf. on 495.

1063. For E.'s ragged heroes cf. on 842. βασιλεύοντας: 'playing a kingly part'.

1065-6. 'Well anyway it's your fault [-ουν . . . διὰ ταῦτα] that not a single [οὐκ- . . . οὐδεὶς] rich man is willing to equip a trireme. . . .' The equipping of a warship (τριηραρχία) was, like the χορηγία, one of the public duties (λειτουργίαι) of rich Athenians. Ar. blames E. here for what was doubtless mainly due to wartime stringencies (cf. on 404 ff.). περιλλόμενος: 'wrapped round in'. This is a reading in R : there are many variants. For this surprisingly polymorphous verb see L.-S.-J. on εἵλω and Radermacher (who follows Solmsen in preferring περιειλλόμενος here).

1068. ἐξαπατήσῃ : 'deceives' : sc. the officers in charge of investigating whether a citizen was rich enough to be liable for the trierarchy. περὶ τοὺς ἰχθῦς ἀνέκυψεν : 'he pops up [like a fish : cf. L.-S.-J. : the aorist is 'gnomic'] round the fish-stalls in the market'. Fish was a favourite, but expensive, food in 5th-century Athens. The household marketing was usually done by the master of the house accompanied by a slave. Note this Attic use of 'the fish', 'the wine', 'the cheese', etc., for the parts of the market where they were sold : cf. *Lysis.* 557.

1070-1. 'Which emptied the wrestling-schools and effeminized the youths with their babbling, and persuaded the Paralians. . . .' The *Paralos* (cf. on 204) was the flag-ship of the Athenian navy : its crew were strongly democratic (cf. Thucydides 8, 73 and 86).

1073. 'They knew nothing except how to call for grub and to say Yo-ho.' μᾶζα from μάττειν 'knead' (cf. on 1040), a coarser kind of bread than ἄρτος.

1074-5. This may be paraphrased : 'Yes, and disgust the rowers on the lower benches, and mess up the man who eats

with them, and, when they go ashore, rob someone'. **θαλάμᾱκι**:
the form θαλάμαξ occurs only here in Greek: a comic perversion
(see on 909) of θαλαμίτης, one of the three ranks of rowers in a
trireme.

1078-98. (*Antipnigos* : see § 13 n. 72.) METRE : anapaestic
dimeters, with catalectic forms in **1088** and **1098**, marking the
ends of the rhythmical groups. **1097** is exceptional, consisting of
two anapaests only.

ACTION. Aeschylus and Dionysos in turn mock the degenerate
citizens whose moral decline A. blames on E.

1079-82. **προαγωγοὺς**: 'panders'; or perhaps feminine, 'pro-
curesses', here as in *Thesm.* 341. The Nurse plays this part in
Hippolytus. 'Bearing children in temples' : so Auge in E.'s lost
Auge. 'Mating with brothers' : Canace in *Aeolus* (but *cf. Odyssey*
10, 7 and my note there) : *cf. Clouds* 1371-2. 'Saying life is not
life' : as stated by characters in E.'s *Polyidus, Erechtheus,* and
Phrixus (*cf.* 1477).

1084-5. 'Filled up with under-secretaries and scurrilous demo-
crat-apes.' The Σ says that civil-service secretaries were exempt
from military service : hence the popularity of this profession in
wartime. For contempt for these under-secretaries see Lysias
30, 27-9, and Demosthenes 19, 98. **βωμολόχων** [see on 358] **δημο-
πιθήκων** : people who use the shameless antics and flatteries of
monkeys (see on 708-9) to get popular power : for the form *cf.*
δειπνοπίθηκος.

1088-96. A.'s reference to the torch-race (see on 131) leads D.
to describe a scene (which may actually have occurred at the last
Panathenaia). He 'laughed himself dry [with ἀφαναίνομαι here
cf. 194] when a slow, pallid, fat fellow, with his head down
[**κύψας**: contrast 1068], was running on [**ἴθει**] far behind the
rest, and doing very badly' (**δεινὰ ποιῶν** : ποιούμενος would have
implied 'feeling very badly about it'). 'Then the people of the
Kerameikos [see on 129] at the gates [**πύλαις** : plural presumably
for the double gate, the Dipylon, which led out of Athens in that
district] slapped him with the flat of their hands' (**ταῖσι πλατείαις**
sc. χεροί). Apparently it was the custom of the Kerameikans to
treat slow runners like this : hence, says the Σ, the proverbial
phrase Κεραμεικαὶ πληγαί.

1096-8. The present participle **φυσῶν** implies blowing his
torch to keep it alight (since the draught caused by *this* man's
running—or his πορδή—would be insufficient to fan the flame), not
blowing it out. **ἴφευγεν** : 'continued his flight '.

1099 ff. ACTION. To introduce the third round of the literary

contest the Chorus sings (and no doubt excitedly dances : see
§ 12) another ode of exhortation to stimulate the protagonists.
METRE. 1099-1108 = 1109-1118 : see Dale 88. The longer
lines are catalectic trochaic tetrameters (see on 686 ff. : resolu-
tion is much more frequent here). The shorter lines are trochaic
dimeters with ∪ ∪ ∪ often for ∪ − as usual.

1099. πρᾶγμα : see on 759. **ἁδρὸς :** 'thick-set'.

1101-4. Note the military *Metaphors* : **τείνῃ** 'press on';
ἐπαναστρέφειν : 'wheel round to attack again'; **ἐπερείδεσθαι**
[*cf.* on 914] **τορῶς :** 'smartly bring a force against' : **κάθησθον**
[dual. imperat. *κάθημαι*] **ἐν ταὐτῷ ;** 'remain inactive' (*cf.* Thucy-
dides 5, 7) ; **εἰσβολαί :** 'invasions, attacks' : (but also 'introduc-
tions', perhaps in a rhetorical sense like *προσβολαί*, as in 958).

1106. The MSS. have ἀναδέρετον, but the metre (= 1116, with
resolution) needs another short syllable. It is easy to read ἀνά
τε δέρετον with Dobree or (with Thiersch) ἀνὰ δὲ δέρ. (*Tmesis* :
cf. Starkie on *Wasps* 784.) But δέρω 'skin, flay, beat' (*cf.* 619)
makes poor sense with the objects in 1107. I have adopted
δὲ φέρετον 'then bring up (as weapons)' from M. Platnauer in
American Journal of Philology lxvii (1946), 265.

1108. ' And desperately dare to say something subtle and skil-
ful ' : see on 99, 828, 1118.

1111. ὡς = ὥστε. **γνῶναι :** 'appreciate, discriminate between'
as in 964, 1210. **λεγόντοιν :** 'while you two are talking'.

1113-14. 'For they have served in the wars, and each one has
a book and understands the witty points.' The first phrase im-
plies 'they are veterans in literary criticism', which I take to
mean 'they have experienced plenty of literary criticism in
previous comedies'. But what is the 'book' ? Explanations
are : (*a*) copies of the first edition of the *Frogs* (but see § 7 n. 25) ;
(*b*) some current manual of military tactics (there is no evidence
for this) ; (*c*) 'his book' : a gibe at the growing bookishness of
the Athenian public in the late 5th century. The last view seems
best : *cf.* 943, *Birds* 974 ff., and fr. 490. Critical treatises of
various kinds were then current in Athens. See further in Sedg-
wick, E. G. Turner, *Athenian Books* etc. (London, 1951), Ehrenberg
287 (who emphasizes that Ar. was no friend of bookishness and
pedantry), and Radermacher : also especially Plato, *Apology* 26 D,
Phaedrus 274 B, Xenophon, *Mem.* 4, 2, 1, Eupolis, fr. 304. We
may, then, translate 'and each one has his text-book', like earnest
play-goers. But the reference remains uncertain and vague.

1115-18. Flattery of the *Audience*. **παρηκόνηνται :** 'have
been sharpened' (ἀκονάω : *cf.* ἀκόνη 'whetstone'). **θεατῶν γ'**

οὕνεχ': 'so far as the spectators are concerned, anyway': see on 189 and 2. σοφῶν: 'skilled' (*i.e.* in the poetic art), as in 1108, 766. This limited meaning of σοφία, as 'technical knowledge', seems to be older than the general notion of 'wisdom'.

1119-22. Euripides now 'wheels again to the attack' (καὶ μὴν indicating a new departure: see on 285). He will turn to Aeschylus's 'very prologues' (*i.e.* even the opening speeches of A.'s plays which at least should be clearly expressed: E. himself took special trouble in making his own prologues lucid). To begin with he will examine the beginning (τὸ πρῶτον . . . πρώτιστον) of A.'s work (E. changes here from σοι to αὐτοῦ, because he has begun to address Dionysos). Following Meineke, Bergk, and van Leeuwen, I have marked 1122 as an interpolation (perhaps an editor's remark which has slipped into the text). Dramatically it is more effective to let the audience wonder what E.'s criticisms would be. The Greek, also, is awkward (for πραγμάτων Σ mentions a variant ῥημάτων, which is no improvement).

1124. τὸν ἐξ 'Ορεστείας: 'the ‹well-known› one from the Orestes-saga'. For the ending -εια in this sense *cf.* 'Οδύσσεια. Since, as Denniston (MS.) notes, this ending is not found elsewhere in titles of single plays, it is unlikely that the *Choëphoroe* alone is meant. Presumably it is the group of four plays by Aeschylus, *Agamemnon-Choëphoroe-Eumenides-Proteus*, is intended: *cf. Lycourgeia* in *Thesm.* 135 with reference specially to the satyr-play. (But *Aristarchus*, acc. to Σ, used *Oresteia* of the trilogy, not the tetralogy: see in Pickard-Cambridge, *Dramatic Festivals* 81.)

1126 ff. Aeschylus now recites the first three lines of the *Choëphoroe* (which are preserved only here: not in the MSS. of Aeschylus). The phrases which E. will attack for ambiguity and redundancy are πατρῷ' ἐποπτεύων κράτη 'overseeing paternal powers' and ἥκω καὶ κατέρχομαι 'I have come, and return' (see on 1138 ff.).

1132-4. A. has apparently made a gesture as if about to speak (unless we accept Bergk's attribution of 1130 to him: but the pres. infin. σιωπᾶν rather implies 'remain silent'). προσοφεί-λων: 'in debt for more than the three lines': *i.e.* in addition to losing your three lines you'll have to pay more as well' (see on 1151), ἐγὼ σιωπῶ: 'Am I to . . .': deliberative subjunctive: see on 1. Note τῷδε followed by D.'s ἐὰν (MSS. disagree here, but this reading has the strongest support): probably not pronounced as -ε ε- with *Hiatus*, but (in this quick dialogue) with the beginning of D.'s answer blending with the end of A.'s question. Many editors (but not Radermacher) prefer to elide the first ε. *Cf.* 56, 1229, and on 1220.

1135. γάρ : 'He'd better [keep silent] because right away [**εύ-θύς**, *i.e.* at the very beginning of his play] he has made an error that reaches to high heaven' (*i.e.* a colossal 'howler' : *cf.* 781).

1136. ἀλλ' ὀλίγον etc. : 'Well it's of small concern to me, anyway'. All MSS. give this remark to Dionysos, except U, which gives it to Euripides (which seems best : perhaps with reference to what I suggest on 1151). Tucker gives it to Aeschylus.

1138 ff. Euripides complains (justly) that A.'s phrase **πατρῷα κράτη** is unclear, since 'paternal' may refer to Orestes's father, Agamemnon, or to Hermes's father, Zeus. (The ambiguity is increased by the fact that **κράτος** can mean 'strength, power, rule, sovereignty, authority, mastery, victory' : see L.-S.-J. and Fraenkel on *Agamemnon* 104. But E. does not emphasize this.) In other words, does the phrase mean 'watching over *my* father's dominions' (*i.e.* Argos) or 'watching over *thy* father's dominions' (*i.e.* acting as Zeus's emissary). A. indignantly (**δῆτ'** in 1144) replies : 'Certainly not in that sense [**ἐκείνως** is my emendation of the MS. **ἐκεῖνος/ον** : see *Hermathena* lxxxix] : for he addressed the Luck-bringing Hermes in his function as watcher over the dead [**χθόνιον** : lit. 'in his underground aspect'], and he made it clear in what he said [**λέγων**] that Hermes held this function from his father (Zeus)'. Others have adopted different interpretations but this seems the most satisfactory view of a much disputed passage. (Σ complicates it further by suggesting that **δόλοις** in 1143 points to a third cult-title of Hermes, namely, **δόλιος.**) We must remember that Ar.'s object is humour, not serious literary criticism. In fact *both* explanations may be intended to seem absurd or far-fetched—as a *Parody* of sophistic hair-splittings. It is impossible to say whether Ar. really had any further objection in mind in E.'s interrupted remark in 1147-8. For fuller discussion of **πατρῷα κράτη** see I. G. Kidd, *Classical Review* n.s. viii (1958), 103-5.

1149-50. To D.'s buffoonish remark, 'On that supposition he would have been a tomb-rifler [**τυμβωρύχος**, from **τύμβος** and **ὀρύττω** 'dig open' : *cf.* **τοιχωρύχοις** 'house-breakers' in 773] on his father's side', A. replies 'the wine you drink has no flowery aroma' (*cf. Plutus* 807), *i.e.* 'cheap stuff'. **ἀνθοσμίαν** : Athenaeus 29 e quotes the 5th-century comic poet Hermippus's description of a wine that smelt of violets, roses, and hyacinths. This diversion ends E.'s first attack.

1151. ἕτερον : 'the other bit'. **σὺ δ'** : Euripides, **ἐπιτήρει** : 'watch out for'. **τὸ βλάβος** : editors have tried to explain this as 'the flaw' (Merry), 'the fault' (Blaydes), and suchlike : but neither this word nor the commoner **βλάβη** means anything like

this elsewhere. The normal meaning is 'harm, damage'. Hence
Σ explains 'how you can do him harm': but this seems unsatis-
factory. I suggest that the underlying notion here and in 1121
(βασανιῶ) and 1133, is that A.'s verses are being examined like
slaves under torture. So E. must 'watch out for the harm' in
the sense that he must not overdo the torturing (cf. 623-4).

1154 ff. E. now attacks what he considers to be another
fault : repetition of meaning through synonyms, as in Aeschylus's
'arrive and come', 'hear and listen'. This is a common feature of
both elevated and popular literature and is frequently used in
liturgical language (e.g. 'pray and beseech', 'give ear and
hearken'). Euripides himself uses it at times (e.g. Hippolytus 380,
Ion 1446-7, Cyclops 210 : cf. van Leeuwen and on 1173 below).
Later rhetoricians disputed whether it should be admired as
adding to grandeur of style (e.g. Demetrius, On Style 103 : ἐν
διλογίαις γίνεται μέγεθος) or condemned as a source of confusion :
see further in Radermacher. Probably the basis of E.'s criticism
was Prodicus's book On Synonyms : cf. Plato, Charmides 163 D.

1159. 'Lend me a kneading-trough—or else, if you like a
trough for kneading' (which is as if someone today were to say
'Lend me half a crown—or else two and six') : cf. Pherecrates
137 πρόσαιρε τὸ κανοῦν, εἰ δὲ βούλει, πρόσφερε. Ar. makes the
repetition seem all the more absurd by applying it to the humble
borrowing of a kitchen vessel : for the frequency of such loans in
Athens see Theophrastus on ἀγροικία and Jebb's note.

1160-1. ὦ κατεστωμυλμένε : 'you bejabbered creature' (i.e. over-
powered or debased by στωμυλία : cf. on 841): probably a
Coined Word (first found in Thesm. 461). ταῦτ' (RVM ταῦτ'): τὸ
αὐτό. ἄριστ' ἐπῶν ἔχον : 'with excellent phrasing' (genitive of
respect : cf. 1181), hardly 'most excellent of verses' (Tucker) : cf.
on 862.

1163-5. A., instead of defending the use of synonyms as a
feature of the grand style (cf. 1058-62), argues that ἥκω and
κατέρχομαι are not synonymous, since the first means 'come'
without implying any other circumstance (συμφορᾶς), such as
dubious citizenship, while the second means 'return', especially
in the case of one who, like Orestes, has been in exile.

1167-8. E. characteristically makes the problem more complex.
He takes A.'s statement in 1165 to mean that Orestes was
formally recalled from exile, and denies the accuracy of this, as
he had not got the permission (πιθών) of the authorities (τοὺς
κυρίους, here Clytaemnestra and Aegisthus). In other words, he
turns for a moment from the question of repetition to a question
of verbal correctness (cf. on 1181).

1171. ἀνύσας: 'and hurry up': cf. 606. **τὸ κακὸν:** 'the harm':
see on 1151.

1172-3. A. continues the opening lines of *Choëphoroe*. Here
his phrase **κλύειν, ἀκοῦσαι,** is liturgical in style (cf. 'Give ear . . .
hear . . . hearken' in Isaiah 28, 23. It recurs in *P.V.* 448 and
Euripides's *Phoenissae* 919 (and cf. *Troades* 1303 κλύετε, μάθετε,
and *Hippolytus* 362 ἄιες, ἔκλυες). It is obviously a legitimate
way of emphasizing urgency and solemnity.

1175-6. D. intervenes with an ingenious explanation: why
complain about repetition when 'even with triple supplications
we do not reach the dead'? Orestes, he emphasizes, is addressing
his dead father now. For triple salutations to the dead cf. Virgil,
Aeneid 6, 506 : *magna manes* ter *voce vocavi*, and Pindar, *Pythians*
4, 61. **οἷς** for **οὕς** by attraction to **τεθνηκόσιν.** This remark ends
E.'s attacks (quite inconclusively). It is now A.'s turn.

1178. στοιβὴν: 'stuffing, padding' (literal or metaphorical :
cf. Shakespeare's 'bombast'). **κατάπτυσον:** 'spit on me', *i.e.*
show your utter contempt. E.'s self-confidence (which is not at
all the tone of his plays) increases the comic effect of his *débâcle* in
1471 ff.

1180-1. 'For to be sure I must hear the correctness of the
wording of your prologues.' **οὐ γὰρ . . . ἀλλ':** see on 58. **ἀκου-
στέα:** neuter pl. for singular is common in this construction.
ὀρθότητος: the Sophist Protagoras was specially interested in
ὀρθοέπεια: cf. Plato, *Phaedrus* 267 c.

1182-86. E. recites the first line of his *Antigone* (now lost). A.
seizes on the word **εὐδαίμων** which in its fullest sense means
'having a beneficent guardian spirit'. How could a man, pro-
claimed in an oracle before his birth as doomed to kill his father,
be such? **πρὶν καὶ γεγονέναι** ('even before he had been born')
is an emphatic repetition of **πρὶν φῦναι.** (But van Leeuwen,
rather attractively, gives it to D. as a buffoonish misinterpreta-
tion: 'Be a killer before he was even born?') **εὐτυχής:** 'fortu-
nate', not so strong a word as **εὐδαίμων.** Note **μὲν** *solitarium* in
1184, implying an intended contrast which is later omitted :
Denniston 380.

1187-95. E. adds another line : 'Then in turn he became most
wretched of mortals'. 'Emphatically not', replies A. 'On the
contrary [**οὐ μὲν οὖν :** see on 241] he never stopped being it.'
He recalls O.'s many misfortunes : his exposure as a baby in a
potsherd (**ὄστρακῳ** here for χύτρα, the vessel usually used for this
grim practice : cf. *Wasps* 289 and A. C. Cameron in *Classical
Review* xlvi, 1932, 105-14), his mutilated feet (**οἰδῶν τὼ πόδε :** an
etymology of Οἰδί-πους), his exile (**ἤρρησεν :** ἔρρω = 'go painfully,

unhappily' here) with Polybos, king of Corinth, his marriage as
a young man with a woman who, besides being old, was also his
mother (so Ar. comically presents the tragedy of Oedipus's mar-
riage with Jocasta), and his final self-blinding. γραῦν : old
women are a frequent butt of Aristophanes's less youthful
humour.

1195-6. 'Then he *was* [imperfect of discovery] happy after
all, *if* [to complete his perfect happiness !] he also was a general
with *Erasinides*' (and consequently condemned to death with
him after *Arginusae*). Here I follow Denniston (MS.), who notes
that ἦν should not be taken = ἦν ἄν, while the γε implies 'but only
if'.

1198-9. κατ' ἔπος γε : 'just word by word' : *cf.* on 862. κνίσω :
'scratch at'. ῥῆμ' : 'phrase' as in 97, 821.

1200. ἀπὸ ληκυθίου (*Diminutive*) : 'with (*cf.* on 121) a little
oil-jar '. A. no doubt meant E.'s astonished repetition of the
phrase to reflect the bewilderment of the audience too (*Mystifica-
tion*). The λήκυθος, a slender narrow-necked jar, was commonly
carried about by Athenians or their slaves, even in the theatre :
cf. Ar. fr. 472 and Knox-Headlam on Herodas 3, 20. See further
on **1208**.

1202-3. '. . . so that everything fits on—little fleece and little
oil-jar and little bag—in your iambics.' For the depreciatory
Diminutives here—'fleecelet and flasklet and baglet'—see Aris-
totle, *Rhetoric* 1405 b 29 ff. and Peppler. A. is mocking the
alleged triviality of E.'s subject matter with this contemptuous
list of commonplace articles. θῠλᾰκῐὄν gives a tribrach or ana-
paest in the 6th foot (as in 1216, 1231, *Acharnians* 777 : see
Tucker xxxix, White 44, and Descroix 130-1). As Harrison
suggests, the line with its 3 trisyllabic feet may parody E.'s
fondness for resolved feet in his trimeters ; and the jerky rhythm
(strong diaeresis after 2nd and 4th foot, no caesura : *cf. Kn.*
100) enhances the effect of oddity and triviality. Harrison para-
phrases : 'By bolster and beer-bottle and brown-paper-bag'. *Cf.*
Descroix 177-8.

1205. ἰδού (see on 200) : sardonically here, with a repeated
word (a usage confined to Ar.) : 'See here, you're going to show
us, are you ?' καὶ δή : 'Well, then . . . '.

1206-8. The beginning of E.'s lost *Archelaus* according to one
tradition ; but a Σ says *Aristarchus* denied this : see van Leeu-
wen. Fritzsche suggests that some of E.'s prologues were altered
by editors after Aristophanes's ridicule of them in this scene : *cf.*
on **1238**.

1208. ληκύθιον ἀπώλεσεν : 'lost his little oil-jar'. What criticism of E.'s poetry is implied by this tag (repeated in 1216 etc.) ? Three aspects must be considered : metre, subject matter, syntax. In metre the tag introduces a tribrach in the 4th foot, and in general E. is fonder of tribrachs than Aeschylus : but this is hardly a matter for concentrated ridicule. (The pause after the 5th half-foot is not, of course, peculiar in any way.) In subject matter the reference to a little oil-jar might parody E.'s alleged fondness for introducing everyday things into his tragedies (see 959) and his triviality of detail (cf. 976 ff.) : but the prologues quoted do not obviously suggest this. In syntax the tag suggests that E.'s opening sentences were constructed on a monotonous pattern, beginning with a proper name (all here except 1217) and containing an early participle. This syntactical criticism seems the likeliest : cf. Σ, διαβάλλει δὲ τὴν ὁμοειδίαν τῶν εἰσβολῶν, though in fact it only strictly applies to one, the I.T. (see 1232-3), of E.'s extant plays : see further in Murray 122-5, van Leeuwen, and O. Navarre in Revue des Études Anciennes xxxv (1933), 278-280. (I cannot agree with J. H. Quincey's view in Classical Quarterly xliii, 1949, 37-44, that ληκύθιον here is equivalent to the Latin ampulla in the sense of swelling, turgid style : but cf. Pfeiffer on Callimachus, fr. 215). But there may be little more than comical foolery here. The repetition of a phrase like this is a recognized comic device : cf. λαβὲ τὸ βιβλίον five times repeated in Birds 974 ff. ; and we know that Hegemon of Thasos 'when he was in difficulties with his parodies would add "and the leg of a partridge" ' (καὶ τὸ πέρδικος σκέλος : cf. Schmid 351 n. 5). For lecythion as a metrical term (derived from this passage) see on the metre of 209.

1209. 'What's the point of this oil-jar ?' For the imperfect cf. on 37. Note Deictic Iota.

1211-13. From Hypsipyle. The thyrsos (a rod tipped with a pine-cone) and fawn-skin were the usual equipment of a votary of the Dionysiac cult. καθαπτὸς seems to be used loosely here in the sense 'equipped with' or 'fitted out with' (but Σ offers other curious renderings). ἐν πεύκῃσι (for this form of dat. pl. in tragedy see Radermacher : RU read πεύκαισι) : probably 'among torches' (cf. Clouds 604, Bacchae 307, and further parallels in Blaydes), not 'among the pine-trees'. Parnassus was Dionysos's precinct during the winter months.

1214. This mock-tragic cry perhaps parodies the King's death-cries in Agamemnon 1343 and 1345.

1216. προσάψαι : Tucker and Radermacher think this indicates that the use of the ληκύθιον tag is derived from a game of 'capping'

a quotation (as described in Athenaeus 457 e). For the metre
see on 1202-3.

1218. The beginning of *Stheneboia* (*cf.* 1043). **ἐσθλὸς**: 'noble'
here (*pace* Tucker). **βίον**: 'livelihood'.

1220. τί ἐστι; ὑφέσθαι μοι δοκεῖ (Kuster for MS. δοκεῖς): 'What
is it?' 'I think it's best to lower sail' (a more drastic precau-
tion against the coming storm than that described in 999).
All MSS. read ἐστιν in this line (or ἐστίν, V), which gives an unlikely
type of 'broken anapaest' (see Arnott as cited on 77). Rader-
macher reads ἐστ': I prefer ἐστι, assuming that the last syllable
merges into the beginning of D.'s reply : *cf.* on 1134.

1221. πνευσεῖται: Doric future (for others in Ar. see Starkie
on *Wasps* 157). For the storm *Metaphor cf.* on 825.

1223. 'For now this one at any rate [*i.e.* the beginning of the
Phrixos cited in 1225-6] will knock it from his hand.'

1228-32. τὸ τί: *cf.* on 7 : 'Just what do you mean ? Am I to
buy it to please him ?' τῷδ': dative of interest : *cf. Acharnians*
812. For the elision see on 1134. E. goes on to quote the opening
lines of his *Iphigeneia among the Tauri*.

1235-6. ἀπόδος : this is much disputed, and A gives a variant
ἀπόδου. The meaning depends on the person addressed. The
many editors who believe it is Aeschylus (translating 'give it to
E.' or, with ἀπόδου, 'sell it to E.') can hardly be right, since E.
in his reply (1237) uses οὔπω ('I won't yet'), which could not mean
'don't do it yet' (which would require μήπω) ; while Tucker's 'he
won't do it yet' is weak with the following γὰρ . . . μοι. Ad-
dressed to E. the remark might possibly mean 'give Pelops
(1232) back his oil-jar' (so Σ, van Leeuwen, and Murray take it).
But it seems best (with Bothe, Fritzsche, and Radermacher) to
take ἀπόδος = 'give him (Aeschylus) the price', *i.e.* 'pay him in
return for it', though ἀποδίδωμι is generally used in connexion
with services already rendered (*cf.* 270). ἔτι καὶ νῦν : 'there's
still time' (Denniston). πάσῃ τέχνῃ : 'by every means in your
power' (since A. is in no accommodating mood). λήψει etc. :
'you will get it for an obol'. πάνυ καλήν τε κἀγαθήν : 'and it's
very fine and good' : salesman's talk : *cf.* the parallels at the
end of Blaydes's note.

1238. From Euripides's *Meleager* (but a scholiast says not the
very first lines : see Fritzsche and Radermacher).

1242. 'While he was sacrificing ? Then who filched it ?' D.'s
remark emphasizes the incongruity of the oil-jar tag. In real life
irreligious thieves would find easy game at crowded sacrifices.

1243-4. ἔασον: 'let it go'. (VAU give ἔα αὐτόν in which the first word could be scanned as a monosyllable as in *Lysistrata* 945.) ὦ τᾶν: 'old chap': Wilamowitz's view (*loc. cit.* on 559) that this is a contraction of ὦ τάλαν makes good sense here and in 952: but for objections see Björck 277. πρὸς τοδὶ γὰρ εἰπάτω: 'for let him reply to this one'. E. now quotes the beginning of *Melanippe the Wise.* (For the papyrus fragment giving the lines following these see Page 116 and Pickard-Cambridge in Powell, *New Chapters* 3, 113.) In the first eight lines the ληκύθιον could only have been attached after the third word, λέλεκται (*cf.* 1238).

1245. With ἀπολεῖς (the reading of RAU) we must understand με: 'You'll destroy me (with your futile efforts)'. The idiom is paralleled in *Wasps* 1202 and (with similar omission of the object) *Eccl.* 775. VM read ἀπολεῖ σ': 'he'll destroy you'.

1247. σῦκ': 'styes' or 'warts' here (*cf.* Hippocrates, *Epidem.* 3, 17). ἔφυ: 'grow' ('gnomic' aorist).

1249. οἷς is Dobree's emendation of ὡς: *cf.* οἷοις in 909.

1251-60. Choral interlude marking a change in the contest.

METRE. Two groups of 3 lines consisting of 2 glyconics (⏑⏑ ⏑ −⏑⏑− ⏑−)+ 1 pherecratean (⏑⏑ ⏑ −⏑⏑− −). In 1256 τῶν μέχρι νυνί is Meineke's emendation (from a scholium) of the un-metrical ἔτι νῦν ὄντων of RVAM and νῦν ἔτ' ὄντων of U. Then in 1257-60 (see note below) come a glyconic + 3 pherecrateans. (Radermacher divides 1259-60 καὶ | δέδοιχ' to make a glyconic + telesillean.)

1253. 'What blame we may expect [ἆρα] E. to bring against . . .'

1257-60. This quatrain has been bracketed as spurious by many editors because it repeats the sense of 1252-6 and separates E.'s sarcastic μέλη θαυμαστά in 1261 from κάλλιστα μέλη in 1255. Possibly here, as Radermacher suggests, we have evidence of a second edition of the play (see § 7 n. 25). In 1260 αὐτοῦ could refer to either E. or A.

1261. 'Yes, very wonderful indeed, as will soon, let me tell you [δή], become clear.' The subject of δείξει is presumably something like 'the actual performance' as in *Lysistrata* 375, τοὔργον τάχ' αὐτὸ δείξει (see further in Blaydes).

1262. 'For I shall reduce all his lyrics down to one pattern.' (Possibly, as Tucker's edition suggests, there is a pun here with μέλη = 'limbs': E., like Procrustes, will cut down A.'s gangling limbs to fit one bed.) Unfortunately for our judgement of E.'s accusation that A.'s lyrics are monotonous (*cf.* 1250) their accompaniment (*Music*) has not survived and we can only consider the metre.

1263 f. 'Well, then, I'll take some pebbles and keep count' (of the score against A.). Note the following παρεπιγραφή (as at 312) here : 'Someone plays an interlude [δι-αύλιον from αὐλός 'pipe'] on the pipe'. But Denniston (MS.) prefers to punctuate διαύλιον· προσαυλεῖ τις : 'a flute interlude : ⟨then⟩ someone plays the accompaniment on the flute'.

1264 ff. What exactly is E. mocking in the following excerpts from A.'s plays ? Not A.'s use of refrains (though possibly they are hinted at as a secondary source of monotony), but apparently A.'s tendency to slip into dactylic rhythms in his lyrics. This is not, however, a marked feature of A.'s work as now extant (see White 147). Possibly it was more noticeable in lost plays. Or, more likely, E.'s accusation is as unfair as A.'s ληκύθιον attack : in other words, it may be another example of Aristophanes's readiness to exaggerate things for comic effect. Note that, contrary to the practice in the previous scene, the critic (not the criticized author) recites the lines, doubtless with horrid over-emphasis of their faults. But a catastrophic retaliation from A. will soon follow.

1264-77. METRE. Although the basic rhythm is dactylic, I follow White 146 in taking the 'fatal cadence' to be the part of a dactylic hexameter following the penthemimeral caesura (*i.e.* ∪∪ −∪∪ −∪∪ −⌣) which, scanned as anapaests, is a paroemiac (but see also Fraenkel, *Lyrische Daktylen* 321). This seems to be indicated by the fact that D. interrupts twice in this metre (1268, 1272). All the 'Aeschylean' lines slip into this paroemiac rhythm thus :

1264 : − − ∪ − − + paroemiac.

1265 (= 1267, 1271, 1275, 1277) : ∪ − + paroemiac.

1266 : − − − ∪∪ − + paroemiac.

1268 : paroemiac.

1269/70 : − − ∪ − − ∪∪ − + paroemiac.

1272 : paroemiac.

1273/4 : − ⌣ − ∪∪ − ∪∪ − + paroemiac (= dactylic hepta-meter !).

1276 : − ∪∪ − ∪∪ − ∪∪ − ∪∪ − ∪∪ − − : dactylic hexa-meter or − ∪∪ − ∪∪ − + paroemiac.

1264-5. From Aeschylus's *Myrmidons.* 'Why, when thou hearest—Oho !—the man-slaughterous beating [of battle], approachest thou not to the rescue ?' (At that time Achilles had withdrawn in anger from the fighting against the Trojans.) ἰή, used in grief here, is commoner as an exclamation of joy.

1266. From A.'s *Ghost-raisers.* λίμναν : the Stymphalian lake in Arcadia. The Arcadians claimed descent from Hermes.

1270. From A.'s *Telephus* or *Iphigeneia.* μάνθανέ μου : as in archaic English, 'learn of me'.

1273/4. From A.'s *Priestesses.* μελισσονόμοι : lit. 'Beetenders' or possibly, as Denniston (MS.) suggests, 'attendants on the Bee-priestesses'. This curious title seems to belong to some cult-association between Artemis and bees : see Radermacher. But Dindorf on the basis of the gloss in Σ, οἱ διανέμοντες τὰ τῆς πόλεως, conjectured πολισσονόμοι (as in Aeschylus, *Choëph.* 864, *Pers.* 853). πέλας οἴγειν : understand πάρεισι : 'are at hand to open'.

1276. From *Agamemnon* 104 (see Fraenkel's note there) : 'I have authority to give utterance of the fateful command, ruling the expedition'. For κράτος see on **1138.** ὅδιον is restored here (for ὃς δῖον in R, ὅσιον in other MSS.) from the MSS. of *Agamemnon.*

1278. D.'s remark begins with a metrical joke : the first two feet suggest anapaests, but παρὰ προσδοκίαν he switches into iambics to form a regular trimeter.

1279-80. Buffoonishly D. inserts a crude remark (presumably to prevent the less literary members of the *Audience* from becoming bored). He pretends that he is suffering physically from a 'monstrous heap of beatings'. (For χρῆμα in this colloquial sense see L.-S.-J., especially the meanings in ii 3 and 3 b, which I take to be jointly implied by Ar. here.) For his intention of going to the bath-house to cure the alleged swelling of his kidneys *cf.* Aristotle, *Problems* 1, 39 τοὺς μὲν θερινοὺς κόπους ['fatigues' here] λουτρῷ ἰᾶσθαι. With 1278-9 *cf. Clouds* 1-2.

1281-3. The omission of ἄν after πρίν is unusual in this construction, but see van Leeuwen. στάσιν : here (contrast on 359) a 'set, row' of lyrics (μελῶν), an apt term for the choral lyrics called στάσιμα (because the chorus stayed in a fixed order as they sang them). **1282**: 'Constructed from his compositions for the lyre'. **1283**: 'Go to it then. Carry on : only don't keep on adding [μὴ προστίθει : see *Present Imperative*] "beating".'

1284-95. Here the loss of the *Music* is probably even more serious than in 1264-77, since the nonsensical refrain in 1286 etc. seems to indicate musical rather than metrical monotony. The Σ's reference to A.'s use of the ὅρθιος νόμος, 'the high-pitched melody' invented by Terpander (*cf.* 'Plutarch', *De musica* 3), gives a tantalizing hint of what we have lost here by the absence of any musical record. The metre of the long lines remains, however, monotonously dactylic (with a preliminary iambic metron in 1284 and 1291: *cf.* on the metre of 1264 etc. above). For the refrain see on 1286 below.

1285-9. 1285 and 1289 are from *Agamemnon* 109-11. But to increase the joyful confusion Ar. inserts words from A.'s *Sphinx* in 1287. The following mad meaning emerges : 'How the furious bird sends, with spear and avenging hand, the twin-throned [referring to the two kings Agamemnon and Menelaus] lordship of the Achaeans, of the Greek prime manhood, the Sphinx, presiding she-dog of unlucky days'.

1286 (=1288 etc.): as one might expect in meaningless *Onomatopoeia* of this kind, the MS. readings vary greatly in accentuation, spelling, and word division : and they are not consistent in the subsequent repetitions (see the wonderful display in von Velsen's apparatus). I have followed the lettering of VU (which R seems to accept in 1296) but have left out all divisions and diacritic signs (which beg dubious questions). Since the τοφλαττ- etc. rhythm seems to be iambic, not dactylic, we must distinguish the musical from the metrical monotony here : see further in Radermacher (who points out that Ar. is obviously being unfair, since if *Agam*. 104, *i.e.* 1276 above, was accompanied by the flute, it is most unlikely that *Agam*. 109 ff. was accompanied by the lyre, or *vice versa*). The normal accompaniment for tragic choruses seems to have been the flute, not the lyre (see Pickard-Cambridge, *Dramatic Festivals* 164). Probably in this scene E. pretends to strum a lyre as he sings. With the refrain *cf.* English 'ti-tum' or 'tra-la', and Ar.'s θρεττανελό in *Plutus* 290.

1291. Source unknown. 'Having granted to the eager air-ranging dogs to light upon . . .': various other versions are possible. The 'dogs' here are presumably vultures or eagles (*cf.* 1289 and *Agam*. 136, *P.V.* 1022).

1294. 'The joined force that leans on Ajax': from A.'s *Thracian Women*. The scansion is ∪ – ∪ – ∪ – – ∪, which echoes the metre of the refrain (except in the last foot) but jars with the dactylic lines. Σ says the line was missing from some MSS.: so some editors delete it as an interpolation (but its intrusion has not been satisfactorily explained). Radermacher may be right in explaining it as a burst of triumph from E. who thinks that A. is now as sorely pressed by the combined weight of evidence against him as Ajax in his direst straits.

1296-7. 'Was it from Marathon, or where, that you collected your rope-twister's songs ?' Marathon is perhaps mentioned

because of the abundance of a kind of reed (φλέως, possibly sug-
gested by the previous -φλατ-) that grows in the marshes there.
But some editors think this too far-fetched and explain it as a
reference to the battle of Marathon (at which A. fought), implying
that φλαττοθρατ sounds barbaric enough to be Persian. The
implication in 'songs of a rope-twister' is equally disputed.
Tucker takes it as being connected with the making of ropes from
rushes (he assumes that φλέως and σχοῖνος are interchangeable
terms) : hence it is the kind of monotonous work-song that rope-
makers may have sung (cf. Athenaeus 618 d and 619 b on the
ἱμαῖος ᾠδή of millers and other work-songs). But van Leeuwen
denies that ἱμονιοστρόφου could refer to the making of a rope
from rushes, since ἱμονιαί were made from leather ἱμάντες : he
prefers to take it as referring to the drawing of water from a deep
well by a rope, and compares Callimachus (as quoted by Σ here)
ἀείδει . . . ἀνὴρ ὑδατηγὸς ἱμαῖον (Pfeiffer, fr. 260, 66). But
-στρόφου seems wrong for this process of pulling (if a wheel was
used, it was not the rope that was 'turned', and cf. the meaning
of καλωστρόφος). There is also the possibility that 'songs of a
rope-twister' is intended to suggest 'songs as long-stretched-out
as a rope' as in Pindar's use of σχοινοτένεια ἀοιδά (cf. ἱμονίαν used
of something long-drawn-out in Eccl. 351). Non liquet.

1298-1300. ἀλλ' οὖν : used in remonstrances and protests :
'Well, anyway, in reply to that, I brought it from a noble source to
a noble end'. Presumably the 'noble source' vaguely describes
Terpander and the Aeolic style of lyric : cf. on 1284. For Phry-
nichus the tragedian see on 910. The Metaphor in 1300 is a
variation on Birds 748-50 where Phrynichus is compared to a
bee.

1301. The mss. have . . . μὲν φέρει πορνιδίων, in which μὲν
is hard to explain and πορνιδίων seems to be unmetrical. I have
printed Palmer's μέλι, which makes good (ironical) sense with the
reference to a meadow in 1300 (cf. Plato, Ion 534 ἀπὸ κρηνῶν
μελιρρύτων δρεπόμενοι . . . τὰ μέλη : perhaps an unemphasized
pun on μέλι and μέλη is intended both by Plato and Ar. here :
for the notion of honey in connexion with Phrynichus see Birds
748-50, Wasps 220). As to the metre : L.-S.-J. accepts a unique
lengthening of the first ι in πορνιδίων (as if from a conjectural
πορνίον) ; but against Petersen's arguments in favour of such
lengthenings see Arnott as cited on 77. I print Meineke's conjec-
ture (for others see Blaydes and van Leeuwen) πορνῳδίων : though
not attested in extant Greek it is a likely Aristophanic formation
from πόρνη and ᾠδή. See Wilamowitz as cited in next note.

1302-3. 'From Meletos's drinking-songs, Carian flute-tunes,
lamentations, dance-tunes.' Wilamowitz (Gr. Vers. 226) thinks

that this cannot be Meletos the third-rate tragedian who accused
Socrates (see Plato, *Apology* 23 E), as he is described as young
and unknown in *Euthyphro* 2 B (399 B.C.) and so could hardly
have been said to have influenced Euripides (as here). W. thinks
Ar. means Meles the Colophonian (Plutarch, *De Musica* 5). But Ar.
mentions the anti-Socratic Meletos in frs. 149 and 114 (*cf. Apology*
23), so perhaps we cannot rely on *Euthyphro* 2 B. For examples
of σκόλια see Athenaeus 694 c. **Καρικῶν**: evidently a depreciatory
term, but it is not clear in what precise sense : perhaps 'lewd,
lascivious' (as in Athenaeus 580 d) ; or 'cheap' (see L.-S.-J. on
Καρικός and Κάρ) ; or 'dirgelike' (*cf.* Plato, *Laws* 800 E and
Pollux 4, 75 θρηνῶδες γὰρ τὸ αὔλημα τὸ Καρικόν : but this would
be tautological with θρήνων in 1303). Wilamowitz, citing Hesy-
chius, thinks that **Καρικῶν** here refers specially to lyrics in
choriambic rhythm. In general, on the corrupting moral effect
of mixing up the traditional forms of music see Plato, *Laws* 700 E.
Plutarch, *Moralia* 795 D says that Euripides encouraged the
notoriously 'modernistic' musician Timotheos. See further in
Schmid-Stählin 1, 3, 1, 816, and Schönewolf 17-26, 37-44, Kranz,
228 ff.

1305-6. 'Where is the woman who beats time with the casta-
nets ?' ὄστρακα can mean either 'shells' or 'potsherds': despite
L.-S.-J. and Tucker, I think the first seems more likely to be used
for the purpose of marking dance-rhythms, as here : *cf.* Athenaeus
636 e. αὕτη : presumably contemptuous·(see L.-S.-J., C 3).
Possibly there is a reference here (as Σ and Photius on κροταλίζειν
suggest) to Hypsipyle's use of a rattle to soothe the infant
Opheltes in E.'s *Hypsipyle* : *cf.* Page 84 *v.* 23. (For pictures of
dancers using castanets see Bieber 8, fig. 11 and G. M. A. Richter,
*Handbook of the Greek Collection in the Metropolitan Museum of
Art*, New York, 1953, plate 55 C.) After A.'s question apparently
a grotesque character representing the Muse of Euripides comes
on the scene : *cf.* Euripides, fr. 184 μοῦσάν τιν' ἄτοπον εἰσάγεις,
ἀσύμφορον, | ἀργόν, φίλοινον. She marks the rhythms in 1309 ff.
with castanets, and dances comically in accompaniment (see on
1323-4) : *cf.* the beautiful Σπονδαί in *Kn.* 1389, who are intro-
duced with δεῦρο, as here. Pherecrates in his *Cheiron* introduced
a female character called Μουσική who complained of ill-treatment
by the younger musicians.

1308. 'This Muse certainly wasn't playing the Lesbian part.'
At sight of the ugly creature who enters to represent the Muse of
Euripides, D. emphatically (repeated οὐ) denies that *she* could
make any profit by her charms (as Lesbian women notoriously
did in the 5th century : *cf. Wasps* 1346). At the same time (since
Terpander, *cf.* on 1298, came from Lesbos) he implies that E.'s

lyrics had no Aeolic charm about them. The excellence of
Lesbian music is implied by the proverb (Cratinus, fr. 243)
'second to the Lesbian singer'. (A reference to Sappho or to the
specific malpractices of other Lesbian women seems unlikely
here.)

1309-22. In the following wonderful farrago of parody and
quotation Aeschylus is primarily mocking the irregular rhythms
of E.'s lyrics. E. has accused him of monotony : he replies by
accusing E. of turning the stately rhythms of the tragic chorus
into a wild chaos in which the basic patterns of the established
rhythms are wilfully destroyed. The lines are also selected so as
to give a kind of mad sense. But the main criticism (as the
accompaniment by the castanets indicates) seems to be metrical.
There are many uncertainties in the identification of the rhythms :
cf. White, Radermacher, and Dale.

METRE. The first part (1309-28) is aeolic in rhythm.

1309 : − ∪ ∪ ∪ − ∪ − − ∪ ∪ − − ∪ − − : rhythm uncertain. Rader-
macher, scanning ă- in ἀενάοις, takes it as iambic : I prefer
(following a suggestion by Miss Dale) to scan ā and take it as
aeolic (choriambus in sylls. 7-10).

1310 : catalectic trochaic dimeter (a 'lecythion' for Euripides).

1311 : − − − ∪ ∪ − ∪ − : glyconic (regular).

1312 : ∪ ∪ ∪ ∪ ∪ ∪ (= − ∪ ∪ −) − ∪ ∪ ≤ : choriambic dimeter.

1313 : − ∪ − ∪ ∪ − ∪ ∪ − ∪ − : ? aeolic.

1314 : − − − − | − − − ∪ ∪ − ∪ − ∪ − − : if we ignore the first
four ει's as A.'s own exaggeration this is an aeolic hendecasyllable
('phalacean' as in Catullus's *passer deliciae meae puellae*) : but
see Wilamowitz 225 for a re-division of 1313-14 to give a glyconic.

1315 : − ∪ ∪ ∪ − − ∪ ∪ : possibly a lecythion or else aeolic poly-
schematist dimeter (White 230-1).

1316 : − ∪ ∪ ∪ − − ∪ ∪ − : choriambic dimeter.

1317 : ∪ ∪ ∪ − ∪ ∪ − ∪ − : glyconic.

1318 : − − − ∪ ∪ − ∪ − : glyconic.

1319 : − − ∪ − ∪ ∪ − : acephalous choriambic dimeter.

1320 : − − − ∪ ∪ − ∪ − : glyconic.

1321 : ∪ ∪ ∪ ∪ ∪ ∪ − ∪ ∪ − : choriambic dimeter (= 1312).

1322 : ∪ ∪ − − ∪ ∪ − ∪ − : glyconic with anapaest in 1st foot.

1323 : ∪ − − ∪ ∪ − ∪ ∪ − : ? irregular glyconic with anapaestic
ending.

1324 : ∪ − − ∪ ∪ − ∪ − : glyconic.

1325 : – – – – – ∪∪ –: choriambic dimeter.

1326 : – – – ∪∪ – ∪ –: glyconic.

1327 : ∪∪∪ – ∪∪ – ∪ –: glyconic.

1328 : – – – ∪∪ – –: pherecratean.

1329-30 : Two regular iambic trimeters.

For 1331 ff. see below.

1309-12. The Σ attribute these lines to E.'s *Iphigeneia at Aulis*, but they are not to be found in the text as it now survives. Perhaps *Iphigeneia among the Tauri* 1089 ff. was vaguely Ar.'s model (see Blaydes). στωμύλλετε: 'babble', an indirect hit at E. himself : *cf*. on 841. With 1311-12 *cf*. Euripides, *Ion* 117 (and note ἀέναος in 118 as 1309 here).

1313-14. ὑπωρόφιοι . . . φάλαγγες: 'spiders under the roof [ὄροφος]', *i.e.* living on the ceiling : possibly an echo (perhaps *via* a lost play of Euripides) of Pindar's φόρμιγγες ὑπωρόφιαι (*Pythians* 1, 97).

1314. ειειειειειειλίσσετε: 'wi-i-i-i-i-ind' (the MSS. vary in the number of repetitions of ει). This parodies the musical device (which Σ calls ἐπέκτασις ' prolongation ') by which a singer prolongs a syllable of a word in the lyric to allow for the singing of several different notes, or else repetitions of the same note, on it. On this and other innovations of the later fifth-century musicians see especially Schönewolf : for a frag. of a musical accompaniment to E.'s *Orestes* see Mountford in Powell, *New Chapters* 2, 146 ff. Ar. probably took ειει- etc. from E.'s *Electra* 437 (see on 1317), where there is a variant reading εἰειλισσόμενος. (The breathing varies on this word, which is a favourite of E. in his lyrics.) For similar devices in modern music see Grove's *Dictionary of Music and Musicians* (1954) at *Ornaments* B.

1315-16. 'Threads for stretching on the loom, the care of the tuneful weaving-rod.' ἱστότονα recurs only in E.'s *Hypsipyle* (Page 84 *v*. 25) : ἱστόπονα, the reading of R, seems to be a late word. πήνισμα (πήνη) is the thread spun from yarn on to a spool (πηνίον : *cf*. on 577-8 and 1348) for weaving. For objections to taking κερκίς as 'shuttle' here and elsewhere see G. M. Crowfoot in *Annual of the British School at Athens* xxxvii (1936-7), 36-47 : she thinks a 'pin beater' is meant, which when stuck between the warp-threads would give out a soft tuneful sound (ἀοιδοῦ here : *cf*. Sophocles, frs. 595, 890). 1316 is from E.'s *Meleager*, according to Σ.

1317-18 = Euripides's *Electra* 435-7. ἔπαλλε [intransitive here] πρῴραις : 'leaps to the bows', as dolphins still do in Greek seas.

184 ARISTOPHANES: FROGS

The dative may be locative (as in Sophocles, *O.C.* 411) or, as Tucker suggests (and *cf.* Denniston on *Electra* 436), may mean 'in honour of'. φίλαυλος 'flute-loving' (used in parody of E. also by Axionikos, fr. 4): for ancient belief in the dolphin's love of music *cf.* the legend of Arion (Herodotus 1, 23-4) and Pliny, *Natural History* 9, 8.

1319. 'Oracles and race-courses': source (if any) unknown: probably without syntactical connexion with the context. But Coulon and others try to construe it with ἵππαλλε.

1320-2. 1320 and 1322 are from E.'s *Hypsipyle*, according to Σ (with 1322 *cf. Phoenissae* 165-6, 306-7).

1322. Source unknown: but perhaps Ar. has supplied some Euripidean concoctions of his own in this medley (see § 10 n. 46). περίβαλλ': an anapaest as the 1st foot of a glyconic is very rarely found. Mr. G. W. Bond has pointed out to me that in van Leeuwen's examples from Euripides (*Hel.* 526 and *I.T.* 1132) the reading and colometry are doubtful (and so, too, the colometry in *Bacchae* 144). And probably Ar. is parodying E.'s fondness for περιβάλλω and for using ὠλένη in place of χείρ.

1323-4. τὸν πόδα: 'foot', but probably not just the monstrous anapaest but the whole glyconic in 1322. (See White 312.) When Dionysos answers 'I see it', he presumably looks at the foot of Aeschylus or of the 'Muse' (or possibly even of Euripides). A. replies 'What are you up to?' τί δαί, the reading of UAM for R's δέ (V omits 1324), gives an apt metrical responsion to 1323 and stronger idiom: Tucker thinks A. means the Muse's other foot. H. L. Crosby in *Classical Philology* xx (1925), 66-8 deprecates the notion that the dignified Aeschylus should be made play the buffoon here, and gives the first part of 1324 to Dionysos and the ὁρῶ to Aeschylus. This is so much a matter of comic *Business* that no certain interpretation is possible. (There is some further discussion of these lines by V. Coulon in *Rheinisches Museum* cv, 1962, 29-30.)

1325-8. A. turns to denounce E. ἀνὰ τὸ δωδεκαμήχανον Κυρήνης (a parody of a phrase in E.'s *Hypsipyle*): 'on the twelve-variety system of Cyrene'. The Σ says she was a notorious and versatile prostitute: *cf. Thesm.* 98 and Plato Comicus, fr. 134. Possibly some reference to the twelve-stringed lyre mentioned by Pherecrates, fr. 145, is intended.

1330 ff. τῶν μονῳδιῶν . . . τρόπον: 'the style of your solo lyrics'. In what follows (partly quotation, partly invention: *cf.* Schroeder in *Philologus* lxiv, 1905, 147-8), A.'s mockery is aimed less at metrical extravagances and more at the general style and mood of E.'s monodies (*cf.* 849, 944)—especially their exaggerated emotionalism, sensationalism, triviality of association, lapses into prosaic style, and quick changes of feeling (reflected in the rhythms). For a discussion of these solo performances see Radermacher : Timotheos's *Persians* is an outlandish example and *cf.* the solo of the Phrygian in Euripides, *Orestes* 1369-1502, which is obviously in Aristophanes's mind in what follows here. Many stylistic features are parodied, notably E.'s emotive repetitions (1336, 1352-5), *Oxymoron* (see on 1331), references to dimness and gloom (in the manner of 19th-century 'gothic' romanticism : see on 1331). The touches of *Bathos* in 1342, 1345, 1360, 1364, are, as Denniston (MS.) notes, not typical of E.'s lyrics elsewhere and may be simply Ar.'s method of throwing the hysterical character of the rest into relief. The narrative is in seven parts : the Dream (1331-7 : E. was fond of describing dreams), the Purification (1338-41), the Discovery of the Theft (1342-5), the Lonely Vigil (1346-51), the Flight of the Bird (1352-5), the Call for Aid (1356-1360), the Invocation (1361-4). A woman describes how she saw in a dream a terrible, darkly shrouded vision, 'with murder, murder, in its eyes and long finger-nails'. She calls her servants to bring water for her purification. Suddenly she cries out : she has discovered that the crime predicted by the vision has actually occurred : her maid Glyke has stolen her pet cock—leaving her (alas and alack !) naught but woe upon woe and tears upon tears. Recovering from her deep emotion, she summons guards and a goddess to help her catch the thief red- (or at least feathery-) handed. There is an excellent version of this superb parody by T. F. Higham in *The Oxford Book of Greek Verse in Translation* (Oxford, 1938), 508-9.

The metre is an extraordinary medley reflecting the sharp changes of mood. There are many uncertainties. See especially White 277 ff.

First period (1331-7) :

1331 : – – – ∪ – ∪∪ – : choriambic dimeter.

1332 : – – ∪∪ – – – ∪∪ – : anapaestic dimeter.

1333 : – – – – ∪∪ – ∪∪ – : anapaestic dimeter.

1334 : ∪∪ – – – : anapaestic monometer.

1334a : – – ∪∪ – ∪∪ – – : ? paroemiac (Radermacher 'enoplion').

1335-7 : ? ? Here the clear anapaests disappear, leaving a highly uncertain set of rhythms (? anapaestic, or enoplion, + dochmiac : see especially van Leeuwen, Radermacher, Dale). Perhaps, as Miss Dale has suggested, the lines should be divided to follow the rhetorical sense, as in Hall and Geldart.

Second period (1338-41):

1338: dactylic tetrameter ($\mu o\acute{\iota}$ before $\dot{\alpha}\mu$- by *Correption*).

1339: dactylic hexameter.

1340: dactylic tetrameter (spondee in 1st foot: $\dot{\alpha}\pi o\kappa\lambda\acute{\upsilon}\sigma\hat{\omega}$ before $\acute{\iota}\grave{\omega}$). See Radermacher.

1341: $--\ -\cup\cup\ --$: dactylic (or possibly $\underset{\smile}{-}-\ -\cup\cup-\ -$: pherecratean).

Third period (1342-5: note -ϵ unelided at end of **1345**, marking end of period). The rhythms and divisions of these lines are very uncertain.

1342: trochaic dimeter.

1343-44a: ? ?: for various possibilities see Schroeder, White, Radermacher, Dale.

1344b: $-\cup\cup-\cup\cup-\wedge$: dactyls.

1345: $--\ \cup-\ \cdot-\ \cup\cup$: syncopated iambic dimeter.

Fourth period (1346-51).

1346: $\cup--\ \cup-\cup$: ? 2 bacchiacs (= Iacchos cry in **316** ff.) or dochmiac.

1347: $\cup\cup-\ \cup\cup\cup-\ -$: ? pherecratean.

1348: $--\ \cup\cup--\ \cup\cup-\cup$: ? ionics a minore.

1349: $-\ ---\ -\cup\cup-$: ? choriambic dimeter (ignoring first $\epsilon\iota$-: *cf.* **1314**).

1349a: $-\ -\cup\cup-\ \cup-$: telesillean (= acephalous glyconic).

1350: $\cup-\cup\ -\cup\cup-$: ? acephalous choriambic dimeter.

1351: $\cup-\cup\cup--$: reizianum.

Fifth period (1352-5):

1352: $\cup\cup-\ \cup\cup-\ \cup\cup-\ \cup\cup$: anapaests (approximating to a paroemiac).

1353: $-\cup\cup\ -\cup\cup\ --\cup-$: ? Ibycean (dactylic).

1354: $\cup-\ \cup\cup\cup\ \cup\cup\cup\ \cup\cup\cup$: iambic dimeter.

1354a: $\cup\cup\cup\ \cup\cup\cup\ \cup-\ \cup-$: iambic dimeter.

1355: $\cup\cup\cup\cup\cup\cup---$: ? (Miss Dale notes its identity with Euripides's *I.T.* 213 and suggests it is a 'Euripidean' paroemiac.) The contrast between the flighty shorts and sedate longs may be intended to seem ludicrous here.

Sixth period (1355–60): mainly cretic rhythm.

1356: − − −∪− −∪∪∪(▬−∪−): spondee + 2 cretics.

1357: −∪∪∪ −∪∪∪ −∪∪∪: 3 paeons (*i.e.* resolved cretics).

1358: −∪− −∪∪∪ −∪ −− −∪ − ∧ : 2 cretics + catalectic trochaic dimeter.

1359: ∪∪∪− −∪− −∪−: cretics (for text see n. on 1359 below).

1360: −∪− −∪− −∪− ∪∪∪− −∪−: cretics.

Seventh period (1361–4): iambs and anapaests, ending in an iambic dimeter + a spondee. (So Radermacher: Schroeder divides so as to have a final cretic and spondee.)

1361: ∪− ∪− ∪∪− ∪∪−

1362: ∪− ∪∪− ∪∪− ∪−

1363: ∪∪− ∪∪− ∪− ∪−

1364: ∪− ∪− −− ∪− −−

It is difficult but necessary to remember that all this metrical complexity was intended to be *funny*. Hence we may expect parts of it to be metrically nonsensical and impossible to reduce to metrical laws based on serious poetry.

1331–2. *The Dream.* 'O darkly bright gloom of the night': for other 'romantic' references to gloom and darkness *cf.* 1336, 1350: for genuine examples from Euripides see, *e.g.*, *Hecuba* 68–72 (which may be parodied here: see Σ) and in Blaydes. For the *Oxymoron* in κελαινοφαής 'darkly shining', *cf.* ψυχὰν ἄψυχον in 1333–4a. This figure is remarkably common in E. (for 36 examples see Mitchell). E. is fond of compounds from φάος : see O. Hense, *Philologus* lx (1901), 389.

1333–4a. πρόπολον : 'a herald, announcer' (*cf.* Aesch. *Choëph.* 357, Eur. *Hel.* 570). This seems the best reading here (*cf.* van Leeuwen): RVMU have πρόμολον from which Wilamowitz conjectured προμολῶν 'approaches, entrances'. If 'spiritless spirit' is intended to be anything more than pretentious nonsense, it presumably refers to the feebleness of ghosts (as described in *Odyssey* 10, 495). μελαίνας : a favourite 'atmospheric' term in E., see Allen-Italie, *Concordance to Euripides*, and *cf.* in 1336.

1335–6. With the repeated φόνια *cf.* the repeated ἀνέπτατ' in 1352 and δάκρυα in 1354a. Note that these all scan ∪∪∪, a subtle mockery of E.'s rhythms: *cf. Hel.* 195, 214, 1118 and *Or.* 986, 1414, 1416 (see further in Descroix 153). μελανο- also repeats μελαίνας in 1334a. E. was addicted to using repetitions to stimulate emotion. In the *Orestes* monody (1369-1502) he uses eighteen of them. In *Hecuba* 689-90 we find ἄπιστ' ἄπιστα, καινὰ καινὰ δέρκομαι. ἔτερα δ' ἀφ' ἐτέρων κακὰ κακῶν κυρεῖ: *Helena* 648-51 is almost as bad. *Cf. Thesm.* 915. (But, as van Leeuwen notes, Aeschylus was not guiltless of this : see, *e.g.*, the seven repetitions in *Suppl.* 836-63.) μελανο-νεκυ-είμονα: 'black-corpse-clad' is a comic inflation for 'black-shrouded', *cf.* the φάντασμα μελανόπτερον in *Hecuba* 705. 'With great finger-nails' : a mockery of E.'s trivial detail and also of his sensationalism.

1338-41. *The Purification.* Ritual cleansing of this kind (ἀπο-διοπομπεῖσθαι) was customary after an evil dream : sea water or fresh running water (as here) was used. The heating mentioned here is perhaps a deliberately trivial touch. The 'oceanic divinity' is presumably Oceanus, the traditional father of all rivers (note ποταμῶν in 1339) : *cf. Iliad* 21, 196.

1342-3. *The Discovery.* τοῦτ' ἐκεῖνο: 'that's it' (*cf.* 318), *i.e.* this is what the dream meant : a sudden lapse into everyday speech (*Bathos: cf.* Starkie on *Acharnians* 41). τέρᾱ: 'portents', Dindorf's emendation for R's τὰ δ' ἔτερα and V's τάδε τέρατα. But the metre is uncertain.

1344-5. We now discover the cause of all this tragic fussification. A slave called Glyke ('Sweetie') has stolen a cock (see on 935). The *Bathos* is gloriously deepened by the following joint invocation of the Nymphs and a slave with the barbarous name Μᾱνία. This was a Phrygian prostitute's name according to Machon as cited by Athenaeus, 578 b : *cf.* 965 above and *Thesm.* 728. The name is not linguistically cognate with μανία 'madness' : but Ar. may be taking a side-crack at E.'s fondness for mad-scenes : *cf.* 'Longinus', περὶ ὕψους 15. There is a similar pun in Machon as quoted by Athenaeus, 578 d. The source of Νύμφαι ὀρεσσίγενοι is discussed by M. P. Nilsson, *L'Antiquité Classique* xxiv (1955), 336-40.

1346 ff. *The Lonely Vigil.* 1348: women in ancient Greece spent much time in spinning (as their modern successors still do). A bundle of unspun wool (τολύπη) was stuck on a distaff (ἠλακάτη) which was held in the left hand : from it the right hand drew off the fibres, twisted them between finger and thumb, and wound them as yarn (*cf.* on 1315) on to a spindle (ἄτρακτος: conn. w. *torqueo* 'twist') or spool (πηνίον: *cf.* 578). The skein of spun yarn ready for weaving was called a κλωστήρ (from κλώθω 'spin' : see in 1349). This was later woven on a loom (ἱστός: *cf.* in 1315) with the help of a κερκίς (see on 1316) into cloth.

1349. *Cf.* on 1314. Again the number of εἰ's varies in the mss.

I follow Bothe in reading three. The musical gibe is not strictly relevant here. But if Ar. thinks he can get a second laugh for a good joke he generally goes for it.

1352-5. *The Flight of the Bird.* For the repetitions see on 1336. Here the style is mock-dithyrambic in its descriptions of 'soaring' (*cf.* the mockery in *Birds* 1383 ff. and *Peace* 830 ff. : for E.'s fondness for it see Blaydes and Rogers). κουφοτάταις πτερύγων ἀκμαῖς : ' on the lightest tips of his wings ' : a characteristic lyrical periphrasis for ' on his very nimble wings ' (*cf.* Aeschylus, *P.V.* 125-6 ἐλαφραῖς πτερύγων ῥιπαῖς). In sober fact the domestic bird presumably departed in a bag carried by Glyke : *cf.* 1364.

1356-60. *The Call for Aid.* As a climax to this masterpiece of bathos Aeschylus now makes the hapless, cock-bereft female summon (in stirring cretic metre) a posse of Cretans and a goddess to help her catch the thief. Σ says that 1356 is a quotation from E.'s *Cretans* (*cf.* on 849) and that there is some parody of the same play in the following lines. Ἴδας : the Cretan mountain of that (frequent) name. 1358 : with τόξα Ar. perhaps wishes (wickedly) to suggest the Athenian police : see on 608. But for the survival of the bow in Crete *cf.* Plato, *Laws* 625 D.

1358. 'And nimbly ply [ἀμπάλλετε : syncopated for ἀναπάλλετε : *cf.* on ἔπαλλε in 1317] your limbs.'

1359. Δίκτυννα (popularly explained as 'Lady of the δίκτυον, hunting-net', but perhaps a word of pre-Greek origin) is an epithet of Artemis as goddess of the hunt. καλά (*Doric* for -ή) : an epithet specially applied to Artemis : *cf.* *Agamemnon* 140 and Fraenkel's note (I follow him in deleting Ἄρτεμις as a gloss and inserting ἁ, for the stylistic and metrical reasons he gives there).

1360. κυνίσκας : 'bitchlets' : a deliberately incongruous *Diminutive* in this mock-solemn context. Tragedy generally avoids such forms.

1361-4. *The Invocation.* διπύρους . . . λαμπάδας ὀξυτάτας : 'twin fiery torches most keenly bright' : *cf.* ἀμφιπύρους ἀνέχων πεύκας of Dionysos in *Ion* 716. Hecate, goddess of the underworld (*cf.* in 366), regularly carried these. παράφηνον (-φαίνω) ἐς Γλύκης (*cf.* on 69) : 'accompany me [παρα-] with light to Glyke's house'. φωράσω 'discover the theft, catch her in the act' (of retaining the cock) : the prosaic word (*Bathos*) for detecting a thief (φώρ : *cf.* φέρω 'carry off', Latin *fur*, and English 'furtive').

1364a-69. Without further argument about lyrics and music A. and E. agree to pass on to another test, namely to judge the merit of their verses by weighing them on weighing-scales. ἐξελέγξει in 1366 = 'put to the proof, test', not 'refute' as in

960. 1367 = 'for the weight of our phrases will test us' or possibly 'for it will test us with regard to the weight of our phrases'. For solemn weighing-scenes in earlier literature *cf. Iliad* 22, 209 ff. (where Zeus weighs the fates of Achilles and Hector) and Aeschylus's *Psychostasia* in which Zeus weighed the lives of Achilles and Memnon while their mothers stood pleading beside each scale-pan (like A. and. E. in 1378 ff.): further in G. Björck, *Eranos* xliii (1945), 58-66.

1368-9. εἴπερ γε etc. : 'If I really and truly must ⟨do⟩ this, namely treat the art of poets like cheese for sale'. The construction of τοῦτο δεῖ with an infinitive is paralleled in Demosthenes 10, 15 : but Radermacher, following Velsen, prefers to mark a lacuna after 1368. For the homely comparison *cf.* 798.

1370-7. A short ode in praise of cleverness.

METRE. Catalectic trochaic dimeters (lecythia) in 1370, 1371, 1372 ; full trochaic dimeters in all other lines except the final ‒ ∪ ‒ ∪ ‒ ‒ (ithyphallic) in 1377.

1370. ἐπίπονοί γ': 'Yes, painstaking are the clever ones', *i.e.* they will go to infinite trouble to achieve their intention, the ἐπι- (as in 1373) implying a renewed effort. *Cf.* the definition of genius as 'an infinite capacity for taking pains'.

1374-5. μὰ τόν : 'Good gracious'. The name of a deity is omitted (only here in Ar., but occasionally elsewhere, *e.g.* Plato, *Gorgias* 466 E : see further in Werres 9) as in English 'Oh my !' and 'Oh dear !' (originally with 'God' added). Tucker may be right in finding a παρὰ προσδοκίαν joke in the parenthetical phrase 'not even if I had been told by someone who . . . happened to meet me' (instead of 'someone who had actually witnessed it'), together with a gibe at Athenian credulity.

1378 ff. ACTION. A pair of scales—probably grotesquely huge and ungainly, for comic effect—has meanwhile been set up (doubtless with much *Business*) in the *Orchestra*. D. commands each poet to recite a single line into one of the scale-pans. A. was, of course, the likelier to win in any contest on the basis of sheer weight (see 940 ff.). But Radermacher rightly warns against assuming that the results of successive scenes in Aristophanes's plays follow logically from one another.

1378. 'Come on, then. You two take your stand beside the two scale-pans.' A. and E. do so and reply together (see Radermacher for such simultaneous remarks), 'there you are' : *cf.* on 200.

1379. εἴπατον : 'speak' : contrast the *Present Imperative* λέγετον 'recite' in 1381. So, too, in 1389-90.

1380. μεθῆσθον : 2nd pers. dual 2 aor. subj. mid. of μεθίημι :
cf. on 1384. κοκκύσω : 'yell out' : this verb is used to represent
(by *Onomatopoeia*) shrill cries in general or, in particular, the
cock's crow or (less frequently) the cuckoo's call.

1381. τοῦπος : this is the only place in Ar. where ἔπος seems
at first to be best translated 'verse' (see on 862). But since τὸ
ῥῆμα in 1379 seems to be a synonym (as in 882, 1198) and D.
judges the weight in terms of word-meaning alone (*cf.* on 1386-8),
not rhythm or phonetic quality, it is better to take it here (as in
1387, 1388, 1395, 1407, 1410) as 'word' or 'phrase'.

1382-3. The first line of E.'s *Medea* and a line from A.'s lost
Philoctetes. διαπτάσθαι (2 aor. mid. διαπέτομαι) : 'winged
through', *sc.* the Clashing Rocks on the way to Colchis : *cf.* on
1388.

1384. Here and in 1393 the MSS. have μεθεῖτε which is an un-
paralleled form. *Porson* conjectured μέθεσθε : but it is hard to
see why this should be corrupted to μεθεῖτε. I have followed
Coulon in accepting Wilamowitz's μεθεῖται : 'it [the πλάστιγξ]
has been released', spoken by A. and E. together. This is closer
to the MS. reading and gives point to both 1384 and 1393.

1386-8. ἐριοπωλικῶς : 'like wool-sellers', who wet their wool
(τἄρια = τὰ ἔρια) to make it heavier : *cf.* adding sand to sugar,
slate to coal, water to milk, chicory to coffee, and irrelevant
quotations to editions of classical authors. D.'s argument is, of
course, quite absurd—that a line mentioning a river is bound to
be heavier than a line that refers to wings. τοῦπος ἐπτερωμένον :
'the word that has wings' (διαπτάσθαι in 1382) : *cf.* Homer's
phrase 'winged words' (ἔπεα πτερόεντα). Verrall notes (*Classical
Review* xxii, 1908, 172-5) that from the phonetic point of view
E.'s lines here on the whole have weightier groups of consonants
and long vowels than A.'s (though the reverse is true of these
authors' general usage) : so subtle critics in the audience might
have expected E. to win. But D. judges only by subject matter.

1390. ἤν : an exclamation (*cf.* Latin *en*) : 'Look'. ἰδού : 'there
you are' : *cf.* on 200.

1391-2. From E.'s *Antigone* and A.'s *Niobe* (see further in
Nauck, Aesch. fr. 161, 4 for a subsequent reference to πειθώ
there). For E.'s interest in 'persuasion' *cf. Hecuba* 816. οὐ
δώρων ἐρᾷ : normally in Ar. the negative would immediately
precede its verb in a sentence like this (but *cf. Kn.* 474) : this
order here is Aeschylean. (I owe this information to Mr. A. C.
Moorhouse : *cf.* on 866.)

1393. μέθετε is Blass's emendation for μεθεῖτε. For this word
see on 1384.

1395-6. 'Yes, but I put in Persuasion : it made a perfectly expressed phrase.' *Cf.* **1161.** D.'s reply is in regular tragic metre and sounds like a quotation.

1399-1400. When E. ruminates on what would be the most effective line for him to quote, D. mischievously supplies a trivial line probably from E.'s *Telephus* : ' Achilles threw two singles and a four '. D.'s following remark shows that he knew it was quite unsuitable. The line describes a bad throw—the triple six being the highest : *cf.* Fraenkel on *Agamemnon* 32-3—in the dice-and-board game called κυβεία (κύβος, English 'cube', being used to denote both the die itself and the single 'pip', the μονάς) : for details and comparisons with modern games see H. J. R. Murray, *A History of Board Games other than Chess*, Oxford, 1952.

1401-3. 'You'd better recite, since this is the ⟨only⟩ remaining weighing for the pair of you.' λέγοιτ' ἂν : polite optative like the Hiberno-English use of the subjunctive for imperative : 'Let you say it'. στάσις : *cf.* on 359. E. now quotes from *Meleager*, A. from *Glaukos Potnieus.* νεκρῷ : a locative dative (*cf.* on 1318 : but M has νεκρῶν) or else it depends on the ἐπὶ in the next line in A.'s play—ἵπποι δ' ἐφ' ἵπποις ἦσαν ἐμπεφυρμένοι.

1406. 'Which not even a hundred Egyptians could raise.' The Egyptians had a reputation for strength (*cf. Birds* 1133), mainly, perhaps, owing to their colossal buildings : *cf.* Herodotus 2, 124 on the building of the pyramids.

1408-9. I follow Radermacher in reading παιδία χἠ (see on 508) γυνή as the best explanation of R's unmetrical παιδία ἡ γυνή and παιδία χἠ γυνή of other MSS. 'Children-and-wife' is a natural group in itself, hence the intrusive καί. For the gibe at Cephisophon and at E.'s books see on 943-4.

1411. D. brusquely interrupts A. (see on 1414 below) and addresses Pluto. ἄνδρες (=οἱ ἄνδρες) is Seager's correction of the MS. ἄνδρες (M² has οἱ ἄνδρες).

1413. 'The one I consider clever [or 'skilful' or 'wise'], the other I enjoy.' Which is which ? There is no clear indication. Perhaps Ar. deliberately made it ambiguous to leave the audience in uncertainty about D.'s final decision. The ambiguity of σοφόν (see on 1118) increases the vagueness. The evidence earlier in the play is inconclusive : *e.g.* 66 ff., 916-17, 968, 1028-9. *Aristarchus* thought Euripides was the 'clever' one here. See further in Dörrie as cited on 1437-41 below. On the whole, I am inclined to agree with Denniston (MS.) that D.'s association with Aeschylus has re-awakened an old fondness for Aeschylus which becomes decisive in 1468. If so, σοφόν here refers to Euripides (*cf.* 71).

1414 ff. ACTION. Pluto intervenes to induce the wavering D. to decide between A. and E. Pluto was present since 830—as a silent figure, humorously enough in view of 911. ff.—or else, as Radermacher thinks, he may have entered, announced perhaps by a clap of thunder from the βροντεῖον, after 1410. The second view would better motivate the sharp interruption there. For refutation of the ancient view that the Chorus speaks 1414 and presumably 1415-16 see Radermacher : at any rate the invitation in 1479-80 must come from Pluto. The competition in tragic skill is now abandoned and a political test substituted. (On this whole passage to l. 1467 see D. MacDowell, *Classical Quarterly* n.s. ix, 1959, 261-8.)

1417 ff. εὐδαιμονοίης : 'God bless you' (*sc.* for your kindness) : used in accepting an offer with gratitude. 'I came down in search of a poet.' The fickle D. has changed his purpose : in 66 ff. his desire was only for Euripides : but *cf.* end of n. on 1413.

1419. 'So that the City may be saved and may keep on conducting the choruses' (*i.e.* the dramatic festivals). This is Aristophanes's rather perfunctory way of converting D.'s original literary and personal motive into a political one. (Perhaps a specific reference to the financial difficulty of providing choruses is intended : *cf.* on 405.) See Schmidt 76 ff.

1421-2. The test question is to be : 'What do you think about *Alcibiades* ?' Political opinion in Athens in 405 was sharply divided on this brilliant, ostentatious, charming, unscrupulous, unpredictable, and dissolute aristocrat. Should he be recalled from the Thracian Chersonese (where he had voluntarily withdrawn in 406) ? Undoubtedly he had the ability to defeat the Peloponnesians : his recent victories had shown it. But could a man who had gone over to the enemy after his recall from Syracuse be trusted now ? He was not in fact recalled, and was mysteriously assassinated in 404. *Cf.* § 5.

1423-4. δυστοκεῖ : 'is in difficult labour with the question', *i.e.* finds it hard and painful to produce a decision. For the *Metaphor* from childbirth *cf.* Theognis 39 and 1081. In 1424 I follow Brunck in attributing the first part to Euripides.

1425. An adaptation of a line from Ion's *Guards*, where Helen says to Odysseus (on a spying expedition in Troy) σιγᾷ μέν, ἐχθαίρει δέ, βούλεταί γε μήν. For such mixed feelings *cf.* Catullus's *odi et amo*.

1427-9. 'I hate any citizen who will . . .' These lines are in tragic metre—quotations or parodies. The variant πέφυκε for φανεῖται may, as Tucker suggests, come from the tragic original : πάτρα, *cf.* 1163, belongs to elevated style. E. is fond of beginning

lines with words like μισῶ, στυγῶ etc.: see Schmid 353 n. 4.
Note the rhetorical antitheses, 'slow . . . swift . . . resource-
ful . . . helpless . . .'. *Cf.* Euripides, fr. 905 μισῶ σοφιστήν,
ὅστις οὐχ αὐτῷ σοφός.

1431a-b. The lines are tautological. Perhaps the duplication
is due to a revision of the play by Ar. (see § 7 n. 25 ; but why
should he re-write a perfectly good line ?) or possibly one is the
line as originally found in Aeschylus (inserted by a commentator)
and the other its adaptation by Ar. ; or possibly, as Radermacher
suggests, one is an interpolation from Eupolis's *Demoi*. **1431b**
is omitted by VA, but **1431a** is omitted by Plutarch, *Alcibiades*
16 and is apparently ignored by Valerius Maximus 7, 2, 7. I
follow Coulon in bracketing the first. Erbse, however, suggests
an ingenious solution : he places **1431a** after **1429** as the last
line of E.'s statement ; then in **1431b** A. agrees with E.'s view,
but goes further in **1432.**

1431b. The metaphor of the lion cub—charming and harmless
at first but fierce and destructive when it grows up, as described
in *Agamemnon* 717 ff.—is common in 5th-century literature, the
earliest known example being cited by Herodotus 5, 92 (in a
Delphic oracle to the Corinthians : so perhaps Ar. intends some
parody of Aeschylus's 'oracle-style' : see Stanford, *Aeschylus* 29).
It seems to have had some special significance for Alcmaeonids (see
Plutarch, *Pericles* 3, 2 and *Alcibiades* 16, 3). (A reference to the
contemporary general named Leon is unlikely.)   On lion-oracles
see G. W. Dyson, *Classical Quarterly* xxiii (1929), 186-95.

1433-4. 'By Zeus the Saviour': an apt oath in a matter that
concerns the safety of Athens (*cf.* **1419**). δυσκρίτως γ' ἔχω: 'I
am in a difficulty of judgement' : a quotation from Euripides,
Erechtheus 12. 'For one has spoken cleverly, the other plainly' :
this is as ambiguous as **1413.** While E.'s language in **1427-9** is
clearer than A.'s metaphor in **1431-2**, he offers no clear advice on
policy. (What follows later in **1445** and **1451** can hardly be taken
as relevant to the meaning here.)   The ambiguity is perhaps in-
tentional and not to be resolved : as Higham notes, political
caution might be advisable for Ar. on this.   Meineke ingeniously
suggests that we should read σοφῶς again for the following σαφῶς,
giving a deliberate anti-climax : 'and the other—cleverly'. But
possibly, as Platnauer has suggested, Ar. intends to mock Euripides,
Orestes 397 σοφόν τοι τὸ σαφές, οὐ τὸ μὴ σαφές.

1436. ἥντιν' ἔχετον: on this division of the dactyl see White
43 and Descroix 183 ff.

1437-41. These lines were rejected by *Aristarchus* as vulgar
and cheap (presumably for Euripides, not for Ar. in general) and

by Apollonius as out of place, since D. asks for *one* opinion in
1435 and E. gives a series of opinions in **1437** ff. Certainly **1442**
seems to be phrased to follow directly after **1436**. Editors have
suggested various re-arrangements and deletions. Coulon accepts
the text without alteration, and R. E. Wycherley has defended
it in *Classical Review* lix (1945), 34-8, suggesting a pause for
laughter after **1441** and arguing that comic relief was needed in
the serious political discussion. Though I agree with Wycherley
and others that the humour of the whole passage is Aristophanic,
the present syntax seems impossible to me : so I have bracketed
the lines as out of place. Others have preferred to re-arrange the
text. Most recently H. Dörrie in *Hermes* lxxxiv (1956), 296-319
has made a detailed re-examination of **1433-66**, reviewing previous
interpretations. He concludes that owing to some mechanical
error in transmitting the text twelve lines were interchanged, and
that **1451-62** should come after **1441**, and **1442-50** (+ a two-line
lacuna after **1450**) after **1462**. He also suggests different speakers
for several of these lines (his main contention being that the
advice given in **1443-4** and **1446-50** should be given to Aeschylus :
which has much to recommend it). The chief objection to his
theory is the need to assume a lacuna after **1450**. Failing further
evidence, no final agreement on the authentic text is likely to be
reached. See also Süss, *Scheinbare* etc., Schmid 354 n. 3, Schmidt
76 ff., and Erbse 277.

1437 ff. The fantastic suggestion curiously anticipates modern
methods of aerial and chemical warfare. *Cinesias* was tall and as
thin as a lath (and for his 'flightiness' see *Birds* 1373 ff.), so he
would make long, light wings for Cleocritus who, according to
Birds 877, somehow looked like an ostrich : and, as Pausanias 9,
31, 1 confirms, ostriches' bodies are so weighty that their own
wings cannot lift them into the air. ὀξίδας : 'vinegar-jars'.
πτερώσας has no main verb agreeing with it : but, as Tucker
notes, unattached participial clauses of this kind are found else-
where. The diction of **1438** is highly poetical, perhaps parodying
Euripides, *Palamedes*, fr. 578, 4 ποντίας ὑπὲρ πλακός. τίνα : the
last word in a Greek sentence is sometimes emphatic like this
(see Fraenkel on *Agamemnon* 1436), though usually the emphasis
comes at the beginning.

1443-5. Pronounced quickly ἀπιστατίσθ' and -τάπιστάπιστα
are pretty near to gibberish : cf. *Hecuba* 689 as quoted on **1335**.
D. pardonably asks for something phrased 'less learnedly',
ἀμαθέστερον (cf. on **839**).

1448. σωθείημεν : this form, long suspected as being un-Attic,
can now be accepted : see Radermacher.

1450. τἀναντί' ἀν is Dobree's correction of the unmetrical τἀναντία πρ. (Ar. does not lengthen syllables before mute and liquid letters of this type in iambic trimeters, but he often does so in lyrics : cf. on 814.) πράξαντες (R) seems better for the sense 'if we do' than πράττοντες (V).

1451. Palamedes, a hero who took part in the early stages of the Greek expedition against Troy, was credited with great inventiveness and ingenuity—hence the reference here. But it is a bad omen for Euripides, since Palamedes met a tragic fate before the Greeks reached Troy. *Cf.* the mockery of E.'s *Palamedes* in *Thesm.* 770 ff., and on **1438**.

1452-3. See on **1437**. For Cephisophon see on **944**.

1455. Aeschylus has not been in Athens for over 50 years, having died abroad in 456 B.C. **πόθεν :** 'Nonsense !' (like the colloquial 'How come ?') used to denote incredulity or disbelief. *Cf.* the scornful ποῖος in **529**.

1459. 'When neither city coat nor country cloak suits it.' The χλαῖνα was the city-man's fashionable ἱμάτιον made from carefully worked wool. The σισύρα was a rough covering made from sheep- or goat-skin with the hair left on it, as still worn by Greek shepherds. The phrase sounds like a proverb.

1460-1. εἴπερ ἀναδύσει : 'at any rate if you are going to rise up again'. ἐκεῖ : in Athens.

1462. 'Oh please don't do *that*, but send up your good counsels from here.' The second phrase seems to be formulaic for the sending up of good gifts by spirits and divinities in the underworld : cf. Ar. fr. 488, 11 ff. and in Radermacher.

1463-5. Schmid (354-5) thinks, with Wilamowitz, that these lines are spurious, as A.'s recommendation of Pericles's policy (to concentrate Athenian strength on naval attacks while allowing the enemy to invade Attica freely : cf. Thucydides 1, 143, 4) was out of date in 405. But perhaps A. is being made to appear old-fashioned deliberately : and an interpolation of this kind is not likely. *Cf.* on **1437-41**.

1465. 'Let ships be riches, riches wretchedness' (D. W. Lucas's translation). The line with its *Oxymoron* and jingling repetition is Euripidean rather than Aeschylean : cf. *Iphigeneia in Tauris* 897 πόρον ἄπορον. Possibly a hit at the recently appointed Revenue Commissioners is intended : cf. on **1505**.

1466. 'Yes, except that the juryman alone gobbles up the money' (αὐτὰ = τὰ χρήματα τοῦ πόρου: cf. in 1025). The jurymen's pay had been raised to 2 obols by *Cleophon* in 409. Ar. mocks the jurymen's rapacity elsewhere, especially in *Wasps*.

1469-70. Euripides, sensing his imminent defeat, makes a wild appeal to D. In fact D. has not, within the play at least (and we are hardly justified in assuming off-stage conversations, as van Leeuwen suggests), sworn by any gods to bring E. back to Athens (though *cf.* 66 ff.). See p. xxiv.

1471. 'My tongue has sworn [but not my mind]: so I shall choose Aeschylus.' Here again (*cf.* 102 and *Thesm.* 275-6) Ar. refers to E.'s *Hippolytus* 612 ἡ γλῶσσ' ὀμώμοχ', ἡ δὲ φρὴν ἀνώμοτος. Ar. uses it as a justification of perjury (*cf.* ἐπιορκήσασαν in 102). This is unfair to E., since Hippolytus in his play kept his oath faithfully to the end. But Ar., in so far as he intended any serious criticism, might have argued that E. by making a distinction between oath and intention opened the door to unscrupulous mental reservations and evasions. Note that Ar. uses the New Attic γλῶττα here for E.'s Old Attic γλῶσσα (§ 11 n. 56).

1473. τίη: a strengthened form of τί (for uncertainties or accent see L.-S.-J.): 'Why on earth . . . ?'

1474-5. 'Do you look me in the face after doing a deed most shameful ?': tragic diction and metre (so, too, **1468**). It leads up to another crushing reply taken directly from E.'s *Aeolus* with the substitution of τοῖς θεωμένοις for τοῖσι χρωμένοις. This line 'What is shameful if the doers think it not so ?' caused moral indignation in Athens : see much further in Fritzsche.

1476. σχέτλιε: see on 116. δή: indignant 'do you mean to say'. These are E.'s last words in the play.

1477-8. A third and final blow against E. For the first line see on 1082. The second line mocks it in a comic jingle (*Assonance*), 'And breathing's broth and sleep a pillow-slip' (lit. '. . . is dinner . . . a fleece': *cf.* 107 and 1203). The 'dinner' part prompts Pluto's invitation in the next line.

1479. χωρεῖτε . . . ὦ Διόνυσ': the plural is frequently so used for a person together with his companions (here it includes Aeschylus) : *cf.* Knox-Headlam on Herodas 3, 87.

1480. ἵνα ξενίζω is Meineke's correction of the unmetrical ξενίσω of the mss. : *cf.* 618. Coulon prefers Bergk's ξενίσω 'γώ.

1480-1. 'A good suggestion, by Zeus. I've no objection to the deed' : this nonchalant remark expressed in tragic style and metre aptly ends D.'s talk in the play. Complacently accepting Pluto's invitation as his natural due, and probably without a glance at the flabbergasted Euripides, he strolls in to the feast.

1482-99. The Chorus sings an ode in praise of the man of true intelligence, who, they claim, will avoid Socratic subtleties and bring practical benefit to his kinsmen and to the citizens in general.

METRE : trochaic : 3 lecythia + 5 trochaic dimeters + 1 ithyphallic (1490 : ∪ ∪ ∪ ∪ ∪ ∪ − −) + 3 lecythia + 1 trochaic dimeter + 1 lecythion + 3 trochaic dimeters + 1 ithyphallic (∪ ∪ ∪ − ∪ − ⤳).

1482-4. 'Yes [γ' assents to the decision in the previous scene], blessed is the man with accurate intelligence. This fact one can [πάρα = πάρεστι] learn in many ways.' μακάριος denotes the highest state of happiness, as in the opening phrase of the Beatitudes (St. Matthew 5, 3 ff.) : μακάριοι οἱ . . .

1485. δοκήσας (for δόξας : cf. in 737) : 'having shown himself to have good sense'.

1487-8. ἐπ' ἀγαθῷ . . . ἐπ' ἀγαθῷ : 'bringing good to . . .' : the repetition gives a liturgical effect. Ar. often ends his comedies with this kind of 'Happy Christmas' atmosphere, as befitted a religious festival.

1491. χαρίεν οὖν etc. : 'The elegant thing, then, to do is not to sit chattering beside Socrates . . .'. Here Ar. makes an opportunity of mocking his old victim Socrates (cf. Clouds 144 ff., Birds 1555), adopting the popular but misguided view that he was a typical Sophist, a pedantic, over-ingenious, arrogant (σεμνοῖσιν in 1496) quibbler (cf. in 1497), and an enemy of established custom in religion, ethics, and education (cf. 1493-5 and § 6). In private life Ar. and Socrates may well have been good friends, as Plato in his Symposium seems to imply. Ar. could hardly have foreseen that his comic attacks on Socrates would help to bring on his indictment and execution in 399 B.C. (see Plato, Apology 18 D and 19 C). In the present passage (as in fr. 376) Ar. implies that Euripides had been influenced by Socrates (who was the younger by 12 years), which may or may not be true : see further in Ehrenberg 274-8, E. Angelopoulos, Aristophane et ses idées sur Socrate (Athens, 1933), R. Stark in Rheinisches Museum xcvi (1953), 77-9, T. Gelzer, Museum Helveticum xiii (1956), 65-93.

1497. σκαριφησμοῖσι : 'verbal scratchifications' : the word (perhaps cognate with scribo) occurs only here and its precise meaning is uncertain. I have connected it with σκαρίφασθαι and compounds, with reference to a bird scratching in the ground : see Athenaeus 507 c and further in Blaydes ; and for another opprobrious comparison between mental ability and the habits of hens cf. Acts of the Apostles 17, 18, where St. Paul is called by the Athenians a 'seed-picker' (σπερμολόγος). But Σ explains σκαριφησμός as an artist's preliminary sketch (σκιαγραφία), implying vagueness or subtlety of line.

1498. διατριβὴν ἀργὸν : 'idle time-spending'. In its neutral sense this noun simply meant 'a way of passing the time' (διατρίβω). In Plato and later writers it has the meaning 'discourse, ethical lecture or treatise', hence our 'diatribe'.

1499. 'Is the sign of a man going out of his mind' : for the genitive *cf.* 534 ff.

1500-27. The preceding chorus has marked a lapse of time long enough for Pluto's feast to be finished. Aeschylus, Pluto, and Dionysos come out from the *Scene-building* in high spirits. What follows is the *Exodos*.

METRE : anapaestic dimeters, with the catalectic forms (paroemiacs) in 1513/14, 1523, 1527 (and see on 1505).

1501. 'Our city' : strictly, of course, Pluto's own place was Hades not Athens, but Scaliger's emendation ὑμετέραν is unnecessary. Pluto is in the convivial mood of the drinking-song 'Your friends are my friends, And my friends are your friends'. Pious folk in the audience would remember that Attica was specially under the protection of Pluto's wife, Persephone.

1504-6. δὸς τουτὶ . . . τουτουσὶ . . . τόδε (I have adopted Bergk's τουτουσὶ which accounts for the variation in the MSS. and removes the anomalous paroemiac in the middle of a sentence) : what exactly Pluto had in his hands when he said this, is uncertain. But since the proverbial three roads to death were the sword, the halter, and the hemlock (with the variation of throwing yourself off a cliff instead of poison : see on 121 ff. and Fritzsche), we may take it that Pluto handed Aeschylus a sword, several halters, and a bowl of hemlock. The πορισταί were special Revenue Commissioners appointed during the war to raise emergency taxes to meet war expenditure (*cf.* Antiphon, *De chor.* 49). Myrmex and Archenomos are unknown, unless Myrmex ('the Ant') means Philoxenus the dithyrambist (see *Suidas s.v.*, Pherecrates frag. 145, and *Thesm.* 100). Nicomachos is probably the legal innovator and 'secretary' (*cf.* on 1084-5) denounced in Lysias 30, 10 ff.

1511. στίξας . . . ξυμποδίσας : 'when I've branded them [like slaves, *cf. Birds* 760 : or possibly just 'marked them by beating' as in *Wasps* 1296, *cf.* on 756] and tied their feet together'.

1512. Adeimantos was one of the 'generals' in the present year (405) and was later accused of betraying the Athenian fleet at Aegospotami. According to Xenophon, *Hellenica* 1, 4, 21, his father's name was Λευκολοφίδης : this Ar. changes to Λευκόλοφος 'Whitecrest' here, perhaps hinting at ostentation or pretentiousness (*cf.* 1016, 925), as well as for the sake of the metre. For an alternative view on the basis of the ref. to a Λευκολόφας in *Eccl.* 645 see Fritzsche.

1515-16. θᾶκον : this is *Bentley's* emendation here and in 1522 for RVAM's unmetrical θρόνον and U's θῶκον (the epic and Ionic form which is out of place here). For *Sophocles's* succession to the Chair of Poetry see 787 ff.

1520. 'That blackguardly, scurrilous liar' : Euripides. It was not the Greek custom to be kind to the vanquished in words or deeds. μηδ' ἄκων : 'not even unintentionally'.

1524-5. φαίνετε . . . λαμπάδας ἱεράς : 'show your mystic torches' (*cf.* 313, 340). Platt, with some reason, argues (*Journal of Philology* xxxiv, 1918, 246) that we would expect 'Show light [intransitive] *with* your torches' and emends to λαμπάσιν ἱεραῖς. προπέμπετε : 'escort'. The torchlight processional *exeunt omnes* is paralleled in *Lysis.* 1295 ff. Perhaps here it is meant to recall the great torchlight, triumphal procession at the end of Aeschylus's *Eumenides.*

1526-7. 'Celebrating his fame with his own songs and dances' : presumably a reference to the final hexameters (1528 ff. : contrast Euripides's strictures in 1261 ff.) and possibly to some Aeschylean phrases (*cf.* on 1528) in the concluding lines : some of the Chorus's gestures as they went out may also have recalled Aeschylean choreography.

1528 ff. Final part of the *Exodos.*

METRE : dactylic hexameters. Note the strong caesura in the 4th foot of every line except **1529**, the infrequency of spondees in the first 5 feet, and the complete absence of short syllables at the end of the line (see further in Dale 28).

1528-32. εὐοδίαν ἀγαθὴν : '*bon voyage*' : according to the scholiast a quotation from Aeschylus's *Glaukos Potnieus.* With **1530** *cf. Eumenides* 1012-13 εἴη δ' ἀγαθῶν ἀγαθὴ διάνοια πολίταις. **1532** : 'harsh concurrences in arms' : this also sounds like an Aeschylean phrase : but ἀργαλέος (from ἄλγος 'pain', the first λ being changed to ρ by dissimilation from the second) does not occur in extant tragedy, according to L.-S.-J.

1532-3. '*Cleophon* and anyone else (of these fellows) who wants to fight . . .' Ar. ends with a slash at the war-mongers, accusing them as usual (*cf.* on 679 ff.) of not being pure-blooded Athenians (πατρίοις ἐν ἀρούραις implies 'out of our country', and, in Cleophon's case, Thrace, which was also the homeland of Ares, the war-god) : *cf.* 680 ff. and *Birds* 1368-9. According to Aeschines 2, 76, when the Peloponnesians offered terms of agreement after Arginusae, Cleophon said he would cut the head off anyone in

Athens who even mentioned peace. The play's last phrase, τούτων
πατρίοις ἐν ἀρούραις, 'in *their* [οὗτος contemptuous as in 1308]
ancestral (ploughed) lands', would especially appeal to the Attic
farmers in the audience (see § 3), and at the same time (since
Homer uses similar phrases : see L.-S.-J.) suggest an epic spirit
to the more literary spectators.

So Aristophanes ends his play by giving the Athenians the
comfortable feeling that their errors and sufferings are due to
foreigners and aliens. 'If only we were left to ourselves,' he
implies, 'how happy, peaceful, and prosperous we would be.' This
was no doubt gratifying to the Athenians' self-esteem, but, as
their history shows, it was not in fact entirely true.   However, the
Dionysiac festivals (see § 2) and their comedies were there to give
a sense of well-being and confidence, not to promote self-criticism
or introspection. The final mood then is : 'For we are jolly good
fellows . . . and so say all of us'—but with a religious fervour
and exaltation to sustain it.

INDEX TO INTRODUCTION
AND NOTES

203

LIST OF BOOKS AND ARTICLES [1]

Américo da Costa Ramalho : 'Dipla onomata no estilo de A.',
  Humanitas, supplement iv. 1952
Anti, Carlo : *Teatri greci arcaici.* Padua, 1947
Bernhardi, C. : 'De incisionibus anapaesti in trimetro comico
  Graecorum', *Acta Soc. Phil. Lipsiensis* (1872), i, 2, 245 ff.
Bieber, M. : 'The Entrances and Exits of Actors and Chorus
  in Greek Plays', *American Journal of Archaeology* lviii
  (1954), 277-81
  The History of the Greek and Roman Theater. Princeton
  and London, 1939
Björck, G. : 'Das Alpha impurum und die tragische Kunst-
  sprache', *Acta Soc. Litt. Hum. Reg. Upsaliensis* xxxix,
  1 (1950)
Blass, F. : 'Zu A.'s *Fröschen*', *Hermes* xxxii (1897), 149-59,
  xxxvi (1901), 310-12
Blaydes, F. H. M. : *Ranae.* Halle, 1889
Boudreaux, P. : *Le Texte d'A. et ses commentateurs.* Paris,
  1919
Brunck, R. F. P. : *A. comoediae.* 2nd edn., Oxford, 1810
Cantarella, R. : *Le 'Rane'.* Como, 1943. Vols. i-iii
  Le commedie. Milan, 1949–54
Cataudella, A. : *La poesia di A.* Bari, 1934
*Cornford, F. M. : *The Origin of Attic Comedy.* 2nd edn.,
  Cambridge, 1934
Couat, A. : *A. et l'ancienne comédie attique.* 3rd edn., Paris,
  1902
Coulon, V. : *Aristophane.* Vols. i-v. Paris, 1952–4
  *Essai sur la méthode de la critique conjecturale appliquée au
  texte d'A.* Paris, 1933

[1] Mainly of those cited summarily in the introduction and com-
mentary : for some other publications see the footnotes to the
introduction and notes on the text. Books marked with an asterisk
are recommended for preliminary reading. Select bibliographies will
be found in Dover, Murphy, Pickard-Cambridge, Schmid, Starkie, Web-
ster, and Dover, *Lustrum* ii (1957), 52-112.

*Croiset, M.: *A. and the Political Parties at Athens.* Translated by J. Loeb. London, 1909
*Dale, A. M.: *The Lyric Metres of Greek Drama.* Cambridge, 1948
Denniston, J. D.: 'Technical Terms in A.', *Classical Quarterly* xxi (1927), 113-121
    The Greek Particles. 2nd edn., Oxford, 1954
    Also: ms. lecture notes (latest date, Nov. 1949): see preface
Descroix, J.: *Le Trimètre iambique* etc. Paris, 1931
Dover, K. J.: 'Greek Comedy'. *Fifty Years of Classical Scholarship,* ed. Maurice Platnauer (Oxford, 1954), 96-129
Drexler, H.: *Die Komposition der 'Frösche' des A.* 100. Jahresbericht der Schlesischen Gesellschaft für vaterländische Kultur, 1927. Breslau, 1928
Earp, F. R.: *The Style of Aeschylus.* Cambridge, 1948
*Ehrenberg, V.: *The People of A.* 2nd edn., Oxford, 1951
Erbse, H.: Review of Radermacher's *Frogs, Gnomon* xxviii (1956), 272-8
*Fitts, Dudley: *The Frogs: an English Version.* London, 1957
*Flickinger, R. C.: *The Greek Theatre and its Drama.* 4th edn., Chicago, 1936
Fraenkel, E.: 'Lyrische Daktylen', *Rheinisches Museum* lxxii (1917/18), 161 ff., 321 ff.
Fritzsche, F. K.: *Ranae.* Zürich, 1845
*Gomme, A. W.: 'A. and Politics', *Classical Review* lii (1938)
Green, W. C.: *The Frogs.* Cambridge, 1879
Grene, David: 'The Comic Technique of A.', *Hermathena* l (1937), 87-125
*Guthrie, W. K. C.: *The Greeks and their Gods.* London, 1950
Hall, F. W., and Geldart, W. M.: *A. comoediae.* Vols. i-ii. Oxford, 1906-7
Handley, E. W.: '*-sis* nouns in A.', *Eranos* li (1953), 129-42
Harrison, J. E.: '*Frogs* 1203, and a Point of Tragic Metre', *Trans. Cambridge Phil. Soc.* xcv-xcvi (1913), 18
Hope, W. E.: *The Language of Parody.* Baltimore, 1906.
Householder, F. W.: 'Paroidia', *Classical Philology* xxxix (1944), 1-9
Hugill, W. M.: *Panhellenism in A.* Chicago, 1936
Humbert, J.: *Syntaxe grecque.* 2nd edn., Paris, 1954
Jernigan, C. C.: *Incongruity in A.* Menasha, 1939
Kock, T.: *Die Frösche.* 4th edn., Berlin, 1898
Koster, W. J. W.: *Traité de métrique grecque.* Leyden, 1936

Kranz, W.: *Stasimon*. Berlin, 1933

'Zur Komposition der *Frösche*', *Hermes* lii (1917), 584-91

Kraus, W.: 'Testimonia Aristophanea cum scholiorum lectionibus', *Denkschr. Akad. Wien*, lxx, 2 (1931)

See also Radermacher below

Krause, F.: *Quaestiones Aristophaneae scaenicae*. Rostock, 1903

Lapalus, E.: 'Le Dionysos et l'Héracles des *Grenouilles*', *Revue des Études Grecques* xlvii (1934), 1-20

Leeuwen: see van Leeuwen

*Lever, Katherine: *The Art of Greek Comedy*. London, 1956

Maas, Paul: *Griechische Metrik*. 2nd edn., Leipzig, 1929

Mazon, P.: *Essai sur la composition des comédies d'A.* Paris, 1904

*Merry, W. W.: *The Frogs*. 5th edn., Oxford, 1905

Miller, H. W.: 'A. and Medical language', *Transactions of the American Philological Association* lxxvi (1945), 74-84

'Comic Iteration in A.', *American Journal of Philology* lxvi (1945), 398-408

Mitchell, T.: *The Frogs*. London, 1839

Murphy, C. T.: 'A. and the Art of Rhetoric', *Harvard Studies in Classical Philology* xlix (1938), 69-113

'A Survey of Recent Work on A. and Old Comedy', *Classical Weekly* xlix, no. 15 (23 April 1956), 201-11

Murray, A. T.: *On Parody and Paratragoedia in A.* Berlin, 1891

*Murray, Gilbert: *Aristophanes*. Oxford, 1933

The Frogs (translation and notes). London, 1908

Neil, R. A.: *The Knights*. Cambridge, 1901

*Norwood, G.: *Greek Comedy*. London, 1931

Oxford Classical Dictionary, edited by M. Cary and others. Oxford, 1949

Pack, R. A.: *The Greek and Latin Literary Texts from Greco-Roman Egypt*. Ann Arbor, 1952

Page, D. L.: *Greek Literary Papyri*. Vol. i. London, 1942

Paley, F. A.: *Ranae*. Cambridge, 1877

Paronzini, V.: 'L' ideale politica d' A.', *Dioniso* xi (1948), 26-42

Pascal, C.: *Dioniso, saggio sulla religione e la parodia religiosa in A.* Catania, 1911

Peppler, C. W.: *Comic Terminations in A. and the Comic Fragments*. Diss. Baltimore, 1902

'The Suffix -μα in A.', *American Journal of Philology* xxxvii (1916), 459-65

'The Termination -κός as used by A. for Comic Effect', *American Journal of Philology* xxxi (1910), 428-44

210   ARISTOPHANES: FROGS

*Pickard-Cambridge, A. W. : *Dithyramb, Tragedy and Comedy.*
Oxford, 1927
    The Dramatic Festivals of Athens. Oxford, 1953
    The Theatre of Dionysus in Athens. Oxford, 1946
Platnauer, Maurice : 'Antistrophic Variations in A.', *Greek
Poetry and Life* (Oxford, 1936), 241-56
'Comedy', in *New Chapters in the History of Greek Litera-
ture*, third series (Oxford, 1933), 156-80
Poultney, J. W. : *The Syntax of the Genitive Case in A.*
Baltimore, 1936
Powell, J. U., and Barber, E. A. : *New Chapters in the History
of Greek Literature.* Oxford, 1921-33
Radermacher, L. : *Frösche.* 2nd edn. by W. Kraus. Vienna,
1954
'Zur Geschichte der gr. Komödie', *Akad. Wien phil.-hist.-
Sitzungsberichte* 202, 1. Vienna, 1924
Richards, H. : *A. and Others.* London, 1909
Richter, F. : *Die 'Frösche' und der Typ der aristophanischen
Komödie.* Frankfurt, 1933
Rogers, B. B. : *The Comedies of A.* Vol. v (*Frogs* and *Eccle-
siazusae*). London, 1902
Römer, A. : 'Zur Kritik und Exegese der *Frösche* des A.',
Rheinisches Museum lxviii (1908), 341 ff.
*Rose, H. J. : *A Handbook of Greek Literature.* 4th edn.,
London, 1950
Ruppel, A. : *Konzeption und Ausarbeitung der aristophanischen
Komödien.* Darmstadt, 1913
Schlesinger, A. C. : 'Identification of Parodies in A.', *American
Journal of Philology* lviii (1937), 294-305
Schmid, W. and Stählin, O. : *Geschichte der griechischen
Literatur*, I, iv, 2, 1. Munich, 1946. (Cited as 'Schmid')
Geschichte der griechischen Literatur, 1, ii and iii. Munich,
1934, 1940. (Cited as 'Schmid-Stählin')
Schmidt, J. : *A. und Euripides.* Greifswald, 1940
Schönewolf, H. : *Der jungattischen Dithyrambos.* Giessen, 1938
Schwyzer, E. : *Griechische Grammatik.* 3 vols. Munich,
1939, 1950, 1953
Sedgwick, W. B. : 'The *Frogs* and the Audience', *Classica et
Mediaevalia* ix (1947), 1-9
Snell, B. : *The Discovery of Mind.* Oxford, 1953
Stanford, W. B. : *Aeschylus in his Style.* Dublin, 1942
Starkie, W. J. M. : *The Acharnians.* London, 1909
    The Clouds. London, 1911
    The Wasps. London, 1897
Steiger, H. : 'Die Groteske und die Burleske bei A.', *Philo-
logus* lxxxix (1934), 161-84, 275-85, 416-32

Stevens, P. T.: 'Euripides and the Athenians', *Journal of Hellenic Studies* lxxvi (1956), 87-94

Süss, W.: *A. und die Nachwelt.* Leipzig, 1911

De personarum antiquae comoediae usu et origine. Bonn, 1905

Die 'Frösche' des A. Berlin, 1935

'Scheinbare und wirkliche Incongruenzen in den Dramen des A.', *Rheinisches Museum* xcvii (1954), 115-59, 229-54, 289-316

Tierney, M.: 'The Parodos in A.'s *Frogs*', *Proceedings of Royal Irish Academy,* xlii (1935), C 199-218

Todd, O. J.: *Index Aristophaneus.* Cambridge (Mass.), 1932

*Tucker, T. G.: *The Frogs.* London, 1906 (reprinted 1913, 1930)

van Daele, H.: French translation of Aristophanes's plays in Coulon's edn. (as listed above)

van Leeuwen, J.: *Prolegomena ad A.* Leyden, 1908

Ranae. Leyden, 1896

von Velsen, A.: *Ranae.* Leipzig, 1881

*Webster, T. B. L.: *Greek Theatre Production.* London, 1956

Wecklein, N.: *Studien zu den 'Fröschen' des A.* Munich, 1872

Werres, J.: *Die Beteuerungsformeln in der attischen Komödie.* Bonn, 1936

White, J. W.: *The Verse of Greek Comedy.* London, 1912

Wilamowitz-Moellendorff, U. von: *Griechische Verskunst.* Berlin, 1921

'Lesefrüchte cclviii', *Hermes* lxiv (1929), 470-6

Lysistrate. Berlin, 1927

Wüst, E.: 'Skolion und γεφυρισμός in der alten Komödie', *Philologus* lxxvii (1921), 26-45

Wycherley, R. E.: 'A. and Euripides', *Greece and Rome* xv (1946), 98-107

Zielinski, T.: *Die Gliederung der altattischen Komoedie.* Leipzig, 1885

THE END